U.S. ENVIRONMENTAL POLICY

DOMESTIC AND GLOBAL PERSPECTIVES

DIANNE RAHM, Ph.D.

PROFESSOR OF POLITICAL SCIENCE
HONORARY PROFESSOR OF INTERNATIONAL STUDIES
TEXAS STATE UNIVERSITY

WEST
ACADEMIC
PUBLISHING

© 2019 LEG, Inc. d/b/a West Academic
    444 Cedar Street, Suite 700
    St. Paul, MN 55101
    1-877-888-1330

West, West Academic Publishing, and West Academic are trademarks of West Publishing Corporation, used under license.

Printed in the United States of America

ISBN: 978-1-68328-908-1

Table of Contents

U.S. ENVIRONMENTAL POLICY

DOMESTIC AND GLOBAL PERSPECTIVES

CHAPTER 1

Domestic and Global Environmental Policy Institutions and Actors

INTRODUCTION

An inquiry into environmental policy must involve the identification of the main actors and stakeholders. This chapter will identify both the key global actors and the important domestic ones. At the domestic level, the main federal institutions and actors include the president, the Congress, and the courts. The powers of each and how they may impact the making of environmental policy is discussed. Several executive agencies are central players in environmental policy including the Environmental Protection Agency, the Department of Interior and its various departments, the Department of Energy, the Forest Service, and the Army Corps of Engineers. At the domestic level, consideration also needs to include the states and the role they play in a system dominated by regulatory federalism. Domestically as well as internationally, the role of the nonprofits sector and environmental interest groups is important. Finally, the role the media plays both in setting the nation's environmental agenda and framing the narrative of environmental issues is discussed.

On the international level, the main player is the United Nations (UN) System which includes the General Assembly of Nations, the Security Council, and several UN organizations that function to

1

support human health and the environment. United Nations conferences, held since 1972, that focused on the environment as well as sustainable development have been important not only in setting the international agenda but also in creating a further subset of environmentally focused international organizations and international environmental regimes. Nongovernmental organizations are also important actors for global environmental issues because they play a critical role in the complex network of organizations that are vital to the making of global environmental policy.

U.S. ENVIRONMENTAL POLICY INSTITUTIONS AND ACTORS

The United States has many institutions and actors that deal with environmental policy at the federal and state and local levels. Of key importance at the federal level are the president and the executive branch agencies, the Congress, and the courts. Each state also has a structure that mirrors the federal structure, to some extent, although states may differ in how they organize their efforts. Finally, nonprofit organizations and the media play important roles. Each of these will be discussed below.

The Chief Executive

The president of the United States has several powers that make the chief executive a key player in environmental issues. These powers allow the president several ways to set or influence the environmental policy agenda. First, the president is required by the Constitution to provide Congress with an address on the state of the nation from time to time. This has become what today is the annual State of the Union Address. It is through this address that the president can inform Congress and the nation of executive priorities for the coming year including policies that concern the environment.[1] While the Constitution does not require the president to submit an annual budget, the Budget and Accounting Act of 1921 does. This act requires the president to submit a budget message to Congress at the beginning of the congressional session. Although there is no legal mandate to provide a statement of policy agenda priorities in the federal budget, the chief executive typically includes a policy message at the beginning of the budget document to announce the administration's policy objectives. Additionally, the chief executive indicates policy priorities in the budget by suggesting to Congress what level of funding the executive branch would like to see for agencies and programs.[2] Presidents, as managers of the federal government agencies, have the power to issue Executive Orders to agency personnel that may specify procedures and policies to follow in daily operations. This power influences the behavior of agencies. For instance, when President Clinton issued an executive order instructing all executive agencies to take environmental justice into consideration, he was able to use this managerial power of the president to influence environmental policy. The chief executive is given power in the Constitution to veto legislation. If Congress passes environmental laws that the president does not approve of, this power allows the president to stop that legislation unless Congress has enough votes to override the veto. The president also has the power to appoint the heads of cabinet-level and other executive agencies, with the advice and consent of the Senate, and to create White House advisory commissions. This authority allows the president to put in place the political heads of said agencies under the assumption that those selected will be loyal to the chief executive's policy framework. Finally, the president has the authority to negotiate international treaties. Since most transboundary environmental issues must be negotiated among a group of nations, the power of negotiation is important in environmental policy.[3] Together, all of these powers make the chief executive a critical player in environmental politics and policy.

Congress

Congress possesses many powers that make it a key player in environmental policy. First and foremost, Congress crafts and passes legislation. This lawmaking can be specific environmental legislation, or it may be law that impacts the agencies that have a heavy role to play in environmental policymaking. The most important of this type of legislation would be the annual budget of the United States which determines the funding level of all government agencies. Through the authorization-appropriation process, Congress establishes, modifies, or continues programs or policies and then funds them.[4] While the president can suggest a budget, it is Congress that ultimately votes for a budget and determines funding levels.

Both the House of Representatives and the Senate organize themselves into numerous committees. Table 1.1 shows the standing committees for the second session of the 114th Congress. As Table 1.1 shows, many committees have some say in environmental affairs. This fragmentation creates considerable complexity for the many environmental agencies in the federal government as each of these committees will have some sway over environmental legislation as well as oversight of the specific executive agency charged with implementing and enforcing U.S. environmental statutes. Oversight activities of the committees include holding hearings, conducting investigations, and issuing reports. Congressional oversight focuses the attention of the media and the public on the specific issues under consideration.

Table 1.1

Committees of the U.S. Congress

House	Senate
Agriculture	Agriculture, Nutrition, and Forestry
Appropriations	Appropriations
Armed Services	Armed Services
Budget	Banking, Housing, and Urban Affairs

Education of the Workforce	Budget
Energy and Commerce	Commerce, Science, and Transportation
Ethics	Energy and Natural Resources
Financial Services	Environment and Public Works
Foreign Affairs	Finance
Homeland Security	Foreign Relations
House Administration	Health, Education, Labor, and Pensions
Judiciary	Homeland Security and Government Affairs
Natural Resources	Judiciary
Oversight and Government Reform	Rules and Administration
Rules	Small Business and Entrepreneurship
Science, Space, and Technology	Veterans' Affairs
Small Business	
Transportation and Infrastructure	
Veterans' Affairs	
Ways and Means	

Source: Library of Congress, "Standing Committees of the U.S. Congress," accessed February 1, 2017, https://www.congress.gov/committees.

The Courts

The federal courts that have some engagement with environmental policy include the district courts, the court of appeals, and the Supreme Court. Decisions of the U.S. Supreme Court affect the entire nation, but the decisions made in other courts affect environmental policy as well. Decisions made in federal district courts provide the initial frame for many environmental policy issues. As these cases move forward, key arguments are developed, special interests are organized, and baseline judicial decisions are made that will provide the foundation for subsequent reviews, if any, by appellate courts.[5]

An important role of the courts in environmental policymaking involves the use of citizen suits. Most environmental laws allow environmentally minded individuals or groups to sue to compel enforcement actions when governments fail to act. Under citizen suit provisions, individuals and organizations can sue anyone or any organization thought to be in violation of an environmental law. Under citizen suit provisions individuals or groups can also sue the Environmental Protection Agency administrator or other government officials who are not carrying out a non-discretionary legal obligation.[6]

The Executive Office of the President

There are two important organizations within the Executive Office of the President that have a good deal to do with environmental policy. The first is the Council on Environmental Quality (CEQ). CEQ was created by the National Environmental Policy Act of 1969. It is headed by three members appointed by the president and its function is to advise the president and others in the Executive Office of the President regarding environmental issues of importance. CEQ, however, can provide no more advice to the president than the president wishes to get, therefore, CEQ's influence varies based upon the environmental stance of the president. The second unit to consider is the Office of Management and Budget (OMB). As its name suggests, OMB is responsible for management and budgeting, giving it considerable power. Since the Reagan administration, the OMB has also been the organization responsible for reviewing required Cost Benefit Analyses for potential new regulations that might have a major impact on the economy. OMB also houses the Office of Information and Regulatory Affairs (OIRA) which reviews draft and final regulations coming from agencies.[7]

The Environmental Protection Agency (EPA)

As the nations of the world began to become concerned over the state of the environment in the 1960s and 1970s, the American public shared that concern. Accordingly, in 1970 EPA was created through a reorganization of the federal government undertaken by then President Richard Nixon. The circumstance that the agency was cobbled together from pieces of other agencies and the fact that Congress has passed many environmental laws which necessitate that EPA be organized in ways that emphasize programs developed to implement those laws, has led some to conclude that EPA is not a well-integrated organization.[8]

EPA also suffers from fragmentation due to the heavy role that regulatory federalism plays in environmental policy. Many environmental laws allow the states to share in, if not lead, the implementation of environmental policy. EPA also exists within the wider system of separation of powers. While EPA's authority is established by Congress through the passing of laws, EPA is an executive agency and therefore is directly accountable to the president. If a president has an anti-environmental perspective, this can put EPA career staff directly in conflict with leadership.[9]

EPA's headquarters is located in Washington, D.C. but EPA also has ten regional offices located in Boston, New York, Philadelphia, Atlanta, Chicago, Dallas, Kansas City, Denver, San Francisco, and Seattle. Both the headquarters and the regional offices are organized in separate offices that reflect its programmatic organization, including the offices of air and radiation, chemical safety and pollution prevention, land and emergency management, and water.[10] As of 2016, EPA had a budget of over $8 billion and a workforce of 15, 376.[11] EPA's budget and resources are typically strained, a perennial problem stretching back to the Reagan administration when the then president, believing he had an anti-regulatory and anti-environmental mandate, used resource restriction as a means to constrain the agency.

EPA's mission is "to protect human health and the environment." They do this by enforcing the nation's environmental laws and by creating regulations written to provide critical details necessary for enforcement. EPA is responsible for enforcing all or parts of many laws, as shown in Table 1.2.

Table 1.2

Major Environmental Laws EPA Enforces

Law	EPA's Responsibility
Atomic Energy Act (AEA) (1946)	When EPA was formed, it was given the responsibility to issue environmental radiation standards.
Beaches Environmental Assessment and Coastal Health (BEACH) Act (2000)	Amended the Clean Water Act to authorize EPA to give grants to eligible states, territories, tribes, and local governments to support testing, monitoring, and notification of the public of disease-causing microorganisms in coastal waters.
Clean Air Act (CAA) (1970)	EPA to establish air emission standards and regulate stationary and mobile sources of air pollution.
Clean Water Act (CWA) (1972)	EPA to regulate the discharge of pollutants into the waters of the United States and establish quality standards for surface waters.

Comprehensive Environmental Response, Compensation and Liability Act (CERCLA, or Superfund) (1980)	EPA to oversee a federal "Superfund" to clean up uncontrolled or abandoned hazardous waste sites.
Emergency Planning and Community Right-to-Know Act (EPCRA) (1986)	EPA to help local communities protect themselves from chemical hazards through local planning and data made available in the Toxic Release Inventory (TRI).
Energy Policy Act (2005)	EPA to regulate underground storage tanks to prevent releases and leaks.
Federal Insecticide, Fungicide, and Rodenticide Act (FIFRA) (1947)	When EPA was formed, EPA was given control over distribution, sale, and use of pesticides through registration (licensing).
Food Quality Protection Act (FQPA) (1996)	Amended FIFRA and the Federal Food, Drug, and Cosmetic Act to allow EPA to set risk-based standards for pesticides.
Ocean Dumping Act (1988)	EPA to develop ocean dumping criteria to be used in permitting.
National Environmental Policy Act (NEPA) (1969)	EPA to review Environmental Impact Statements prepared by other federal government agencies.

Noise Control Act (1972)	EPA to coordinate the programs of all federal agencies related to noise research or control.
Oil Pollution Act (1990)	EPA to regulate aboveground storage facilities to prevent and respond to oil spills.
Toxic Substances and Control Act (TSCA) (1976)	EPA to regulate toxic substances.
Frank R. Lautenberg Chemical Safety Act for the 21st Century (2016)	Amended TSCA to strengthen EPA's ability to control toxic substances.

Source: EPA, "Major Laws and Executive Orders," accessed October 31, 2016 https://www.epa.gov/laws-regulations/laws-and-executive-orders#majorlaws.

The Department of the Interior (DOI)

DOI has a large role to play in natural resources. Its mission is "protecting America's great outdoors and powering our future."[12] Included within DOI are several subdivisions that have specific authority and jurisdiction. Under the Assistant Secretary for Fish, Wildlife and Parks are the National Park Service (NPS) and the U.S. Fish and Wildlife Service (FWS). Under the Assistant Secretary for Land and Minerals Management are the Bureau of Land Management (BLM); the Office of Surface Mining, Reclamation and Enforcement (OSMRE); the Bureau of Ocean Energy Management (BOEM); and the Bureau of Safety and Environmental Enforcement (BSEE). Under the Assistant Secretary for Water and Science are the U.S. Geological Survey (USGS) and the Bureau of Reclamation (USBR).

Established in 1916, NPS is responsible for the National Park System which is made up of the many national parks, national preserves, national heritage areas, national monuments, national historic trails, and national historic parks in the U.S. NPS employs about 22,000 people and in 2016 had a budget of about $3 billion.[13]

FWS, along with the National Oceanic and Atmospheric Administration (NOAA) Fisheries Service, have the responsibility of implementing the Endangered Species Act of 1973. FWS is also involved with fish and aquatic conservation, migrating birds, climate change, invasive species, and landscape conservation. Under its International Affairs program, FWS has responsibilities under many treaties, such as the Convention on International Trade in Endangered Species of Wild Fauna and Flora (CITES).[14] FWS employs about 9,000 people and had a 2016 budget of about $3 billion. FWS manages the 150 million-acre national Wildlife Refuge System and operates 70 National Fish Hatcheries, 65 fishery resource offices and 86 ecological services field stations.[15]

BLM has control over more than 245 million surface acres of U.S. federal lands and 700 million acres of sub-surface mineral estate owned and managed by the federal government. BLM was given authority by Congress under the Federal Land Policy and Management Act of 1976 and its amendments to control this land by using the policies of multiple use and sustained yield. Accordingly, BLM leases rights to energy, minerals, timber, and grazing lands. They also offer recreational opportunities for the public interested in using these public lands for that purpose.[16] BLM has an annual budget of more than $1 billion and a workforce of 10,000 employees. BLM also generates revenue through its activities. For example, in FY 2012 it produced nearly $5 billion in revenue most of which came from onshore oil and gas development.[17]

The Office of Surface Mining, Reclamation and Enforcement is responsible for regulating surface coal mines and dealing with the restoration of abandoned coal mines.[18] It was created in 1977 when Congress passed the Surface Mining Control Reclamation Act. OSMRE works with the states to protect the land during surface mining of coal and to safely restore the land after mining is done. A small agency, OSMRE had a 2016 budget of just over $150 million, although it has access to funds exceeding $1 billion through the Abandoned Mine Reclamation Fund, which OSMRE can use to assist communities affected by abandoned mines. OSMRE employs only about 500 people.[19]

The Bureau of Ocean Energy Management manages the development of the U.S. Outer Continental Shelf energy and mineral resources. Much of this work involves the leasing of offshore oil and gas wells.[20] The Bureau of Safety and Environmental Enforcement was created in aftermath of the Deepwater Horizon oil spill to separate regulatory efforts from promotion efforts. BOEM now functions to promote energy development while BSEE is the regulatory arm that works to assure environmental safety of offshore drilling.[21] BOEM, a small agency, had a 2016 budget of just over $170 million and employed 574 people.[22] BSEE had a 2016 budget of just under $190 million and employed 785 people.[23]

USGS, created by Congress in 1879, is the only science agency in the Department of Interior. The nation's largest mapping agency, its mission is "providing reliable scientific information to describe and understand the Earth; minimize loss of life and property from natural disasters; manage water, biological, energy, and mineral resources; and enhance and protect our quality of life."[24] In 2016, USGS had a budget of just over $1 billion and employed just over 8,000 people.[25]

The Bureau of Reclamation is responsible for managing water in America's arid West. Established in 1902, USBR is famous for its many dams and power plants, including Hoover Dam and Grand Coulee Dam. It provides water to many millions, generates energy, and provides many recreational opportunities for the public.[26] In 2016, USBR had a budget of $1 billion and employed 5,300 people.[27]

The Forest Service (FS)

Located within the Department of Agriculture, the Forest Service manages 154 national forests and 20 national grasslands in the U.S. The first leader of the FS was Gifford Pinchot, who established the mission of multiple use for the national forests and grasslands.[28] Pinchot was an advocate of conservation and "wise use." With the help of his friend and supporter, Theodore Roosevelt, Pinchot's influence expanded as did the amount of forest land set aside for conservation under the authority of the FS. Today the FS has jurisdiction over 191 million acres of land. It has a 2016 budget over $2 billion and employed 38,000 people.[29]

The Department of Energy (DOE)

Established as a cabinet-level agency in 1977 by President Carter, DOE was supposed to become the focus of national energy policy. DOE was established at a time when the nation was confronting a global energy crisis and was seen as necessary to coordinate national energy efforts including energy production, distribution, research and development (R&D), regulation, and conservation. While most of the efforts of DOE are focused on nuclear material safety and security, DOE does have a large role to play in environmental issues. DOE must address the cleanup of the DOE facilities that were part of the nuclear weapons complex and DOE continues to run the country's national laboratories where a great deal of R&D is done. DOE also promotes energy efficiency and the development of emerging clean energy technologies that may be critical to dealing with climate change.[30] In 2016, DOE had a budget of $29.6 billion and employed more than13,000 federal employees and over 90,000 contractors.[31]

Army Corps of Engineers (USACE)

The Army Corps of Engineers is one of the two large water managers in the federal government, the Bureau of Reclamation being the other. USACE began in the Revolutionary War and has continued as an engineering unit ever since. In 1794, it was split into civilian and military branches. Its civilian branch, the larger of the two, is charged with a variety of activities. To assist the nation to accommodate water traffic, USACE dredges rivers. Flood control is another role, and this is done through building levees, dikes, and reservoirs.[32] Many of these reservoirs now also provide recreation sites. USACE employs about 37,000 civilians and military personnel and had a 2016 civil works budget exceeding $4.6 billion.[33]

National Aeronautics and Space Administration (NASA)

Established by President Dwight D. Eisenhower in 1958, NASA's mission expanded from satellite technology to space exploration after President Kennedy established the goal of astronauts landing on the moon. NASA is a government agency with a R&D mission and a scientific base. NASA is headquartered in Washington, D.C. but has ten field centers spread across the United States. NASA contributes to environmental policy in several ways. It studies the Earth and is helping to answer critical questions regarding climate change, sea-level rise, freshwater resources, and extreme weather events. NASA had a 2016 budget of $18.5 billion and employed approximately 19,000 government workers along with about 60,000 contractors.[34]

National Oceanic and Atmospheric Administration (NOAA)

Located in the Department of Commerce, NOAA is a science agency. NOAA monitors climate and weather, assists with the building of resilient communities, and participates in fisheries management. NOAA is a central science agency player in providing data to monitor climate change and to track severe weather events. NOAA had a 2016 budget of nearly $6 billion and employed over 12,000 people.[35]

The Role of the States

Almost all environmental laws include a special role for the states that is based in the U.S. system of regulatory federalism. Since the earliest federal environmental laws were passed, stress has been placed on the states creating their own implementation mechanisms that will bring the state into compliance with federal standards set by law. To accomplish this, most states have established a state-based environmental agency. While the names of these agencies vary state by state, they share the common responsibility of being the state-level focus for environmental issues.[36]

The states vary in their commitment to environmentalism. Some states have a very strong environmental ethos while other states do not. Research suggests that states with substantial economic dependency on extractive industries and manufacturing tend to have a lower commitment to high environmental standards than do states with an economy based on tourism and white-collar jobs.[37] Studies have also shown that states with liberal public opinion, strong environmental groups, and liberal state legislatures are the most committed to environmentalism.[38] States with a strong commitment to environmentalism include Oregon, Vermont, Washington, and California. States that lead in opposition to environmentalism include Texas, Louisiana, Wyoming, and Oklahoma.

Environmental Interest Groups

There are many environmental interest groups functioning both in the United States and worldwide. Their missions vary as do their strategies and tactics. Major environmental interest groups include: Defenders of Wildlife, Ducks Unlimited, Environmental Defense Fund, Greenpeace, National Audubon Society, National Resources Defense Council, National Wildlife Federation, Nature Conservancy, Sierra Club, Wilderness Society, and the World Wildlife Fund.

Nonprofit environmental interest groups engage in an array of activities and actions to promote the issues and solutions to which they are committed. Some specialize in taking legal action, like the Sierra Club. Others prefer to engage in non-violent direct action, like Greenpeace. Some hold demands for environmental protection without regard to the cost of solutions or the preservation of the capitalist system while others, like Environmental Defense Fund, seek solutions that are cost effective and within the frame of western market-based systems.[39]

In addition to these large national groups, there are numerous local groups that form around particular local issues. Examples include such groups as the Texas-based AGUA that seeks to protect the large Edwards Aquifer which underlies part of south central Texas[40] or Environment California which focuses on issues of importance to the state.[41]

The Media

The media is an influential actor in environmental policy and politics. It often carries stories that promote environmental action by creating awareness on the part of the public to issues that may affect their health or well-being. The media can also be a powerful force in inhibiting environmental action when, under the excuse of presenting the audience with a balanced narrative, they provide undue time and credit to views that do not represent legitimate scientific perspectives. Opponents of taking action to confront climate change, for instance, have been successful in distributing their message in this way. The wide array of media outlets includes social media, broadcast media, news magazines, and newspapers. They provide many paths for environmental issues to gain salience. Media coverage has the power to focus the public's and politicians' attention on an issue which may result in some action or response, thus influencing agenda setting. The media also has a powerful role to play in framing issues and constructing narratives through which the public and politicians will view issues.[42]

GLOBAL ENVIRONMENTAL POLICY INSTITUTIONS AND ACTORS

By the late 1960s, worldwide concern with growing levels of pollution and environmental deterioration had emerged. Awareness of the devastating effects of some chemicals on animal and human life grew after Rachel Carson published *Silent Spring* in 1962, a book which detailed the impacts of pesticides (particularly DDT) on bird populations. The 1968 book, *The Population Bomb*, raised the issue of the growth of human populations and the dire consequences that might occur if population growth continued unchecked. These two American-based publications had global reach. A 1972 European study, *Limits to Growth*, also raised the issue of population increases and consumption patterns in a world with finite resources. Together these books are credited with raising awareness and setting the stage for the modern global environmental movement.

The United Nations System

The United Nations and key actors within it are central players in world environmental issues. The UN was created in the aftermath of the Second World War as a global security institution. It is organized into a General Assembly, representing the 193-member states, and the Security Council, which consists of representative from 15 states including the permanent representatives from China, France, Russia, the United States, and the United Kingdom. From its foundation, and through the Cold War, the UN focused primarily on keeping world peace. In the 1950s, 1960s, and early 1970s the UN began to focus on global scientific concerns that moved it closer to a direct interest in the environment. For instance, the World Meteorological Organization (WMO) got involved with the 1956–7 International Geophysical Year as well as the Global Atmospheric Research Program.[43] The Food and Agricultural Organization (FAO) was concerned with scientific issues surrounding food production. The World Health Organization (WHO) maintained an interest in human health and was concerned with correlation between exposure to pollution and heath affects. In 1972, the UN turned to a direct interest in the environment.

UN Conferences

The world's first major meeting that focused on the environment, the United Nations Conference on the Human Environment, was held in Stockholm, Sweden in 1972. A Declaration resulted from the Stockholm Conference elaborating many fundamental principles that would become central to the emerging environmental movement. These include: the idea that humans are both a "creature and molder" of the environment, that human well-being depends on our environment, that humans have an obligation to protect the environment, that in developing countries most environmental problems emerge from lack of development therefore the primary obligation of developing countries is to develop, that in developed countries most environmental problems result from industrial processes and technology so developed countries have an obligation to reduce pollution, and that developed countries should devote efforts to assisting developing nations to progress in a sustainable manner. The Declaration spoke to the need to protect and improve the environment for current populations and future generations, that humans have the responsibility to protect wildlife and habitat, that the discharge of toxic substances must be controlled, that steps must be taken to protect the seas from pollution, and that environmental education, science, and technology should be widely deployed.[44] Many of these key principles would be revisited in future UN conferences. The Stockholm Conference also underscored the important role that the United Nations institutions would play in global environmental governance.

Since the Stockholm Conference, the UN has hosted a series of global environmental conferences. These conferences have served as a critical mechanism to bring together world governmental and civil sector leaders to discuss policy on specific environmental issues or regimes. These conferences have resulted in elaboration of international expectations often expressed as conference declarations. These meetings have also resulted in the creation of specific UN institutions focused on the environment and development. The first of these institutions, the United Nations Environment Programme (UNEP), was created by the Stockholm Conference. Since 1972, the UN environmental conferences and agencies have been key players in the making of multilateral environmental agreements (MEAs).[45]

Major UN conferences on the environment and sustainable development have been held since the UN Conference on the Human Environment in 1972. In 1987, the World Commission on Environment and Development drafted a report to the General Assembly called *Our Common Future*, also known as the Brundtland Report, which created a definition of sustainable development. The UN Conference on Environment and Development, also called the Earth Summit, was held in Rio de Janeiro in 1992. It created the Commission on Sustainable Development (CSD). The Earth Summit also created the Rio Declaration which, like the Stockholm Declaration, contained a list of principles and obligations for states to adopt and follow. Another product of the Rio meeting was Agenda 21, a global action plan to stimulate sustainable development. Two very important MEAs were created by the Rio meeting: the UN Framework Convention on Climate Change (UNFCCC) and the Convention on Biological Diversity (CBD). Under the direction of the secretariat of the UNFCCC and various other working groups, a series of conferences have been held to address the issue of climate change since the UNFCCC took effect in 1994 (after ratification by enough parties to the agreement). The two major agreements negotiated have been the Kyoto Protocol in 1997 and the Paris Agreement in 2015. The CBD, also signed at Rio, promotes the conservation of biological diversity and the sustainable use of Earth's biological resources. Rio's Agenda 21 was reviewed at the World Summit on Sustainable Development held in Johannesburg, South Africa in 2002. This meeting was also known as Rio+10. The UN Conference on Sustainable Development, also known as Rio+20, held again in Rio de Janeiro in 2012 produced a paper called *The Future We Want*, reformed UNEP's institutional form, and set up a process to replace CSD with a High-Level Political Forum (HLPF) for sustainable development.[46]

United Nations Environment Programme

UNEP was supposed to be the anchor organization in the UN system for environmental issues. However, the design of the UNEP did not structure it as an organization well-equipped for centralized administration of environmental issues. Rather, the designers of UNEP saw it more as a flexible integrative body that would influence the already functioning UN organizations that had control over traditional UN policy areas including agriculture, health, labor, transportation, and industrial development. UNEP also ended up receiving inadequate funding and, for political reasons, was located in Nairobi, Kenya. The Nairobi location worked against UNEP fulfilling its role of integration as the other organizations with overlapping policy jurisdictions were not similarly located. UNEP's founders tasked it with a progression of functions to use to grapple with the world's environmental problems. Its mandate is fourfold: problem identification using scientific data, establishing policy goals and methodology, coordinating environmental action within the UN system, and building national institutional capacity. UNEP was generally seen as unsuccessful at fulfilling this mandate fully. Rather than becoming the single leading environmental organization in the UN system, UNEP was often viewed as just one of many actors in a fragmented system.[47] These failings were addressed to some extent in Rio+20. At that conference, UNEP's Governing Council was expanded to include all the member nations of the UN, in essence transforming it into the UN Environmental Assembly. This change is likely to give its actions more legitimacy. Rio+20 also put UNEP in a better financial position by increasing its budget. Together these changes greatly enhanced UNEP's ability to become the central coordinating body for environmental issues in the UN system.[48]

The Commission on Sustainable Development and the High-Level Political Forum

CSD was created by the Rio Earth Summit to implement the outcomes of the conference. After some early successes, CSD became increasingly unable to accomplish its mission of turning discussions into actions. Dissatisfaction with CSD led to the establishment of HLPF after much discussion regarding other possibilities such as creating an independent sustainable development council. Efforts to develop such a council failed. At the suggestion of the G77/China, a state-led forum in which developing countries would have control was considered. In the end, compromises resulted in the HLPF's organizational form. It is an inter-state forum that meets under the auspices of the UN General Assembly, at the head of state level, every 4 years. It also meets annually at the ministerial level under the auspices of the United Nations Economic and Social Council (ECOSOC). This hybrid structure and 'forum' status forces HLPF to adopt an orchestration strategy—a mode of indirect or soft governance in which the orchestrator (HLPF) enlists intermediary actors (nongovernmental organizations and other UN organizations) to bring a third set of actors (the world's nations) in line with its goals. HLPF has been given ambitious goals including providing political leadership for action on sustainable development, setting the sustainable development agenda, coordinating the agenda across the UN system, and following up on the progress in implementing UN sustainable development goals. HLPF does this with modest resources. While HLPF has legitimacy and political prestige which puts it in a good position to bring leadership within the UN system, it also must compete with many other UN system organizations that deal with sustainable development.[49]

The Global Environment Facility

Other international environmental organizations exist. For instant, the Global Environmental Facility (GEF), established just before the Earth Summit, is a unique organization that works with many partners to deal with pressing global environmental issues. Partners of the GEF include developed and developing nations, nongovernmental organizations (NGOs), and agencies of the United Nations. GEF is administered jointly by the UNEP and the United Nations Development Programme (UNDP) with funding coordinated by the World Bank. One important role of GEF is to make funds available to developing nations and to provide capacity building so that they can fulfill their requirements under several international environmental agreements, such as: the Minamata Convention on

Mercury, the Stockholm Convention on Persistent Organic Pollutants, the United Nations Convention on Biological Diversity, the United Nations Convention to Combat Desertification, and the United Nations Framework Convention on Climate Change.[50]

Environmental Regime Secretariats and Environmental Departments in Non-Environmental Organizations

A good way to envision the organization of environmental programs in the United Nations is to consider each major area of environmental concern, for which an international treaty has been negotiated, a regime. For instance, there are regimes for ozone, hazardous waste, toxic chemicals, ocean pollution, climate, transboundary air pollution, global biodiversity, endangered species, wetlands, desertification, and whaling. Each environmental regime has its own secretariat, which is a permanent international governmental body with a permanent staff that reports to the regime's Conference of Parties. Many of the secretariats are located within UNEP, but some, like the secretariat for the UNFCCC, are managed directly by the UN. Others, such as the toxic waste regime secretariat exist outside of the UN completely (for example, the Ramsar Convention secretariat). Many treaty-based environmental regimes have scientific and technical support organizations. For instance, the UNFCCC has the Intergovernmental Panel on Climate Change (IPCC), which advises the climate change regime on new scientific findings periodically.[51]

In addition to the secretariats of international environmental treaties, there are other international governmental institutions to consider. Specifically, these include environmental departments located within international organizations that do more than just environmental policy. These would include such units as environmental departments and subdivisions of the World Bank, the environmental department of the secretariat of the International Maritime Organization, and the environmental directorate of the

Organization for Economic Cooperation and Development (OECD) secretariat.[52] It is also important to remember that many groups with a wider mission, such as the International Monetary Fund (IMF) or the World Trade Organization (WTO), have enormous influence on environmental issues whether or not they have set up a dedicated bureaucracy within their organizations to handle specific environmental issues.

Nongovernmental Organizations

In addition to the formal governmental institutions in the international network system, there are many NGOs that play an important role. The UN formally recognizes NGOs as official observers for its processes and many NGOs without official observer status take part in UN environmental proceedings. Most NGOs are advocacy organizations that work to advance policy outcomes they desire. These groups can work to represent the interests of the environment, business and industry, trade unions, local governments and municipal authorities, and indigenous peoples. NGOs play a prominent role in UN side events which are officially sanctioned discussions and panels held at the periodic meetings of the Conference of Parties organized around an environmental regime.[53]

Together these groups form a complex network at the global, regional, and sub-regional levels. The growing number of these groups with an environmental focus and the lack of a yet fully functional centralized coordination mechanism create a major challenge for international environmental policymaking.[54]

CONCLUSION

This chapter has introduced the main players for both global and domestic environmental policymaking. How well these institutions and actors function determines the outcomes of policy for natural resources and the environment.

From the domestic context, these include the president, the Congress, the courts, several executive agencies, the states, environmental interest groups, and the media. The president is a key player in setting the environmental agenda. Presidential administrations use a variety of powers to do this including providing clear priorities in the State of the Union, the budget message of the president and proposed funding for environmental activities and agencies, nomination of agency heads, and representing the U.S. at international environmental meetings. Congress passes environmental laws and provides funding for the implementation of those laws through annual appropriations. Congressional committees play a critical role by exercising oversight. The courts play a key role in environmental policy because they ultimately decide questions of enforcement, including cases brought by citizen suits allowed by many environmental statutes. Many executive agencies have a role to play in environmental policymaking, but EPA is by far the most influential as it has the responsibility to enforce most of the nation's environmental statutes. Critical roles are also played by the land management agencies including BLM, FWS, FS, and NPS. Other agencies have a more limited role including NOAA, NASA, USBR, OSMRE, BSEE, DOE, USACE, USGS, OMB, and CEQ. The sheer number of agencies involved with environmental issues in the U.S., however, shows the extent of fragmentation of policy efforts. The system of regulatory federalism whereby states exercise considerable autonomy further adds to policy division and complexity. Finally, domestic environmental policymaking cannot be understood without consideration of the wide array of environmental interest groups and the role played by the media.

From the global perspective, the United Nations System and its various conferences and subgroups are key global policymakers. Beginning in 1972, the UN has held summits on the environment and sustainable development. These various summits and their subsequent meetings have created a variety of environmental groups including the UNEP, the Commission of Sustainable Development and the High-Level Political Forum, the Global Environment Facility, and UNDP.

Each of these actors makes up part of the complex and intricate network of institutions and organizations that provide the basis for global environmental policymaking. Since 1972, global multilateral agreements have emerged to deal with ozone, hazardous waste, toxic chemicals, ocean pollution, climate change, transboundary air pollution, global biodiversity, endangered species wetlands, desertification, and whaling.

---

[1]   Norman J. Vig, "Presidential Leadership and the Environment," in *Environmental Policy: New Direction for the Twenty-First Century*, eds. Norman J. Vig and Michael E. Kraft (Washington, D.C.: CQ Press, 2006), 102–103.

[2]   John L. Mikesell, *Fiscal Administration: Analysis and Applications for the Public Sector* (Boston: Wadsworth Cengage Learning, 2014), 198.

[3]   Walter A. Rosenbaum, *Environmental Politics and Policy* (Thousand Oaks, CA: Sage/CQ Press, 2017), 85–86.

[4]   Walter J. Oleszek, *Congressional Procedures and the Policy Process* (Washington, D.C.: CQ Press, 2007), 42.

[5]   Christopher E. Smith, *Courts and Public Policy* (Chicago: Nelson-Hall Publishers, 1995), 3.

[6]   James Salzman and Barton H. Thompson, Jr., *Environmental Law and Policy* (St. Paul, MN: Foundation Press, 2014), 99.

[7]   Rosenbaum, *Environmental Politics and Policy*, 90.

[8]   Daniel J. Fiorino, "Environmental Protection Agency," in *A Historical Guide to the U.S. Government,* ed. George T. Kurian (Oxford: Oxford University Press, 1998), 203–204.

[9]   Fiorina, "Environmental Protection Agency," 204.

[10]   "EPA Organizational Chart," EPA, accessed November 7, 2016, https://www.epa.gov/aboutepa/epa-organizational-chart.

[11]   "Planning Budget Results," EPA, accessed August 10, 2018, https://www.epa.gov/planandbudget.

[12]   "Who We Are," DOI, accessed October 31, 2016, http://www.doi.gov/whoweare/Mission-Statement.

[13]   "Frequently Asked Questions," NPS, accessed November 7, 2016, https://www.nps.gov/aboutus/faqs.htm.

[14]   "Conserving the Nature of America," FWS, accessed October 31, 2016, https://www.fws.gov.

[15]   "About the U.S. Fish and Wildlife Service," FWS, accessed August 10, 2018, https://www.fws.gov/help/about_us.html.

[16]   "The Federal Land Policy and Management Act of 1976: As Amended," BLM, accessed August 10, 2018, https://www.blm.gov/or/regulations/files/FLPMA.pdf.

[17]   "About the BLM," BLM, accessed August 10, 2018. https://www.blm.gov/about.

[18]   "Office of Surface Mining Reclamation and Enforcement," OSMRE, accessed October 31, 2016, http://www.osmre.gov.

[19] "Budget and Planning," OSMRE, accessed November 7, 2016, http://www.osmre. gov/budget/docs/FY17_Proposed_Budget.pdf.

[20] "About BOEM," BOEM, accessed October 31, 2016, http://www.boem.gov/About-BOEM/.

[21] "History," BSEE, accessed October 31, 2016, http://www.bsee.gov/who-we-are/ history.

[22] "Office of Budget and Program," BOEM, accessed November 7, 2016, https://www. boem.gov/BOEM-FY-2017-Budget-Justification/.

[23] "Budget Justification," BSEE, accessed November 7, 2016, https://www.bsee.gov/ sites/bsee.gov/files/budget-justifications//bsee-fy-2017-budget.pdf.

[24] "Who We Are," USGS, accessed October 31, 2016, http://usgs.gov/about/about-us/ who-we-are.

[25] "Budget Justification," USGS, accessed August 10, 2018, https://www.doi.gov/sites/ doi.gov/files/migrated/budget/appropriations/2016/upload/FY2016_USGS_Greenbook. pdf.

[26] "About Us," USBR, accessed August 10, 2018, https://www.usbr.gov/main/about/.

[27] "Budget Justification," USBR, accessed November 7, 2016, https://www.usbr.gov/ budget/2017/fy2017_budget_justifications.pdf.

[28] "About the Agency," FS, accessed October 31, 2016, http://www.fs.fed.us/about-agency.

[29] Rosenbaum, *Environmental Politics and Policy*, 324.

[30] "Mission," DOE, accessed October 31, 2016, http://www.energy.gov/mission.

[31] "Department of Energy: FY 2017 Congressional Budget Request," DOE accessed November 7, 2016, http://www.energy.gov/sites/prod/files/2016/02/f29/FY2017Budgetin Brief_0.pdf.

[32] Marc Reisner, *Cadillac Desert: The American West and Its Disappearing Water* (New York: Penguin Books, 1993), 172–173.

[33] "President's Fiscal 2017 Budget for U.S. Army Corps of Engineers Civil Works Released," USACE, accessed November 7,2016, http://www.usace.army.mil/Media/News-Releases/News-Release-Article-View/Article/652668/presidents-fiscal-2017-budget-for-us-army-corps-of-engineers-civil-works-releas/.

[34] "About NASA," NASA, accessed November 16, 2016, www.nasa.gov/about/index. html.

[35] "About our Agency," NOAA, accessed November 16, 2016, www.noaa.gov/about-our-agency.

[36] Rosenbaum, *Environmental Politics and Policy*, 119–121.

[37] Samuel P. Hays, *A History of Environmental Politics Since 1945* (Pittsburgh: University of Pittsburgh Press, 2000), 109–119.

[38] Scott P. Hays, Michael Esler, and Carol E. Hays, "Environmental Commitment among the States: Integrating Alternative Approaches to State Environmental Policy," *Publius* 26, no.2 (1996): 41.

[39] Michael Kraft, *Environmental Policy and Politics* (Boston: Pearson, 2015), 116.

[40] "Welcome to AGUA," Aquifer Guardians in Urban Areas, accessed November 16, 2016, www.aquiferguardians.org.

[41] "About Us," Environment California, accessed November 16, 2016, www.environment california.org.

[42] Deserai A. Crow and Andrea Lawlor, "Media in the Policy Process: Using Framing and Narratives to Understand Policy Influences," *Review of Policy Research* 33, no. 5 (2016): 472.

[43] Kate O'Neill, "Architects, Agitators, and Entrepreneurs," in *The Global Environment: Institutions, Law, and Policy* eds. Regina S. Axelrod and Stacy D. VanDeveer (Los Angeles: Sage, 2015), 27–28.

[44] "Declaration of the United Nations Conference on the Human Environment," United Nations Environment Programme, accessed August 10, 2018, http://legal.un.org/avl/ha/dunche/dunche.html.

[45] Steinar Andresen, "The Effectiveness of UN Environmental Institutions," *International Environmental Agreements: Politics, Law and Economics* 7, no. 4 (2007): 317–336.

[46] "Conferences and Reports on the Environment," United Nations, accessed Sep 8, 2016, http://research.un.org/en/docs/environment.

[47] Maria Ivanova, "UNEP in Global Environmental Governance: Design, Leadership, Location," *Global Environmental Politics* 10, no.1 (2010): 31–45.

[48] Maria Ivanova, "The Contested Legacy of Rio+20," *Global Environmental Politics* 13, no.4 (2013): 4–6.

[49] Kenneth W. Abbott and Steven Bernstein, "The High-Level Political Forum on Sustainable Development: Orchestration by Default and Design," *Global Policy* 6, no.3 (2015): 222–225.

[50] O'Neill, "Architects, Agitators, and Entrepreneurs," 34.

[51] O'Neill, "Architects, Agitators, and Entrepreneurs," 33.

[52] Frank Biermann and Bernd Siebenhuner, "The Role and Relevance of International Bureaucracies," in *Managers of Global Change: The Influence of International Environmental Bureaucracies*, eds. Bernd Siebenhuner and Frank Biermann (Cambridge, MA: The MIT Press, 2009), 9–10.

[53] O'Neill, "Architects, Agitators, and Entrepreneurs," 38.

[54] Jacqueline Peel, "International Law and the Protection of the Global Environment," in *The Global Environment: Institutions, Law, and Policy*, eds. Regina S. Axelrod and Stacy D. VanDeveer (Los Angeles: Sage, 2015), 56.

CHAPTER 2

Domestic and Global Environmental Policymaking

INTRODUCTION

U.S. domestic policymaking is the result of actions taken by several key players within our national system of governance. These include the Congress, which passes legislation; the bureaucracy, which tailors programs and regulations to enable this legislation and enforce it; the president, who often uses the power of the executive office to forge the agenda; and the judiciary, which interprets the law when disputes are brought to the courts. Accordingly, domestic policymaking is made through four distinct processes, each one associated with the institution that is the key force behind the policymaking: congressional policymaking, bureaucratic policymaking, presidential policymaking, and judicial interpretation of law. Each of these is discussed below. The approaches used in environmental policymaking have varied over time. The traditional method has been a command-and-control regulatory approach but in the 1990s and thereafter other approaches have been experimented with and adopted including market-based approaches, voluntary compliance, and a variety of incentive systems. These are discussed below.

In considering global environmental policymaking, the key concern is how nations work together to assure that our planet is not destroyed by pollutants or poor practices which spill over borders and have negative impacts on other sovereign countries. Every nation is assured, under international law, the sovereignty to control its own internal processes and procedures, however, problems develop when the actions taken by one nation have negative consequences on other nations. How do nations work together to prevent such dilemmas? How do nations solve collective action problems? Understanding the answers to these questions is central to approaching an understanding of global environmental policymaking and the negotiation of multilateral environmental agreements (MEAs). These issues are more fully explored in this chapter.

DOMESTIC ENVIRONMENTAL POLICYMAKING

Congressional Policymaking

Public policy scholars typically emphasize the central role of Congress in policymaking. This is because Congress writes the statutes that form the foundation of policy. The process of congressional policymaking has a series of key stages including agenda setting, policy formulation and legitimation, implementation, and evaluation.

Agenda setting, or getting the attention of policymakers so that they begin consideration of legislation, is the beginning of policymaking. For environmental issues, a crisis may precede and fast-track an issue gaining it legislative attention. For instance, the quick passage of the Superfund law came in the wake of the crisis at Love Canal, a focusing event that catapulted toxic waste to the center of national attention.[1] Crisis can affect agenda setting by exposing previously hidden relationships between various actors and participants in the policy process, sometimes called issues networks or iron triangles. A crisis can expose the members of these groups and affect the way they interact with each other and the bureaucratic agency they seek to manipulate.[2] A focusing event can cause the public to demand that elected officials do something to respond to the crisis, and thus acts to trigger the beginning of the policymaking cycle.

Policy formulation and legitimation occur when the legislation is drafted and voted upon. The exact framework for the law, or the policy response, is the result of the work of policy entrepreneurs who are spoken advocates of specific proposals for action.[3] These policy entrepreneurs, who may be elected officials, legislative staff, or members of advocacy groups, typically have a formulation prepared for a program that they would like to see implemented, and they await the opportunity to convince others of its merits. When a focusing event such as a crisis occurs, the policy entrepreneur is given the opportunity to push his or her idea onto center stage. If there is political will to do something about the crisis or focusing event, the policy entrepreneur may be successful in getting legislation drafted and voted upon. If the vote is positive, a program is established, and an administrative agency is given the responsibility to implement the law's requirements. While legislation is being drafted and voted upon, members of Congress and their staff are subject to a great deal of pressure from outside groups who wish to have some influence over the proposed law. This lobbying may be effective in defeating the proposed statute or in modifying it to meet the demands of the outside interests.

Implementation involves the daily activities of the program that Congress has authorized and appropriated money to support. In many cases, environmental programs as specified in their enacting legislation tend to be very vague, leaving the agency with jurisdiction over the program the responsibility for specifying the details of the policy. A key activity that allows this to occur, especially in regulatory agencies such as the Environmental Protection Agency (EPA), is rulemaking (discussed below). As the details of programs and the regulations that are drafted to support the program are articulated, the implementing agency is often subject to a great deal of political and interest group pressure stemming from the desires of agency outsiders to influence outcomes.[4] This form of lobbying, typically called administrative lobbying, can have significant influence on the form the program and its regulations take.

The final stage of the policy process model is often considered to be evaluation. At this point in policymaking, the program implementing the policy has typically been in place for a substantial amount of time to have established a track record. Evaluation is the formal process of investigating the program's outcomes to determine if the program is achieving the goals it has set out to achieve. The results of such an inquiry are program continuation in the event of success, program modification if some changes are called for, or program termination if the outcomes do not show that program goals have been achieved.[5]

Congress also plays a significant role in policymaking through its oversight role. Congressional committees that have jurisdiction over executive agencies hold hearings that investigate the activities of those agencies and the programs they run. Most importantly, these committees have considerable power to recommend levels of budgetary appropriations that, in the end, determine what executive agencies can actually accomplish.

Bureaucratic Policymaking

The main avenue through which administrative agencies make policy is through rulemaking. Rulemaking is the way executive agencies provide the necessary detail to implement a law that Congress has passed. Typically, when Congress passes a statute, it provides the policy goals that it wishes to see achieved and perhaps a framework that authorizes and directs a regulatory agency to fill in the details of the framework. Members of Congress ordinarily expect the agency experts to provide the details, especially on technical and scientific matters.

Rulemaking as a process must comply with the Administrative Procedure Act (APA) which stresses information, participation, and accountability. Information is given to the public when notice is provided in the *Federal Register* of draft rulemaking and again when the rule is finalized. For proposed rules, agencies need to inform the public of what it is proposing to do and the authority under which it is acting. Agencies are expected to inform the public of the time and place of rulemaking discussions and give the public time to respond to proposed rules. Participation is achieved by the public being able to interact with the agency in such a way as to allow the public the opportunity to influence the agency's actions. That is, agencies are supposed to take comments on the proposed rule into consideration and perhaps alter the rule based on those comments. Accountability is achieved by the APA by allowing judicial review of rules on both substantive and procedural grounds for those that wanted to challenge a rule.[6]

Since the passage of the APA, government agencies have tended to do far more to promote public participation than just issue a written notice in the *Federal Register*. Indeed, government agencies typically attempt to reach out to the public, and the likely affected regulated community, in myriad ways. These include the holding of face-to-face public forums in a variety of geographic locations to explain issues and receive feedback, seeking reaction from the public and the regulated community regarding a forthcoming rulemaking process from neutral third parties, and engaging the public using electronic communications, social media, and the like.

In 2002, Congress passed the E-Government Act, which calls on agencies to enhance public participation using information and communication technology (ICT). As part of this effort, the portal www.Regulations.gov was launched and it serves as the key to federal government e-rulemaking. E-rulemaking builds upon and modernizes the participation processes envisioned by the APA. This website allows users to search for all proposed rules and provides a time frame for comments. Using e-rulemaking has enabled agencies to provide more information to the public and receive more extensive feedback. Commenting on proposed rules through the portal is quite simple. It has been shown that public comments on proposed rules using ICT are numerous, that commenters also view the comments of others, and that commenters say they gained an understanding of other positions by reading the posted comments. For example, the U.S. Department of Agriculture's rulemaking on organic foods received more than 250,000 comments.[7]

While the impact of ICT certainly does hold hope for greater and more meaningful public participation in rulemaking, some scholars suggest that there are also drawbacks. E-rulemaking imposes a financial burden on regulatory agencies in the sense that they must devote resources to the technology needed as well as the personnel requirements. If the number of comments received is great, the agency either must devote more resources to process the comments in a meaningful way or the mountain of comments will be only superficially dealt with and will not improve the quality of the rulemaking process.[8] There is also a growing concern about the submission of fake comments or participation by bots.

Rulemaking is not only a federal issue. State regulatory agencies also use rulemaking as a process through which they establish state-based rules for many issues that are unaddressed by the federal government. Less is known about the process undertaken within states but in many of them, it mirrors the federal process in that there are common patterns of informal pre-process information dissemination and community consultation, formal draft rule publication in a state-based government register similar to the *Federal Register*, comment periods, and finalized rules.[9] However, some states vary significantly in how they undertake rulemaking.[10]

Presidential Policymaking

Presidents also have a critical role to play domestically in environmental policymaking, as presidential desires strongly affect the directions that domestic policy will take. Along with the constitutional power to veto legislation, presidents can influence the agenda of Congress by suggesting legislation or using the media and other forms of communication, including the State of the Union address, to press Congress for desired legislation. There is substantial evidence showing presidents have had influence over environmental agenda setting for the past 50 years.[11]

Presidential preferences for or against the use of the federal government's regulatory authority greatly inform what a president will support or oppose when it comes to environmental policy. The role that the executive plays in suggesting initial budget amounts for agencies communicates a great deal about the administration's willingness to support certain policy areas.[12] For example, President Trump's decision to request fewer dollars for the EPA resulted in the president sending a clear message that his deregulatory and anti-environmental agenda was underway.

In a similar way, presidential appointment powers can greatly influence domestic environmental policy. Should a president select an individual hostile to the policy area to run an agency, this too signals the president's agenda. For example, President Trump's selection of Scott Pruitt to run the EPA signaled his willingness to embark on an anti-environmental agenda. An earlier example of this occurred when President Reagan selected Anne Gorsuch to run the EPA.[13] But the fact that Gorsuch and her lower-level appointee, Rita Lavelle, eventually found themselves in conflict with Congress and were eventually forced out demonstrates that presidential power is not without check. Like Gorsuch, Pruitt was also forced out of EPA's leadership.

Presidents play a key role in foreign policymaking and in that capacity the president is the lead U.S. negotiator on any international environmental agreement that will have consequences on the nation. Whether a president seeks a strong role in international policymaking or chooses to keep the U.S. on the side lines or completely out of international environmental discussions, presidential actions have large consequences on bi- and multi-lateral environmental agreements. For instance, the fact that President Clinton so strongly supported the inclusion of cap-and-trade provisions in the Kyoto Protocol had enormous influence in the shaping of that treaty. The fact that

President Bush subsequently withdrew the U.S. from the Kyoto process also had major consequences for international relations over climate change.[14] Similarly, the decision of President Obama to reinvigorate U.S. involvement in climate change negotiations was instrumental in the successful adoption of the Paris Agreement in 2015, the successor treaty to the Kyoto Protocol. President Trump's announcement that the U.S. would withdraw from the Paris Agreement is yet another example of presidential power in international matters.

Judicial Interpretation of the Law

The courts play an influential role in the environmental policy through their interpretation of the law. The courts are often asked by industry, environmental groups, and other parties to review agency rules to determine whether such rules represent permissible exercises of an agency's statutory authority. These rules are often challenged pursuant to the judicial review provisions of the APA, which authorizes persons aggrieved by agency actions to seek judicial review of final agency actions. The upholding or invalidating of agency rules by the courts is a determination of whether the agency acted in accordance with the law. If the court invalidates an agency regulation, it remands the matter back to the agency to issue a new rule. This is one way that courts have an impact on environmental policy.

Another way that courts influence environmental policy is through citizen suits which are typically used to enforce existing laws and rules against entities subject to those rules and laws. Many of the nation's environmental laws contain provisions for citizen suits. Under these citizen suits, individuals and groups can sue anyone or any organization alleged to be in violation of an environmental law. Environmental groups have used this option widely. Citizen suits also permit individuals or groups to sue government officials who are not carrying out a statutory obligation, such as a rulemaking deadline. Environmental groups have used this strategy widely to force the EPA and other environmental regulatory agencies to meet the deadlines that Congress set in many of the nation's laws.[15]

Because of this, advocates have been able to use a strategy of appealing to the judiciary to enforce environmental laws. In 2000, the U.S. Supreme Court in *Friends of the Earth v. Laidlaw* held that the environmental plaintiffs had standing to sue an alleged polluter for civil penalties (even though any penalties assessed would go to the federal government and even though the plaintiffs' asserted injuries only involved lessened recreational value of the river). The courts also play a role of setting standards for review, including whether they will defer to the expertise of an executive agency, or if the court will more fully scrutinize the decisions an agency makes. The courts also interpret the Constitution, the language of laws, treaties, and earlier court decisions.[16]

Approaches to Environmental Policymaking

Traditional domestic policymaking has largely consisted of command-and-control regulatory approaches in which a regulator specifically directs polluters on how they must reduce pollution. Most of the nation's environmental laws follow this approach. Command-and-control regulation is rooted in a series of procedural steps. First, Congress sets the goals to be achieved by stating them in the legislation. Second, the agency—typically the EPA—formulates technical and scientific criteria to assure the achievement of those goals. Once criteria are established, the agency then establishes quality standards aligned with the criteria. Finally, the agency sets emission standards for sources of pollutants primarily through rulemaking and the agency enforces the emission standards largely through imposition of fines for noncompliance. Over time, considerable controversy arose regarding the command-and-control regulatory approach. Opponents argued it was too heavy-handed. Several of the early environmental laws implemented using command-and-control regulatory processes were seen as highly prescriptive, for instance, applying exacting regulations for each smokestack or telling the regulated community exactly what technology they had to purchase and install or face fines for noncompliance. Industry argued it was too inflexible and expensive. Economists suggested other approaches might be more efficient.[17]

The response to these critics was experimentation with other possible approaches. Beginning the 1980s, the EPA began experimenting with changes to the Clean Air Act. The earliest approaches involved two schemes to lower the cost of pollution control called netting and bubbling. To explain these ideas, consider a company with four plants, each with its own smokestack that emits 10 tons of a regulated pollutant for a total of 40 tons. The company is going to be required to reduce emissions by 10% or 4 tons. Under traditional command-and-control approaches, EPA would have required a per smokestack reduction of 1 ton for a total of 4 tons. But suppose some of the company's plants are more efficient than others so that a 1-ton reduction per smokestack would be more expensive than if it could reduce the full 4 tons more cheaply by reducing the full amount from one plant. Using such an approach would mean that the overall air "bubble" surrounding the plants would still produce the required emission reductions, but the company would only have to modify one plant's smokestack. Netting was similar, but it experimented with allowing companies to increase emissions from one smokestack while simultaneously reducing them from another smokestack but keeping the overall air "bubble" at the same level of emissions. These concepts were widened to include offsets which create a "bubble" over an air quality region and require that no new source of pollution could enter the region unless it offset its emissions by reducing already existing pollution sources within the region. One way to get these offsets would be for the entering company to pay already existing companies in the region to reduce their emissions.[18]

The success of these experiments resulted in the use of market-based approaches, which found form in what became the cap-and-trade regulatory approach as part of the 1990 Clean Air Act Amendments. Under a cap-and-trade system, the government sets a limit, or cap, on the total amount of emissions for an air quality region. It then distributes emission allowances to operating companies within the region which allow a certain amount of emissions. Typically, an emission allowance is for a ton of a regulated pollutant. Emissions are tracked, and when a company reaches its maximum, they either must cease production or purchase additional emission allowances from a company that has some to spare. More than likely, companies will have spare emission allowances because they are more efficient. The overall idea is to permit flexibility while at the same time encouraging economic growth. Pollution reduction in the air quality region can be accomplished by reducing the cap in the subsequent cap-and-trade cycles. This approach was first used to regulate sulfur dioxide emissions under the 1990 Clean Air Act Amendments. In 1994 the Chicago Board of Trade created a national trading market to facilitate trading under the law.[19] The perceived success of cap-and-trade resulted in the expansion of its use to other pollutants including nitrogen oxide under the Clean Air Act and carbon dioxide under the Kyoto Protocol as well as several U.S. regional greenhouse gas reduction agreements.

In addition to these approaches, several others have been considered and used. Federal, state, and local governments use market incentives in the form of taxes or subsidies to change behavior. These include such things as subsidies for purchasing fuel-efficient cars, low-water use appliances, and energy efficient lighting. Providing information and education to the public has provided empowerment. One example is the use by advocacy groups of the Toxic Release Inventory (TRI) data to get local polluters to reduce their emissions. TRI data enables local advocates to do zip code searches for many toxic emissions. Many governments and businesses have procurement standards in place to encourage the use of energy efficient and recycled products. Providing money for research and development efforts has led to innovation in many products and services that reduce resource use and prevent pollution. Voluntary approaches have encouraged many firms to adopt ISO 14000 environmental management standards which have resulted in many firms becoming more environmentally friendly.[20]

GLOBAL ENVIRONMENTAL POLICYMAKING

Sovereign Nations and Collective Action Problems

Just as the U.S. has its independent and unique way of policymaking, so too do all nations. What nation's do within their own borders remains their sovereign decision, within certain norms of international agreements. For instance, Principle 21 of the Stockholm Declaration states that: "States have, in accordance with the Charter of the United Nations and the principles of international law, the sovereign right to exploit their own resources pursuant to their own environmental policies, and the responsibility to ensure that activities within their jurisdiction or control do not cause damage to the environment of other States or of areas beyond the limits of national jurisdiction."[21] Clearly what this principle outlines is the obligation of nations not to interfere with the internal policy processes of any other country. At the same time the principle is somewhat contradictory for it also suggests that sovereign state actions must be limited to exclude practices that impose a burden on other countries. It begs the question of how such limitations shall be enforced.

The problem is that the Earth is a global commons and protection of the commons is a problem with a long and troubled history. The nature of this issue was elaborated by Garrett Hardin in his 1968 article in *Science*, "The Tragedy of the Commons," which called for a limit to population increases in a finite world. Hardin describes the world as 'a commons' and as an illustration of the concept he describes an open pasture shared by many herdsmen. He argues that the rational herdsman will add as many cattle as possible to the commons to increase individual wealth. But since the commons is limited, the adoption of such behavior by all the herdsmen will result in the destruction of the shared resource. Hardin goes on to describe the same problem in reverse fashion regarding pollution. Here the problem is not the taking of something from the commons but rather the introduction of something into the commons—polluting wastes. Since each rational person understands that the cost of cleaning individual wastes before disposing of them in the commons is greater than dumping them into the commons without treatment, the commons becomes polluted. Hardin concludes his argument by asserting that reliance on conscience will not be effective. The tragedy of the commons can only be averted by "mutual coercion mutually agreed upon."[22]

Some have argued against the conclusions drawn by Hardin and others who contend that natural resources held in commons would be overused or exhausted without intervention of a central regulator. Notably, Elinor Ostrom, winner of the 2009 Nobel Prize in Economic Sciences, argues that there are many cases of successful management of local resources by local communities that self-organize to control their own common pool goods, like fisheries.[23] Ostrom, however, restricted most of her study to small groups. Some suggest that given the sheer number of actors involved in trying to solve current global ecological problems, the option of a self-regulating organization posed by Ostrom would be unworkable.[24] For example, the negotiation of the Paris Agreement, to deal with the global problem of climate change, involved nearly 200 countries as well as many thousands of advocacy organizations and multinational corporations. Problems of this sort are the epitome of the collective action problem and they require a global environmental governance solution.

About MEAs

A Multilateral Environmental Agreement (MEA) is an agreement among several nations. The specific language used for MEAs varies and includes treaty, protocol, convention, covenant, and agreement. The term protocol is often used to designate a subsequent agreement to a framework agreement, where the framework convention contains obligation of general nature such as gathering information while the protocol imposes specific obligations such as timelines, targets, and mechanisms. Not all MEAs are legally binding. The factor that establishes an MEA as legally binding is the clearly stated intent of the parties that it is binding. MEAs also are described by the terms "hard law" and "soft law" which designate, respectively, specific and legally binding obligations versus no legally binding obligations, flexibility, or lack of specificity. Soft law approaches are typically taken to encourage broader participation and collective action.[25]

When states initially organize a meeting to discuss the possibility of a new MEA, one of the first items of business is to set the rules that will be used in the negotiation. These rules include such matters as how often the parties will meet—typically at an annual Conference of Parties (COP). In addition to frequency of meetings, the parties must work out who can attend the meetings as observers, that is, those who may attend the meetings but not have the right to vote. Management of the agenda for each COP shapes what will be discussed at each meeting, and while the initial agenda should be drafted and circulated by the secretariat, all parties to the meeting should have ample time to add agenda items. When there is no agreement on a suggested agenda item, it can be "held in abeyance," or set aside, so that work on agreed upon agenda items can begin at the start of the meeting. Such items may be moved to the agenda of a subsequent COP if they fail to be discussed at the COP for which they were held in abeyance.[26] This process continues for a series of COPs over an extended period of time, until a final agreement or binding treaty emerges.[27]

After the negotiation of a MEA at a diplomatic conference, states or regional alliances such as the European Union (EU) may sign the agreement. The time period allowed for signatures is typically limited by statement within the agreement. After signing a nation or regional alliance uses its own internal processes to ratify the MEA. Each party then must send to the depository of the treaty a written copy of ratification. After the requisite number of parties have ratified the agreement, it goes into force.[28]

Agenda Setting, Negotiation, and Operationalization of Multilateral Environmental Agreements: The Climate Change Example

Just as movement toward a domestic law requires getting the attention of leaders, MEAs begin with agenda setting. World leaders need to be convinced that some issue exists that requires action. An illustration from the climate regime may help to clarify how this occurs. In the case of climate change, scientists beginning in the late 19th century discovered the greenhouse effect and the relationship between increasing levels of carbon dioxide (CO_2) and temperature rise. Monitoring of atmospheric CO_2 began in Mauna Loa in the 1950s. Within the next several decades, the scientific community began to grow concerned about the implications of building levels of CO_2 and temperature rise. Acting on concern, the Intergovernmental Panel on Climate Change (IPCC) was created in 1988 by the World Meteorological Organization (WMO) and the United Nations Environment Programme (UNEP). The IPCC gave its first assessment to world leaders in 1990, an assessment that was concerning enough to begin negotiations among nations.[29]

In 1992, the United Nations Framework Convention on Climate Change (UNFCCC) was adopted. This convention made it clear that there was enough information to confirm that climate change might pose a problem and so all parties to the agreement were to publish an inventory of their emissions as the nations continued to consider what to do about the issue. The UNFCCC established a secretariat which took on the task of arranging subsequent meetings to be held on the topic. In 1997, the member states signed the Kyoto Protocol, which was a binding MEA specifying action to be taken by signatory nations.[30]

After ratification by the appropriate number of states, the Kyoto Protocol went into operation in 2005. Continuing post-Kyoto COP meetings were held to report on the progress as well as to negotiate a successor treaty. That successor was finally achieved at Paris in 2015, providing a relatively seamless continuation in operations.[31] Although there is variation in the process from environmental regime to regime, this example serves as a simplified model of how policymaking occurs using the framework-protocol approach at the international level. Of course, in actual negotiations there are many complexities to sort out and disagreements to settle. Achieving a successful outcome of negotiations is often a vexing process.

MEAs in Chronological Context

Most MEA's have taken form after or as a result of a large UN meeting or international conference but not all have originated in this way. For example, the 1973 Convention on International Trade in Endangered Species of Wild Fauna and Flora (CITES) was the result of a 1963 draft resolution at the International Union for the Conservation of Nature (IUCN).[32] Moreover some environmental agreements date back to the 19th century, such as the convention to protect fur seals[33] but the vast majority of MEAs have been adopted in the aftermath of the 1972 United Nations Conference on the Human Environment (UNCHE). Some of the key MEAs that have been implemented in the wake of UNCHE and their objectives are listed in Table 2.1.

Table 2.1

Major MEAs Adopted After UNCHE

Name and Adoption Date	Objectives
Convention on the Prevention of Marine Pollution by Dumping of Wastes and other Matter (London Dumping Convention) (1972)	To prevent ocean dumping.

Convention on International Trade in Endangered Species of Wild Fauna and Flora (CITES) (1973)	To assure that trade in animals and plants does not endanger their survival.
International Convention for the Prevention of Pollution by Ships as modified by the Protocol of 1978 (MARPOL) (1973/1978)	To prevent pollution from ships.
Convention on the Conservation of Migratory Species of Wild Animals (Bonn Convention) (1979)	To conserve migratory species and their habitat.
United Nations Convention on the Law of the Sea (UNCLOS) (1982)	To set seaward boundaries for international waters and specify exclusive economic zones for nations.
Convention on the Protection of the Ozone Layer (Vienna Convention) (1985)	To protect human health and the environment from adverse effects that might accompany depletion of the ozone layer.
Montreal Protocol on Substances that Deplete the Ozone Layer (Montreal Protocol) (1987)	To protect the ozone layer by managing and eliminating substances that deplete it.
Convention on the Control of Transboundary Movement of Hazardous Wastes and their Disposal (Basel Convention) (1989)	To assure that management, handling, and disposal of hazardous wastes is consistent with protection of human health.

Source: Environment Canada, UNEP, and University of Joensuu, *MEA Negotiator Handbook* (Joensuu, Finland: University of Joensuu, 2007), 1.3–1.4 available at: https://unfccc.int/resource/docs/publications/negotiators_handbook.pdf.

Just as many MEAs were adopted in the aftermath of UNCHE, so too were a number adopted after the next major conference, the United Nations Conference on Environment and Development (UNCED) held in Rio in 1992. Table 2.2 provides detail of the MEAs that were negotiated after the UNCED.

Table 2.2

Major MEAs Adopted After UNCED

Name and Adoption Date	Objectives
United Nations Framework Convention on Climate Change (UNFCCC) (1994)	To provide an inventory of greenhouse gas emissions and to move toward a binding agreement to reduce greenhouse gas emissions.
Convention on Biological Diversity (CBD) (1993)	To conserve biological diversity and the fair and equitable use of genetic resources.
Convention to Combat Desertification in those Countries Experiencing Serious Drought and/or Desertification, particularly in Africa (Desertification Convention) (1994)	To fight drought and desertification, especially in Africa.
Kyoto Protocol to the United Nations Framework Convention on Climate Change (Kyoto Protocol) (1997)	To set binding limits to greenhouse gas emissions by countries listed in Annex A.

Rotterdam Convention on Prior Informed Consent Procedure for Certain Hazardous Chemicals and Pesticides in International Trade (Rotterdam Convention) (1998)	To promote shared responsibilities and cooperation among nations involved in the international trade of chemicals and pesticides.
Cartagena Protocol on Biosafety to the Convention on Biological Diversity (Biosafety Protocol) (2000)	To assure safety in the transfer and handling of genetically modified organisms
Stockholm Convention on Persistent Organic Pollutants (POP Stockholm Convention) (2001)	To protect human health and the environment from persistent organic pollutants.

Source: Environment Canada, UNEP, and University of Joensuu, *MEA Negotiator Handbook* (Joensuu, Finland: University of Joensuu, 2007), 1.7–1.8 available at: https://unfccc.int/resource/docs/publications/negotiators_handbook.pdf.

The World Summit on Sustainable Development was held in Johannesburg, South Africa in 2002. It focused on the three pillars of sustainable development: environmental protection, social equity, and economic development. Ten years after, in 2012, the United Nations Conference on Sustainable Development or Rio+20 was held in Rio de Janeiro primarily to review the world's progress since UNCED. Both of these major meetings produced action on MEAs. Table 2.3 provides details of these agreements.

Table 2.3

Major MEAs Adopted After World Summit
on Sustainable Development

Name and Adoption Date	Objectives
Minamata Convention on Mercury (Minamata Convention (2013)	To protect human health and the environment from releases of mercury and mercury compounds.
Protocol on Liability and Redress to the Cartagena Protocol on Biosafety (2010)	To provide rules and procedures for redress of grievances related to the use of genetically modified organisms.
Protocol on Access to Genetic Resources and the Fair and Equitable Sharing of the Benefits Arising from their Utilization to the Convention on Biological Diversity (The Nagoya Protocol) (2010)	To share the benefits coming from the use of genetic resources in a fair manner, including access to genetic sources, transfer of technologies, funding and conservation.
The Paris Agreement under the United Nations Framework Convention on Climate Change (Paris Agreement) (2015)	To provide cooperation in the reduction of greenhouse gases as a successor to the Kyoto Protocol.

Source: "International Issues: Multilateral Environmental Agreements," European Commission, accessed February 1, 2017, http://ec.europa.eu/environment/international_ issues/agreements_en.htm.

Weaknesses of Multilateral Environmental Agreement Policymaking

Achieving cooperation on MEAs is not easy. All parties need to be convinced of several key ideas before negotiations will be successful. First, nations need to overcome a level of scientific uncertainty. They need to be convinced that there is enough compelling evidence to take action. They need to believe that it is necessary for them to cooperate in order to avoid a real threat to them. It is not enough that they fear having diminished access to a resource, rather they must feel some sense of risk that if nothing is done they will be in eminent danger. Second, they need to believe that the costs of ignoring the problem are more than taking some action. This is typically a difficult threshold to surpass especially if they suspect some nations will try to free ride on the actions of other nations. Finally, they need to be convinced that there is an equitable distribution of regulatory burden. This typically fits into a polluter pays model of action. Nations that did not cause the problem will resist taking action if those that are responsible fail to take a fair share of the burden of fixing the problem.[34] Even if these conditions are met, a country may not be willing to enter into a MEA because of domestic concerns. The U.S., for instance, has failed to join several MEAs because of presidential opposition or the difficulty of obtaining Senate approval.

If a MEA reaches the point of being operational, barriers still exist to its success. One large barrier is that nations need to be held accountable. This is very difficult to do short of one superpower guaranteeing to police compliance with its military might, which would be exceptional. MEAs, like other multilateral treaties and agreements, tend to rely on a system of pre-specified punishments, like public shaming or the imposition of economic sanctions, should a nation not meet its obligations. For a fractious group of competing nations, any penalties specified may be too weak to compel compliance. Moreover, nations may make reservations or provide interpretative statements which exclude or modify specific provisions of the agreement on the state. International law recognizes the sovereign rights of nations. Although it is not common, some MEAs have specific provisions that allow for parties to withdraw. Most MEAs specify dispute settlement procedures. While parties are required to follow the processes established, they are not required to accept the decision.[35]

CONCLUSION

This chapter has explored U.S. domestic policymaking and global environmental policymaking. Domestic policymaking is the outcome of actions taken by key players within our national system of governance: Congress, the bureaucracy, the president, and the judiciary. Each plays a different role in the process with Congress making the law, the bureaucracy implementing it, the courts interpreting it, and the president advocating for particular policies. The ways policy has been thought of and implemented has changed over time. The traditional command-and-control regulatory approach remains but has been supplemented by market-based approaches including cap-and-trade, voluntary compliance, and a variety of incentive systems.

Global environmental policymaking must deal with the central problem of how to get sovereign competing nations to cooperate when international law assures their rights to do as they will within their own borders. In modern times, though, we are all too keenly aware of the transboundary nature of pollution. Finding ways for nations to work together to deal with collective action problems and forge meaningful international solutions is the critical problem. Establishment of MEAs as prominent activity of the United Nations has been explored in this chapter. The weakness of enforcing those agreements and obtaining compliance remains a central problem of international environmental policymaking.

---

[1]   Dianne Rahm, *United States Public Policy: A Budgetary Approach* (Belmont, CA: Thomson Wadsworth, 2004), 37.

[2]   Barry Pump, "Beyond Metaphors: New Research on Agendas in the Policy Process," *Policy Studies Journal* 39, no. S1 (2011): 3.

[3]   John W. Kingdon, *Agendas, Alternatives, and Public Policies* (New York: HarperCollins College Publishers, 1995), 122–123.

[4]   Michael E. Kraft, *Environmental Policy and Politics* (Boston: Pearson, 2015), 82–83.

[5]   Rahm, *United States Public Policy*, 39.

[6]   Cornelius M. Kerwin, *Rulemaking: How Government Agencies Write Law and Make Policy* (Washington, D.C.: CQ Press, 2003), 52–55.

[7]   Christopher G. Reddick, *Public Administration and Information Technology* (Burlington, MA: Jones & Bartlett Learning, 2012), 64–65.

8　Ann Marie Johnson and Alexandru Roman, "Reflections on E-Rulemaking: Challenges, Limitations and Unrealistic Expectations," *The Electronic Journal of e-Government* 13, no. 1 (2015), 53.

9　Deserai A. Crow, Elizabeth A. Albright, and Elizabeth Koebele, "Environmental Rulemaking across States: Process, Procedural Access, and Regulatory Influence," *Environment and Planning C: Government and Policy* 34, no.7 (2016), 1222.

10　Sara Rinfret, Jeffrey Cook, and Michelle C. Pautz, "Understanding State Rulemaking Processes: Developing Fracking Rules in Colorado, New York, and Ohio," *Review of Policy Research* 31, no.2 (2014), 88.

11　Paul E. Rutledge and Heather A. Larsen Price, "The President as Agenda Setter-in-Chief: The Dynamics of Congressional and Presidential Agenda Setting," *Policy Studies Journal* 42, no.3 (2014): 453.

12　Dianne Rahm, *United States Public Policy*, 34–35.

13　Craig Collins, *Toxic Loopholes: Failures and Future Prospects for Environmental Law* (Cambridge: Cambridge University Press, 2010), 90–91.

14　Dianne Rahm, *Climate Change Policy in the United States: The Science, the Politics and the Prospects for Change* (Jefferson, North Carolina: McFarland & Company, Inc. Publishers, 2010), 69–70.

15　James Salzman and Barton H. Thompson, Jr., *Environmental Law and Policy* (St. Paul, MN: Foundation Press, 2014), 99.

16　Kraft, *Environmental Policy and Politics*, 95.

17　Walter A. Rosenbaum, *Environmental Politics and Policy* (Thousand Oaks, CA: Sage/CQ Press, 2017), 181–186.

18　Salzman and Thompson, *Environmental Law and Policy*, 123–125.

19　Rosenbaum, *Environmental Politics and Policy*, 186–188.

20　Kraft, *Environmental Policy and Politics*, 257–258.

21　"Declaration of the United Nations Conference on the Human Environment." UNEP, accessed September 12, 2016, http://www.un-documents.net/unchedec.htm.

22　Garrett Hardin, "The Tragedy of the Commons," *Science* 162, no. 3859 (1968): 1243–1248.

23　Elinor Ostrom, *Governing the Commons: The Evolution of Institutions for Collective Action* (Cambridge: Cambridge University Press, 1990), 2–28.

24　Peter J. Stoett, *Global Ecopolitics: Crisis, Governance, and Justice* (Toronto: University of Toronto Press, 2012), 6.

25　Environment Canada, UNEP, and University of Joensuu, *MEA Negotiator Handbook* (Joensuu, Finland: University of Joensuu-UNEP Course Series 5, 2007), 2.1–2.3.

26　Environment Canada, UNEP, and University of Joensuu, *MEA Negotiator Handbook*, 3.2–3.5.

27　Jacqueline Peel, "International Law and the Protection of the Global Environment," in *The Global Environment: Institutions, Law, and Policy*, eds. Regina S. Axelrod and Stacy D. VanDeveer (Los Angeles: Sage, 2015), 62–63.

28　Environment Canada, UNEP, and University of Joensuu, *MEA Negotiator Handbook*, 2.4–2.8.

[29]   Michele M. Betsill, "International Climate Change Policy," in *The Global Environment: Institutions, Law, and Policy*, eds. Regina S. Axelrod and Stacy D. VanDeveer (Los Angeles: Sage/CQPress, 2015), 236.

[30]   Dianne Rahm, *Climate Change Policy in the United States*, 42–43.

[31]   "Paris Agreement—Status of Ratification," UNFCCC, accessed January 23, 2017, http://unfccc.int/2860.php.

[32]   Stoett, *Global Ecopolitics*, 56.

[33]   Denise K. DeGarmo, *International Environmental Treaties and State Behavior: Factors Influencing Cooperation* (New York: Routledge, 2005), 33.

[34]   Craig Collins, *Toxic Loopholes*, 153.

[35]   Environment Canada, UNEP, and University of Joensuu, *MEA Negotiator Handbook*, 2.11.

CHAPTER 3

Population, Consumption, and the Carrying Capacity of the Earth

INTRODUCTION

The growth in population and how those growing numbers of people choose to consume goods and services are the two key factors that determine the environmental future of our country and planet. A sustainable future is not possible unless population growth and consumption can be balanced with the ability of the Earth and its natural systems to recover from human impacts. To survive, human populations need fresh water, access to land to produce food, and energy.

Natural freshwater supplies are limited and often the water is not located where the population is. As a result, many people spend a considerable amount of their time and effort simply transporting water from where it is to where it is needed. The burden of this transport frequently falls to women and girls. In developed areas, a great deal of infrastructure is devoted to freshwater collection and transport. As populations grow, the per capita amount of naturally occurring freshwater goes down, threatening water security. Wealthy societies can adapt by turning to technological solutions, such as desalination, but such technology remains very expensive and is largely out of the reach for poor societies.

Agricultural production is heavily dependent on access to adequate water supplies. When rainfall is insufficient, irrigation allows arid land to become cropland. Irrigation, however, has the negative side effect of causing the land to become salinized thus eventually rending it unsuitable for crops. The amount of land available to grow crops is limited and with growing populations cropland must compete with land used for human settlements and industrial production.

Energy is necessary for transport of water and crops as well as the growing of crops. In wealthier societies, fossil fuel energy supports mechanized food production, fertilizers, and pesticides. In poorer societies, human and animal energy provide the basis for access to water and crop production. Use of fossil fuel energy is problematic because its use emits carbon dioxide, a greenhouse gas, which is causing climate change. This chapter explores each of these in greater detail.

POPULATION

Population Growth and Carrying Capacity

Population growth has long been an issue of concern. We can date the beginning of the debate on population growth and its consequences back to the late 18th century. Most famously, Thomas Malthus, in a 1798 publication called *An Essay on the Principle of Population*, described population growth as exponential, while the growth of food production was expected to be arithmetical or linear. Malthus predicted that if efforts were not taken to control population growth, calamity would ensue, and many would suffer from poverty and starvation.[1] Malthus, however, did not consider the role that technological change has on production of food and so his dire predictions have not materialized to date. But concern about populations growing to a point where they exceed the ability of the environment to support them has not disappeared. It is also of importance to note that Malthus had enormous influence on thinkers of the time, including Charles Darwin, and subsequent biologists. Darwin's theory of natural selection was heavily influenced by Malthus. Darwin stated that it occurred to him

that under the pressure of such a struggle for existence, strong species
would survive while weak species would be destroyed, and new species
would emerge to replace them. Darwin's concepts provided the bases
for the science of evolutionary biology. Malthus' concepts can also be
seen as the driving impetus for the establishment of demography as a
field of study.[2]

Malthus' idea was expressed in an equation form by the Belgian
mathematician, Pierre Verhulst, who fit census population data for
several decades in early 19th century France, Belgium, Russia, and
England to the logistic or sigmoid curve. This equation included a term
that Verhulst called carrying capacity, which captured what Malthus
referred to as a shortage of food. At carrying capacity, Verhulst's
equation showed that births would equal deaths and population size
would be at equilibrium. In the early 20th century, Raymond Pearl and
Lowell Reed, professors of Biometry and Vital Statistics in Baltimore,
Maryland also formulated a logistic growth curve for population
growth and fit it to U.S. Census data. The curve is now widely known
as the Verhulst-Pearl logistic equation. It has been verified in laboratory
settings and in simple populations. However, many subsequent
attempts to empirically verify that human population growth actually
matches the predictions have not been forthcoming, in large part
because the equation does not consider other related factors, such as
increasing food supplies and population migration.[3]

The concept of carrying capacity was used in ecological studies by
Hawden and Palmer in 1922 in their study of reindeer populations in
Alaska. Reindeer herds had grown rapidly, creating a large population,
which then fell off quickly before eventually stabilizing at equilibrium.
They defined carrying capacity as the number of reindeer the range
would support without injury to the range.[4] The term was used shortly
thereafter, also in application to the natural world, by Aldo Leopold.[5]
In his work for the U.S. Forest Service, Leopold studied the number of
animals a range could successfully support without creating an
environmental imbalance and he referred to this as the ranges' carrying
capacity. Leopold's idea was that managers could identify factors, such

as available forage and water, or reduction in the numbers of predators, that could be manipulated through good management practices to increase the carrying capacity of a range.

The idea of carrying capacity was further advanced by Eugene Odum in the 1950s. Odum theorized that population growth mirrored the logistic curve, in which low populations would at first grow slowly but as their numbers increased, growth rates would surge exponentially until they reached the upper asymptote of the curve. That asymptote was described by Odum as the saturation level or carrying capacity.[6] Odum argued that using logistic analysis would enable scientists to infer the eventual size of a growing population, so long as they did not experience a shortage of environmental resources. Odum acknowledged that environmental restrictions could limit the growth of populations, thus affirming the ideas much earlier expressed by Malthus, but Odum also insisted that human innovation could result in increases to carrying capacity. Odum was keen to point out that population size was dynamic rather than deterministic as a result of many variables that might interact and affect the outcome.

The concept of carrying capacity, in regard to human populations, was revived in the middle 20th century by Garrett Hardin and Paul Ehrlich, who both followed in the neo-Malthusian tradition. Hardin used the metaphor of the limited pasture to describe the finite capacity of the environment to support life[7] while Ehrlich stated that population density alone was not the concern, rather, what needed to be considered was population size in the context of resources available for use by humans or carrying capacity. Ehrlich concluded that overpopulation occurs when a given population cannot maintain itself without depleting nonrenewable resources, a situation he contended existed worldwide in his influential 1968 book, *The Population Bomb*. The book reignited the debate over the pressures increasing populations have on the environment and the Earth's finite capacity to provide for growing numbers of humans.[8] Ehrlich is also known for his contribution to the widely-used formula I=PAT where I represents impact of human activity on the planet, P represents population, A

represents affluence (or average consumption), and T represents
technology (transporting and disposing of goods consumed). Devised
in the 1970s, this equation has been broadly used to depict the
relationship between population and consumption. It has also been
criticized for its over-simplicity, especially in assuming the
independence of population, affluence, and technology.

The Limits to Growth: A Report to The Club of Rome (1972) followed
in this trend although it modified the Malthusian assumptions to allow
for technological change. It used a System Dynamics model to analyze
population, industrialization, food production, pollution, and depletion
of nonrenewable natural resources. It assumed that pollution and
population would grow exponentially, while improvements in
technology necessary to increase food production would grow only
linearly. The result was a prediction of "sudden and uncontrollable
decline in both population and industrial capacity" by 2070.[9] Later
studies by the Club of Rome found that only under extreme
technological progress can population and the economic system avoid
collapse and keep growing. Other studies, however, have suggested that
survival of human populations, even without extreme advances to
technology, is possible as long as people are concerned and react to
news about the deterioration of the environment enough to change
their consumption patterns.[10] These more recent studies suggest a more
hopeful future in which not just the number of people, but their choices
determine the future of the global environment.

Projected Population Growth and Environmental Impacts

World human population growth has been historically very slow.
The total world population was less than one billion by the beginning
of the industrial era.[11] By 1700, the doubling time for population was
about 1,200 years. This rate picked up speed in the 18th and 19th
centuries. Much of this population increase occurred in Europe and its
colonies. The growth in population there was owed in large part to a
rising standard of living that brought improved nutrition and control

of infectious diseases. Globally, however, life expectancy and population growth remained low until about 1950. World population numbers have seen an amazing increase since 1950 as better food supplies and modern preventive health methods spread to Asia, Latin America, and Africa. World life expectancy in 1950 was 30 years, but by 1960 it had grown to 48 years and reached 67 years in 2010. Between 1950 and 2000, world population increased from 2.5 billion to an incredible 6.1 billion. This growth has varied in the different regions of the world, for instance, European populations increased only about 35 percent while sub-Saharan populations grew by 4.6 times. The population of the U.S. and Canada doubled, in part because of heavy migration. Asia's population increased by 3 times and Latin America's by 3.5-fold.[12] According to the United Nations Population Division, by 2015 world population had reached 7.3 billion.[13]

Projections for future growth differ based upon the various assumptions used in the forecasting models. To provide these estimates, the UN Population Division uses a low, median, and high estimating technique. Barring a widespread pandemic, the UN Population Division's 2015 estimate for a world population in 2050 was 8.7 billion using the low estimate, 9.7 billion using the median estimate, and 10.8 billion using the high estimate. By 2100, population will decline to 7.2 billion using the low estimate, increase to 11.2 billion using the median estimate, or climb to 16.5 billion using the high estimate.[14] Since the variation between the measures is great, and since there is reason to believe that both the low and high estimates may be both too low and too high, a more reasonable range might be between 9.2 and 10.2 billion in 2050 and between 9.2 and 13.8 billion by 2100.[15]

The environmental impact the increasing population will have by 2050 will depend on where the growth occurs. Since North America will experience slight growth, the main environmental impact will be an increase in carbon dioxide (CO_2) emissions, as the growing population adopts North American consumption patterns. The largest regional growth, however, will be in sub-Saharan Africa. That population increase will not impact climate change because most of that population will likely be relatively poor and contribute far less per capita to CO_2 emissions than do North Americans. The pressing environmental impacts in sub-Saharan Africa will most likely stem from the need to feed the growing population, which will necessitate increased water use. Likely consequences will be aquifer depletion, loss of bio-diversity and natural habitats, and ecosystem degradation due to the need to grow more crops.[16]

The Politics of International Population and Development Conferences and Institutions

The growth of the world's population over time has resulted in considerable controversy and disagreement among nations regarding the causes and consequences of population increases. Over time, a split emerged between developed and developing nations whereby developed nations insisted that large increases in population in poor countries stalled development efforts and increased poverty. Most developing nations, however, rejected the notion that their nations should focus on population reductions, arguing instead that the developed countries should reduce their consumption. Domestic policy efforts eventually undertaken by China to reduce its population added to the controversy and triggered a U.S. response that mirrored U.S. political divisions over abortion.

Beginning in 1954, the United Nations (UN) convened a number of international conferences that focused on population growth. Two early conferences held in Rome and Belgrade, in 1954 and 1965 respectively, were of a different sort than later conferences. These early conferences were dominated by demographers and population experts who were not drafted to represent their respective nations. These two conferences sought only to bring together experts to discuss scientific matters related to population. By the 1970s, however, contraceptives had become widely available and political concerns about rapid population growth was on the rise. The United States had become particularly concerned with population growth and began diverting its international aid to specifically target population control programs and policies. To assist countries to achieve their population goals, the United States contributed several millions of dollars in 1967 to create the United Nations Fund for Population Activities, now called the United Nations Population Fund (UNFPA).[17]

The United Nations responded to the increasing concerns over population by bringing nations together with the clear goal of identifying population policies. The Bucharest Population Conference in 1974 was the first of these. It took place at a time very favorable to the establishment of government programs to lower the rate of population growth, especially in developing nations. But to the surprise of those that drafted the *World Population Plan of Action* to be introduced in Bucharest, opposition from developing countries was strong. The main theme of the draft plan was that overpopulation was a main cause of underdevelopment. The developing nations present at Bucharest, however, moved the discussion away from population and argued that there was a need to establish a new world economic order that would narrow the gap between developed and developing nations. The developing nations expressed sincere concern that they might lose their sovereignty and be subjected to some global plan for reduction in population growth rates. The final *Plan of Action* agreed to in Bucharest reflected these concerns.[18]

While publicly calling international attempts of control over the population growth of developing nations part of the imperialist agenda, China implemented its controversial one-child policy in 1979 to cut its population growth. The policy was launched both over Malthusian fears of overpopulation and as a mechanism to raise living standards within China. This policy imposed a penalty on most families that had more than one child. Allegations of coercion including forced abortion and involuntary sterilization attached to the policy.[19]

A decade later, at the Mexico City Population Conference in 1984, the developing nations continued to express their concerns over fear of loss of national sovereignty and the imposition of a global population policy. Eighty-eight recommendations were adopted at the

Mexico Conference. Several of them emphasized the need to integrate population and development planning as well as to increase international efforts to fight hunger, illiteracy, and unemployment. But the Mexico Conference also called for the improvement of the status of women and a number of development strategies were recommended to achieve this goal. Population goals and policies elaborated the need for countries to consider programs to reduce population growth rates, especially in regions where fertility was particularly high.[20]

At the Mexico City Population Conference, President Reagan announced a new policy called the Mexico City Policy which expanded the ban begun during the Carter administration on the use of foreign aid for abortion or involuntary sterilization. The Mexico City Policy included withdrawal of U.S. funds for all organizations that undertook abortion activities, even those using non-U.S. funds for those purposes. Concerned with China's one-child policy, the Reagan administration required UNFPA to provide clear assurances that it did not provide abortions or support coercive family planning programs. In 1985, the U.S. Congress amended the Foreign Assistance and Related Programs Appropriations Act to include a ban on funding any organization or program that manages, supports, or participates in coercive family planning. President Reagan used this law to deny all U.S. funding to UNFPA. This policy remained in place through the first Bush administration.[21]

By the late 1980s, a vocal political international split emerged between the developed and developing nations over the issue of population and its impact on the environment. The developed nations tended to argue that population growth was a key factor in increasing environmental degradation, while developing nations argued that environmental destruction was due primarily to overconsumption by the wealthy nations. By the late 1980s, evidence supported the claim that on a per capita basis, resource use in the developed world was far greater than in the developing world. While the developed nations held only one quarter of the world's population, collectively they consumed near three quarters of the world's resources. The split was first seen in

1987, when the Bruntland Commission could not come to agreement on the causal significance of population growth on sustainable development. In 1990, a preparatory committee for the 1992 United Nations Conference on Environment and Development (UNCED) failed to put population issues on the agenda for the meeting. Because of this, no official working group was established to study the issue coming out of the Rio Earth Summit. Also, in preparation for the Rio meeting, environmental delegates from Latin America published a separate agenda called *Our Own Agenda* which specifically called population control efforts deliberate interference on the part of the rich, industrialized countries. The G77 conference of developing countries also opposed population control discussions in international meetings.[22]

During the same period of time, the developed nations under the leadership of the U.S. made a strong claim that rapid population growth in developing nations was correlated with lack of development and poverty. The rich nations claimed that population growth was linked with poor health conditions, low status of women, high rates of unintended pregnancy, and lack of access to family planning services. Low childhood survival rates put pressures on poor populations to have many children so that some would survive into adulthood. Further, the rich nations argued that rapid population growth created a stress on infrastructure, including hospitals and schools, and strained the economies of poor nations that were unable to create jobs for the growing population. The rich nations pressed the poor nations to curb their population growth so that they could develop.[23]

With the election of President Clinton in 1993, the U.S. reversed the Mexico City Policy and in the Foreign Operations Appropriation Act of 1994 Congress allocated $50 million for the UNFPA. For the duration of the Clinton administration the policy that was followed assumed that UNFPA provided no direct support for any coercive family planning policies, including China's one-child policy, and so funding was maintained. However, the Clinton administration required UNFPA to assure that its funding was not being used in China.

Funding for UNFPA remained in place until the election of President George W. Bush, who reinstated the Mexico City Policy.[24]

In 1994, the United Nations International Conference on Population and Development (ICPD) was held in Cairo. ICPD reframed the issue of population to focus on the use of reproductive health services to improve women's health. More than 1,500 nongovernmental organizations (NGOs) attended the Cairo Conference and their interests spanned a wide range of concerns including development, women's health, women's empowerment, violence against women, family planning, and rights of indigenous peoples. At Cairo, traditional population topics such as the determinants and consequences of overpopulation were not paid any serious attention.[25] The strong influence of NGOs, many dominated by women advocates, moved the discussion firmly away from population control toward women's human rights and reproductive health. The activists were able to forge an unlikely alliance with advocates of population control by linking women's empowerment with fewer children and therefore population growth declines.[26]

U.S. efforts to fund UNFPA since the Cairo conference have continued in an on-again off-again way, based on whether the U.S. had a Republican or Democratic president. The willingness of the U.S. to fund international population control and family planning efforts has mirrored the internal dynamic that has played out over domestic abortion rights. Republican presidents reinstate the Mexico City Policy while Democratic presidents reverse the restriction.[27] Thus, in the wake of the Bush administration, the Obama administration reversed the restrictions and funded UNFPA. When Donald Trump took office, he reinstated the Mexico City Policy.

While there has not been a population conference since the meeting in Cairo, there are policy efforts underway that may very well hold a key to lowering population. The adoption of the Sustainable Development Goals (SDGs) in 2015, if actually implemented, could foster reductions in population growth. Specifically, the SDGs emphasize reproductive health and female education, both of which have been shown to result in smaller families. More educated women consistently have fewer and healthier children.[28]

It is also important to note that several of the world's fastest growing population centers, China and India, have taken domestic political steps to deal with their own populations numbers. China's one-child policy, while successful in slowing population growth, also created considerable unexpected outcomes. The preference for male children resulted in infanticide and abandonment of female children, eventually creating a situation whereby males outnumbered females in large number. This, in turn, created a situation where marriage became problematic since there were too few women. Additionally, the overall population shifted from having a balance between young and old to a heavily older population. This put pressure on social services to deal with the large elderly demographic. By 2015, these negative consequences led to the end of the policy. In 1952, India became the first country to institute national family planning but despite its long history, India still struggles to control its population growth. The unmet demand for contraceptives remains high and this along with early marriage and inadequate spacing of childbirths, means India's population continues to surge.[29]

CONSUMPTION

Water

As populations grow, freshwater demands will increase vastly. By 2025, it is estimated that 38 percent of the global population will live in water-stressed countries. Freshwater depletion is already readily observed with the over pumping of many aquifers and depletion of river flows. As the world population increases, access to naturally occurring freshwater will, by definition, go down on a per capita basis. By 2050, given the growth projections, the amount of naturally occurring freshwater available per capita will decrease by one third from 2000 levels. Concerns over water are myriad. The distribution of natural freshwater does not mirror population concentrations. For instance, Asia supports more than 60 percent of the world's population and yet it has access to only 32 percent of the world's freshwater. South America, home to only 6 percent of the world's population, holds 28 percent of the world's freshwater supplies. About 60 percent of the world's freshwater supply runs directly into the sea without being collected for human use. The only way to prevent this is to build more water retention dams but worldwide such construction is declining due to economic, social, and environmental costs.[30] The rate of water use is unsustainable. Groundwater supplies are dropping and, as demand increases, aquifers will be further overdrawn, resulting in lower water tables and land subsidence. The world's major rivers are increasingly running dry. Globally, agriculture is the largest user of water, consuming over 70 percent. But as cities grow and more human populations concentrate in urban areas, competition for water between agriculture, industry, and urban populations becomes more intense. Water-stressed regions are on the increase and as regions becomes water-stressed they tend to import their food, so they can use what water they do have for industrial and household purposes. This creates food insecurity. Most water-stressed populations are in sub-Saharan Africa and South Asia and it is here that populations are growing the most rapidly.[31]

Demand for water in the future will depend on consumption choices. Dietary choices, in particular, play a key role. Countries that move from a current plant-based diet to one that consumes more meat and dairy products will increase their water footprint substantially.[32]

Food

Many historical concerns with the need to increase food production were silenced by the Green Revolution, a series of initiatives deployed mostly in the developing world that resulted in massive increases in food production. These initiatives included introduction of high-yielding varieties of cereals, use of fertilizers, pesticides, irrigation, and mechanized cultivation. The results, emerging largely in the late 1960s, were alleged to save millions from starvation. Food production outpaced population increases through the turn of the 21st century. Norman Borlaug, the "father" of the Green Revolution, accepted the Nobel Peace Prize in 1970 for his efforts. Borlaug, however, warned in that the Green Revolution had bought some time but if world population growth continued unabated, food production would not be able to keep up. In 1970, he said that the world's leaders had about 30 years to find ways to reduce population before the issue re-emerged as critical.[33]

There is evidence that as early the start of the 21st century trends in food scarcity were emerging. The World Health Organization (WHO) in 2003 estimated that more than 3.7 billion people were malnourished. Cereal grains make up more than 80 percent of human food and are therefore essential for human survival. Yet the UN Food and Agriculture Committee indicates that per capita availability of cereal grains have been in decline since the 1980s. This is despite the increasing use of biotechnology and other agricultural technologies. The ability to produce more food is also limited by the lack of cropland, which also is declining on a per capita basis. Cropland is being lost to wind and soil erosion as well as salinization due to irrigation. Per capita fertilizer use worldwide is declining, further decreasing yields of crops.[34]

The likely availability of adequate food supplies into the future in large part depends on the extent to which populations choose to rely on animal protein. Animal diets are far less efficient than plant-based diets and they also contribute to higher rates of climate change through the production of methane emissions.[35] Increased populations by 2050 and shifts in consumption patterns, particularly toward a meat-based diet, will require agricultural production to at least triple.[36]

Energy

Energy is necessary for almost all human activities, including food production and storage, industrial production, transportation, mineral extraction, heating, air conditioning, refrigeration, and delivery of water where it is needed. Agriculture, especially in industrialized nations, uses large amounts of fossil fuels for fertilizers, pesticides, powering irrigation systems, and the manufacture and use of farm machinery. In developing countries, expensive fossil fuel use is replaced to a large extent by human and animal power.[37] Provision of energy, especially to poor populations, can lead to improvements in quality of life, which in turn may result in reduced populations. In this sense, providing energy to populations may be a key to reducing population growth rates.[38]

Over the last four decades, the industrialization of many developing countries and population increases have led to increases in global energy consumption. Between 1971 and 2011, global energy consumption was increasing on average by 2.2 percent per year. Consumption of coal during this time period on average increased by 2.4 percent per year, oil consumption increased on average by 1.2 percent per year, and natural gas consumption grew on average by 2.9 percent per year. While renewable sources of energy such as wind, solar, and geothermal also increased, the overall consumption of fossil fuels decreased only slightly from 86.6 percent in 1971 to 81.6 percent in 2011.[39] As populations continue to increase and as the world continues to develop, the use of more energy every year is to be expected.

The heavy reliance on fossil fuels is problematic because the burning of fossil fuels is the primary contributor to global warming. As the Intergovernmental Panel on Climate Change (IPCC) states:

> The atmospheric concentrations of carbon dioxide, methane, and nitrous oxide have increased to levels unprecedented in at least the last 800,000 years. Carbon dioxide concentrations have increased by 40% since pre-industrial times, primarily from fossil fuel emissions and secondarily from net land use change emissions.[40]

Increases in these greenhouse gases in the atmosphere have raised the Earth's temperature on average by half a degree Celsius over the past century and this warming is expected to continue. This warming will result in significant and destructive effects on human health and the environment, including rising sea levels, extreme storms, wildfires, extinctions, droughts, degradation of ecosystems, etc.[41] Climate change will also be costly because both mitigation, or reductions in greenhouse gas emissions, and adaptation strategies, or finding ways to live in a warmer world, impose large financial burdens.

While some suggest that heavy reliance on fossil fuels is problematic because fossil fuels will eventually be depleted, coal is abundant, and it is clear from the history of the oil and gas industry that technological innovation continues to provide access to new resources as well as to extract more from existing known reservoirs.[42] The real problem is not that fossil fuels will be exhausted, but rather that the world needs to transition from reliance on fossil fuels to energy sustainability, while still increasing the amount of energy produced to accommodate continued development and population growth.

Herman Daly defines several principles that provide appropriate parameters for energy sustainability. Daly argues that renewable resources should be used at rates equal to their regeneration. Non-renewable resources should be paired with, or used no faster than, renewable substitutes for them can be put into place.[43]

Energy sustainability involves both energy efficiency and use of renewable resources. For renewable energy, Daly's first principle applies to sources such as biomass, which should be used only as quickly as they regrow and therefore are available to the next generation. For sources like the sun and the wind, which cannot be exhausted, the first principle does not apply except to the extent that use of these resources involves investment in production technologies. These investments should be managed in a manner so that production investment does not overwhelm investment in research and development to assure greater efficiency in the next generation of production.[44] Daly's second principle might suggest that non-renewable energy sources, such as fossil fuels, should be used no more

rapidly than renewables can be substituted for them, however, the costs
of climate change should also be taken into consideration. A warming
globe imposes costs in the form of damage to human health and the
environment, and there are costs associated with adaptation and
mitigation.

As the world seeks to transition from dependence on fossil fuel to
sustainable energy, access to energy coming from any source remains a
primary concern for many. Adequate supply of energy is already an
issue for billions. According to the International Energy Agency (IEA),
1.2 billion people in 2016 lacked access to electricity, almost as many
have power only intermittently, and about 2.7 billion still rely on
biomass, dung, or coal for cooking and heating. Use of biomass, dung,
or coal for cooking creates smoky indoor environments which were
linked to 3.5 billion premature deaths in 2016. The IEA continues to
see inadequate supply problems far into the future. They estimate that
by 2040 there will be a 30 percent increase in energy demand, which
will mean increasing consumption of all available fuels, including fossil
fuels. They also estimate that by 2040 many hundreds of millions will
still be without basic energy services.[45]

As we approach the middle of the 21st century, renewable energy
will see the fastest growth of use. Nearly 60 percent of new power
generation will come from renewables and most of those renewables
will be cost-competitive without subsidies. As to fossil fuels, natural gas
use is projected to increase by 50 percent. Growth in demand for oil
will slow but the world will still rely on more than 100 million barrels a
day. Coal use is projected to decline sharply in developed countries, by
60 percent in the European Union and 40 percent in the U.S. However,
coal use will decline by considerably less in developing countries,
especially China and India. Nuclear energy use will increase, mostly in
China. Overall, world energy consumption is projected to be on the
decline in the developed countries over the next several decades but on
the rise in the developing world. But even with increase provision of
energy, many will lack adequate energy supply. Nearly half a billion
people, mostly in sub-Saharan Africa, will still lack access to electricity

in 2040 and about 1.2 billion will still be reliant on biomass, dung, or coal for cooking and heating.[46]

CONCLUSION

The size of population and how that population consumes are the two drivers of worry for a sustainable future world. Concern over population growth dates back to the late 18th century with the publication of Thomas Malthus' *An Essay on the Principle of Population*. Malthus predicted dire outcomes if population growth was not limited. His ideas were echoed by many through history including Charles Darwin, Pierre Verhulst, Raymond Pearl and Lowell Reed. Each of these thinkers was focused on some aspect of the concept of carrying capacity in human populations. Ecologists Hawden, Palmer, and Leopold later expanded the concept through their studies of animal populations. The idea of carrying capacity was further advanced by Eugene Odum, who pointed out that population size was dynamic rather than deterministic as a result of the numerous variables that might interact and affect the outcome.

The concept of carrying capacity in regard to human populations was revived in the middle 20th century by Garrett Hardin and Paul Ehrlich who both followed in the neo-Malthusian tradition. Hardin's *Tragedy of the Commons* and Ehrlich's *The Population Bomb* renewed the debate over the pressures increasing populations have on the environment and the Earth's finite capacity to provide for growing numbers of humans. *The Limits to Growth: A Report to The Club of Rome (1972)* added to the discussion by suggesting an environmental collapse by the late 21st century if population was not controlled.

Concern over population growth moved into the political arena in the 1970s. The United States had become particularly anxious about population growth and began diverting international aid to specifically target population control programs and policies. The U.S. was instrumental in funding what is today the United Nations Population Fund. In turn, the United Nations responded to the increasing apprehension over population growth by bringing nations together with the clear goal of identifying population policies. The Bucharest Population Conference in 1974, the first of these conferences, exposed a split between developed and developing countries over efforts to control population growth. China, in alliance with the developing countries, nevertheless established its own domestic program to reduce its population. China's one-child policy provoked alarm over forced abortion and involuntary sterilization which prompted the U.S., under the Reagan administration, to articulate the Mexico City Policy at the Mexico City Population Conference in 1984. The Mexico City Policy has shifted over time and mirrors the domestic abortion rights debate within the U.S. As a consequence, when those who support abortion rights are in power they try to fund UNFPA while when those who oppose abortion rights are in power they de-fund UNFPA. In 1994, the United Nations International Conference on Population and Development, held in Cairo, reframed the issue of population to focus on the use of reproductive health services to improve women's health. The advocates that attended Cairo were able to create an alliance with advocates of population control by linking women's empowerment with fewer children and therefore population growth declines. In the aftermath of the Cairo conference, the UN has relied on its development goals to provide support for population policies.

World population numbers have grown enormously since the middle of the 20th century. It is likely that several billion more people will be added to the world's population by the middle of the 21st century. The addition of that many more people to the world will have enormous consequences for provision of food, water, and energy.

Population growth will stress water supplies. By 2050, given the population growth projections, the amount of naturally occurring freshwater available per capita will decrease precipitously. Groundwater supplies will drop as demand increases. The world's major rivers are at risk of running dry. Global agriculture, the largest user of water, will have to compete with growing urban areas for water in the future. The most water-stressed populations are in sub-Saharan

Africa and South Asia, and it is there that populations are growing the most rapidly. Demand for water in the future will depend on consumption choices, particularly dietary choices.

While fears about the need to increase food production were briefly silenced by the Green Revolution, there is evidence that as early the start of the 21st century trends in food scarcity were emerging. Many billions of people suffer from malnourishment. Production of cereal grains, which make up a large percent of human diets, are in decline. The ability to produce more food is also limited by the lack of cropland. The likely availability of adequate food supplies into the future in large part depends on the extent to which populations choose to rely on animal protein, as animal diets are far less efficient than plant-based diets.

Energy, which is required for nearly all human activities, is unevenly distributed throughout the globe. Energy use is necessary for food production and storage, industrial production, transportation, mining, heating, air conditioning, refrigeration, and delivery of water where it is needed. Agriculture, especially in industrialized nations, uses large amounts of fossil fuels for fertilizers, pesticides, powering irrigation systems, and the manufacture and use of farm machinery.

Recent decades show increased global energy consumption and a heavy reliance on fossil fuels. Fossil fuels account for more than 80 percent of the energy sources. As populations continue to increase and as the world continues to develop, the world will use of more energy every year. If reliance on fossil fuels is continued, the impacts coming from climate change will be far worse than if the world makes a successful transition to sustainable energy. Efforts must focus on energy efficiency and increased use of renewables if the worst effects of global warming are to be avoided. Rising sea levels, extreme storms, wildfires, extinctions, droughts, degradation of ecosystems, and human health impacts are all to be expected. Climate change will also be costly to the world's economy.

Adequate supply of energy is already an issue for billions and while some improvements are expected to be made in the future, expectations are for a future scenario where many hundreds of millions will still be without basic energy services. There will be shifts in the mix of energy sources as we approach the middle of the 21st century. Renewable energy will see rapid growth of use with nearly 60 percent of new power generation coming from renewables. With the exception of coal, fossil fuel use also is projected to increase. Overall, world energy consumption is projected to be on the decline in the developed countries over the next several decades but on the rise in the developing world. But even with increased provisions of energy, many will lack adequate energy supply.

[1]   Thomas Malthus, *An Essay on the Principle of Population, as it Affects the Future Improvement of Society with Remarks on the Speculations of Mr. Godwin, M. Condorcet, and Other Writers*. (London: printed for J. Johnson, in St. Paul's Church-yard, 1798), accessed February 3, 2017, http://www.esp.org/books/malthus/population/malthus.pdf.

[2]   Irmi Seidl and Clem Am Tisdell, "Carrying Capacity Reconsidered: From Malthus' Population Theory to Cultural Carrying Capacity," *Ecological Economics* 31 (1999): 397–398.

[3]   Seidl and Tisdell, "Carrying Capacity Reconsidered," 399.

[4]   Seidl and Tisdell, "Carrying Capacity Reconsidered," 401.

[5]   Aldo Leopold, *Game Management* (New York: Charles Scribner Sons, 1933), 50–51.

[6]   Eugene P. Odum, *Fundamentals of Ecology* (Philadelphia: Saunders, 1953), 122.

[7]   Garrett Hardin, "The Tragedy of the Commons," *Science* 162, no. 3859 (1968): 1243–1248.

[8]   Paul R. Ehrlich and Anne H. Ehrlich, "The Population Bomb Revisited," *The Electronic Journal of Sustainable Development* 1, no. 3 (2009): 1, accessed February 6, 2017, www.ejsd.org.

[9]   Donella H. Meadows et. al., *The Limits to Growth: A Report to The Club of Rome*. (New York: Universe Books 1972), accessed February 6, 2017, http://www.clubofrome.org/report/the-limits-to-growth/.

[10]   Peter Berck, Amnon Levy, and Khorshed Chowdhury, "An Analysis of the World's Environment and Population Dynamics with Varying Carrying Capacity, Concerns and Skepticism," *Ecological Economics* 73 (2012):104.

[11]   Berck, Levy, and Chowdhury, "An Analysis of the World's Environment and Population Dynamics," *Ecological Economics* 73 (2012):103.

[12]   John Cleland, "World Population Growth; Past, Present and Future," *Environmental and Resource Economics* 55, no. 4 (2013), 544–545.

[13]   "World Population Prospects, the 2015 Revision," United Nations Population Division, accessed February 8, 2017, https://esa.un.org/unpd/wpp/Download/Standard/Population.

[14]   "World Population Prospects, the 2015 Revision."

[15] Cleland, "World Population Growth," 548.

[16] Cleland, "World Population Growth," 553.

[17] Jason L. Finkle and C. Alison McIntosh, "United Nations Population Conferences: Shaping the Policy Agenda for the Twenty-First Century," *Studies in Family Planning* 33, no. 1 (2002): 12.

[18] Finkle and McIntosh, "United Nations Population Conferences," 14.

[19] Junsen Zhang, "The Evolution of China's One-Child Policy and Its Effects on Family Outcomes," *Journal of Economic Perspectives* 31, no. 1 (2017): 144.

[20] George F. Brown, "United Nations International Conference on Population, Mexico City, 6–13 August 1984," *Studies in Family Planning* 15, no. 6 (1984): 297.

[21] Rachel Farkas, "Recent Developments: The Bush Administration's Decision to Defund the United Nations Population Fund and Its Implications for Women in Developing Nations," *Berkeley Women's Law Journal* 18, no.1 (2003): 245.

[22] R. Paul Shaw, "The Impact of Population Growth on Environment: The Debate Heats Up," *Environmental Impact Assessment Review* 12 (1992): 11–12.

[23] USAID, "USAID's Strategy for Stabilizing World Population Growth and Protecting Human Health," *Population and Development Review* 20, no. 2 (1994): 483–484.

[24] Farkas, "Recent Developments," 246.

[25] Finkle and McIntosh, "United Nations Population Conferences," 14.

[26] Carmen Barroso, "Beyond Cairo: Sexual and Reproductive Rights of Young People in the New Development Agenda," *Global Public Health* 9, no. 6 (2014): 639.

[27] Denise M. Horn, "U.S. Foreign Policy, Population Control and International Family Planning Programs," *International Feminist Journal of Politics* 15, no.2 (2013): 195.

[28] Guy J. Abel, et al., "Meeting the Sustainable Development Goals Leads to Lower World Population," *Proceedings of the National Academy of Sciences* 113, no. 50 (2016): 14295.

[29] Janmejaya Samal and Ranjit Kumar Dehury, "Family Planning Practices, Programmes and Policies in India Including Implants and Injectables with a Special Focus on Jharkhand, India: A Brief Review," *Journal of Clinical & Diagnostic Research* 9, no.11 (2015): 2.

[30] Sandra L. Postel, "Water and World Population Growth," *Journal off the American Water Works Association* 92, no. 4 (2000): 131–132.

[31] Postel, "Water and World Population Growth," 134.

[32] A. Ertug Ercin and Arjen Y. Hoekstra, "Water Footprint Scenarios for 2050: A Global Analysis," *Environment International* 64 (2014): 80.

[33] Bernard Gilland, "World Population and Food Supply: Can Food Production Keep Pace with Population Growth in the Next Half-Century?" *Food Policy* 27, no. 1 (2002): 48.

[34] David Pimentel and Marcia Pimentel, "Global Environmental Resources Versus World Population Growth," *Ecological Economics* 59, no. 2 (2006): 195–196.

[35] X.P.C. Verge, C. De Kimpe, and R.L. Desjardins, "Agricultural Production, Greenhouse Gas Emissions and Mitigation Potential," *Agriculture and Forest Meteorology* 142 (2007): 255.

[36] Christy L. van Beek et al., "Feeding the World's Increasing Population While Limiting Climate Change Impacts: Linking N_2O and CH_4 Emissions from Agriculture to Population Growth," *Environmental Science & Policy* 13 (2010): 90.

[37] Pimentel and Pimentel, "Global Environmental Resources Versus World Population Growth," 196.

[38] John Sheffield, "World Population Growth and the Role of Annual Energy Use per Capita," *Technological Forecasting and Social Change* 59 (1998): 56.

[39] Vaclovas Miskinis et al., "Aspirations for Sustainability and Global Energy Development Trends," *Journal of Security and Sustainability Issues* 3, no. 4 (2014): 17–18.

[40] IPCC, "Summary for Policymakers," in *Climate Change 2013: The Physical Science Basis. Contribution of Working Group I to the Fifth Assessment Report of the Intergovernmental Panel on Climate Change*, ed. T.F. Stocker et al. (Cambridge University Press, Cambridge, United Kingdom and New York, NY, USA, 2013): 11.

[41] Miskinis et al., "Aspirations for Sustainability and Global Energy Development Trends," 18.

[42] Daniel Yergin, *The Quest: Energy, Security, and the Remaking of the Modern World* (New York: Penguin, 2012): 239.

[43] Herman E. Daly, "Toward Some Operational Principles of Sustainable Development," *Ecological Economics* 2 (1990): 2–4.

[44] Marko M. Mihic, et al., "Comparative Analysis of Global Trends in Energy Sustainability," *Environmental Engineering and Management Journal* 13, no. 4 (2014): 948–949.

[45] IEA, *World Energy Outlook 2016: Executive Summary*, 2.

[46] International Energy Agency, *World Energy Outlook 2016: Executive Summary* (Paris, France: International Energy Agency, 2016): 2.

CHAPTER 4

Air Quality and Clean Air Policies

INTRODUCTION

Clean air has been a concern of governments and the public both domestically and internationally since the 1940s. Several incidents that occurred in the 1940s and 1950s of extreme smog that resulted in sickness and death raised awareness of the seriousness of air pollution. In the U.S., smog events in Los Angeles, California and Donora, Pennsylvania resulted in the first state efforts to reduce air pollution. A major smog event in London, U.K., which killed thousands, brought the issue into international dialog.

After California launched a state-based structure to battle air pollution, the U.S. federal government also took on the issue nationally. Beginning in the late 1950s, the federal government began enacting laws to research the causes and seek regional solutions to air pollution. These early efforts were too weak to provide any viable solution, so a change in policy was undertaken in 1970 when the first air pollution control act with considerable power was passed. That law, the Clean Air Act of 1970, used a command-and-control approach to air pollution, mandating that each state put forth a plan to reduce pollution for six criteria pollutants. This law was amended in 1977 and again in 1990 to improve air quality even further and to address other issues including visibility, hazardous air pollutants, acid rain, and ozone depletion.

Nations were aware that air pollution emitted in one nation often crossed borders to cause harm in another nation. This first became an issue with the discovery of declining fish populations in Scandinavia. Research proved that acidification of water bodies in Scandinavia was the result of European emissions of sulfur dioxide. In North America, Canada claimed forest damage and water body acidification because of sulfur dioxide emissions from the northeastern U.S. states. Seeking a solution to transboundary issues associated with air pollution, the nations came together under the auspices of the United Nations in 1979 to forge the first international agreement on air pollution, the Convention on Long-Range Transboundary Air Pollution. This successful agreement first addressed the issue of acid rain by seeking to control sulfur dioxide and was later extended to other substances after several amendments. As knowledge of transboundary pollutants grew globally, further agreements were adopted. The Stockholm Convention on Persistent Organic Pollutants, negotiated in 2001, sought to extend the controls on persistent organic pollutants already adopted under the Convention on Long-Rang Transboundary Air Pollution.

Scientific discovery of potential harm to the protective stratospheric ozone layer by certain chemicals highlighted the need for an international agreement to ban these chemicals. Several international meetings, first in Vienna and then in Montreal, resulted in negotiation of the Montreal Protocol on Substances that Deplete the Ozone Layer in 1987. The Montreal Protocol was amended several times to expand it to other chemicals, adjust it to new scientific discoveries, and to hasten the phaseout implementation time frame.

Concern about the warming of the planet due to emission of greenhouse gases resulted in negotiation of the United Nations Framework Convention on Climate Change in 1992. This framework convention, which only required parties to provide an annual inventory of emissions, was eventually followed by a binding treaty in 1997, the Kyoto Protocol. The Kyoto Protocol required the developed nations to reduce their greenhouse gas emissions but contained no requirement for developing nations to do the same. The U.S., however, never ratified the Kyoto Protocol. When the Kyoto Protocol ended it was replaced by the Paris Agreement, negotiated in 2015. The Paris Agreement consisted of voluntary pledges from all nations regarding emissions reduction efforts. Championed by then President Obama of the U.S. and Xi Jinping of China, it was agreed to by 195 countries. The Trump administration, however, announced a planned U.S. withdrawal from the agreement June 1, 2017.

Beginning with domestic consideration, this chapter provides a detailed description of the major U.S. legislation to control air pollution as well as an assessment of how successful domestic laws have been. The chapter then proceeds to a discussion of the international air pollution agreements and their amendments.

DOMESTIC CONSIDERATIONS

The initial impetus for concern over air pollution came as a result of several focusing events that occurred in the 1940s and early 1950s. In the summer of 1943, Los Angeles, California experienced the earliest instance of severe smog. Visibility was reduced to 3 blocks and people suffered stinging eyes, nausea, vomiting, and overall discomfort. As a result of this event, California's Governor Earl Warren signed into law the Air Pollution Control Act of 1947 which established pollution control districts in every county in the state. The first was established that year in Los Angeles and it became the first pollution control district in the U.S.[1] In 1948, smog engulfed Donora, Pennsylvania, killing nearly two dozen people. In 1952, world attention focused on London as what came to be called 'The Great Pea Soup' descended on the city. An inversion of cold air aloft held smog over the city for four days, trapping the smoke from coal heating stoves, diesel exhaust from vehicles, and industrial smokestack emissions. The Great Pea Soup killed twelve thousand people.[2] The response in the U.S. was to raise public concern and interest in air pollution to the federal level.

Early Federal Legislation

The first federal law governing air pollution was the Air Pollution Control Act of 1955. Its key provision was to provide funding for air pollution research. It was followed by the Clean Air Act of 1963, the first in a series of laws that would come to be known collectively as the Clean Air Act (CAA). This act provided for the development of a national program to control air pollution as well as for expanded research under what was then the Department of Health, Education, and Welfare (HEW). The Air Quality Act of 1967 established programs for control of interstate air pollution and again expanded research. It was the first law that required states to establish outdoor or ambient air standards based on federal criteria for air quality control regions designated by HEW. These early laws were relatively weak, lacked enforcement, and did not provide for a unified national approach. Rather, they expanded research and sought regional solutions for air pollution. One major accomplishment of these early laws, however, was the establishment of federal-state partnerships, or what would later become a system of environmental federalism, whereby the states have major responsibility for implementation while the federal government has the leading role for establishing regulatory standards.[3]

The Clean Air Act of 1970

The Clean Air Act of 1970 departed decidedly from earlier laws, marking the beginning of the modern era of air pollution prevention. The act was drafted at a time of high national concern over the environment. General public sentiment that produced the first Earth Day and compelled Richard Nixon to establish the Environmental Protection Agency (EPA) and the Council on Environmental Quality (CEQ) also drove Congress to pass a national law that had some strong provisions. The 1970 CAA contained several provisions of considerable importance.

The first was the creation of National Ambient Air Quality Standards (NAAQS) which were to be established by EPA to protect human health and the environment. The primary standards were to protect human health and the secondary standards were to protect buildings, crops, forests, water, and other creatures or objects. The EPA was to set the NAAQS at levels to provide the public with "an adequate margin of safety" from criteria pollutants: sulfur dioxide, carbon monoxide, nitrogen dioxide, ozone, and particulate matter. Lead was added in 1977. Hydrocarbons were eliminated in 1978.[4] The NAAQS were to be set to safe levels regardless of the cost of achieving those levels. Table 4.1 shows the NAAQS for the criteria pollutants.

Table 4.1

National Ambient Air Quality Standards

(in Effect in 2017)

Pollutant	Averaging Time	Standard Level	Standard Type
Carbon Monoxide (CO)	8 hour	9 ppm	Primary
	1 hour	35 ppm	Primary
Lead (Pb)	Rolling 3 month average	$0.15 \mu g/m^3$	Primary and secondary
Nitrogen Dioxide (NO$_2$)	1hour	100 ppb	Primary
	1 year	53 ppb	Primary and secondary
Ozone (O$_3$)	8 hours	0.070 ppm	Primary and secondary
Particle Pollution 2.5 (PM$_{2.5}$)	1 year	$12.0 \mu g/m^3$	Primary
	1 year	$15.0 \mu g/m^3$	Secondary
	24 hours	$35 \mu g/m^3$	Primary and secondary

Particle Pollution 10 (PM_{10})	24 hours	150 $\mu g/m^3$	Primary and secondary
Sulfur Dioxide (SO_2)	1 hour	75 ppb	Primary
	3 hours	0.5 ppm	Secondary

Source: EPA, NAAQS Table, accessed May 26, 2017, https://www.epa.gov/criteria-air-pollutants/naaqs-table.

The primary sources of emission of sulfur dioxide and other sulfur oxides are fossil fuels burned by power plants as well as by industrial facilities. Smaller sources include some industrial processes, locomotives, ships, and heavy equipment that burn fuel with a high sulfur content. SO_2 can harm both health and the environment. Short-term exposure can cause respiratory problems, and this is particularly an issue for those who suffer from asthma. Elevated levels of SO_2 in the air can lead to the formation of other sulfur oxides which may react with other substances in the air to form small particulate matter (PM) (discussed below). If these particles remain in the air, the result is lowered visibility due to haze. SO_2 can cause damage to plants as well as decrease their growth. SO_2 is a primary cause of acid rain which harms crops and fish, as well as causing damage to buildings, statues, and monuments.[5]

Carbon monoxide is a colorless, odorless gas that is released by combustion. For ambient air, the greatest sources of CO are cars, trucks, and other vehicles or machinery that burn fossil fuels. When humans or animals breathe air with substantial amounts of CO, the amount of oxygen that can be carried by the blood stream is reduced. At very high levels, which are possible in enclosed environments or indoors, CO can cause symptoms from dizziness and confusion to unconsciousness and death. Elevated levels of outdoor CO can be an issue for people with heart disease because those individuals may already have reduced capacity for their blood stream to carry oxygen.[6]

Nitrogen dioxide is a gas in the family of highly reactive gases known as nitrogen oxides (NO_x) which also includes nitrous acid and nitric acid. NO_2 gets into the air mainly by the burning of fossil fuels and so it can be found in auto, bus, and truck emissions as well as from power plants and equipment that burns fossil fuels. Breathing air with elevated levels of NO_2 can cause respiratory difficulties especially for those who suffer from asthma or for those with other respiratory diseases. Symptoms include coughing, wheezing, and difficult breathing which may necessitate hospital admissions. Long-term exposure will increase the likelihood of developing asthma or respiratory infections. Nitrogen dioxide and nitrogen oxides react with other substances in the air to form particulate matter and ozone, both of which can cause harmful effects on the respiratory system. NO_2 and NO_x combine with water, oxygen, and other substances in the atmosphere to form acid rain. The particulate matter formed by NO_2 and NO_x causes haze and lowers visibility. NO_x in the air can also contribute to nutrient pollution in water bodies.[7]

Ozone is harmful to air quality when it exists outside the protective stratospheric ozone layer. Ground-level ozone is not emitted but rather is created by a chemical reaction between NO_x and volatile organic compounds (VOCs) in the sunlight. Major sources of NO_x and VOCs are industrial facilities, power plants, auto exhaust, gasoline vapors, and chemical solvents. Breathing ozone can cause airway inflammation, chest pain, coughing, throat irritation, and reduced lung function. It is particularly bad for people with asthma or suffering from emphysema or bronchitis as well as for children and the elderly. Ozone can harm plants and reduce their growth.[8]

Particulate matter, or particle pollution, is a mixture of liquid droplets and solid particles in the air. Some of the solid particles may be visible to the human eye such as dirt, smoke, and dust while other particles are too small to be visible without magnification. There are two designations of PM: PM_{10} and $PM_{2.5}$. PM_{10} consists of inhalable particles (dust, mold, pollen, etc.) that are 10 microns and smaller. $PM_{2.5}$ consists of fine inhalable particles (combustion particles, organic compounds, metals, etc.) that are 2.5 microns and smaller. To visualize the size, it is useful to compare it to the average human hair, which is 50–70 microns in diameter. Another useful comparison is to fine beach sand, which measures 90 microns in diameter. The sources of PM vary. Some are emitted directly from a source such as construction sites, fields, smokestacks or fires while others are formed in the atmosphere as a result of chemical reactions. Important sources of PM include sulfur dioxide and nitrogen oxides. PM is a health hazard because it can be inhaled. PM_{10} is a health problem because it can get deeply into human lungs and may even be able to pass into the bloodstream. $PM_{2.5}$ is the main cause of haze and reduced visibility.[9]

Lead air pollution comes from a variety of sources including lead smelters, ore and metal processing, piston-engine aircraft using leaded aviation fuel, waste incinerators, utilities, and lead-acid battery manufacturers. Lead in the air has decreased 98 percent between 1980 and 2014 primarily as a result of EPA regulations to remove lead from gasoline. Lead's health effects are quite serious. Once taken into the body, lead circulates in the blood and eventually accumulates in the bones. Lead can cause damage to the nervous system, kidneys, immune system, cardiovascular system, reproductive and development systems. The most common problem seen is neurological effects in children, including lowered IQ, learning deficits, and behavioral problems. Lead in the environment can result in neurological effects in vertebrates as well as decreased growth rates and reproductive rates in plants and animals.[10]

Aside from the NAAQS, the Clean Air Act established a number of regulatory programs. Clean Air Act of 1970 required that "an ample margin of safety" be provided for hazardous air pollutants (HAPs) such as arsenic, chromium, hydrogen chloride, zinc, radioactive substances, and pesticides. Finally, the law established standards for mobile sources of air pollution including cars, trucks, and buses that would reduce hydrocarbon and carbon monoxide emissions by 90 percent. Stationary sources of hydrocarbon and carbon monoxide emissions including refineries, chemical companies, and industry were regulated. New sources of pollution were to be held to rigorous ("best available technology") New Source Performance Standards (NSPS) and were to be regulated industry by industry. Existing sources were to be held to lower standards.[11]

The Clean Air Act was implemented using a system of regulatory federalism under which the federal government sets a national standard that serves as a regulatory floor. States are free to adopt more environmentally protective standards if they so desire. Using this concept of regulatory federalism, each state was to draft a State Implementation Plan (SIP) to implement the federal standards. This provided the states flexibility in deciding how to meet federal standards and accounts for geographic variation. The EPA was to approve the SIPs. If a state failed to get EPA approval, the EPA was given authority to impose a federal implementation plan on the state. SIPs had to include enforceable emission limitations along with plans for monitoring, compiling, and analyzing data. The EPA would not accept a SIP that did not provide regulations that were enforceable, quantifiable, and accountable. Overall, the 1970 CAA was legislation with ambitious goals to be achieved in a tight time frame. Congress provided specific dates by which goals were to be attained. To meet the levels specified in the NAAQS, state SIPs adopted specific strategies and rules based on the environment and economic situation of each state. Monitoring of the NAAQS was to be done via geographically specified air quality control regions (AQCRs) that may or may not align with traditional political geographic divisions. The AQCRs were to be identified as either attainment or nonattainment. For attainment regions, the goal was to remain in attainment. For nonattainment regions, states were required to implement strategies and rules to bring the area into attainment.[12]

The Clean Air Act Amendments of 1977

Public concern over clean air was quite intense in 1970. Acting on behalf of public sentiment, the Sierra Club insisted that the CAA required programs not only to clean up dirty air but also programs to prevent further degradation in areas with already clean air. The EPA did not move on this strategy, prompting the Sierra Club to sue, and the courts agreed with the Sierra Club's interpretation of the law. This resulted in a wide public debate about preventing the worsening of air quality in regions with relatively clean air and the major "prevention of significant deterioration" programs in the 1977 Clean Air Act Amendments. The 1977 law established three classes of air quality. Class 1, the cleanest, was to have the strongest protection against deterioration. National parks and wilderness areas were given Class 1 designation, but all classes were to be protected from major loss of quality. Because concerns had been raised about visibility across the Grand Canyon, the law also specified that EPA and the National Park Service (NPS) define visibility standards and decide to what lands they should be applied.[13] The act contained a controversial provision that required the use of scrubbers to remove sulfur dioxide from new power plants. This provision was written into the law to protect the high-sulfur coal industry. The 1977 act also pulled back on some of the more aggressive deadlines imposed in the 1970 law, giving polluters more time to come into compliance.[14]

While some progress was made in cleaning the nation's air due to the 1970 and 1977 CAAs, problems remained. Hazardous air pollutants proved to be difficult to clean up and needed to be reconsidered. Many cities continued to experience unhealthy levels of pollutants. New problems also emerged including acid rain, the hole in the ozone layer, the rising importance of mobile sources of pollution, and greenhouse gas emissions that were contributing to climate change. As the country moved politically to the right with the election of Ronald Reagan, concern grew regarding the burden of regulations on the economy both in terms of costs to industry, slowed innovation, and reduced economic growth.

The Clean Air Act Amendments of 1990

The amendments passed in 1990 continued the environmental federalism of the 1970 and 1977 acts while also including major new programs to address emerging problems. The 1990 amendments continued the practice of the EPA setting levels for the NAAQS for carbon monoxide, lead, ozone, nitrogen dioxide, sulfur dioxide, and particulate matter as well as implementation in the states through the SIPs. NAAQS continued to be monitored via the AQCRs. Title I of the 1990 amendments added new provisions for regulating air quality in nonattainment areas by creating a new classification of areas that failed to comply with NAAQs for ozone, carbon monoxide, and particulates. Depending on the severity of the pollution, areas were given between 3 and 20 years to come into compliance. Title II of the law also set more than 90 new emission standards for automobiles and trucks. Cleaner or reformulated fuels were also mandated for selected areas of the country where carbon monoxide levels, primarily in winter, were a problem. Title III required the EPA to create national standards for all major sources of hazardous air pollutants. Tired of the lack of seriousness the Reagan administration's EPA had taken towards environmental protection, the law specifically identified 189 chemicals to be regulated by specific deadlines.[15] Since 1990, the EPA has made changes to the list through rulemaking and now lists 187 hazardous air pollutants. Examples of hazardous air pollutants include benzene, perchloroethylene, methylene chloride, dioxin, asbestos, toluene, cadmium, mercury, chromium, and lead compounds.[16] Major changes were introduced in the 1990 amendments through both Title IV, Title V, and Title VI. Title IV dealt with the acid rain, Title V established a new permit program to enforce the act, and Title VI addressed ozone depletion.

Acid rain includes any form of precipitation with acidic components, primarily sulfuric acid or nitric acid, that fall to the ground either in wet or dry forms. Acid rain is caused when sulfur dioxide and nitrogen oxides are emitted into the air and transported by wind. These substances react with water, oxygen and other chemicals to create sulfuric and nitric acids. Most of the SO_2 and NO_x in the atmosphere comes from 3 sources: the burning of fossil fuels, vehicle and heavy equipment emissions, and manufacturing or oil refineries. Nearly two thirds of the SO_2 and one quarter of the NO_x comes from electric power generation. This acid can fall to the Earth as precipitation or it can be deposited in dry form. When the acid particles deposit in dry form, they cover surfaces that will be washed off in the next rain storm and this runoff can be harmful to plants and animals. The acid particles can also form larger particles during transport and these larger particles can be harmful to human health.[17]

Title IV of the 1990 amendments dealt with acid rain using an innovative new approach to regulation. Departing from its typical use of command-and-control regulations, the program set up by Title IV instead sought to use market mechanisms to control acid deposition. The program created a new emissions trading program for SO_2. This was accomplished by allotting to each coal burning power plant an allowance for each ton of SO_2 emitted. This allocation was to be reduced in subsequent years with the intention of putting pressure on inefficient power plants to improve their operations. Power plants were permitted to bank, trade, or sell their excess allowances thus creating a cap-and-trade market for SO_2. Title IV required that national sulfur emissions be cut in half by 2000. In addition, the largest SO_2 emitters in the utility sector were required to meet stricter standards.[18] This program proved successful and was subsequently used as a model for the cap-and-trade program for carbon pollution established by the Kyoto Protocol to deal with climate change.

Title VI of the act addressed the issue of the depletion of the ozone layer. The ozone layer protects plants and animals from the sun's harmful ultraviolet (UV) light. Exposure to UV light can cause crop damage, skin cancer, and cataracts. The ozone layer is in the stratosphere, which is the layer of the atmosphere that extends from about 6 miles to 31 miles above the Earth. The ozone layer is concentrated in the stratosphere between 9 and 19 miles above the Earth. The ozone layer absorbs part of the sun's UV light thus acting as a sunscreen. Beginning in the 1970s, scientific studies showed that the ozone layer was being depleted by chlorine and bromine atoms. Ozone depleting substances (ODS) release chlorine or bromine when exposed to UV light and these include chlorofluorocarbons (CFCs), hydrochlorofluorocarbons (HCFCs), carbon tetrachloride, methyl chloroform, halons, and methyl bromide. While these substances are released at the Earth's surface, they eventually make their way into the stratosphere where they can cause ozone depletion.[19]

During the 1970s, the U.S. scientific community, led by the National Academy of Sciences (NAS), National Aeronautics and Space Administration (NASA), National Oceanic and Atmospheric Administration (NOAA), and leading universities conducted a broad range of research on ODS. By 1975, they had established that CFCs were reaching the stratosphere and that they were being hit by UV light causing them to release chlorine. In 1985, British scientists reported that they had found a thinning of the ozone layer over Antarctica. This thinning was widely reported by the press worldwide as a "hole" in the ozone layer, thus creating considerable dread and demand that action be taken. International action on ODS resulted in the negotiation of the Montreal Protocol on Substances that Deplete the Ozone Layer (discussed below) in 1987.[20] The extensive public anxiety that resulted from the discovery of the ozone hole moved U.S. lawmakers to strengthen the provisions established in international law and to speed the phaseout of ODS beyond what the U.S. had agreed to as a party to the Montreal Protocol.

Since 1970, air pollution in the U.S. has been vastly reduced. From 1990 to 2016, the six criteria pollutants showed the following reductions: 22 percent for ozone, 42 percent for $PM_{2.5}$, 39 percent for PM_{10}, 99 percent for lead, 56 percent for nitrogen dioxide, 72 percent for carbon monoxide, and 85 percent for sulfur dioxide.[21] In 2011, the third evaluation report of the Clean Air Act by the EPA estimated that the 1990 amendments had prevented 160,000 cases of premature mortality due to poor air quality. Further, the Office of Management and Budget (OMB) reported that the benefits of implementing the Clean Air Act are far greater than the costs.[22]

Greenhouse Gas Reporting

While no national domestic legislation has addressed the issue of climate change, the United States is a party to the United Nations Framework Convention on Climate Change (UNFCCC). To fulfill our responsibilities to that global agreement, the EPA has been maintaining and reporting the inventory of U.S. greenhouse gas (GHG) emissions and sinks since the early 1990s. The annual report provides the UNFCCC secretariat with an accounting of all anthropogenic sources of carbon dioxide, methane, hydrofluorocarbons, perfluorocarbons, nitrous oxide, sulfur hexafluoride and nitrogen trifluoride. The report also provides information on carbon dioxide emissions removed from the atmosphere through sinks such as forest, soils, and vegetation. In 2015, the U.S. released 6,587 million metric tons of greenhouse gases. The actual release was reduced via sinks to 5,828 million metric tons. Greenhouse gas emissions in 2015 were 11.5 percent below releases in 2005 but still slightly higher than 1990 levels. In 2015 the electric sector accounted for 29 percent of those emissions, transportation 27 percent, industry 21 percent, commercial and residential 12 percent, and agriculture 9 percent.[23]

GLOBAL CONSIDERATIONS

A variety of nations began to consider air pollution an issue for multinational environmental agreements (MEAs) in the late 1960s when Scandinavian scientists observed a marked decline in local fish populations. Research revealed the culprit to be lake acidification, owed to acid rain tied to SO_2 emissions in continental Europe. In the early 1970s, the issue also arose in North America as Canadian scientists claimed damage to Canadian forests and lakes as a result of U.S. SO_2 emissions.

Convention on Long-Range Transboundary Air Pollution

In 1972, the notion of transboundary transport of air pollutants became an issue for discussion at the United Nations Conference on the Human Environment in Stockholm. Several years later a meeting was held in Geneva, Switzerland under the auspices of the UN Economic Commission for Europe (UNECE), which resulted in the Convention on Long-Range Transboundary Air Pollution (CLRTAP) in 1979. CLRTAP was the first international agreement to address the problem of transboundary air pollution. CLRTAP focused initially on sulfur dioxide, with the expectation that it would expand later to other pollutants. Initial parties to the treaty included all of Western Europe, Eastern Europe, Russia, Canada, and the United States. CLRTAP went into force in 1983. CLRTAP has been extended by a series of protocols, the last of which was adopted in 1999. These protocols expanded the substances to include nitrogen oxides, VOCs, persistent organic pollutants, heavy metals, and ground-level ozone. Parties to the agreement grew over time to fifty-one nations.[24]

Stockholm Convention on Persistent Organic Pollutants (POPs)

Beginning in 1998, international negotiations began on a new multilateral treaty on POPs. Those negotiations resulted in the Stockholm Convention on Persistent Organic Pollutants, which was agreed to in 2001 and entered into force in 2004. It includes 170-member nations. POPs are toxic chemicals that are easily transported across borders via the wind or water. POPs generated in one country can readily affect people and wildlife of other countries. POPs last in the environment for extended periods and they bioaccumulate, passing from one species to another through the food chain. The Stockholm Convention initially targeted twelve key POPs known as the "dirty dozen." These include: aldrin, chlordane, dichlorodiphenyl trichloroethane (DDT), dieldrin, endrin, heptachlor, hexachlorobenzene, mirex, toxaphene, polychlorinated biphenyls (PCBs), polychlorinated dibenzo-p-dioxins (dioxins), and polychlorinated dibenzofurans (furans). Since the initial list was created, other chemicals have been added. POPs were widely used in industry in the years after the Second World War and while they had properties that made them useful, they also had unintended human health effects. Perhaps the best known of the POPs are DDT, PCBs, and dioxin. The Stockholm Convention was convened in large part because of the finding of POPs in remote regions of the Arctic. This finding made nations aware of the easy transport of dangerous substances via global dust storms that have been observed by satellite imagery.[25]

Montreal Protocol on Substances That Deplete the Ozone Layer

As mentioned above, the negotiation of the Montreal Protocol was undertaken after the discovery of the "hole" in the ozone layer which caused considerable anxiety among nations. However, intense objection to regulating CFCs initially existed in the U.S. and in Europe, the top two centers of production. The chief blocking group in the U.S. was led by DuPont in alliance with the Chemical Manufacturer's Association while European opposition was led by the U.K. The newly elected Reagan administration argued that the science was not certain enough to justify a ban. In response, the United Nations Environment Programme (UNEP) established a Coordinating Committee on the Ozone Layer (CCOL) comprised of representatives of many governmental and nongovernmental organizations conducting ozone research. Leadership changes in the EPA made the U.S. more receptive to tackling the ozone threat and the agency sponsored international meetings to discuss the issue. The first meeting took place in Vienna in 1985, where a framework agreement to continue to study the issue was adopted. In the same year, British scientists found the "hole" in the ozone layer and NASA satellites confirmed the finding.[26] In addition to high-levels of trepidation driving the negotiations, DuPont also dropped its opposition to banning CFCs because it was suffering from poor public relations and it had a lead on developing a more profitable alternative. When negotiations began in Montreal, the opposition to eliminating CFCs collapsed and the treaty was agreed to.[27]

The Montreal Protocol, adopted in 1987, included provisions that allowed parties to the Protocol to respond quickly to new scientific evidence and accelerate the phaseout of ODS when necessary. Since its initial adoption, the Protocol has been adjusted 6 times and formally amended 4 times. The amendments have allowed the treaty to include new chemicals and to financially assist developing nations to comply. The amendments include the London Amendment of 1990, the Copenhagen Amendment of 1992, the Montreal Amendment of 1997, and the Beijing Amendment of 1999. Parties to the agreement meet annually to discuss and make decisions on implementation. Over 720 decisions on implementation have been made since the Protocol was adopted.[28] The Montreal Protocol is discussed more fully in chapter 13.

United Nations Framework Convention on Climate Change

The Rio Earth Summit of 1992 led to the adoption of several international treaties to deal with perceived problems. One was the United Nations Framework Convention on Climate Change. The goal of the UNFCCC is to prevent dangerous human interference with the Earth's climate. By the late 1970s, a growing number of scientists had begun to warn of the dangers of greenhouse gas emissions. These concerns were prominently backed by a series of reports from government agencies. In 1981, NASA's Institute for Space Studies issued a forecast that predicted warming trends that might be sufficient to melt the West Antarctic Ice Sheet causing massive sea-level rise. In 1983, the EPA predicted the globe would warm 2 degrees Celsius by 2050. The same year the National Academy of Sciences issued a report agreeing with the EPA. In 1988, James Hansen of NASA told a Congressional committee that there was evidence that global warming had begun. In response to these scientific warnings, the World

Meteorological Organization and the United Nations Environment Program organized the Intergovernmental Panel on Climate Change (IPCC). IPCC's task was to gather scientific information and present to the world's governments periodic reports on the status of climate change. The First Assessment Report (FAR) was released in 1990 and it played a pivotal role in the creation of the UNFCCC at the Rio Earth Summit.[29]

The goal of the UNFCCC was to stabilize GHGs at a level that would prevent serious anthropogenic contributions to climate change within a time frame that would allow ecosystems to adapt naturally to rising temperatures, to make sure that food production was not affected, and to allow for continued sustainable development. The UNFCCC put the responsibility for doing this in the hands of the developed countries, who were responsible for most past and then current emissions. While the UNFCCC did not put binding reductions in place, it provided the structure for negotiation of a subsequent treaty, the Kyoto Protocol, that would. The UNFCCC only required reporting of GHG emissions on an annual basis. Under the Kyoto Protocol, the developed countries, termed Annex I countries, were by 2000 to reduce GHG emissions to 1990 levels. In addition, they were to provide financial assistance and technology to developing countries so that they could take action on climate change. A system of loans and grants was set up and managed by the Global Environment Facility.[30]

The Kyoto Protocol was succeeded in 2015 by the Paris Agreement, which continues to function under the UNFCCC to reduce GHG emissions.[31] The Paris Agreement consists of voluntary pledges from all parties regarding emissions reduction efforts. Championed by then President Obama of the U.S. and Xi Jinping of China, it was agreed to by 195 countries, essentially making the fight against climate change an issue for almost every nation on Earth. The Trump administration, however, announced U.S. withdrawal from the agreement June 1, 2017. According to the terms of the agreement, that withdrawal procedure will take nearly four years. Since the U.S. was a party to the agreement, it will have to abide by the terms of the agreement which says parties must wait three years after the treaty comes into force to begin a one-year formal withdrawal process. The Paris agreement came into force November 4, 2016, so the U.S. cannot formally begin withdrawal until November 4, 2019. Final withdrawal cannot happen until after November 4, 2020. Climate change is discussed more fully in chapter 14.

Air Pollution: A Global Health Risk

In a report released in 2014, the World Health Organization (WHO) reported that in 2012, 7 million people died prematurely as a result of global air pollution. Said another way, air pollution deaths accounted for 11.6% of all deaths in 2012. This number doubled previous estimates, confirming that air pollution had become the world's single largest environmental health risk. The new estimates were the result of new global data mapping techniques incorporating satellite data, ground-level monitoring measurement, and data on pollution emissions from key sources. In addition to the known association between air pollution exposure and respiratory disease, the data underpinning the report revealed a strong link between exposure to air pollution and cardiovascular diseases, such as stroke and heart disease, as well as between exposure to air pollution and cancer. The report indicated that low- and middle-income groups in Southeast Asia and the Western Pacific had the largest exposure to air pollution, with a total of 2.6 million deaths related to ambient air pollution and 3.3 million deaths associated with indoor air pollution. Worldwide, WHO attributes 3.7 million deaths annually to outdoor air pollution and 4.3 million deaths to indoor air pollution. Table 4.2 shows the specific diseases linked to both indoor and outdoor air pollution.[32]

In a 2016 follow up study, WHO claimed that 90 percent of urban populations worldwide continued to be exposed in 2014 to particulate matter in outdoor air in excess of WHO air quality guidelines. Regional variations persist. High-income regions, including Europe and North America, continue to see improvements in air quality, largely due to efforts to reduce smog and particulates. However, outdoor air pollution has increased in low- and middle-income regions over the past decade. In particular, Southeast Asia has experienced such increases largely due to population growth and increasing industrialization without adequate laws to regulate the release of pollutants. As the success of the wealthy countries shows, setting standards and enforcing regulations, along with careful monitoring, results in cleaner air and fewer deaths from air pollution.[33]

Table 4.2

Indoor and Outdoor Air Pollution-Caused Deaths

Percent by Disease

Outdoor Air Pollution-Caused Deaths	Indoor Air Pollution-Caused Deaths
40% of ischaemic hearth diseases	26% of ischaemic hearth diseases
40% of strokes	34% of strokes
11% of chronic obstructive pulmonary disease (COPD)	22% COPD
6% of lung cancers	6% lung cancers
3% of lower acute respiratory infections in children	12% of lower acute respiratory infections in children

Source: "7 Million Deaths Annually Linked to Air Pollution," World Health Organization, accessed April 17, 2017, http://www.who.int/mediacentre/news/releases/2014/air-pollution/en/.

CONCLUSION

U.S. domestic alarm over air pollution resulted after several extreme smog events that occurred in the 1940s and early 1950s. While California became the first U.S. state to enact air pollution control legislation, the first federal law was the Air Pollution Control Act of 1955 which provided funding for air pollution research. It was followed by the Clean Air Act of 1963, which provided for the development of a national program to control air pollution and further research. The Air Quality Act of 1967 established programs for interstate air pollution, expanded research, and required states to establish ambient air quality standards. These initial laws were weak in several ways. Enforcement was lax, and they did not create a unified national approach to air pollution. They did, however, initiate a system of federal-state partnerships that would become the basis of later laws.

The Clean Air Act of 1970 was the first federal air pollution law that was significantly different from earlier laws. Its enactment marked the beginning of the modern era of air pollution prevention. The law required EPA to set primary and secondary National Ambient Air Quality Standards. The primary standards were to protect human health and the secondary standards were to protect the environment. The law provided NAAQS for six criteria pollutants: sulfur dioxide, carbon monoxide, nitrogen dioxide, ozone, particulate matter, and lead (added in 1977). While the law did specify the regulation of some hazardous air pollutants, enforcement of that provision was not forthcoming, and the issue would have to be readdressed in the 1990 CAA Amendments. The intent of Congress was clear in that they expected the law to clean up the air regardless of cost.

The Clean Air Act of 1970 was designed using regulatory federalism. Each state was required to create a SIP, that the EPA approved, to implement the federal standards. The law set ambitious dates by which goals were to be achieved. To reach the levels established in the NAAQS, each state had to put in place rules based on the specific situation in its state. The law required monitoring, by air quality control regions, of the air quality to assure the NAAQS were being met. The regions were identified as either attainment or nonattainment. For attainment regions, the law required the region to stay in attainment. For nonattainment regions, states were obligated bring the area into attainment.

One of the main drivers of the 1977 amendments of the CAA was poor visibility in the national parks so the amendments focused on prevention of significant deterioration. The amendments set three classes of air quality and national parks were put in the highest category. The 1977 act also recognized that the 1970 law had been unrealistic in terms of deadlines, so the amendments extended the time limit for compliance.

The CAA Amendments passed in 1990 continued the regulatory federalism of the 1970 and 1977 acts while also adding two major new programs to address acid rain and ozone depletion. Title I of the 1990 amendments added requirements for regulating air quality in nonattainment areas, which were given between 3 and 20 years to come into compliance. Title II of the law set new emission standards for vehicles. Reformulated fuels were mandated for some areas of the country where carbon monoxide levels were high. Title III addressed hazardous air pollutants by naming 189 specific chemicals to be regulated by clear deadlines. Title IV set up a new cap-and-trade program to deal with the acid rain by reducing SO_2. The program proved effective and became a model for the future use of market mechanisms in environmental law and agreements. Title V established more effective permitting requirements. Title VI addressed stratospheric ozone depletion by speeding up the phaseout of ODS.

The effectiveness of domestic air pollution programs has been demonstrated, at least by reviewing the levels of criteria pollutants in the air. Since the 1970s, air pollution levels have declined, although many people, especially in cities, continue to experience higher levels of smog than they should. As a party to the UNFCCC the U.S. is required to keep an inventory of greenhouse gas emissions. They, too, have declined. Emissions in 2015 were nearly 12 percent below 2005 levels despite the fact that the U.S. never joined the Kyoto Protocol, the international treaty in place during that time span.

International interest in air pollution dates to the same focusing events that brought greater awareness to Americans. Europe was particularly motivated to deal with its air pollution after the London smog event. One of the first issues to be dealt with in a multinational manner was acid rain. CLRTAP of 1979 focused initially on sulfur dioxide and later expanded to other pollutants including nitrogen oxides, VOCs, POPs, heavy metals, and ground-level ozone.

The problem of persistent organic pollutants was insufficiently addressed by amendments to the Convention on Long-Range Transboundary Air Pollution and so further negotiations resulted in the Stockholm Convention on Persistent Organic Pollutants of 2001. The Stockholm Convention was motivated by scientists finding POPs in remote regions of the Arctic.

The discovery of the "hole" in the ozone layer moved nations to negotiate the Montreal Protocol of 1987 that banned CFCs and other ODS. Since its initial adoption, the Protocol has been adjusted and amended to include new chemicals and to provide financial assistance to developing nations so that they could also comply with the treaty.

Concern over increasing levels of GHGs in the atmosphere and associated temperature increases led to the UNFCCC, which seeks to prevent dangerous human interference with the climate. The UNFCCC did not put binding reductions of greenhouse gases in place, but it provided the structure for negotiation of a subsequent treaty, the Kyoto Protocol, that did. Under the Kyoto Protocol, the developed countries were by 2000 to reduce GHG emissions to 1990 levels. The Kyoto Protocol was succeeded in 2015 by the Paris Agreement, which will continue to operate under the UNFCCC despite the announcement in 2017 of the U.S. intention to withdraw.

Despite efforts to improve air quality, many millions die prematurely from dirty air. Indoor and outdoor air remains a problem worldwide, but it is a more severe problem in poorer countries. A 2016 World Health Organization study reported that 90 percent of urban populations worldwide continued to be exposed to particulate matter in ambient air in excess of WHO air quality guidelines. The poor suffer more than the wealthy. Europeans and North Americans continue to see improvements in ambient air quality mostly because of their environmental regulations that reduce smog and particulates. Ambient air pollution has increased in poorer regions and indoor air pollution remains a persistent problem.

1   "Key Events in the History of Air Quality in California," California Environmental Protection Agency Air Resources Board, accessed August 10, 2018, https://ww2.arb.ca.gov/about/history.

2   Luke Fowler, "Assessing the Framework of Policy Outcomes: The Case of the U.S. Clean Air Act and Clean Water Act," *Journal of Environmental Assessment Policy and Management* 16, no. 4 (2014): 2, accessed May 18, 2017, doi:10.1142/S1464333214500343.

3   Fowler, "Assessing the Framework of Policy Outcomes," 3–4.

4   Michael E. Kraft, *Environmental Policy and Politics* (Boston: Pearson, 2015), 137–138.

5   "Sulfur Dioxide Basics," EPA, accessed May 25, 2017, https://www.epa.gov/so2-pollution/sulfur-dioxide-basics.

6   "Carbon Monoxide (CO) Pollution in Outdoor Air," EPA, accessed May 25, 2017, https://www.epa.gov/co-pollution/basic-information-about-Carbon-Monoxide-co-outdoor-air-pollution.

7   "Nitrogen Dioxide (NO₂) Pollution," EPA, accessed May 25, 2017, https://www.epa.gov/no2-pollution/basic-information-about-no2.

8   "Ozone Pollution," EPA, accessed May 25, 2017, https://www.epa.gov/ozone-pollution/ozone-basics.

9   "Particulate Matter (PM) Pollution," EPA, accessed May 25, 2017, https://www.epa.gov/pm-pollution/particulate-matter-pm-basics.

10   "Lead Air Pollution," EPA, accessed May 25, 2017, https://www.epa.gov/lead-air-pollution/basic-information-about-lead-air-pollution.

11   Kraft, *Environmental Policy and Politics*, 137–138.

12   Fowler, "Assessing the Framework of Policy Outcomes," 4–6.

13   Samuel P. Hays, *Beauty, Health, and Permanence: Environmental Politics in the United States, 1955–1985* (Cambridge: Cambridge University Press, 1987), 121–122.

14   Kraft, *Environmental Policy and Politics*, 138.

15   Walter A. Rosenbaum, *Environmental Politics and Policy* (Thousand Oaks, CA: Sage/CQ Press, 2017), 206–207.

16   "What Are Hazardous Air Pollutants?" EPA, accessed May 26, 2017, https://www.epa.gov/haps/what-are-hazardous-air-pollutants.

17   "What is Acid Rain," EPA, accessed May 25, 2017, https://www.epa.gov/acidrain/what-acid-rain.

18   Rosenbaum, *Environmental Politics and Policy*, 207.

19   "Ozone Layer Protection," EPA, accessed May 25, 2017, https://www.epa.gov/ozone-layer-protection.

20   Craig Collins, *Toxic Loopholes: Failures and Future Prospects for Environmental Law* (Cambridge: Cambridge University Press, 2010), 161–162.

21   "Our Nation's Air," EPA, accessed November 6, 2017, https://gispub.epa.gov/air/trendsreport/2017/#highlights.

22   Fowler, "Assessing the Framework of Policy Outcomes," 13–14.

[23] "Greenhouse Gas Emissions," EPA, accessed May 26, 2017, https://www.epa.gov/ghgemissions/inventory-us-greenhouse-gas-emissions-and-sinks.

[24] Peter J. Stoett, *Global Ecopolitics: Crisis, Governance, and Justice* (Toronto: University of Toronto Press, 2012), 89–91.

[25] "International Cooperation," EPA, accessed May 26, 2017, https://www.epa.gov/international-cooperation/persistent-organic-pollutants-global-issue-global-response.

[26] Collins, *Toxic Loopholes*, 164–170.

[27] Collins, *Toxic Loopholes*, 194–196.

[28] "Ozone Secretariat," UNEP, accessed August 10, 2018, http://ozone.unep.org/.

[29] Dianne Rahm, *Climate Change Policy in the United States: The Science, the Politics, and the Prospects for Change* (Jefferson, NC: McFarland & Company, Inc. Publishers, 2010), 15–16.

[30] "First Steps to a Safer Future: Introducing the United Nations Framework Convention on Climate Change," UNFCCC, accessed August10, 2018, https://unfccc.int/resource/docs/publications/handbook.pdf.

[31] "Paris Agreement—Status of Ratification," UNFCCC, accessed May 30, 2017, http://unfccc.int/2860.php.

[32] "7 Million Deaths Annually Linked to Air Pollution," World Health Organization, accessed April 17, 2017, http://www.who.int/mediacentre/news/releases/2014/air-pollution/en/.

[33] World Health Organization, *World Health Statistics 2016: Monitoring Health for the SDGs* (Geneva: WHO Press, 2016), 94.

CHAPTER 5

Clean Water Policies

INTRODUCTION

Clean water has been a public policy concern since physicians linked diseases with contaminated water. In the 19th and early 20th century, clean water was considered a local or state issue. It was not until the nation's environmental awakening in the 1970s that the federal government would become involved in protecting the nation's surface waterways and groundwater.

The two most important federal laws involving clean water are the Clean Water Act and the Safe Drinking Water Act. Both are discussed in this chapter in considerable detail. Like the Clean Air Act, both are implemented using regulatory federalism. The federal government acknowledges the need to oversee the setting of standards, but it is the obligation of the states to achieve those standards.

Early federal efforts to control water pollution tended to be weak with reliance on voluntary approaches and only requiring that states study the issue. By the time the Cuyahoga River caught on fire, public outrage demanded a solution. The result was the Clean Water Act and its subsequent amendments, which set the regulatory framework for clean water. It applied only to surface water bodies, though, leaving the nation's groundwater largely uncontrolled by this federal law. However, about half of all drinking water comes from groundwater, therefore the federal government does regulate much of the nation's groundwater through the Safe Drinking Water Act.

The question of how effective each of these laws is in guaranteeing clean and safe water is a complicated one. While the CWA had shown considerable success in changing attitudes towards waste disposal in the nation's waterways, many bodies of water continue to be impaired. This persistence of high levels of impairment and failure to make progress on cleanup suggests the Clean Water Act has, at best, a mixed record of success. While the U.S. has by far safe and clean drinking water, issues have arisen. The Flint Michigan water crisis of 2015, when the tap water was contaminated by lead, raised the visibility of clean drinking water and made safe drinking water a politically charged issue. Problems include not only instances of lead contamination but wider issues of other potential hazards including pharmaceuticals and agricultural runoff.

Access to safe and clean water is a major international issue. Much of the world's population suffers daily from lack of access to clean water and adequate sanitation. Achieving access to safe and clean water is a major goal of the United Nations (UN), however, population increases, rising pollution, and climate change pose significant challenges. In turn, lack of access to clean and safe water threatens already unstable nations with more volatility and disruption.

The nations of the world have long recognized the importance of water resources. Several multilateral agreements have attempted to create international cooperation, especially over shared water resources. Two of the most important, the Convention on the Law of the Non-Navigational Uses of International Watercourses and the UN Economic Commission for Europe Convention on the Protection and Use of Transboundary Watercourses and International Lakes, are discussed in this chapter. Nations that share water resources often try to develop cooperative arrangements for water use. Some bilateral arrangements have been very successful but many times these agreements are either not forthcoming or unsuccessful in producing cooperative management. Some of these are discussed in the chapter including the details of U.S. water agreements with Canada and Mexico.

DOMESTIC CONSIDERATIONS

The nation's surface water bodies—its lakes, streams, ponds, rivers, and wetlands—are the most visible source of water for use in agriculture, industry, recreation, transport, electricity production, and for human and wildlife consumption. Because of their visibility, surface water became the first target of federal protection. But the nation also has massive amounts of underground water stored in aquifers that also provide for many of our water needs including drinking water. These underground sources, however, are regulated differently than surface water bodies and much of the regulation is by the states rather than the federal government. Most of the federal regulation of groundwater is capsulated in protections for drinking water.

Early Federal Legislation

The earliest federal interest in water addressed the needs of the arid West. Based upon the lobbying of the National Irrigation Association, mining interests in the West, and the backing of President Theodore Roosevelt, Congress passed the Reclamation Act of 1902. The statute authorized the construction of dams and distribution networks to serve the needs of 16 western states. Later, the federal government took an interest in the generation of electricity from these dams and in 1920 the Federal Power Act was passed creating the Federal Power Commission charged with selling excess electricity generated from federal dams.[1] Since the early 1900s, both the U.S. Bureau of Reclamation (USBR) and the U.S. Army Corps of Engineers (USACE) engaged in water projects to create water reservoirs, irrigation, flood control, and electricity generation.[2]

The earliest regulation of discharges to waterways involved concern with navigation rather than pollution. In 1899 Congress amended the Rivers and Harbors Act of 1890, later known as the

Refuse Act, to require dumpers to obtain Army Corps of Engineers-issued permits before discharging objects or substances into waterways that might interfere with navigation. This law also applied to wetlands. Beginning in the 1960s, the law was occasionally applied to industrial water pollution, but its focus remained on stopping obstructions to navigation.[3]

Regulation of water pollution took the same form as regulation of air pollution in so far as early federal laws focused primarily on research, voluntary actions, and state-lead approaches to cleaning up pollution. The first federal law was the Water Pollution Control Act of 1948 which required research into the condition of the nation's surface waterways. This law did not provide for the federal government to establish quality standards nor did it specifically ban the discharge of wastes into water bodies. Importantly, the law did provide financial assistance from the federal government to state and local governments for water treatment plants. That financial assistance would later be expanded. The Water Quality Act of 1965 went a bit further in requiring states to establish quality standards for interstate water bodies and to establish enforcement mechanisms, but the federal government remained in a passive role, acting only as an overseer of the states' actions.[4] The Clean Water Restoration Act of 1966 gave the federal government the authority to fine polluters $100 per day if they did not comply with reporting requirements. The Water Quality Improvement Act of 1970 further expanded federal authority and established a state certification program to prevent degradation of water quality below certain thresholds.[5]

While the federal role had been increasing incrementally, a dramatic shift occurred in the aftermath of an incident in Cleveland, Ohio. In 1969, an oil slick on the Cuyahoga River caught on fire. This was not the first time the river, used primarily for industrial waste disposal, had burned. When a picture of Cleveland's burning river made the front page of the nationally popular *Time Magazine*, however, it served as a focusing event to raise the importance of water pollution control in the U.S. The mayor of Cleveland became a vocal critic of water pollution and attempted to draw attention to the issue. He eventually was able to testify before a congressional committee investigating water pollution. The Cuyahoga River fire commanded considerable public attention and served to highlight the importance of clean water. Also in 1969, an oil spill off the coast of Santa Barbara focused public attention on the need for protection of water resources. The eventual result was the Federal Water Pollution Control Act Amendments of 1972, now referred to as the Clean Water Act, passed overwhelmingly by Congress after overriding a veto by President Nixon who was concerned about the cost of the proposed legislation.[6]

Clean Water Act and Its Amendments (CWA)

The CWA is the major federal law regulating pollution of navigable surface water bodies in the U.S. The act has jurisdiction over rivers, lakes, coastal waters, and wetlands but does not have control over groundwater. Adoption of the law revolutionized water pollution control law in two ways. First, the CWA reversed the traditional approach to water pollution which was based on the notion that it was acceptable to discharge pollutants into waterways until there were signs of clear problems from such releases. The CWA established a system whereby discharge of effluent into waterways was prohibited unless release was done in compliance with a government-issued permit, which typically would require pre-treatment of wastes to protect human health and the environment. Second, the CWA expanded the definition of what was considered effluent to include not only chemicals and wastes but also any substance that might change the water body's characteristics including its hydrology, sediments, or biodiversity.[7]

Just as the Clean Air Act embraced regulatory federalism as a mechanism to implement federal clean air policy, so, too, did the CWA. The CWA established a permit system for effluent discharge run by the Environmental Protection Agency (EPA) but it also placed the burden on state and local governments to implement water quality standards.[8] The CWA acknowledged that states had the primary responsibility for water pollution control. The law required the states to submit to the

EPA water quality standards for all interstate and intrastate waterways.[9] The Water Quality Criteria (WQC) were to be set using EPA guidelines which specified the levels of contaminants allowable.[10] States were to identify any water bodies that did not meet these standards and designate them as impaired.

The CWA prohibited discharge of any pollutant from a point source, such as a pipe, without a permit either from the EPA or a state agency implementing the program with the EPA's approval. The permits imposed effluent limitations that required that dischargers use the best available technology to pretreat wastes before discharge with the ultimate aim of achieving zero pollution discharge. Dischargers under the law were also required to meet stricter water quality-based limits to assure water quality standards. Those standards designated the use of the water for a purpose, such as swimming, drinking, or for protection of aquatic life. The standards were then set to the appropriate level to protect those purposes. These standards were to be set by the states but required EPA review and approval. For water bodies that remained polluted despite technology and water-quality controls, the law required states to calculate the total amount of pollution a water body could absorb without violating standards, to allocate those amounts between sources within the watershed, and to develop strategies to reduce pollution so as to meet the standards.[11] This part of the law primarily was concerned with nonpoint sources of pollution such as runoff. The statute required states to develop total maximum daily load (TMDL) programs and to address the impairment accordingly.[12]

Since the CWA established that the major responsibility for cleaning the nation's waters rested with the states and localities, Congress authorized large grants to municipalities for the construction of sewage treatment plants. At the time, more than 1,300 U.S. communities had sewer systems that discharged untreated waste directly into waterways and about the same number provided only primary treatment, which eliminated only 30 percent of pollutants, before disposal. The CWA allowed the EPA to make grants of $18 billion for construction of new treatment plants during the fiscal years of 1973–1975. The federal government's share of the costs was 75 percent. States, localities, and industrial users were expected to pay the remaining 25 percent.[13]

The permit system established by the CWA is the National Pollution Discharge Elimination System (NPDES). The CWA prohibits anyone from discharging pollutants from a point source into waterways without a NPDES permit. The NPDES permit specifies amounts of pollutants that may be discharged, monitoring and reporting requirements, and other specific requirements established by the law. The waterways covered include navigable waters, tributaries to navigable waters, interstate waters, the oceans (up to 200 miles offshore), and intrastate waters used by interstate travelers for purposes such as recreation, fishing for fish or shellfish sold in interstate commerce, or for industrial purposes by industries engaged in interstate commerce. The pollutants include waste such as dredged soil, solid waste, incinerator residue, sewage, garbage, sludge, chemicals, radioactive material, and heat. NPDES permits are issued by the states that have EPA approval to issue permits or by regional EPA offices in states without approval. Under the law the states were required to set maximum daily load limits to pollution to assure that aquatic life and wildlife would be protected.[14]

Under the law the EPA Administrator was required to publish a list of toxic pollutants, including those that after discharge and upon contact with an organism may cause death or disease, and effluent limits for those substances. Additionally, the EPA was required to publish pretreatment standards for industry discharging into a municipal sewage treatment plant so that the release would not interfere with the operation of the municipal sewage treatment plant.[15]

The CWA's section 311 addressed spills of oil and other hazardous substances into navigable waters of the U.S. as well as adjoining shorelines. It established procedures for preventing, reporting, and responding to spills.[16]

The CWA was amended in 1977 to expand regulations and the EPA's authority as well as to provide more federal funding for wastewater treatment plant construction. The 1981 Municipal Wastewater Treatment Construction Grants Amendments also provided for improvements in the capacity of municipal treatment plants. After many years of providing federal government grants for construction and expansion of wastewater treatment plants, the 1987 Water Quality Act reversed the trend by replacing the grants with a Clean Water Revolving Fund. The 1987 amendments also required the states to develop nonpoint pollution management plans and strategies.[17]

The CWA was amended in 2000 by the Beaches Environmental Assessment and Coastal Health (BEACH) Act. The goal of the amendments was to reduce health risks to users of the nation's beaches and coastal recreation areas by authorizing the EPA to award grants to support testing for microbes in coastal recreational waters. The amendments also provide for a public notification system of pollution occurrences, the Beach Advisory and Closing Online Notification (BEACON) system.[18]

Evaluation of the CWA

The CWA legislation had very ambitious goals. The primary objective of the act was not just to clean up the nation's water but to "restore and maintain the chemical, physical, and biological integrity of the nation's waters."[19] The law set a deadline date of 1985 by which time all discharges of wastes into navigable waterways were to be fully eliminated. Second, the law set an interim goal to "provide for the protection of fish, shellfish, and wildlife and recreation by July 1, 1983."[20] This second goal is often referred to as "fishable and swimmable." These goals were clearly overly ambitious. The zero-discharge goal, although only a goal and not required under the law, has not been met in the nearly half decade of CWA enforcement.

The CWA did produce noteworthy progress in reducing some forms of water pollution since its adoption. In particular, the construction of sewage treatment plants across the U.S. has resulted in the decrease of outbreaks of water-borne infectious disease. The CWA has reduced the direct release of industrial chemicals into waterways. However, neither of these problems has been solved entirely and other forms of water pollution have received far less attention. At best, the CWA must be considered a partial success as there is much work to be done to guarantee clean water in the U.S.[21]

The EPA maintains a list of over 100 pollutants that need to be monitored to assure water quality. There has not been consistent measurement of these substances geographically, so evaluation of the CWA is problematic. While the EPA claims the evidence is overwhelming that the CWA has achieved success, some studies suggest that cleanup of the nation's waterways has been spotty, with some states making more progress than others.[22]

The CWA requires states to designate waters that do not meet state quality standards as impaired and to devise for those waters a TMDL for pollutants causing the impairment. Early in the laws implementation, few such recovery plans were developed. This resulted in a number of citizen suits in the 1980s requiring the EPA to develop those TMDL programs. As of 2015, nearly 42,500 water bodies were on the impaired waters list. Despite the high number of waterways on the impairment list, few have been de-listed. This failure to clean impaired waters so that they might be de-listed is a strong indicator of the dubious success of the CWA.[23] Finally, the CWA left regulation of non-point sources of pollution almost exclusively to the states, which explains much of the difficulty in achieving water quality objectives.

Safe Drinking Water Act of 1974 and Its Amendments (SDWA)

The second important law dealing with water in the U.S. is the Safe Drinking Water Act. Americans get their drinking water from over

150,000 public water providers which are regulated by the EPA under the act. The law was initially passed in 1974 and was amended in 1986 and 1996. It was first passed into law after widespread public apprehension over drinking water contamination. The more specific concerns were over industrial pollutants found in the drinking water supplies in the Mississippi River Basin and trihalomethanes discovered in drinking water distribution systems.[24] Trihalomethanes are disinfectant by-products formed when chlorine is used to disinfect drinking water.

The SDWA was passed to assure Americans have access to safe drinking water. The initial law required that the EPA set national standard for drinking water to protect against both naturally-occurring and human-caused contaminants. The EPA was required to specify maximum contaminant levels (MCLs) for all known contaminants, or where MCLs proved impossible, to propose treatment technologies.[25]

EPA efforts to regulate drinking water got off to a very slow start after the passage of the law. Between 1974 and 1986, when the first amendments were passed, the EPA had finalized only one regulation to control water quality and that was to regulate total trihalomethanes for systems serving more than 10,000 people. The other accomplishment for this time period was the successful conversion of 22 already existing Public Health Service drinking water standards.[26]

Congress was dissatisfied with the progress the EPA was making in implementing the SDWA, so it amended the act. The 1986 amendments provided a list of chemicals to be regulated and Congress specifically required that the EPA regulate 25 additional substances every 3 years. The 1986 amendments added the requirement that surface water used as drinking water be filtered. Despite the specificity of the amendments, the EPA fell behind schedule and that resulted in lawsuits. Nevertheless, the EPA eventually finalized rules on 83 contaminants including volatile organic compounds (VOCs), coliform, synthetic organic chemicals, inorganic chemicals, lead, and copper.[27]

In 1993, there was an outbreak of *Cryptosporidium* in Milwaukee which sickened over 400,000. The cryptosporidium parasite is resistant to chlorine, but the problem in Milwaukee was that the filters being used needed the assistance of a coagulant agent to cause the parasites to stick together and that coagulant was inappropriately applied. The parasites gained entry to the water system eventually causing $96 million in medical costs and loss of productivity.[28] This occurrence drew national attention and increased public demand for assurances that their drinking water was safe. Congress responded with the 1996 amendments to the SDWA.

The 1996 SDWA amendments stressed three predominant features: pollution prevention rather than post-hoc cleanup, public participation and education, and risk management. The later included balancing costs with relative risks to set priorities.[29]

The 1996 amendments required the EPA to produce a contaminant candidate list (CCL) every five years and to determine if five of those on the CCL met the criteria to be regulated. The criteria for regulation included whether the contaminant causes adverse health effects, determination that the contaminant exists in public water systems, and if regulation of the contaminant will result in meaningful reduction in health risks. Additionally, the 1996 amendments also required the EPA to establish criteria to monitor at least 30 unregulated contaminants every five years.[30] Under the later adopted Unregulated Contaminants Monitoring Rule (UCMR), the EPA must periodically draft a list of unregulated potential contaminants and monitor them at several locations to determine their risk.[31] The amendments require the EPA to review and revise each National Primary Drinking Water Regulation (NPDWR) at least every 6 years with the goals of improving public health.[32]

The 1996 amendments also included provision for source water assessment and informational reporting, as well as creation of a fund to make money available to water providers to maintain and improve infrastructure. All water suppliers were required to identify any potential sources of contaminants in the source waters they use for drinking water supplies and to make adequate plans to test for likely contaminants in the water provided. The informational requirements were to be achieved through Consumer Confidence Reports (CCRs). CCRs are an annual notification to consumers of contaminants found and noncompliance events. Funding to provide for infrastructure was accomplished by establishing the Drinking Water State Revolving Fund (DWSRF) program. These loans were to be made available to water providers to assist them with capital improvements to keep up with newly identified contaminants.[33]

Evaluation

Between 1975 and 2017 the EPA identified and regulated nearly 90 contaminants in drinking water including microorganisms, disinfectants, disinfection by-products, inorganic chemicals, organic chemicals, and radionuclides. The National Primary Drinking Water Regulations apply to all public water systems.[34] The EPA continues to assess threats, such as contaminants like perchlorate, which are in the process of being regulated.

Waterborne diseases have decreased since the passage of the SDWA, however, the portion of diseases associated with plumbing or infrastructure has risen since passage of the law. This fact shows that water leaving the tap is not as safe was water leaving the water plant. This is primarily associated with U.S. aging infrastructure. This situation points to the need to focus on repairing and maintaining infrastructure, reducing leaks, and avoiding contamination in delivery systems.[35]

The 2015 health crisis in Flint, Michigan, with the exposure of the population to unsafe levels of lead, underscored the importance of maintaining infrastructure to protect human health. In Flint, a decision on the part of community leaders to save money by switching to the Flint River as the water source, rather than the more expensive Lake Huron water, resulted in lead leaching from the pipes as the new more caustic water flowed. The result was a health emergency for the entire community.[36]

Other substances continue to be of concern for drinking water quality. One is agricultural pollution, such as during the 2014 contamination of Toledo, Ohio's water supply as result of an algal bloom in Lake Erie that resulted from agricultural fertilizer runoff and animal waste.[37] Public anxiety also focuses on the continued detection of chemicals in drinking water from many widely used consumer, health, and personal-care products. Of particular alarm are pharmaceuticals, surfactants, and pesticides. Many of these substances have been documented as surviving wastewater treatment and have been discharged to surface water bodies. This class of substances is generally referred to as "contaminants of emerging concern."[38]

Wetlands Protections

As mentioned earlier in the chapter, the Rivers and Harbors Act and the Clean Water Act both apply to wetlands. The Rivers and Harbors Act regulates the dumping of material into waterways that might affect navigation, including wetlands. Section 404 of the CWA regulates the discharge of dredged and fill material into waterways, including wetlands. Under section 404 the EPA operates programs to regulate fill for development, water projects including dams and levees, infrastructure development, and mining. Section 404 requires a permit before dredged or fill material may be discharged into waterways. Permits are reviewed by USACE. Section 404 is built upon the concept that no dredged or fill material can be disposed of by water discharge if alternatives exist that are less damaging or if the waterway would be significantly degraded by such discharge. But several other domestic laws directly address the issue of wetlands as well. The Federal Agriculture Improvement and Reform Act of 1996 included provisions to conserve wetlands on farm land. It did so by removing potential benefits from established farming programs to farmers who converted wetlands into productive agricultural lands if they did not recompense for the wetland functions that were lost.[39] The Endangered Species Act

(ESA) includes a program to protect endangered or threatened species by protecting their habitat, which may be a wetland. The Transportation Equity Act for the 21st Century (TEA-21) included provisions to improve water quality and to restore wetlands. The Coastal Wetlands Planning, Protection & Restoration Act of 1990 required the identification of wetlands and construction of coastal wetlands restoration projects.[40]

Availability of Clean Water in the U.S. Future

Water availability has long been a problem in the western United States. The land west of the 100th meridian, which stretches from North Dakota to Texas, is arid with most areas getting less than 20 inches of annual rainfall and many areas receiving less. In such a dry climate, agriculture without irrigation is not reliable if it is possible at all.[41] To facilitate further settlement, the federal government historically supported a large system of dams and reservoirs to provide water to a growing population. The Army Corps of Engineers and the Bureau of Reclamation were the two government agencies charged with building and maintaining this infrastructure.[42]

The main river in the Southwest is the Colorado and its resources are distributed between several states including Wyoming, Colorado, Utah, New Mexico, Nevada, California, and Arizona. Division of the water is based on the Colorado River Compact, negotiated under the leadership of then Secretary of Commerce Herbert Hoover in 1922. Hydrologists at the time badly miscalculated the amount of water in the basin, substantially overestimating water availability. For most of the 20th century the error was not a considerable problem because Lake Mead and Lake Powell were full and could be used to provide for compact members' needs. However, by 2017, both reservoirs were more than half empty in large part because of population growth, increasing demand, drought, and the fact that compact members for a decade had been withdrawing all the water originally allowed by the agreement. The problem was addressed in a 2008 report by Scripps

Institution of Oceanography which described the situation as unsustainable.[43]

The circumstances are made worse by the depletion of groundwater supplies. Many regions of the U.S. are pumping water out of aquifers faster than they can recharge, resulting in lowering of the water table, drying up of wells, land subsidence, and saltwater intrusion. According to the United States Geological Survey (USGS), groundwater depletion has been an issue for the Southwest and High Plains for many years, but over pumping is also causing depletion in other regions including the Atlantic Coastal Plain, the Gulf Coastal Plain, the Desert Southwest, and the Pacific Northwest.[44]

Finally, it is important to consider the fact that population growth in the United States continues at a rapid pace. With increasing population numbers, the demand for water will grow because rising populations will require more water consumption for drinking, agricultural production, and industry. Climate change is also likely to impact availability of water resources.[45]

GLOBAL CONSIDERATIONS

Water is a critical international issue. The World Health Organization (WHO) projected that in 2012, an estimated 871,000 deaths worldwide were caused by lack of access to clean water and inadequate sanitation. Specifically, these deaths were owed to contamination of drinking water, water bodies and soil, lack of access to hand washing infrastructure or other necessary services. Unsafe access to water, sanitation, and hygiene services results annually in many deaths from diarrheal diseases and intestinal infections. This problem is most severe in Africa, where nearly half of global deaths from inadequate or unsafe water occurred in 2016 despite the fact that the African population only accounts for 13 percent of global population.[46]

Fresh Water Crisis in Access to Clean Water

The most common measure of water availability is per capita availability by country. Countries are identified as water scarce if availability is less than 1,000 cubic meters per person per year, and as water stressed if there are between 1,000 and 1,667 cubic meters per person per year. By these measures, more than 2 billion people are currently living in countries that are identified as water stressed or water scarce.[47] The World Resources Institute lists 36 countries as facing extremely high levels of water stress: Antigua and Barbuda, Bahrain, Barbados, Comoros, Cyprus, Dominica, Jamaica, Malta, Qatar, Saint Lucia, Saint Vincent and the Grenadines, San Marino, Singapore, Trinidad and Tobago, United Arab Emirates, Western Sahara, Saudi Arabia, Kuwait, Oman, Libya, Israel, Kyrgyzstan, East Timor, Iran, Yemen, Palestine, Jordan, Lebanon, Somaliland, Uzbekistan, Pakistan, Turkmenistan, Morocco, Mongolia, Kazakhstan, and Afghanistan.[48] As population continues to grow, per capita access to fresh water will continue to be a problem.

The Bonn Declaration of Global Water Security released in 2013 stated the problem clearly, saying:

> In the short span of one or two generations, the majority of the 9 billion people on Earth will be living under the handicap of severe pressure on fresh water, an absolutely essential natural resource for which there is no substitute. . . . After years of observations and a decade of integrative research convened under the Earth System Science Partnership (ESSP) and other initiatives, water scientists are more than ever convinced that fresh water systems across the planet are in a precarious state. Mismanagement, overuse and climate change pose long-term threats to human well-being and evaluating and responding to those threats constitutes a major challenge to water researchers and managers alike. Countless millions of individual local human actions add up and reverberate into larger regional, continental and global

changes that have drastically changed water flows and storage, impaired water quality, and damaged aquatic ecosystems. Human activity thus plays a central role in the behavior of the global water system.[49]

The declaration emphasizes the facts that humans have engineered water resources in ways that have resulted in water loss and that pollution further limits the resource.

These conclusions were supported by a U.S. Intelligence Community Assessment requested by the Department of State. The report was an attempt to answer the question of how world water issues would affect U.S. security by 2040. While not a total global assessment, the report did consider a select set of critical water basins including the Nile, Tigris-Euphrates, Mekong, Jordan, Indus, Brahmaputra, and Amu Darya. The key judgement provided by the assessment is:

> During the next 10 years, many countries important to the United States will experience water problems—shortages, poor water quality, or floods—that will risk instability and state failure, increase regional tensions, and distract them from working with the United States on important US policy objectives. Between now and 2040, fresh water availability will not keep up with demand absent more effective management of water resources. Water problems will hinder the ability of key countries to produce food and generate energy, posing a risk to global food markets and hobbling economic growth. As a result of demographic and economic development pressures, North Africa, the Middle East, and South Asia will face major challenges coping with water problems.[50]

In 2011, the United Nations General Assembly passed a resolution declaring 2013 the International Year of Water Cooperation (IYWC). This was done to highlight the importance of water management and the need for peaceful cooperation between nations in regard to shared water.[51] In doing this, the UN recognized a critical factor:

Water, a vital resource unlike any other, knows no borders. For instance, 148 countries share at least one transboundary river basin. That's why water cooperation is key to security, poverty eradication, social equity and gender equality. In addition, water cooperation generates economic benefits, preserves water resources, protects the environment and builds peace. As rapid urbanization, climate change and growing food needs put ever-increasing pressure on freshwater resources, the objective of the Year is to draw attention to the benefits of cooperation in water management. The celebration of this International Year coincides with the twentieth anniversary of World Water Day.[52]

Despite efforts to call for cooperation in water management, many countries continue to suffer water insecurity because they are heavily dependent on river water controlled by an upstream country with which they have uncertain or non-existent water-sharing agreements. While these tensions are not likely to end in conflict within the next decade, it is thought that as water scarcity increases into the future, conflict over disputed water basins may become more likely. In addition, the continued depletion of groundwater supplies in agricultural areas may result in risks to food production in the near future. These water stressors, as well as pollution, are likely to cause economic harm to several countries. Experts assert that of particular economic concern will be their ability to generate electricity to run industry. Over the next several decades, better water management will be key to controlling this water emergency. Since agriculture uses nearly three quarters of the world's fresh water, the most hopeful way to avoid an urgent situation in the future will be investment in technologies that reduce agricultural use of water including drip-irrigation and drought- and salt-tolerant plant varieties.[53]

Multilateral Water Agreements

There are two important multilateral agreements that help establish international approaches to shared water bodies. The first is the Convention on the Law of the Non-Navigational Uses of International Watercourses. It was adopted by the UN in 1997 and took effect in 2014. It provides guidance for the uses and conservation of waters that cross international borders, including groundwater. It imposes notification requirements on states that wish to use a shared waterway and allows states who object to proposed uses a process of mediation, either by neutral nations or through the International Law Commission. It also obligates parties not to cause harm to the waterway and encourages cooperation.[54] The second is the UN Economic Commission for Europe Convention on the Protection and Use of Transboundary Watercourses and International Lakes which likewise provides guidance to states on best ways to cooperatively manage shared water resources.[55] Both of these agreements are relatively weak, although they do provide a framework for accords.

A selected survey of state practices, with a focus on upstream states, reveals how these relations tend to work in reality. Some upstream states serve as models of good behavior, including Switzerland in Europe. China has 14 downstream neighbors and shares waterways and basins with 19 countries. Most of these shared waterways are not covered by treaties and the increased economic development of China has resulted in degraded water quality and diminished quantity of resources to downstream neighbors. India, a rapidly developing country, is home to the three largest transboundary waterways in South Asia (the Ganges-Brahmaputra-Meghna), the Indus, and the Kosi, Mahakali and Gandaki Rivers. India has negotiated bilateral treaties with some of its neighbors but not with others. Treaties have been negotiated with Pakistan, Bangladesh, and Nepal. India does not have a treaty with China and tensions exist between the nations regarding their shared waterways. The world's longest river is the Nile and its basin is shared by 10 countries: Egypt, Sudan, Ethiopia,

Eritrea, Tanzania, Uganda, Burundi, Rwanda, Congo, and Kenya. Since 1999, the Nile Basin Initiative has served as a vehicle to foster cooperation across the region but efforts to move toward a formal binding agreement have not been successful. Tensions over water continue to rise in the region.[56]

U.S. Agreements with Canada and Mexico

The U.S. has bilateral water agreements with Canada and Mexico and a multilateral wetlands agreement with both. The 1944 Treaty on Utilization of Waters of the Colorado and Tijuana Rivers and of the Rio Grande (1944 Water Treaty) is a U.S.-Mexican bilateral agreement governing the Colorado River and the Rio Grande basins. Under this treaty, a binational governing body called the International Boundary and Water Commission (IBWC), originally established in 1889, was charged with addressing issues arising under the treaty. The U.S. part of the IBWC (USIBWC) operates out of El Paso, Texas under the authority of the State Department. Under terms of the 1944 Water Treaty, disputes and changes to the agreements can be made using *minutes*, which are agreed upon interpretations of the treaty.[57]

The history of negotiations over transboundary water between the U.S. and Mexico go back more than a century. A 1906 convention for the sharing of the waters of the Rio Grande for irrigation purposes distributed waters near El Paso. The 1944 Water Treaty defines the basic water distribution agreement between Mexico and the U.S. for both the Colorado River basin and the Rio Grande. For the Colorado River basin, the U.S. is to provide Mexico with 1.5 million acre-feet annually. For the Rio Grande basin (below Fort Quitman, Texas), Mexico has the right to two thirds of the water that feeds into the Rio Grande from the 6 major tributaries that enter from Mexico. The U.S. has the rights to all water flows from Rio Grande tributaries in the U.S. and one third of the flows from the six Mexican tributaries. Mexico's flows are required to average, over 5 years, at least 350,000 acre-feet per year. If Mexico fails to meet these deliveries, they must make up the deficiencies in the next 5-year cycle.[58]

While the treaty established a priority list for water use including domestic and municipal use, agriculture, electric power, industrial uses, navigation, fishing and hunting, and other beneficial uses, it is often criticized for not specifically mentioning ecological needs for maintenance of water levels. Another criticism is that the treaty does not address the issue of water quality resulting in Mexican complaints of water salinity in the water the U.S. delivers.[59] Because the U.S. is allowed water from Mexican tributaries, but Mexico is allowed no water from U.S. tributaries, the treaty has been viewed as unfair and criticized on this account.[60]

The U.S. has two water agreements with Canada. The Columbia River Treaty of 1964 concerns the Columbia River which flows from British Columbia into the Pacific Northwest of the U.S. The other is the Great Lakes Water Quality Agreement of 1972 which, as its name implies, focuses on the water quality in the Great Lakes.

The Columbia River Treaty was negotiated to provide flood control and hydroelectric power. Under the terms of the treaty, the province of British Columbia was to construct three dams (Duncan, Keenleyside, and Mica) and the U.S. was to construct one (Libby Dam in Montana). Together these dams provide flood control and electricity. The terms of the treaty mandated that Canada would provide 15.5 million acre-feet of water storage and would allow the reservoir from Libby Dam to flow 42 miles into British Columbia. The additional electricity produced because of the dams was to be shared by the U.S. and Canada. However, initially Canada did not have a need for the power and did not anticipate the need for it for 3 decades, so Canada sold it to a consortium of utilities in the U.S. for 30 years for a lump sum of $240 million USD.[61]

The Great Lakes Water Quality Agreement (GLWQA), was signed in 1972, the same year the Clean Water Act was enacted by Congress. The stated purpose of the treaty was to restore the chemical, biological, and physical integrity of the Great Lakes ecosystem.[62] The U.S. fulfils its obligations under the GLWQA through the CWA.

GLWQA authority is granted to the EPA which created the Great Lakes National Program Office (GLNPO) to meet its obligations under the treaty. The GLNPO is responsible for monitoring Great Lakes' water quality with a specific focus on toxic pollutants. States that border the Great Lakes are required to include those waters in their CWA obligations, to create water quality standards, and to act to reverse impaired waters.[63]

The U.S. has a multilateral agreement with both Mexico and Canada called the North American Wetlands Conservation Act (NAWCA) of 1989. Within the U.S. the treaty is managed by the U.S. Fish and Wildlife Service (FWS). The treaty funds and provides administration for the North American Waterfowl Management Plan and the Tripartite Agreement on wetlands between the U.S., Canada, and Mexico. Funds provided are to be spent on wetlands conservation projects. The treaty also created the North American Wetlands Conservation Council to recommend projects.[64]

CONCLUSION

The earliest U.S. federal interest in water addressed the needs of the arid American West. The Reclamation Act of 1902 authorized the construction of dams and distribution networks to serve the needs of 16 western states. Since the early 1900s, both the Army Corps of Engineers and the Bureau of Reclamation managed water projects that created water reservoirs, irrigation, flood control, and electricity.

U.S. federal regulation of water pollution took the same form as regulation of air pollution in so far as early federal laws focused primarily on research, voluntary actions, and state-lead cleanup strategies. Early laws included the Water Pollution and Control Act of 1948, the Water Quality Act of 1965, the Clean Water Restoration Act of 1966, and the Water Quality Improvement Act of 1970. Each of these laws marked an incremental increase to federal power to control water policy.

It was not until the public's attention was focused by two events—the Cuyahoga River fire and the Santa Barbara oil spill—that sustained demand for federal action arose. Congress acted by passing the Clean Water Act. The CWA and its amendments revolutionized water pollution control law by prohibiting the unpermitted discharge of waste into waterways and by broadly defining the goal of water cleanup to include not only chemicals and other pollutants but also any substance that could alter a water body's hydrology, sediments, or biodiversity.

The CWA was implemented under a system of regulatory federalism. The CWA's NPDES was overseen by the EPA, but state and local governments are required to draft water quality standards and manage the permits. States were to identify any water bodies that did not meet these standards and designate them as impaired. Once so designated, the statute required states to develop TMDL programs to address impairment. One of the main benefits to the states and localities coming from the passage of the CWA were the large federal grants to municipalities for the construction of sewage treatment plants. The CWA placed emphasis on toxic pollutants by specially listing them. The law required industrial pretreatment of wastes before discharge into a municipal sewage treatment plant. It addressed oil spills and the discharge of other hazardous substances into waters of the U.S. and adjoining shorelines.

The 1977 CWA Amendments expanded regulations and EPA's authority. The 1981 Municipal Wastewater Treatment Construction Grants Amendments provided funds for municipal treatment plants. The 1987 Water Quality Act, however, replaced federal grants with the Clean Water Revolving Fund. The BEACH Act in 2000 provided grants to support testing for microbes in coastal recreational waters that might cause disease and established the BEACON public notification system of beach contamination or closure.

While the ambitious goals of the CWA were not met, the law did reduce some forms of pollution. The construction of sewage treatment plants across the U.S. greatly reduced environmental impacts from the discharge of untreated sewage. The CWA also reduced the direct release of industrial chemicals into waterways. That said, problems persist. The fact that over 40,000 waterways remain listed as impaired speaks to the failure of the act to produce its stated goals.

The SDWA, the second of the major clean water policies, required that the EPA set national standard for drinking water to protect against contaminants, establish MCLs for all known contaminants, and prescribe treatment technologies. The implementation of the law was slow and left Congress dissatisfied, so in the 1986 amendments Congress specified a list of chemicals to be regulated and elaborated a tight time frame for regulation. After the *Cryptosporidium* outbreak in Milwaukee, Congress passed the 1996 amendments to the SDWA, which stressed pollution prevention, public education via the Consumer Confidence Reports, and risk management.

The U.S. generally has an exceptionally safe drinking water system; however, some problems are emerging. Of concern are issues associated with the aging infrastructure as well as drinking water contamination from agricultural runoff, pharmaceuticals, surfactants, and pesticides.

While the CWA and the SDWA largely address issues of water quality, water availability is also an important policy consideration. The arid American West has long struggled with availability issues. To facilitate western settlement, the federal government funded the construction of a large system of dams and reservoirs under the management of the Army Corps of Engineers and the Bureau of Reclamation. The damming of the Colorado River and the creation of Lake Mead and Lake Powell provided adequate water resources through the end of the 20th century. Today, however, both reservoirs are more than half empty. Depletion of groundwater supplies worsens the situation. The fast-growing American population increases the demand for supplies of water. A solution to the availability dilemma remains to be found.

Like in the American West, lack of access to water is a problem in many countries. Nearly 40 nations are water stressed or water scarce, and as world population continues to grow, per capita access to fresh water will become a greater problem. This situation has resulted in international efforts to address the problem, like the Bonn Declaration of Global Water Security. The declaration calls attention to the need to better manage water resources to avoid future problems. Many regions in the world face a future of water shortages, polluted water, and floods which together will escalate regional tensions. It is thought that North Africa, the Middle East, and South Asia will face key tests managing water problems in the coming decades.

International bodies like the United Nations have tried to foster the importance of better water management and the need for peaceful cooperation between nations in regard to shared water resources. Yet many countries continue to suffer water insecurity because of dependence on transboundary water with countries that refuse to negotiate water-sharing agreements. Conflict over disputed water basins may become more likely in the future. Depletion of groundwater supplies in agricultural areas could also result in decreased food production.

There are two significant multilateral agreements that help establish international approaches to shared water bodies: the Convention on the Law of the Non-Navigational Uses of International Watercourses and the UN Economic Commission for Europe Convention on the Protection and Use of Transboundary Watercourses and International Lakes. Both provide guidance to nations on best practices for cooperative management of shared water resources.

There is considerable variance in how nations cooperate on shared water resource. China shares waterways and basins with 19 countries and most of these shared resources are not covered by treaties. The increased economic development of China has resulted in both polluted water and reduced quantity of resources flowing to downstream neighbors. India has negotiated bilateral treaties with some of its neighbors but not with others. India and China do not have a water agreement. As the Nile basin is shared by 10 countries and lacking an agreement over water, tensions continue to rise.

The U.S. has bilateral water agreements with Canada and Mexico and a multilateral wetlands agreement with both. The 1944 Water Treaty is a U.S.-Mexican bilateral agreement governing the Colorado River and the Rio Grande basins. The U.S. has 2 water agreements with Canada. The Columbia River Treaty of 1964 convers the Columbia River, which flows from British Columbia into the Pacific Northwest of the U.S. The other is the Great Lakes Water Quality Agreement of 1972, which focuses on the water quality in the Great Lakes. The U.S. also has a multilateral wetlands agreement with both Mexico and Canada, the North American Wetlands Conservation Act of 1989, which manages wetlands conservation to maintain water fowl habitat.

---

[1] Andrea K. Gerlak, "Federalism and U.S. Water Policy: Lessons for the Twenty-First Century," *Publius: The Journal of Federalism* 36, no.2 (2005): 231.

[2] Marc Reisner, *Cadillac Desert: The American West and Its Disappearing Water* (New York: Penguin Books, 1993), 5.

[3] Robert W. Adler, "Clean Water Act," in *Encyclopedia of Science and Technology Communication,* ed. Susanna Hornig Priest (Thousand Oaks: Sage Publications, Inc., 2010), 139.

[4] Michael E. Kraft, *Environmental Policy and Politics* (Boston: Pearson, 2015), 141.

[5] "EPA History: Water—The Challenge of the Environment: A Primer on EPA's Statutory Authority," EPA, accessed July 14, 2017, https://archive.epa.gov/epa/aboutepa/epa-history-water-challenge-environment-primer-epas-statutory-authority.html.

[6] Michael Rotman, "Cuyahoga River Fire," *Cleveland Historical,* accessed July 13, 2017, https://clevelandhistorical.org/items/show/63.

[7] Robert W. Adler, "Clean Water Act," 139.

[8] Gerlak, "Federalism and U.S. Water Policy: Lessons for the Twenty-First Century," 236–237.

[9] "EPA History: Water—The Challenge of the Environment: A Primer on EPA's Statutory Authority."

[10] Kraft, *Environmental Policy and Politics,* 142.

[11] Adler, "Clean Water Act," 141.

[12] Luke Fowler, "Assessing the Framework of Policy Outcomes: The Case of the U.S. Clean Air Act and Clean Water Act," *Journal of Environmental Assessment Policy and Management* 16, no. 4 (2014):9, accessed May 18, 2017. doi:10.1142/S1464333214500343.

[13] "EPA History: Water—The Challenge of the Environment: A Primer on EPA's Statutory Authority."

14 "National Pollution Discharge Elimination System," EPA, accessed August 10, 2018, https://www.epa.gov/npdes.

15 "EPA History: Water—The Challenge of the Environment: A Primer on EPA's Statutory Authority."

16 Carol Clayton et al., "Minimizing Risk Under the Clean Water Act," *Energy Law Journal* 36, no. 69 (2015): 73–74.

17 Fowler, "Assessing the Framework of Policy Outcomes: The Case of the U.S. Clean Air Act and Clean Water Act," 9.

18 "Summary of the BEACH Act," EPA, accessed July 19, 2017, https://www.epa.gov/laws-regulations/summary-beach-act.

19 "EPA History: Water—The Challenge of the Environment: A Primer on EPA's Statutory Authority."

20 "EPA History: Water—The Challenge of the Environment: A Primer on EPA's Statutory Authority."

21 Adler, "Clean Water Act," 140.

22 Fowler, "Assessing the Framework of Policy Outcomes: The Case of the U.S. Clean Air Act and Clean Water Act," 15.

23 Jill T. Hauserman, "Water, Water Everywhere, But Just How Much is Clean?: Examining Water Quality Restoration Efforts Under the United States Clean Water Act and the United States-Canada Great Lakes Water Quality Agreement," *Georgia Journal of International and Comparative Law* 43, no. 701 (2015): 712.

24 J. Alan Robertson and Michell M. Frey, "An SDWA Retrospective: 20 Years After the 1996 Amendments," *Journal of the American Water Works Association* 108, no.3 (2016): 22.

25 Michael Zarkin, "Unconventional Pollution Control Politics: The Reform of the US Safe Drinking Water Act," *Electronic Green Journal* 1, no.38 (2015): 5, accessed July 17, 2017, http://escholarship.org/uc/item/69s0f9s0.

26 Robertson and Frey, "An SDWA Retrospective," 22.

27 Robertson and Frey, "An SDWA Retrospective," 23.

28 Phaedra S. Corso et al., "Costs of Illness in the 1993 Waterborne Cryptosporidium Outbreak, Milwaukee, Wisconsin," *Emerging Infectious Diseases* 9, no. 4 (2003): 426.

29 Zarkin, "Unconventional Pollution Control Politics: The Reform of the US Safe Drinking Water Act," 2.

30 "Background on Drinking Water Standards in the Safe Drinking Water Act (SDWA)," EPA, accessed August 10, 2018, https://www.epa.gov/dwstandardsregulations/background-drinking-water-standards-safe-drinking-water-act-sdwa.

31 Joseph A. Cotruvo, "The Safe Drinking Water Act: Current and Future," *Journal of the American Water Works Association* 104, no.1 (2012): 58.

32 "Safe Drinking Water Act Requirements for Six-Year Reviews," EPA, accessed July 17, 2017, https://epa.gov/dwsixyearreview/safe-drinking-water-act-requirements-six-year-reviews.

33 Robertson and Frey, "An SDWA Retrospective," 24.

34 "Ground Water and Drinking Water: National Primary Drinking Water Regulations," EPA, accessed July 17, 2017, https://epa.gov/ground-water-and-drinking-water/national-primary-drinking-water-regulations.

35 Cotruvo, "The Safe Drinking Water Act," 57.

[36]   Brent Fewell, "The Failure of Cooperative Federalism in Flint, Michigan," *Journal of the American Water Works Association* 108, no. 3 (2016): 12.

[37]   Margot J. Pollans, "The Safe Drinking Water/Food Law Nexus," *Pace Environmental Law Review* 32, no. 2 (2015):501.

[38]   Susan T. Glastmeyer et al., "Nationwide Reconnaissance of Contaminants of Emerging Concern in Source and Treated Drinking Waters of the United States," *Science of the Total Environment* 501–502 (2017): 909.

[39]   "Wetlands Conservation Provisions (Swampbuster)," NRCS, accessed July 20, 2017, www.nrcs.usda.gov/wps/portal/nrcs/detailfull/national/programs/alphabetical/camr/?&cid=stelprdb1043554.

[40]   "Clean Water Laws, Regulations, Executive Orders," EPA, accessed July 20, 2017, https://www.epa.gov/cwa-404/clean-water-laws-regulations-executive-orders.

[41]   Marc Reisner, *Cadillac Desert: The American West and its Disappearing Water* (New York: Penguin Books, 1993), 45.

[42]   Reisner, *Cadillac Desert*, 5.

[43]   David Owen, *Where the Water Goes: Life and Death Along the Colorado* River (New York: Riverhead Books, 2017), 21–22.

[44]   "The USGA Water Science School," USGS, accessed July 18, 2017, https://water.usgs.gov/edu/gwdepletion.html.

[45]   "Why Population Matters to Water Resources," Population Action International, accessed July 18, 2017, https://pai.org/wp-content/uploads/2012/04/PAI-1293-WATER-4PG.pdf.

[46]   World Health Organization, *World Health Statistics 2016: Monitoring Health for the SDGs* (Geneva: WHO Press, 2016), 72.

[47]   "Why Population Matters to Water Resources," Population Action International, accessed August 10, 2018, https://pai.org/wp-content/uploads/2012/04/PAI-1293-WATER-4PG.pdf.

[48]   "World's 36 Most Water-Stressed Countries," World Resources Institute, accessed July 18, 2017, www.wri.org/blog/2013/12/world's-36-most-water-stressed-countries.

[49]   "The Bonn Declaration on Global Water Security," Global Water System Project, accessed July 18, 2017, www.gwsp.org/fileadmin/documents_news/Bonn_Water_Declaration_final.pdf.

[50]   Intelligence Community Assessment, "Global Water Security," *Intelligence Community Assessment Report ICA 2012-08* (2012): iii.

[51]   "Water Cooperation," UNDESA, accessed July 19. 2017, www.unwater.org/water-cooperation-2013/water-cooperation/en/.

[52]   "United Nations International Year of Water Cooperation," UN, accessed July 19, 2017, http://www.un.org/en/events/worldwateryear/.

[53]   Intelligence Community Assessment, "Global Water Security," 3–6.

[54]   "Convention on the Law of the Non-navigational Uses of International Watercourses," UN, accessed July 19, 2017, http://legal.un.org/ilc/texts/instruments/english/conventions/8_3_1997.pdf.

[55]   Patricia Wouters, " 'Dynamic Cooperation'—The Evolution of Transboundary Water Cooperation," in *Water and the Law: Towards Sustainability*, ed. Michael Kidd et al. (Cheltenham, UK: Edward Elgar, 2014), 36.

⁵⁶ Wouters, "Dynamic Cooperation," 44–59.

⁵⁷ Nicole T. Carter, Stephen P. Mulligan, Clare Ribando Seelke, "U.S. Mexican Water Sharing: Background and Recent Developments," *Congressional Research Service Report 7-5700, R43312* (2017): 5–6.

⁵⁸ Carter, Mulligan, and Seelke, "U.S. Mexican Water Sharing: Background and Recent Developments," 5–6.

⁵⁹ Carter, Mulligan, and Seelke, "U.S. Mexican Water Sharing: Background and Recent Developments," 9.

⁶⁰ Intelligence Community Assessment, "Global Water Security," 12.

⁶¹ "Columbia River Treaty," nwcouncil.org, accessed August 10, 2018, https://www.nwcouncil.org/reports/columbia-river-history/columbiarivertreaty.

⁶² Hauserman, "Water, Water Everywhere, 703.

⁶³ Hauserman, "Water, Water Everywhere," 712.

⁶⁴ "Clean Water Laws, Regulations, Executive Orders," EPA, accessed July 20, 2017, https://www.epa.gov/cwa-404/clean-water-laws-regulations-executive-orders.

CHAPTER 6

Non-Hazardous Solid Waste Policy

INTRODUCTION

Solid waste can be classified as either hazardous or non-hazardous. This chapter deals with non-hazardous solid waste. While it may seem counter intuitive, solid waste does not have to be "solid." Solid waste includes solids, liquids, and contained gases that are disposed of in a variety of ways. Solid waste can be classified as municipal solid waste (MSW) and non-municipal or industrial solid waste (ISW). MSW includes all the garbage and refuse households, offices, retail stores, and schools put at the curb for pickup and disposal. Refuse is made up of such items as scrap metals, building materials, and empty containers. Industrial solid waste comprises the largest part of the non-hazardous solid waste stream and includes discarded material coming from industrial, mining, commercial, and agricultural activities. A large part of ISW is comprised of construction rubble and therefore it does not pose the same threat to human health and the environment as MSW.[1]

The amount of waste produced is tightly linked to the size of the population and its consumption patterns. World population was 2 billion in 1925 and has since grown massively. At the same time, global consumption patterns shifted from modest to more extensive consumption.[2] Domestically, the United States experienced a similar evolution. In 1925, the entire U.S. population was under 116 million.

By 2017, the U.S. population had reached over 325 million.[3] In addition, American appetites changed from modest consumption in the early 20th century to far more wide-ranging consumption. The result is an ever-increasing stream of waste. As populations continue to rise and consume readily, the waste stream will continue to grow unless policies are put in place to reverse the trend. The introduction of new materials in recent decades, including plastics and consumer electronics, has also affected the waste stream.

A large volume of waste is generated in the U.S. The chapter begins with a discussion of the amount of solid waste that needs to be accommodated. In the U.S. solid waste must be disposed of in compliance with the federal statute that specifies appropriate waste management practices, the Resource Conservation and Recovery Act's subtitle D, which is dedicated to non-hazardous waste disposal practices. The chapter provides details of the rules for waste disposal under the act.

Disposal of waste can occur in a variety of ways, including open dumping, landfilling, and incineration. Alternatives to waste disposal include recycling, reuse, and composting. The chapter discusses the evolution of the movement to reduce, reuse, and recycle so that the solid waste stream can be minimized. Statistics on materials recycled and composted are provided.

Solid waste is a significant issue worldwide, but it is particularly problematic in the developing world where nations struggle to collect and properly handle solid waste. Uncollected or mishandled solid waste can result in harm to the environment as well as the spreading of diseases. Poorly managed solid waste sites frequently result in water contamination. They also contribute greatly to climate change as organic material decays and gives off methane gas. It is therefore critical that countries become better at solid waste management. A sound solid waste management paradigm starts with source reduction, reusing and recycling waste, reclaiming waste through such practices as composting and waste-to-energy production, safe incineration and sanitary landfilling. Unfortunately, many developing countries have not yet adopted these sound solid waste management practices and instead rely on uncontrolled open dumping for the waste they do collect. This chapter provides a discussion of these global issues.

DOMESTIC CONSIDERATIONS

In 2014, the U.S. generated 258 million tons of municipal solid waste. Some of that was recycled and some was burned in waste-to-energy plants, but 136 million tons were landfilled. Organic material such as paper, food, and yard trimmings were the largest component of MSW. Paper and paperboard accounted for over 26 percent and food and yard trimmings made up another 28 percent. Plastics made up 13 percent of MSW. Nine percent was rubber, leather, and textiles. Another 9 percent was metal. Wood comprised 6 percent and glass 4 percent. The remaining 3 percent was miscellaneous wastes.[4] The job of managing MSW falls to state and local governments which can decide to handle the waste themselves or to outsource the task to a solid waste management company under contract to the municipality or local government.

The quantity of MSW pales in comparison to industrial solid waste which results from activities of industry, agriculture, manufacturing, or mining. Each year in the U.S. about 7.6 billion tons of ISW are generated and disposed of in industrial waste disposal facilities. States, tribes, and some local governments are required by the Environmental Protection Agency (EPA) to establish and implement programs to assure that this industrial waste is handled in a manner to protect human health and the environment.[5] Management of ISW falls to the organizations that generate it. They can decide to manage their own waste stream or to hire a waste management company to provide solid waste management services.

Disposal Methods

Non-hazardous waste may be disposed of in a variety of ways including open dumping, landfills, and incineration. Open dumping is what its name suggests. Solid wastes are deposited to the land with little or no concern for environmental or health outcomes. Uncontrolled open dumping does not even take into consideration siting which can result in considerable environmental damage and harm to human health. Controlled open dumping at least considers such issues as siting so that environmental damage is reduced. Siting the dump away from water and flood plains lowers the likelihood of water contamination. Controlled open dumping also includes some management of the dump site so that the worst environmental harm is avoided. There has been relatively little uncontrolled or controlled open dumping in the United States since the passage of the Resource Conservation and Recovery Act in 1976.

Sanitary landfills are the cheapest method of disposal if the landfill is sited reasonably close to the source of the waste. Much of the cost of solid waste disposal lies in the pickup and transport of the waste to its disposal site. Once at the site, the waste is spread in a layer of about 10 feet high across the landfill and is topped by a thin layer of dirt. All of this material is compacted using bulldozers. Pollution is minimized by using a liner, correct siting to avoid flooding or high groundwater, and proper venting to avoid the buildup of gases that result from decomposition of organic matter.[6]

There are several landfills used for different purposes. MSW landfills are designed to accommodate household non-hazardous solid waste. In 2009, there were 1,908 MSW landfills in the United States, managed by the states in which they were located.[7] The number of landfills has dropped by nearly 75 percent since the late 1980s when there were nearly 8,000 MSW landfills. There has also been a shift in ownership with the public sector owning only 64 percent of MSW landfills by 2004. Capacity, however, has not changed substantially, as landfills are larger than they were in the past.[8] One specific type of

MSW landfill is a bioreactor landfill which is designed to accept and rapidly degrade organic material. Industrial waste landfills are intended to collect commercial and industrial waste. These consist of construction and demolition (C&D) debris landfills, which are specifically intended to receive debris left over from construction and demolition of buildings, roads, piers, dams, and bridges. C&D landfills often contain bulky material like concrete, wood, asphalt, drywall, metal, bricks, plastics, glass, plumbing fixtures, doors, windows, trees, tree stumps, and rock.[9] Coal combustion residual (CCR) landfills are specifically engineered to hold coal ash. These CCR landfills were mandated by the EPA in 2015 after a determination that poorly constructed coal ash facilities were causing harm to the environment.[10] The EPA also regulates some landfills that dispose of polychlorinated biphenyls (PCBs) in polychlorinated biphenyl landfills.[11]

MSW landfills are regulated by the states in which they are located and must meet EPA standards. The states may impose stricter standards if they so elect. EPA standards include location restrictions to assure that landfills are not built near faults, flood plains, wetlands, or in other sensitive areas. In addition, landfills must have flexible membrane liners overlaying two feet of compacted clay on the sides and bottom of the landfill to protect against leachate releases. Leachate is water that has soaked through the landfill and leached out some of the materials held there. The EPA requires landfills to have leachate collection and removal systems which sit above the liner and remove leachate for treatment and disposal. The EPA requires landfill operators to use certain prescribed practices including compacting and covering waste with several inches of soil to control odor, insects, and rodents. All landfills must test the groundwater to monitor for any released wastes. The EPA requires the control and cleanup of landfill releases to protect groundwater. Finally, the EPA requires that landfills show financial proof of ability to protect the environment during operation and after closure.[12] C&D landfills, however, may be held to lower standards than MSW landfills as they contain mostly inert rubble that poses little threat to human health or the environment.

Incineration involves the burning of materials in suitable facilities. Historically in the U.S. this method was commonly used to deal with solid waste, however, after the passage of the Clean Air Act many of the incineration plants closed due to the expense associated with achieving the new clean air standards. There are some incineration facilities in operation in the U.S. but most of them are only made economical as waste-to-energy plants where the MSW is burned and in the process, electricity is produced. Incineration is more common in countries with limited land for landfills like Japan and across Europe since incineration reduces the amount of remaining ash that needs to be landfilled by about 75 percent by weight. In the U.S. incinerators tend to be unpopular for a variety of reasons. Communities mistrust them because in the past they were the source of considerable pollution. They also increase MSW truck traffic in communities. The largest obstacle, however, is cost. A new MSW combustion facility can cost many hundreds of millions of dollars. Landfills are much cheaper and therefore remain the popular choice in the U.S. where land is available.[13] Waste-to-energy plants also raise fears due to potential air pollutants, including lead and mercury.

Waste Diversion Strategies

Diverting waste material from disposal, or source reduction, is an important solid waste management strategy. Composting and recycling are the two most common management techniques used to accomplish this diversion.

Composting converts organic material to humus, which is the organic component of soil. Composting can be done in a variety of ways and on multiple scales. Small amounts of food waste can be composted onsite using backyard compost piles. Vermicomposting uses worms in bins eat food scraps, grass trimmings, and other organic material and turn it into usable compost. Turned windrow composting is suitable for larger amounts of material, such as those generated by an entire community. This type of composting involves organizing the organic waste into rows, called windrows, and periodically aerating them by turning the piles. The land requirement is fairly large as each windrow should be 4 to 8 feet high and 14 to 16 feet in width. Windrowing also requires either machinery or personnel as the aeration process either involves purchasing equipment to turn the piles or hiring manual labor to physically turn the piles. Aerated static pile composting is similar to windrowing but rather than turning the piles, layers of loosely piled shredded paper or leaves are used to allow air to flow through the pile. In-vessel composting, like windrow composting, can deal with large amounts of materials but it uses less land. Instead of spreading the material in rows, it is placed in specially made vessels that mechanically mix and turn the organic matter. The drawback is cost as the vessels may be expensive.[14]

Recycling is another waste diversion solid waste management strategy. Recycling means the recovery of materials and reprocessing of them into useful materials or products, either for the original or a new purpose. Recycling turns waste into a valuable resource. It is environmentally sustainable because demand for raw materials are reduced, less energy is used to reprocess secondary materials than would be used to process new raw materials, and the waste stream is reduced, leaving fewer wastes to be disposed.[15]

Since the 1970s, more than 9,000 U.S. municipalities have put in place collection of recyclables as part of their MSW management efforts. Over time recycling rates have improved. The components of MSW that are readily recycled include paper and cardboard, plastics, metals, and glass although profitability varies for each material.[16]

MSW recycling involves three steps: collection and processing, manufacturing, and purchasing new products made from recycled material. Collection can happen in a variety of ways. Communities can have curbside collection, there can be recycling drop-off centers, or collection can be facilitated through deposit or refund programs. After collection, the materials are sent to a material recovery facility (MRF) for sorting, cleaning, and processing. Recycled materials are bought and sold on the free market, so prices vary based upon supply and demand.

Recycled content can be used in the manufacturing step. Common products that contain some or all recycled content include paper, aluminum cans, plastic containers, glass containers, and steel. Recycled material can also be formed into new products, such as when recycled plastic is formed into park benches. The final step is the purchase of products containing recycled content.[17]

MSW recycling programs vary by how the materials are collected. Single stream recycling is a system in which all materials are mixed together, or commingled, and are sorted at the MRF using magnets, screens, conveyor belts, air jets, and infrared readers. The separated materials are then bundled and sold to manufacturers and other customers. The advantages of single stream recycling include increased participation rates, less space requirements at the household, reduced collection costs through using less expensive single-compartment trucks instead of more expensive multi-compartment vehicles, and new material can be added to the program without having to make expensive changes.[18] While collection costs are minimized using single stream recycling, separation of the materials in the MRF may result in errors. For instance, if glass ends up in a paper bundle, the contamination may cause the entire bundle to be rejected and sent to a landfill rather than being recycled. This can be avoided if dual stream, or source separated recycling, is used. In this method, the participant separates recycled materials into separate bins.[19]

Much of the C&D waste flow is also recycled. Estimates are that as much as 35 percent of mixed C&D waste is recycled but some items have higher rates. For instance, concrete recycle estimates are 85 percent and reclaimed asphalt has a 99 percent recycle rate. This diverts massive amount of waste from C&D landfills.[20]

Federal Legislation

The first statute passed to deal with solid waste in the U.S. was the 1965 Solid Waste Disposal Act. This act was weak in that it merely encouraged states to develop guidelines for dealing with solid waste.

With the passage of the tougher clean air and water laws in the early 1970s, public and congressional attention also turned to waste. The Resource Conservation and Recovery Act (RCRA) was passed in 1976 as an amendment to the Solid Waste Disposal Act.[21] Many of its sections deal with hazardous waste but subtitle D was devoted to non-hazardous solid waste. The purpose of the law was to deal with the growing amount of industrial and municipal solid waste. Subtitle D imposed restrictions on landfills to assure correct siting so that waste could be adequately disposed. It required liners to protect groundwater. RCRA further required leachate collection and removal systems. Operating procedures were established to assure odor, insect, and rodent control. RCRA imposed groundwater monitoring requirements as well as closure and post-closure monitoring and care. In regard to MSW, the law encouraged states to replace any open dumps in use with sanitary landfills equipped with liners, leachate collection systems, and methane gas controls. States were to handle the implementation of RCRA through an EPA-approved permitting system.[22] An important goal of RCRA was to promote recycling and source reduction.

The 1984 amendment of RCRA, formally called the Hazardous and Solid Waste Amendments (HSWA), had provisions that applied to both hazardous and non-hazardous wastes. The provisions that focused on non-hazardous solid waste resulted from an understanding by Congress that non-hazardous solid waste facilities, particularly MSW landfills, actually did hold an unknown amount of hazardous waste. These wastes were deposited to these facilities by households and by illegal dumping. Households, for instance, commonly throw batteries and empty cans of insecticides into the trash. These items contain small quantities of hazardous materials. Congress recognized the fact that these facilities were under much lighter monitoring and operating restrictions. Incidents of environmental and health problems coming from these sites motivated Congress to act. Studies had revealed that existing MSW landfills violated groundwater protection standards, air standards, and many lacked adequate liners and leachate collection systems. The 1984 amendment required that by 1988, EPA should put in place rules to assure ground water monitoring to detect contamination, establish stricter criteria for the location of new or existing facilities, and provide corrective action where needed. The rule required by this amendment was finally issued nearly 4 years after the legislative deadline and only after significant litigation.[23]

Recycling and Composting Results

Of the more than 258 million tons of municipal solid waste generated in the U.S. in 2014, over 89 million tons were recycled and composted. That amount represents a nearly 35 percent recycling rate. Additionally, more than 33 million tons of MSW were incinerated with energy recovery. In that same year nearly 90 percent of corrugated boxes were recycled and 61 percent of yard trimmings were composted. Recycling and composting of MSW reduced greenhouse gas emissions by 181 million metric tons, or the equivalent of the annual emissions from 38 million vehicles.[24] These results show some successful outcomes but considerable room for improvement remains.

By 2016, curbside recycling served about 53 percent of the U.S. population, however, of those only 44 percent were provided with recycling carts. All curbside recycling programs are local, and variations exist between programs. Some localities provide for public haulers of recycled materials while others use the services of private haulers. On average, nationally, each household recycled 357 pounds of waste in 2016.[25]

Recycling remains controversial. Some suggest that it is typically more expensive for municipalities to recycle household waste than it is to incinerate or bury it. In recent years, prices for recycled materials have dropped due to cheap oil and decreased international demand. This has made recycling plants struggle to maintain profitability. The shift to single stream recycling and the demand on the part of advocates to recycle more and more items has also increased the burden on recycling operations because the ability to separate the valuable items, such as cardboard and aluminum, has been made more difficult by the addition of items such as plastics in the waste stream. Recycling remains politically popular, however, especially in cities that have embraced a "zero waste" goal.[26]

Shift to a No-Waste Paradigm

For most of our history, the creation of waste was seen as a natural part of production. Domestically, that view began to change with the passage of RCRA and its focus on waste reduction. Prevention of waste generation in the first place is now being adopted by many. This change is slowly being accepted by professionals, government officials, and the public as the correct way to deal with solid waste. Rather than landfill or incinerate waste, the "zero waste" movement argues that efforts to avoid producing waste at all should have priority. Advocates say this begins with good product design that will enable easy recycling. It also extends to the use of Life Cycle Assessment or Life Cycle Costing which includes not only the costs of product purchase but also of operation and maintenance as well as disposal.[27] By using this form of accounting for costs, more efficient and environmentally friendly products can be mainstreamed into the economy.

A growing number of communities have adopted the no-waste paradigm including New York, Seattle, Los Angeles, Austin, Minneapolis, Oakland, Washington, D.C., San Francisco, Dallas, and San Diego. Businesses have also joined the movement. A few notable ones include Subaru, Sierra Nevada, Toyota, Unilever, Ford, Fetzer Vineyards, Proctor & Gamble, New Belgium Brewing, Google, and Microsoft. Other organizations are also leaders, including the U.S. Zero Waste Business Council (USZWBC), which provides a third-party Zero Waste Facility Certification program for businesses that meet the standards of The Zero Waste International Alliance (ZWIA).[28] ZWIA defines zero waste as:

> Zero Waste is a goal that is ethical, economical, efficient and visionary, to guide people in changing their lifestyles and practices to emulate sustainable natural cycles, where all

discarded materials are designed to become resources for others to use. Zero Waste means designing and managing products and processes to systematically avoid and eliminate the volume and toxicity of waste and materials, conserve and recover all resources, and not burn or bury them. Implementing Zero Waste will eliminate all discharges to land, water, or air that are a threat to planetary, human, animal or plant health.[29]

ZWIA provides standards, business principles, and community principles to achieve zero waste. In 2013, ZWIA adopted a Hierarchy of Highest and Best Uses based upon the full carbon life cycle of materials, as well as the energy used to extract raw resources, manufacture products, and transport products to market. This hierarchy begins with reduce, reuse, and recycle and ends with landfilling. Prior to landfilling, materials should be analyzed to determine how they should be redesigned in the future to avoid landfilling at all.[30]

GLOBAL CONSIDERATIONS

While solid waste has long been a problem worldwide, throughout most of history it was considered more of an annoyance than a major issue. In the years during and after World War II, that attitude began to shift. First, resources needed to be diverted to the war effort and so populations began to become highly aware of the stream of waste in an attempt to productively use all material wisely. Second, much of the world was devastated by the war and had to deal with massive amounts of construction rubble, military debris, sunken vessels, unexploded weapons, synthetic rubber, electronic equipment and parts, and hundreds of other wastes that were the residue of war. In the post-war period, governments began assessing war damage and beginning cleanup. Attention turned to solid waste and its reuse or disposal.[31]

In the post-war years, the West experienced huge growth as buildings for residencies, industries, factories, and retail establishments boomed. Transportation networks also recovered and expanded. As populations grew, the need for public infrastructure, including schools and hospitals, increased. This growth amplified pollution and drew attention to waste. Source reduction became popular in Europe, and to a lesser extent in America, as individuals like Joseph Ling, vice-president for environmental affairs at 3M Corporation, popularized his PPP (pollution prevention pays) program.[32] Source reduction efforts also came to be applied to waste reduction efforts, particularly through "reduce, reuse, recycle" campaigns and efforts.

Solid Waste Globally

Caution needs to be exercised in making global statements about waste since the data are fairly inconsistent from country to country. However, according to the World Bank's best estimates, current global waste generation (MSW and ISW) is 1.3 billion tons per year and the amount is expected to increase to 2.2 billion tons per year by 2025. Waste generation is higher in urban areas than in rural areas and more in affluent populations than in lower income populations. This is important, because as the world's population grows more urban and wealthier, more waste will be generated. Currently, nearly half (44 percent) of all MSW comes from OECD nations. OECD nations tend to be affluent and include most of Europe and the United States. East Asia and the Pacific (including China) contributes 21 percent, Latin America and the Caribbean 12 percent, Eastern and Central Asia 7 percent, the Middle East and North Africa 6 percent, South Asia 5 percent, and Sub-Saharan Africa 4 percent.[33]

Affluent nations tend to dispose of their waste in landfills or by incineration. They have high rates of recycling and composting that divert wastes from disposal sites. Developing nations, however, tend to dispose of waste in uncontrolled open dumps. They have lower rates of recycling and composting. This has impacts on the environment and human health in communities exposed to uncontrolled waste. Solid waste inappropriately collected or disposed of can create the possibility of disease and environmental contamination.[34]

MSW is a major problem for developing countries. The World Bank estimates that for developing countries it is common for municipalities to spend 20 to 50 percent of their budgets for solid waste management. Even after spending that much of their budget, not all waste is collected. Assessments suggest that only between 40 to 70 percent of solid waste is collected. The rest remains uncollected and unmanaged causing potential harm to the environment and human health. In developing countries, only half of urban dwellers are served by MSW management services. Developing countries tend to take an outdated approach to solid waste management which emphasizes only collection and disposal. However, efforts are underway, led primarily by the United Nations Environment Programme (UNEP), to get municipalities to re-think their strategies and to include recycling as well as waste-to-energy strategies for the handling of MSW.[35]

The European Union (EU), in 2010, adopted a new Waste Framework Directive to all member states very much in sync with UNEP's concept of re-thinking waste as a valued resource. The Directive established a five-step hierarchy for member states with waste prevention as the most desirable option, followed by reuse, recycling, and other forms of recovery including waste-to-energy strategies. Landfilling is denoted in the Directive as the least desirable option. The Directive also encourages member states to use Life Cycle Assessment in their consideration of options.[36] Waste-to-energy plants are common in the EU and when used in conjunction with recycling, they divert much MSW from landfills. There are more than 500 waste-to-energy plants across Europe. In Europe, 72 percent of MSW is handled by recycling or in waste-to-energy plants. Landfills receive only 28 percent of MSW.[37]

CONCLUSION

The collection and handling of solid waste is an important issue because statistics show that the amount of waste produced is correlated with population size and consumption patterns. As the world's population continues to grow, and people become wealthier and more urban, the amount of solid waste generated will be increasing. Finding ways to handle waste safely and economically is important for the environment and human health worldwide.

Non-hazardous waste may be disposed of in a variety of ways, including open dumping, landfills, incineration, and composting. Prior to the passage of RCRA, most waste in the U.S. was openly burned, contributing to air pollution, or openly dumped mostly in uncontrolled dump sites. Once RCRA was passed, open dumping in the U.S. was supplanted largely by the use of sanitary landfills, complemented with a small number of waste-to-energy incineration facilities, recycling, and composting.

Landfill types include MSW landfills designed to accept household non-hazardous solid waste, bioreactor landfills which are designed to rapidly decompose organic material, C&D debris landfills to receive debris left over from construction and demolition of civil engineering projects, CCR landfills to hold coal ash, and polychlorinated biphenyl landfills to hold some of the nation's PCBs.

MSW landfills are regulated by the states in which they are located but they must meet EPA standards or higher standards that the states may themselves impose. EPA standards include location restrictions, required liners and compacted clay on the sides and bottom, leachate collection and removal systems, required operational practices, groundwater testing, control and cleanup of landfill releases, and financial proof of ability to protect the environment during operation and after closure. C&D landfills, because they are less dangerous than MSW sites, can be held to lower standards.

MSW can be incinerated. Incineration involves combusting waste in appropriate facilities. There are a small number of incineration facilities in operation in the U.S. and most of them are waste-to-energy plants. Waste-to-energy is common in Europe, however in the U.S. it is not popular because waste-to-energy plants are very expensive, and landfills remain a cheaper option.

Diverting waste material from disposal, or source reduction, is an important solid waste management strategy. Composting and recycling are the two most common management techniques used to accomplish this diversion. Since the passage of RCRA, thousands of U.S. municipalities have put in place collection of recyclables as part of their MSW management efforts. Over time recycling rates have improved, rising to about 35 percent. Recycling is a three-step process that includes collection and processing, manufacturing, and purchasing new products made from recycled material. Recycling can be single stream, where mixed recyclables are stored and collected in containers and sorted at the MRF, or dual stream where the participant separates recycled materials into separate bins by type. Much of the C&D waste flow is also recycled.

The first law passed to deal with solid waste in the U.S. was the 1965 Solid Waste Disposal Act, however this act only encouraged states to develop guidelines for dealing with solid waste but did not require states to do so. The Resource Conservation and Recovery Act, or RCRA, was passed in 1976 as an amendment to the Solid Waste Disposal Act. While much of RCRA is focused on hazardous waste, subtitle D was devoted to non-hazardous solid waste. The intent of the law was to deal with the growing amount of industrial and municipal waste. The 1984 amendment of RCRA resulted from an understanding by Congress that non-hazardous solid waste facilities, particularly MSW landfills, actually did hold an unknown amount of hazardous wastes. The 1984 amendment required EPA to put in place rules to assure ground water monitoring to detect contamination, establish stricter criteria for the location of new or existing facilities, and provide corrective action where needed. A major contribution of these statutes was the changing perspective on waste. Rather than dispose of waste, the laws emphasized source reduction and diversion from disposal. This, over time, has led to a shift towards a no-waste paradigm.

Rather than landfill or incinerate waste, the "zero waste" movement supports efforts to avoid producing wastes at all. A growing number of U.S. communities and businesses have adopted the no-waste paradigm. Their efforts are supported by the U.S. Zero Waste Business Council and The Zero Waste International Alliance. Zero waste as a goal has been widely embraced by the European Union, especially in its 2010 Waste Framework Directive. The UNEP also supports zero waste strategies and seeks to promote that goal in developing nations. Both UNEP and the EU Directive emphasize re-thinking waste as a valued resource and seek to promote recycling and waste-to-energy incineration.

While inconsistent data collection worldwide makes global statements about solid waste difficult, according to the World Bank's best estimates, current global waste generation (MSW and ISW) is more than a billion tons per year. This amount is expected to double within a decade. Two important patterns have been recognized. First, waste generation is higher in urban areas than in rural areas and, second, waste generation is greater in affluent populations than in lower income populations. This is important, because as the world's population grows more urban and wealthier, more waste will be generated. The world must develop better strategies for dealing with more solid waste. This is particularly true for developing nations that still tend to dispose of waste in uncontrolled open dumps.

MSW is a major problem for developing countries. The World Bank estimates that municipalities in developing countries can spend up to half of their budgets for solid waste management and despite these expenditure levels, not all waste is collected. The UNEP is engaged in efforts to get developing countries to see waste as resource. These programs should increase rates of recycling and the number of waste-to-energy facilities, thus providing waste diversion from dumps and landfills.

---

[1] "Resource Conservation and Recovery Act (RCRA) Overview," EPA, accessed July 26, 2017, https://www.epa.gov/rcra/resource-conservation-and-recovery-act-rcra-overview.

[2] Valerie L. Shulman, "Trends in Waste Management," in *Waste: A Handbook for Management*, ed. Trevor M. Letcher and Daniel A. Vallero (Amsterdam: Elsevier, 2011), 3–4.

[3] "U.S. and World Population Clock," Census Bureau, accessed July 27, 2017, https://www.census.gov/popclock/.

[4] "Advancing Sustainable Materials Management: Facts and Figures," EPA, accessed July 26, 2017, https://www.epa.gov/smm/advancing-sustainable-materials-management-facts-and-figures#USState.

[5] "Guide for Industrial Waste Management," EPA, accessed July 27, 2017, https://www.epa.gov/sites/production/files/2016-03/documents/industrial-waste-guide.pdf.

[6] "Solid Waste Disposal," *Funk and Wagnalls New World Encyclopedia* (2016): EBSCO*host* (Accession number: SO144000).

[7] "What is a Municipal Solid Waste Landfill?," EPA, accessed August 10, 2018, https://www.epa.gov/landfills/municipal-solid-waste-landfills#whatis.

[8] "Municipal Solid Waste Landfills: Economic Impact Analysis for the Proposed New Subpart to the New Source Performance Review," EPA, accessed August 5, 2017, https://www3.epa.gov/ttnecas1/regdata/EIAs/LandfillsNSPSProposalEIA.pdf.

[9] "Sustainable Management of Construction and Demolition Materials," EPA, accessed August 10, 2018, https://www.epa.gov/smm/sustainable-management-construction-and-demolition-materials.

[10] "Basic Information About Landfills," EPA, accessed July 31, 2017, https://www.epa.gov/landfills/basic-information-about-landfills#whattypes.

[11] "Landfills," EPA, accessed July 31, 2017, https://www.epa.gov/landfills.

[12] "What is a Municipal Solid Waste Landfill?" EPA, accessed August 4, 2017, https://www.epa.gov/landfills/municipal-solid-waste-landfills#whatis.

[13] "Energy Recovery from the Combustion of Municipal Solid Waste (MSW)," EPA, accessed July 31, 2017, https://www.epa.gov/smm/energy-recovery-combustion-municipal-solid-waste-msw.

[14] "Sustainable Management of Food," EPA, accessed August 10, 2018, https://www.epa.gov/sustainable-management-food.

[15] Mohamed Alwaeli, "Cost and Cost-Effectiveness of Recycling of Municipal Solid Waste," in *Recycling: Processes, Costs and Benefits*, ed. Charlene J. Nielsen (New York: Nova Science Publishers, Inc., 2011), 15.

[16] Alwaeli, "Cost and Cost-Effectiveness," 19.

[17] "Recycling Basics," EPA, accessed August 2, 2017, https://www.epa.gov/recycling/recycling-basics.

[18] "What is Single Stream Recycling," City of Chicago, accessed August 10, 2018, https://www.cityofchicago.org/content/dam/city/depts/doe/general/RecyclingAndWasteMgmt_PDFs/MultiUnit/FAQs.pdf.

[19] "Understanding Single vs. Dual Stream Recycling," Vangel, Inc., accessed August 10, 2018, https://www.vangelinc.com/single-vs-dual-stream-recycling/.

[20] "Municipal Solid Waste and Construction and Demolition Debris," DOT, accessed August 4, 2017, https://www.bts.gov/archive/subject_areas/freight_transportation/faf/faf4/debris.

[21] James Salzman and Barton H. Thompson, Jr., *Environmental Law and Policy* (St. Paul, MN: Foundation Press, 2014), 232.

[22] Christopher Rizzo, "RCRA's 'Imminent and Substantial Endangerment; Citizen Suit Turns 25," *Natural Resources & Environment* 23, no.2 (2008): 50.

[23] John H. Turner, "Off to a Good Start: The RCRA Subtitle D Program for Municipal Solid Waste Landfills," *Temple Environmental Law & Technology Journal* 15, no. 1 (1996): 1.

[24] "Advancing Sustainable Materials Management: Facts and Figures."

[25] "The 2016 State of Curbside Report," The Recycling Partnership, accessed August 10, 2018, https://recyclingpartnership.org/wp-content/uploads/2018/05/state-of-recycling-report-Jan2017.pdf.

[26] John Tierney, "The Reign of Recycling," *The New York Times,* October 3, 2015, SR2.

[27] Daniel A. Vallero, "Green Engineering and Sustainable Design Aspects of Waste Management," in *Waste: A Handbook for Management*, ed. Trevor M. Letcher and Daniel A. Vallero (Amsterdam: Elsevier, 2011), 13–15.

[28] "Zero Waste Business Council Launces Certification Program," USZWBC, accessed August 10, 2018, https://www.waste360.com/zero-waste/zero-waste-business-council-launches-certification-program.

[29] "ZW Definition," Zero Waste International Alliance, accessed August 3, 2017, http://www.zwia.org/standards/zw-definition.

[30] "Zero Waste Hierarchy of Highest and Best Use," ZWIA, accessed August 10, 2018, http://zwia.org/standards/zero-waste-hierarchy/.

[31] Shulman, "Trends in Waste Management," 5–6.

[32] Samuel P. Hays, *A History of Environmental Politics Since 1945* (Pittsburgh: University of Pittsburgh Press, 2000), 176.

[33] "What A Waste: A Global Review of Waste Management," World Bank, accessed August 1, 2017, http://web.worldbank.org/WBSITE/EXTERNAL/TOPICS/EXTURBAN DEVELOPMENT/0,,contentMDK:23172887~pagePK:210058~piPK:210062~theSitePK: 337178,00.html.

[34] What A Waste: A Global Review of Waste Management," World Bank, accessed August 1, 2017, http://web.worldbank.org/WBSITE/EXTERNAL/TOPICS/EXTURBAN DEVELOPMENT/0,,contentMDK:23172887~pagePK:210058~piPK:210062~theSitePK:3 37178,00.html.

[35] "Integrated Solid Waste Management," UNEP, accessed August 10, 2018, https://sustainabledevelopment.un.org/content/dsd/csd/csd_pdfs/csd-19/learningcentre/presentations/May%202%20am/1%20-%20Memon%20-%20ISWM.pdf.

[36] "Guidelines on the Interpretation of the R1 Energy Efficiency Formula for Incineration Facilities Dedicated to the Processing of Municipal Solid Waste According to Annex II of Directive 2008/98/EC on Waste," European Commission, accessed August 4, 2017, www.ec.europa.eu/environment/waste/framework/pdf/guidance.pdf.

[37] "Confederation of European Waste-to-Energy Plants," CEWEP, accessed August 4, 2017, www.cewep.eu/.

CHAPTER 7

Chemical and Hazardous Substances Policy

INTRODUCTION

Modern economies produce and use a wide array of chemicals and hazardous substances. The agricultural sector uses many pesticides, insecticides, fungicides, and rodenticides to protect crops from infestation by pests, insects, molds, blights, and rodents. Industry uses chemicals in manufacturing processes. The electrical and electronics industry uses many hazardous substances in devices, from transformers to cell phones. All of these substances need to be handled with care to avoid environmental contamination and untoward consequences. Many hazardous substances are toxic and can result in severe health risks upon exposure.

This chapter explores the rise in the manufacture, use, and disposal of hazardous substances in the years following the Second World War. Beginning in the 1970s, the U.S. Congress passed a series of laws to regulate the use of hazardous substances to assure that harm to human health or the environment did not occur. After the discovery of an abandoned hazardous waste site in the late 1970s, Congress passed further legislation addressing the issue of hazardous waste. These laws will be explored in this chapter.

Internationally, the rise in the use of chemicals and pesticides mirrored what the U.S. experienced in the era after the Second World

War. By the 1970s, it became clear that there was a need for multinational and regional agreements to control the transport of hazardous substances between nations. A series of regional and international treaties were negotiated to facilitate this regulation. This chapter discusses these agreements.

The question of inequity for at risk populations of color as well as people of lower socioeconomic status resulted in the rise of the environmental justice movement. Within the U.S. the movement started with evidence of the greater likelihood of exposure to hazardous substances for minority populations. Under President Clinton these concerns became the official policy of the federal government. Internationally, the environmental justice movement also formed around awareness that the wealthy nations were seeking cheaper places to dispose of their hazardous waste and all too often this meant developing nations would take that waste in return for a payment. These patterns resulted in a number of international agreements to provide informed consent. More recently, the environmental justice movement has shifted to a climate justice perspective, given that poor nations and people of color are more likely to experience the most risk from climate change. The chapter discusses environmental justice from both domestic and international perspectives.

DOMESTIC CONSIDERATIONS

The publication of a controversial book, *Silent Spring*, by Rachel Carson in 1962 raised for the first time the issue of the harmful effects of chemicals in the environment. Carson's primary concern was a widely used pesticide called dichlorodiphenyl trichloroethane, or DDT. The book began with a "fable for tomorrow" drawn from real events, which dramatized the impacts of DDT on wildlife in communities using the chemical. The fable appeared as a three-part series in *The New Yorker* the summer before the book's publication where it was read by many. When the book was released, it rapidly became a best seller, and served to introduce the public to the dangers posed by pesticides, like DDT, that persisted in the environment for a long time. Carson accused the chemical industry of incorrectly representing the safety of its products and public officials for so willingly accepting industry claims. The chemical industry, which had blossomed after World War II, responded by launching a vicious personal attack on Carson and the truth of her book. She spent the next two years, until her early death in 1964, defending its scientific accuracy. *Silent Spring* helped to bring about the environmental movement of the 1970s and, in particular, the fear of hazardous substances.[1]

The U.S. uses tens of thousands of chemicals in agriculture, industry, and commerce and develops about 700 new chemicals each year. The chemical industry grew massively after World War II as did the agricultural demand for pesticides. Pesticides are substances intended to destroy or repel pests, to regulate plant growth, or to act as a nitrogen stabilizer. Best known pesticides include insecticides, herbicides, rodenticides, and fungicides. Insecticides kill insects and arthropods such as arachnids. Herbicides kill weeds and other plants growing where they are not wanted. Rodenticides control rodents such as mice. Fungicides kill fungi including mildews, molds, blights, and rusts.[2]

Between 1965 and 1985 the demand for pesticides nearly tripled, and by 1985 more than 6 pounds were being applied per hectare (2.47 acres) per year.[3] According to the Environmental Protection Agency (EPA), in 2012, the U.S. used over 1.1 billion pounds of pesticides. The most commonly used pesticide type was herbicides and plant growth regulators (PGR) (57 percent), followed by fumigants (37 percent), fungicides (9 percent), and insecticides (5 percent).[4] In 2012, the U.S. spent nearly $9 billion on pesticides. In 2012, U.S expenditures accounted for 21 percent of world expenditures on herbicides, 14 percent of world expenditures on insecticides, 10 percent of world expenditures on fungicides, and 23 percent of world expenditures on fumigants.[5]

Concern over exposure to pesticides spans the gamut from agricultural workers to end consumers of the crop. Health effects associated with exposure to pesticides either through breathing them or having skin contact include sickness and death. Consumption of pesticides raises fears of illness, especially after prolonged exposure. The other major issue associated with pesticide use is the impact these chemicals may have on the ecology. Exposure of wildlife to some chemicals has proved dangerous.

Agricultural use of chemicals also includes fertilizers. Fertilizers put nutrients that plants need into the soil. Demand for U.S. crops worldwide since the 1960s has resulted in widespread use of chemical fertilizers including phosphate, potash, and nitrogen. U.S. use of chemical fertilizers peaked in 1981 at 24 million tons. Use declined after then either associated with decreases in demand for U.S. crops or increases in cost for fertilizer. Use of fertilizer in 2011 was 22 million tons. Fertilizer applied correctly will typically be absorbed by the crop, however, if over applied it will runoff and contaminate water bodies with excess nutrients. All too often farmers over apply fertilizer causing adverse environmental impacts.[6]

As agricultural use of chemicals grew in the post-war era, so did the use of industrial and commercial chemicals. The creation of new chemicals after World War II happened at a very fast pace. The American Chemical Society had registered more than 4 million chemicals, many synthetic, by the mid-1960s. Currently, more than 84,000 chemicals are commonly used by industry and commerce in the United States on a regular basis and more than 10,000 new chemicals are pending review by the EPA.[7]

Hazardous waste that requires safe disposal to insure isolation from the environment is also a problem. Copious quantities of hazardous waste are produced in the U.S. each year. Sources of hazardous waste include household waste such as batteries, oil, paints, and solvents. There is a wide array of industrial and commercial hazardous waste produced annually which the EPA tracks in its National Biennial RCRA Hazardous Waste Report. In the late 1980s, massive amounts of hazardous waste were being produced in the

U.S.—estimated at an annual production of 250 million metric tons. That level of hazardous waste production has been reduced substantially in recent decades with the emphasis on source reduction and recycling, but current rates of annual production are still estimated to be about 34 million tons.[8]

Hazardous waste in recent years includes a large quantity of electronic waste, or e-waste. While there are some national variations, e-waste is generally considered discarded electronic devices or appliances. In the U.S., these include computers, monitors, flat panel television, digital cameras, DVD players and recorders, tablets, solar cells, and mobile phones. In 2014, the U.S. generated 7.07 million tons of e-waste.[9] Much e-waste is exported to developing countries where low-wage recycling operations seek to reclaim the valuable metals and rare earth elements in e-waste. Since 2010, the EPA has collaborated with the United Nations (UN) to track global flows of e-waste and to address the e-waste problem in developing nations.[10]

Federal Legislation and Policy

Hazardous and toxic substances are regulated by a number of federal laws passed beginning in the 1960s. These laws include the Federal Insecticide, Fungicide, and Rodenticide Act (FIFRA) and its amendments, the Resources Conservation and Recovery Act (RCRA) and its amendments, the Toxic Substances Control Act (TSCA) and its amendments, the Comprehensive Environmental Response, Compensation, and Liability Act (CERCLA) and its amendments, and the Pollution Prevention Act (PPA). Each are discussed in detail below.

The Federal Insecticide, Fungicide, and Rodenticide Act. FIFRA dates back to the early 1940s when it was under the control of the U.S. Department of Agriculture (USDA). USDA's main interest was how well pesticides worked rather than their potential ecological effects. By the 1960s, especially after the publication of *Silent Spring*, public attention came to focus on the environmental effects of pesticide use. FIFRA was subsequently amended in 1964, 1972, and 1978 to focus on environmental problems associated with pesticide use. When EPA was created in 1970, FIFRA fell under its jurisdiction.[11] FIFRA provides for federal regulation of pesticide sale, use, and distribution. All pesticides used in the U.S. must be registered, or licensed, by the EPA. Before the EPA may register a pesticide for use, the company that is requesting registration must show that the pesticide will perform its intended function and will not cause unreasonable adverse environmental effects if used in accord with widespread and commonly used practice. Additionally, the company must demonstrate that residue left on plants does not pose a risk to humans consistent with restrictions under the Federal Food, Drug, and Cosmetic Act. Under the law, the Office of Pesticide Programs within the EPA establishes maximum levels for pesticide residue on food and regulates all pesticides in use. FIFRA was amended by the Food Quality Protection Act (FQPA) of 1996 and the Pesticide Registration Improvement Act (PRIA) of 2003 and the Pesticide Registration Improvement Extension Act of 2012.[12]

The FQPA passed unanimously by Congress and was signed into law by President Clinton in 1996. It requires that the EPA make a safety finding when setting tolerances for use to assure that the pesticide can be used with "a reasonable certainty of no harm" and that the EPA reassess all pesticide tolerances that were in place before the FQPA was passed. In addition, the law requires that the EPA consider the impact on children by using a tenfold safety factor and consider aggregate risk by considering exposure to multiple sources such as food, water, residential and other non-occupational sources. The FQPA set up a procedure for quick approval of pesticides meeting the FQPA definition of reduced risk. Under the law, the EPA is required to periodically review pesticides due to changes in science and practices over time to assure safety.[13]

PRIA requires that companies pay fees for registration of pesticides based upon the category of their registration. Categories include type of chemical (conventional, antimicrobial, or biopesticide) and type of action requested (new active ingredient, new food use, new registration for an old product). Under the system established, each category ties the EPA to a specific decision review timeline. The goal was to reduce the time frame for registrations thus providing support for companies seeking pesticide reviews.[14]

Resource Conservation and Recovery Act. The Solid Waste Disposal Act of 1965 was later amended by the Resource Conservation and Recovery Act of 1976. RCRA was passed to control solid waste (as discussed in Chapter 6) but also to control hazardous waste. The Hazardous Waste Program was established under RCRA's Subtitle C. It set up a system for controlling hazardous waste from the point of generation to disposal. While the EPA oversees RCRA, the Department of Transportation (DOT) Pipeline and Hazardous Materials Safety Administration regulates the transport of hazardous substances.[15]

Under RCRA, a solid waste is classified as a hazardous waste either by listing or by characteristic. A waste is hazardous if it is listed in one of the 4 lists that are found in title 40 of the Code of Federal Regulations (CFR) section 261. These lists identify known hazardous waste from industrial and manufacturing processes such as solvents or dioxin-bearing waste. Characteristics that identify a waste as hazardous include ignitability, corrosivity, reactivity, and toxicity. A third classification of waste, mixed waste, has a hazardous component and a radioactive component. Mixed waste is regulated both by RCRA and the Atomic Energy Act.[16]

By law, RCRA excluded certain solid waste from being classified as hazardous waste. These include household hazardous waste, agricultural waste, fossil fuel combustion waste, and cement kiln dust waste. Perhaps the most important excluded class of waste included oil, gas, and geothermal waste.[17] Critics argue that this "petroleum exclusion" allows the oil and gas industry a cheap way to deal with the waste that comes from oil and gas extraction. Nevertheless, the powerful oil and gas industry was successfully able to lobby for this provision.[18]

RCRA requires hazardous waste generators to oversee the management of their waste through appropriate identification, monitoring, and treatment prior to disposal. After a hazardous waste is generated, transporters may move the waste to another facility for recycling, treatment, or storage and disposal. The transport is regulated both by the EPA and the DOT. The Treatment Storage and Disposal Facilities (TSDFs) are regulated under RCRA to assure safe handling of hazardous materials.[19] RCRA requires "cradle-to-grave" tracking of materials from point of generation, movement, to final disposal. When a generator of waste produces a specified threshold amount, they are required to contact the EPA to obtain an identification number and to fill out a manifest sheet which accompanies the waste until final disposal. Transporters and TSDFs are required to check the manifest sheet and to verify that the waste being received matches the description on the manifest.[20] Together these activities minimize the risk of illegal dumping of hazardous waste into the environment.

TSDFs are regulated more heavily under RCRA than generators or transporters because historically many TSDFs ended up as Superfund sites. To prevent this, and to speed up the implementation of the law, RCRA was amended in 1984 by the Hazardous and Solid Waste Amendments (HSWA), which gave the EPA the authority to demand that TSDFs clean up present or past contamination in their facilities. These cleanups or "corrective actions" enable the EPA to strictly oversee TSDFs.[21] The HSWA were a response to the slow progress made in implementation of the law by the Reagan administration. It is amongst the most detailed environmental laws passed by Congress. It specified 76 specific deadlines and included 8 "hammer clauses" or legislative prohibitions on disposal that were to take effect if the EPA failed to produce agency regulations in a timely manner.[22]

The Toxic Substances Control Act. TSCA was passed to control toxic substances but it contained many defects that resulted in very weak regulation. It was amended by the Frank R. Lautenberg Chemical Safety for the 21st Century Act of 2016 in an attempt to correct those faults. Many environmentalists sought to change TSCA since its passage in 1976. Rather than requiring safety testing of all chemicals in use when

TSCA was initially passed, the law grandfathered in as safe the 60,000 chemicals then in use. Because of this, TSCA did not follow the precautionary principle (discussed below), but rather took the approach that chemicals should be considered safe until proven harmful. As of 2016, most of those chemicals had still not been tested for safety. The original law gave the EPA very little authority to require proof of safety before allowing a new chemical to go to market. TSCA actually exempted chemical producers from having to show the safety of their products, forcing the EPA to prove a chemical was dangerous before it had power to ban or control its use. Proving that a chemical is dangerous turned out to be very difficult to do since the EPA has limited resources to do its own testing. The original TSCA also required the EPA to consider the costs to the manufacturer before restricting the use of a chemical. All in all, these provisions made TSCA a very weak law.[23]

Understanding the defects in TSCA, the states began to take more aggressive action to restrict what they considered dangerous chemicals. Beginning in the first decade of the 21st century, more than 20 states passed restrictive laws. To override this increasing number of different state-based requirements, the chemical industry after 40 years of opposing changes to TSCA finally agreed that a new federal law would be preferable to a plethora of state laws. As a result, the Frank R. Lautenberg Chemical Safety for the 21st Century Act was signed into law in June 2016.

The new law reformed TSCA in several important ways. For existing chemicals, the EPA was to prioritize assessment of all chemicals in use by designating them high- or low-priority and then to begin evaluation of all high-priority chemicals in use. The law set deadlines for risk evaluations of these existing chemicals. New chemicals must have the EPA's finding of safety before being allowed in the marketplace. Funding is provided through fees on chemical manufacturers when they submit test data to the EPA for review or a premanufacturing notice. The law preserves state laws that were passed prior to April 2016, however, states are prohibited from taking action to ban chemicals once the EPA's risk evaluation is underway. The number of chemicals that the EPA is to evaluate each year is relatively limited, however, and thus will only make a small dent into the vast number of chemicals that are yet to be evaluated.[24]

Comprehensive Environmental Response, Compensation, and Liability Act. In 1978, a small community near Niagara Falls experienced a crisis. Beginning in 1942, Hooker Chemical and Plastics Corporation buried 21,000 tons of chemical waste in Love Canal. In 1953, Hooker sold the site to the city of Niagara Falls for one dollar. The city then proceeded to build an elementary school on the land which soon attracted suburban development. By the 1970s, after a few seasons of heavy rain, the corroded barrels full of chemical waste began to leak. The chemicals oozed into the basements and yards of residential houses. The New York State Health Department, the Department of Environmental Conservation, and the EPA undertook a series of health studies on the local population and their residential surroundings. The results showed that homes tested positive for high-levels of benzene, chloroform, and toluene. Some of the school children had liver problems. In addition, the New York State Department of Health warned that women living near Love Canal had a much higher risk of miscarriage than the general population. In May 1980, the EPA reported that many Love Canal residents had chromosome breakage. The state's refusal to evacuate the neighborhood raised public sentiment that the government had no interest in protecting the health their community. This criticism gained national attention. Eventually the Carter administration intervened and relocated the affected population. The country was shocked by this first instance of the consequences of hazardous waste.[25]

The Love Canal situation resulted in both House and Senate committees holding hearings on the dangers posed by toxic waste. Legislation was introduced in both houses to create a 'Superfund' for dealing with those dangers. While this was being discussed in Congress, a toxic waste site in Elizabeth, New Jersey caught fire. The fire sent a plume of black smoke over a 15-mile area raising considerable local health concerns. State officials closed schools and urged residents to remain in their homes with windows and doors closed. The legislation drafted in both houses made its way to a vote as the Comprehensive Environmental Response, Compensation, and Liability Act or Superfund of 1980. CERCLA's focus was on dealing with the dangers of abandoned or uncontrolled hazardous waste sites. The law allowed the EPA to respond to emergencies, gather data and analyze risks, and hold parties financially responsible for site cleanup of their pollution. CERCLA created the Superfund, through a tax on chemical and oil industries, to respond to emergencies. If a polluter refused to agree to clean a site, the EPA could use the Superfund to pay for cleanup and later charge the polluter triple damages. The first test of CERCLA came the following year when the EPA successfully removed 4,000 drums of waste in Kentucky's Valley of the Drums site. In 1982, the EPA created the Hazardous Ranking System (HRS) as the primary way to determine if a site would obtain Superfund status. The HRS provided a numerical analysis of risks posed by a site to human health or the environment. Once a site scored high enough on the list of factors included in the HRS, it would be eligible for Superfund status. In 1982, the EPA for the first time applied the law to reach a settlement with responsible parties and got South Carolina Recycling and Disposal, Inc. to implement a cleanup of its Bluff Road waste site. Using its HRS screening, in 1983, the EPA generated the first National Priorities List (NPL) with 406 sites prioritized for cleanup.[26]

Once a site is listed on the NPL, it is queued for cleanup. The cleanup process includes site characterization, a decision about what remediation plan will be followed, and the design and implementation of a remediation strategy. Once the strategy is put in place, the site may be listed in the status of construction complete. This would be the case in the event that no further work needs to be done to clean the site but rather that the remedy in place just needs time to operate to complete the cleanup. Once a site is cleaned, it is delisted from the NPL.[27]

Superfund was quite controversial when passed insofar as it was based on the polluter pays principle. Superfund implemented joint, several, and retroactive liability provisions which enabled the EPA to sue polluters but also allowed polluters identified by the agency as primary contributing parties to sue other minor contributors. These lawsuits slowed down the process of cleanup and contributed to excessive litigation. Superfund was also controversial because, even in the absence of lawsuits, the process of cleanup was both costly and lengthy. Site identification to delisting could take decades and the cost of each cleanup averaged about $30 million. The taxes used to fund the Superfund were vigorously opposed by the chemical and oil industry and were finally ended in 1995. The dissatisfaction with Superfund prompted Congress to amend the original law.[28]

The taxes that created the Superfund came at a very high price. To accept the 9.6-cent-a-barrel tax on crude oil, the oil industry asked for and got the exclusion of all of their production wastes from CERCLA liability even though petroleum waste frequently includes quantities of benzene, toluene, xylene, and lead. The petroleum exclusion was built into both RCRA and CERCLA, although the RCRA exclusion is far narrower than the CERCLA exclusion and pertains to only oil and gas field waste. The petroleum exclusions are considered by critics a major loophole in both laws.[29]

The Superfund Amendments and Reauthorization Act (SARA) of 1986 attempted to revise some of the problems with the original law. SARA encouraged voluntary settlements rather than lawsuits. It sought to encourage state and citizen participation in site cleanup. It put increased emphasis on the importance of human health problems caused by hazardous waste.[30]

In December 1984, the largest industrial accident to date occurred in Bhopal, India. A Union Carbide chemical plant exploded killing nearly 4,000 and crippling tens of thousands as toxic gas filled the city.[31] The explosion created consternation in the United States as the public wondered what kinds of plants might be in their localities. As a result, when the Superfund Amendments and Reauthorization Act was passed in 1986, one of its titles was the Emergency Preparedness and Community Right-to-Know Act (EPCRA). EPCRA requires each state to establish a State Emergency Response Commission (SERC). The SERCs are required to divide the state into emergency response districts and to put in place a Local Emergency Response Committee (LERC) for each district. The LERCs work closely with local first responders including police and firefighters to plan for emergency response should a disaster occur. The LERCs maintain an inventory of potentially unsafe sites within communities.[32]

EPCRA also established the Toxic Release Inventory (TRI). The TRI tracks the release of certain toxic chemicals. U.S. facilities in different industrial sectors are required to report annually the amount of their releases to air, land, and water whether accidental or intended. The data is collected by the EPA and put into a database that is publicly searchable so that communities can know what potentially harmful substances are in their localities.[33]

SARA also addressed the issue of toxic sites at federal facilities. Among some of the most polluted sites in the nation are those on public land. These include both military bases and sites associated with the nuclear weapons complex (discussed in chapter 11). Section 120 of CERCLA requires federal facilities to comply with the law in the same manner as non-governmental entities and to identify contaminated adjacent properties. The Defense Base Closure and Realignment Act of 1990 further accelerated cleanup of federal facilities as the transfer of the property would be slowed if they were contaminated.[34]

In 1993, the Brownfields Initiative began. The purpose was to redevelop abandoned, idle, or underused industrial or commercial sites when redevelopment was being slowed or prevented by concern over environmental contamination. In 1995, the EPA introduced the Brownfields Action Agenda to help states and communities redevelop properties. The agenda provided pilot programs with funding, clarified liability issues, encouraged partnerships, and promoted job creation and training. Two years later, the Brownfields National Partnership began. The Partnership brought together more than 25 organizations and the federal government for the purpose of promoting brownfields redevelopment. The Partnership provided $300 million in federal funding for redevelopment of nearly 5,000 properties. Closely linked to the brownfields redevelopment efforts, the EPA announced the Superfund Redevelopment Initiative in 1999. This became a coordinated national program to turn cleaned Superfund sites into community assets. In 2002, President Bush signed into law the Small Business Liability Relief and Brownfields Revitalization Act. This act expanded the EPA's Brownfields Program, increased funding for redevelopment, and clarified liability under Superfund. The law extended Superfund liability protections to landowners of brownfields if they qualified either as prospective property purchasers, contiguous property owners, or innocent land owners.[35] Together these efforts reduced the fear of Superfund liability and promoted redevelopment.

The Pollution Prevention Act. The passage of the Pollution Prevention Act of 1990 established the principle that prevention of pollution was national policy, rather than cleaning up pollution after it occurred. The goals of the act focused on reducing pollution by implementing cost-effective changes in production and operation of industry and government. Emphasis was also placed on reducing raw material use. The law recognized that it was often easier for industry to comply with federal regulations, not through source reduction, but by concentrating on treatment and disposal. The law established as a goal that source reduction be used as a strategy to avoid hazardous material from being released into the environment. Under authority of the law, the EPA evaluates new and existing chemicals seeking ways to prevent or reduce pollution before it gets into the environment.[36]

Environmental Justice. The environmental justice movement was organized in the 1980s, when people of color began to demand that the government address the issue of inequity in environmental matters. The roots of the movement, however, go back farther. As early as 1971, the Council on Environmental Quality (CEQ) raised the issue of race and socioeconomic disparities associated with environmental risk. Social and religious groups soon got involved. The United Church of Christ (UCC) brought attention to the environmental justice movement in 1987 when the UCC Commission for Racial Justice published a study called, *Toxic Waste and Race*. This report focused attention on the correlation between race and likelihood of living or working near a toxic waste site. The movement achieved national attention in 1991 when delegates met at the National People of Color Environmental Leadership Summit in Washington, D.C. The movement's fundamental position is that ethnic and racial minorities have been exposed disproportionately to environmental health and safety risks, especially those associated with hazardous chemicals. The environmental justice movement has grown in size and influence. It now includes hundreds of organizations. In 1994, President Clinton issued executive order 12898 which instructed all federal agencies to ensure that their programs "do not unfairly inflict environmental harm on the poor and minorities." Since then, numerous state and local governments have put in place environmental justice goals and strategies. Robert Bullard's books *Dumping in Dixie: Race, Class, and Environmental Quality* and *Confronting Environmental Racism: Voices from the Grassroots*, both released in the 1990s, further exposed the issue of siting toxic waste facilities and race.[37]

The EPA defines environmental justice as "the fair treatment and meaningful involvement of all people regardless of race, color, national origin, or income, with respect to the development, implementation, and enforcement of environmental laws, regulations, and polices."[38]

GLOBAL CONSIDERATIONS

Production of chemicals worldwide has grown many times since the emergence of the industry in the years after World War II. In 1970, the total global production of chemicals (industrial, commercial, and agricultural) was $171 billion USD. By 2010, global output had increased to $4.12 trillion USD. In only the first decade of the 21st century, total production increased 54 percent. Increasing production of chemicals has varied by country. While the wealthy OECD nations still produce the largest amount of chemicals, China's production has also increased massively. In 2010, China was the world's largest single producer of chemicals with sales of $754 billion USD.[39]

According to the EPA, world use of pesticides totaled nearly 6 billion pounds in 2012. Herbicides accounted for about half of all pesticides used (49 percent), followed by fumigants (19 percent), insecticides (18 percent), and fungicides (14 percent).[40] World expenditure on pesticides in 2012 was nearly $56 billion USD. Of that expenditure, herbicides/PGR accounted for 44 percent, insecticides 20 percent, fungicides 20 percent and fumigants 1 percent.[41]

Global e-waste is also a major problem. E-waste amounts have been increasing globally, but at different rates in different nations. The U.S., in 2014, generated more e-waste than any other nation (7.07 million tons), however, China ran a close second having generated 6.03 million tons. Following in order of generation were Japan (2.2 million tons), Germany (1.5 million tons), the U.K. (1.51 million tons), France, (1.42 million tons), Brazil (1.41 million tons), Russia (1.23 million tons), Australia (0.47 million tons), and South Africa (0.35 million tons). The worldwide production of e-waste in 2014 was 41.8 million tons but of that amount, only 6.5 million tons was properly documented or recycled with exacting standards. Some was recycled in uncontrolled facilities that result in a great deal of human and environmental exposure to toxic materials associated with e-waste including PCBs and heavy metals. Transboundary movement of e-waste from the developed world to the developing world for reprocessing and recycling occurs because of the willingness of low-wage labor in those countries to risk exposure to hazardous material. The problem will magnify in the future as the quantity of e-waste is expected to grow rapidly with estimates of worldwide production of e-waste surpassing 50 million tons by 2018.[42]

Precautionary Principle

Most of the world follows the precautionary principle which was accepted as Principle 15 of the Rio Declaration and reads:

> In order to protect the environment, the precautionary approach shall be widely applied by States according to their capabilities. Where there are threats of serious or irreversible damage, lack of full scientific certainty shall not be used as a reason for postponing cost-effective measures to prevent environmental degradation.[43]

Application of the precautionary principle to chemicals and potentially hazardous substances is widely practiced worldwide, although this by no means suggests that chemicals and other hazardous substances are not handled poorly in many locations. The precautionary principle is the acceptance in international law of some well-known common-sense adages such as "look before you leap" and "an ounce of prevention is worth a pound of cure" and "better safe than sorry." The precautionary principle is the starting point for understanding international environmental agreements on hazardous substances.

International Environmental Agreements

There are several international environmental agreements dealing with several aspects of chemicals and pesticides. The purposes of these treaties vary. Some seek only to provide informed consent to nations regarding the dangers of the substances they are considering importing. Others promote the phaseout of use of certain chemicals that have been determined to be a danger.

Basel Convention. The Basel Convention on the Control of Transboundary Movements of Hazardous Waste was adopted in 1989, after the recognition that hazardous waste was being transported from the developed world to the continent of Africa and other developing countries. As the environmental movement gained following in developed nations in the 1970s and 1980s, public resistance to domestic disposal of hazardous waste grew. This was owed to both the growth of NIMBYism (not in my back yard) and to increasing costs for disposal of such waste. As a result, some hazardous waste operations in the developed world sought out cheap disposal sites in the developing world, where environmental awareness and laws were not yet in force. The goal of the Basel Convention was to end what was termed "toxic trade." The Basel Convention established a system of regulation based on informed consent. It required that before hazardous waste could be transported from one country to another, government authorities from the exporting nation must notify authorities in the importing nation by providing detailed information regarding the shipment.[44]

Bamako Convention. The Bamako Convention was negotiated in 1991and came into force in 1998. It is a treaty of African nations banning the importation of hazardous waste into Africa. It was negotiated in response to Article 11 of the Basel Convention which encouraged nations to enter into regional agreements to help achieve the goals of the Basel Convention. It was also negotiated because of the failure of the Basel Convention to specifically prohibit the trade of hazardous waste to developing countries, which often felt economic pressure to accept waste from the wealthy nations. The Bamako Convention does not allow exceptions for certain hazardous wastes, such as radioactive waste, which were exempted by the Basel Convention. The Bamako Convention also has provisions to minimize and control the movement of hazardous waste within the African continent, to prohibit inland and ocean dumping of hazardous waste, to prohibit incineration of hazardous waste, to ensure hazardous waste is safely handled, and to ensure the precautionary principle is followed.[45]

Rotterdam Convention. The Rotterdam Convention on Prior Informed Consent Procedure for Certain Hazardous Chemicals and Pesticides in International Trade was adopted in 1998 and entered into force in 2004. The treaty provides for the notification of countries regarding the potential problems associated with certain chemicals and pesticides, allowing them time to determine if they wish to ban their import or to allow import subject to restrictions.[46]

European Union (EU) Directives and Regulation of Chemicals and Hazardous Substances. The EU has a number of directives that address various types of hazardous substances and waste. The overall strategy of the EU is to turn waste into a resource, thus enabling a circular economy. The Batteries Directive, adopted in 2006, focuses on minimizing the impact of batteries on the environment by prohibiting the marketing of batteries containing certain hazardous substances and by establishing high-levels of collection and recycling.[47] Restricting hazardous substances in electrical and electronic equipment is addressed by the RoHS Directive of 2002 later revised as the RoHS 2 Directive in 2011. The promotion of collection and recycling of electrical and electronic equipment is addressed by the Waste Electrical & Electronic Equipment (WEEE) Directive of 2002 which was later revised and strengthened. Together these directives create strategies to increase recycling of these products, to keep heavy metals out of the environment, and to encourage substitution of some materials such as polybrominated biphenyls (PBB) and polybrominated diphenyl ethers (PBDE) by safer ones.[48] Polychlorinated biphenyls (PCBs) and polychlorinated terphenyls (PCTs) are in a group of chemicals called Persistent Organic Pollutants (POPs). They were produced and used heavily between the 1930s and 1980s. Due to their human toxicity, they were heavily restricted in Europe in the mid-1980s. European Commission Directive 96/59/EC sets requirements for disposing of equipment containing PCBs and PCTs.[49] Waste oils are also regulated as hazardous wastes under Waste Framework Directive 2008/98/EU.[50]

Beginning in 2007, and phasing in over 11 years, chemicals in Europe have been regulated under REACH (EC 1907/2006). REACH uses a four-step process: registration, evaluation, authorization, and restriction. REACH puts the responsibility on industry to manage risks from chemicals and to provide safety information on chemicals. Manufacturers and importers of chemicals are required to collect data on the characteristics of chemicals that will enable safe handling. That data is entered into a central database maintained by the European

Chemical Agency in Helsinki. REACH also calls for the substitution of the most dangerous chemicals with ones less dangerous as soon alternatives are found.[51]

International Environmental Justice

Concern that developing nations would put their populations in danger in return for economic gain from the importation of hazardous waste, chemicals, or pesticides from the developed countries served as the starting place for the international environmental justice movement. While these issues continue to be of importance, the negotiation of several multinational treaties to address the need for informed consent by importing nations has done much to improve injustice concerns.

The most recent evolution of the movement is toward climate justice. Within this context, the movement argues that climate change is the most threatening environmental issue of the 21st century and that the poor and less powerful nations will bear the heaviest burdens from climate change. Climate models show that the poor nations of the world will be the ones that will see the most negative impacts from climate change (such as heavy precipitation events, extreme storms, flooding, drought, the spread of diseases, and sea-level rise). At the same time, the poor nations have the fewest resources to use to fight climate change or to adapt to its worst impacts. The climate justice movement argues for equity. In particular, the poor nations ask for assistance from the rich countries to help them deal with the impacts of climate change. They say this is equitable since the rich countries are responsible for emitting the bulk of carbon pollution that now impacts the world.

CONCLUSION

Rachel Carson's 1962 book, *Silent Spring*, brought to the world's attention the potentially harmful effects of chemicals in the environment. The book successfully raised domestic U.S. awareness of hazardous chemicals. Many of these chemicals were agricultural fertilizers and pesticides including insecticides, herbicides, rodenticides, and fungicides. There was a swift increase in the use of agricultural fertilizers and pesticides after the 1960s in the U.S. which culminated in mounting cognizance for potential human health and ecological harms. Chemical use in industry and commerce also rapidly increased in the years after World War II. By the 2010s, more than 84,000 chemicals were in common regular use in the U.S. The EPA continues to review requests to register many hundreds of new chemicals each year. Hazardous substances also include the large amount of hazardous waste that is produced each year. This waste includes household waste such as batteries, oil, paints, and solvents as well as a wide array of industrial and commercial hazardous waste produced annually. In recent years an emerging class of hazardous waste is electronic waste, or e-waste.

Hazardous and toxic substances are regulated by a number of federal laws passed beginning in the 1960s. Among the first of these laws was the Federal Insecticide, Fungicide, and Rodenticide Act and its amendments. FIFRA and its amendments provide for federal regulation of pesticide sale, use, and distribution. One of those amendments, the Food Quality Protection Act, requires that the EPA make a safety finding when setting tolerances for pesticide use on food crops. The Resource Conservation and Recovery Act of 1976 is the statute that controls solid and hazardous waste. The Toxic Substances and Control Act initially passed to control toxic substances was amended by the Frank R. Lautenberg Chemical Safety for the 21st Century Act of 2016. TSCA was a weak law in that it allowed more than 60,000 chemicals already in use to remain in use without safety testing. After many years of efforts on the part of environmentalists, the Lautenberg Act put in place a more rigorous procedure for risk evaluation of chemicals.

The discovery of tons of chemical waste in Love Canal prompted the passage of the Comprehensive Environmental Response, Compensation, and Liability Act or Superfund. CERCLA established a means to deal with the dangers of abandoned or uncontrolled hazardous waste sites. Superfund was controversial especially in that it established the polluter pays principle by requiring that polluters be forced to pay for the cost of site cleanup. The Superfund Amendments and Reauthorization Act of 1986 attempted to tone down some of the contentiousness of the original law by encouraging voluntary settlements rather than lawsuits. Provisions were also included in SARA that addressed concerns that arose after the Bhopal disaster struck India. The Emergency Preparedness and Community Right-to-Know Act required each state to establish better procedures for emergency response for chemical releases. EPCRA also established the Toxic Release Inventory which allows communities to track the release of certain toxic chemicals.

The passage of the Pollution Prevention Act of 1990 changed the course of hazardous substances policy by establishing the principle that prevention, rather than cleanup after the fact, was national policy. The law sought to reduce pollution by implementing cost-effective changes in production and operation of industry and government. Other policy changes introduced in the 1990s, such as the Brownfields Initiative, sought to help states and communities redevelop contaminated properties so they could be returned to productive use.

The heavy presence of chemicals and chemical waste sites in communities of color led to the organization of the environmental justice movement in the 1980s. The movement's mission was to address the inequities suffered by minority communities resulting from their disproportionate exposure to environmental health and safety risks. President Clinton's executive order 12898 made environmental justice national policy by ordering all federal agencies to consider the possibility that their actions might cause harm to poor and minority communities.

Hazardous chemicals and waste became an issue of worldwide concern in the years after World War II. Nations expressed their qualms by accepting the precautionary principle in the Rio Declaration.

Application of the precautionary principle to chemicals and potentially hazardous substances has also led to the formalization of several international agreements to address some of the issues associated with worldwide use of chemicals, pesticides, e-waste and other hazardous waste. The Basel Convention on the Control of Transboundary Movements of Hazardous Waste sought to end the "toxic trade" that had resulted from poor nations agreeing to import hazardous materials from developed nations for the revenues they could raise from such trade. The Basel Convention, while it did not prohibit such trade, did establish a system of regulation based on informed consent. African nations subsequently negotiated the Bamako Convention, which banned the importation of hazardous waste into Africa and controlled the transport of hazardous waste within the continent. The Rotterdam Convention on Prior Informed Consent Procedure for Certain Hazardous Chemicals and Pesticides in International Trade provides for the notification of countries regarding the potential problems associated with certain chemicals and pesticides and allows them time to determine if they wish to ban their import or to allow import subject to conditions.

The European Union has a series of directives that address particular types of hazardous substances and waste. The Batteries Directive seeks to minimize the effect of batteries on the environment by barring the marketing of batteries containing certain hazardous substances along with providing for high-levels of recycling. The RoHS Directive restricts the use of hazardous substances in electrical and electronic equipment. The Waste Electrical & Electronic Equipment (WEEE) Directive promotes collection and recycling of electrical and electronic equipment. European Commission Directive 96/59/EC sets requirements for disposing of equipment containing PCBs and PCTs. Waste oils are also regulated as hazardous wastes under the Waste Framework Directive. The REACH Directive seeks to manage chemicals through registration, evaluation, authorization, and restriction. REACH also calls for the substitution of the most dangerous chemicals with ones less dangerous as soon alternatives are identified.

Apprehension that developing nations would put their populations in danger in return for the economic gains that could flow from the importation of hazardous substances from the developed countries launched the international environmental justice movement. The development of many multinational treaties to address the need for informed consent by importing nations has improved injustice concerns, however, the movement continues to evolve as new issues of inequality arise. The realization that the world's poor nations will suffer the largest burdens from the effects of climate change have urged the movement toward climate justice. Climate models predict great devastation from climate change and the poor nations are among the least resilient. The climate justice movement argues for equity in the form of assistance from the rich countries to help poor nations adapt.

[1] "Rachel Carson, Silent Spring," Houghton Mifflin Company, accessed August 9, 2017, www.rachelcarson.org/SilentSpring.aspx.

[2] "Types of Pesticide Ingredients," EPA, accessed August 10, 2018, https://www.epa.gov/ingredients-used-pesticide-products/types-pesticide-ingredients.

[3] Michael E. Kraft, *Environmental Policy and Politics* (Boston: Pearson, 2015), 42.

[4] Donald Atwood and Claire Paisley-Jones, "Pesticides Industry Sales and Usage 2008–2012 Estimates," *Biological and Economic Analysis Division, Office of Pesticide Programs, office of Chemical Safety and Pollution Prevention, EPA* (2017): 9–10.

[5] Atwood and Paisley-Jones, "Pesticides Industry Sales and Usage 2008–2012 Estimates," 4–5.

[6] "Fertilizer Use & Price," USDA, accessed August 10, 2018, https://www.ers.usda.gov/data-products/fertilizer-use-and-price.aspx.

[7] Walter A. Rosenbaum, *Environmental Politics and Policy* (Thousand Oaks, CA: Sage/CQ Press, 2017), 241.

[8] Kraft, *Environmental Policy and Politics,* 45.

[9] Berrin Tansel, "From Electronic Consumer Products to E-Wastes: Global Outlook, Waste Quantities, Recycling Challenges," *Environment International* 98 (2017): 37.

[10] "International Cooperation: Cleaning Up Electronic Waste (E-Waste)," EPA, accessed August 22, 2017, https://www.epa.gov/international-cooperation/cleaning-electronic-waste-e-waste.

[11] Kraft, *Environmental Policy and Politics,* 149.

[12] "Summary of the Federal Insecticide, Fungicide, and Rodenticide Act," EPA, accessed August 26, 2017, https://www.epa.gov/laws-regulations/summary-federal-insecticide-fungicide-and-rodenticide-act.

13 "Summary of the Food Quality Protection Act," EPA, accessed August 26, 2017, https://www.epa.gov/laws-regulations/summary-food-quality-protection-act.

14 "Pesticide Registration Fees and Fee Waivers," EPA, accessed August 26, 2017, https://www.epa.gov/pesticide-registration/pesticide-registration-fees-and-fee-waivers.

15 "Regulatory Information by Topic: Waste," EPA, accessed August 22, 2017, https://www.epa.gov/regulatory-information-topic/regulatory-information-topic-waste.

16 "Defining Hazardous Waste: Listed, Characteristic and Mixed Radiological Wastes," EPA accessed August 22, 2017, https://www.epa.gov/hw/defining-hazardous-waste-listed-characteristic-and-mixed-radiological-wastes#listed.

17 "Criteria for the Definition of Solid Waste and Solid and Hazardous Waste Exclusions," EPA, accessed August 10, 2018, https://www.epa.gov/hw/criteria-definition-solid-waste-and-solid-and-hazardous-waste-exclusions.

18 Craig Collins, *Toxic Loopholes: Failures and Future Prospects for Environmental Law* (Cambridge: Cambridge University Press, 2010), 87.

19 "Learn the Basics of Hazardous Waste," EPA, accessed August 10, 2018, https://www.epa.gov/hw/learn-basics-hazardous-waste.

20 James Salzman and Barton H. Thompson, Jr., *Environmental Law and Policy* (St. Paul, MN: Foundation Press, 2014), 239–240.

21 Salzman and Thompson, Jr., *Environmental Law and Policy*, 241.

22 Kraft, *Environmental Policy and Politics*, 146–147.

23 Kraft, *Environmental Policy and Politics*, 147–148.

24 "Highlights of Key Provisions in the Frank R. Lautenberg Chemical Safety for the 21st Century Act," EPA, accessed August 10, 2018, https://www.epa.gov/assessing-and-managing-chemicals-under-tsca/highlights-key-provisions-frank-r-lautenberg-chemical.

25 Jennifer Thomson, "Toxic Residents: Health and Citizenship at Love Canal," *Journal of Social History* 50, no.1 (2016): 206–207.

26 "Superfund History," EPA, accessed August 27, 2017, https://www.epa.gov/superfund/superfund-history.

27 "Cleaning Up Sites," EPA, accessed August 27, 2017, https://www.epa.gov/superfund.

28 Kraft, *Environmental Policy and Politics*, 153.

29 Collins, *Toxic Loopholes*, 87.

30 "Superfund History," EPA, accessed August 27, 2017, https://www.epa.gov/superfund/superfund-history.

31 Barbara Dinham and Satinath Sarangi, "The Bhopal Gas Tragedy 1984 to ? The Evasion of Corporate Responsibility," *Environment & Urbanization* 14, no. 1 (2002): 89.

32 "Summary of the Emergency Planning & Community Right-to-Know Act," EPA, accessed August 27, 2017, https://www.epa.gov/laws-regulations/summary-emergency-planning-community-right-know-act.

33 "Toxic Release Inventory (TRI) Program," EPA, accessed August 28, 2017, https://www.epa.gov/toxics-release-inventory-tri-program/learn-about-toxics-release-inventory.

34 "Superfund History."

35 "Superfund History."

36 "Summary of the Pollution Prevention Act," EPA, accessed August 28, 2017, https://www.epa.gov/laws-regulations/summary-pollution-prevention-act.

[37] William M. Bowen and Michael V. Wells, "The Politics and Reality of Environmental Justice: A History and Considerations for Public Administrators and Policy Makers," *Public Administration Review* 62, no.6 (2002): 689.

[38] "Environmental Justice," EPA, accessed August 28, 2017, https://www.epa.gov/environmentaljustice.

[39] Rachel Massey and Molly Jacobs, "Trends and Indicators," in Global Chemicals Output: Towards Sound Management of Chemicals (Geneva: UNEP, 2013): 10.

[40] Atwood and Paisley-Jones, "Pesticides Industry Sales and Usage 2008–2012 Estimates," 9–10.

[41] Atwood and Paisley-Jones, "Pesticides Industry Sales and Usage 2008–2012 Estimates," 4–5.

[42] Tansel, "From Electronic Consumer Products to E-Wastes, 36–38.

[43] "Rio Declaration on Environment and Development," UN, accessed August 30, 2017, www.un.org/documents/ga/conf151/aconf15126-1annex1.htm.

[44] "The Basel Convention," UNEP, accessed August 30, 2017, www.basel.int/The Convention/Overview/tabid/1271/Default.aspx.

[45] "The Bamako Convention," UNEP, accessed August 10, 2018, https://wedocs.unep.org/bitstream/handle/20.500.11822/22491/NOTE%20ON%20THE%20BAMAKO%20 CONVENTION.pdf?sequence=1&isAllowed=y.

[46] "Rotterdam Convention," UNEP, accessed September 4, 2017, www.pic.int.

[47] "Batteries & Accumulators," European Commission, accessed August 30, 2017, http://ec.europa.eu/environment/waste/batteries/index.htm.

[48] "The RoHS Directive," European Commission, accessed August 10, 2018, http://ec.europa.eu/environment/waste/rohs_eee/index_en.htm.

[49] "Polychlorinated Biphenyls and Polychlorinated Terphenyls (PCBs/PCTs)," European Commission, accessed August 30, 2017, http://ec.europa.eu/environment/waste/pcbs/index.htm.

[50] "Waste Oils," European Commission, accessed August 10, 2018, http://ec.europa.eu/environment/waste/oil_index.htm.

[51] "REACH," European Commission, accessed August 30, 2017, http://ec.europa.eu/environment/chemicals/reach/reach_en.htm.

CHAPTER 8

Land, Natural Resources, and Wildlife

INTRODUCTION

The United States has an abundance of land, natural resources, and wildlife. How they are managed and protected is an important part of environmental policy. Most of the land in the country is under private ownership, however a considerable amount of land is held by the federal government. This chapter explores how the federal government came to own land and how over time the role of the federal government towards that land changed.

Many of the nation's natural resources are located on privately held lands but many are also located on publicly held land. Access to natural resources on federal land is subject to restrictions set in federal laws. Public lands hold various designations, and these determine to a considerable extent how the land will be protected or managed. How these resources are managed and the conflicts that have arisen over that management are discussed. A conflict at the very core of land management is whether or not the resources on the land should be commercially developed or utilized at all.

An argument is frequently made for the preservation of wilderness. Wilderness by definition remains undeveloped and is accessible only by wildlife and by humans on foot or horseback. Keeping these places roadless guarantees preservation of wilderness.

The quantity of land that should be maintained at this level of preservation is a subject of great debate. This chapter explores the historical evolution of the debate between sustainable use of natural resources and the preservation of wilderness.

Wildlife in the U.S. are treated as a public good and are protected by an array of state and federal laws. Hunting seasons and limits on the amount of wildlife a hunter or angler can take assure that herds and fisheries will not be depleted. Wildlife in threat of extinction are protected under federal laws. This chapter explores those laws and discusses how successful they have been in protecting plant and animal species from extinction.

How the major land management agencies fund their activities is a matter of interest and concern. While Congress provides line item appropriations, the land management agencies for many years have failed to have sufficient resources to pay for the maintenance of assets such as bridges, roads, and buildings. Deferring this maintenance into future years is problematic because it results in greater expense in the future than if timely repairs and maintenance were undertaken. A related funding issue involves how the land management agencies provide compensation to local governments and states that host public land tracts. The chapter discusses these issues.

Serious controversies have arisen over public land and protection of wildlife. The chapter explores several of these controversies. The first is the Sagebrush Rebellion, a movement on the part of several western states to wrestle federal land from Washington, D.C. and return control to the states. While the Sagebrush Rebellion lost support in the late 1980s and was never able to achieve its goals, a modern anti-Washington, D.C. movement continues and is typified by the Bundy family's efforts to oppose federal ownership of land. A bitter conflict also exists over wilderness protection and those who support commercial activities on federal lands. Species protection is also a major area of conflict both on public and private land. The cases of the snail darter and the northern spotted owl illustrate conflicts on public land. The issue of how the Endangered Species Act restricts private property rights is also be explored.

Global considerations for land and species protection include several international agreements. Among these are the Convention on International Trade in Endangered Species of Wild Fauna and Flora, the Migratory Bird Treaty Act, the Convention on Biological Diversity, and the Antarctic Treaty. These are discussed in detail in this chapter. Finally, while many nations have mirrored the U.S. in creating their own domestic national parks, transboundary protected areas and peace parks play a key role in conservation worldwide. The movement toward creation of such protected areas is discussed in the chapter. Controversy over the management of peace parks and transboundary protected areas exists and is also discussed.

DOMESTIC CONSIDERATIONS

The U.S. is the world's third largest country, ranking just behind Russia and Canada in terms of largest land mass. The U.S. consists of a land mass of 9.63 million square kilometers[1] or 2.27 billion acres.[2] About 640 million acres, or 28 percent of all U.S. land, is owned by the federal government. Most of the federal land today is located in the American West.

The federal government acquired what came to be called the National Domain in pieces as America grew from the original 13 colonies to a nation that spanned coast to coast. Wars with native American tribes and the subsequent displacement of most tribes to less desirable land was a large part of the process. Much of the land was also acquired by purchase, such as the Louisiana Purchase, or war with neighboring states, such as the Mexican-American War, or through various treaties with neighboring Canada that defined the Canadian-American border. The initial policy goal of the government was to dispose of these lands to private parties, sovereign tribes, or to the states. Privatization resulted from the Homestead Act of 1862, land allocations to native Americans, and land grants to the railroads in the

19th century. In the beginning of the 20th century, the U.S. changed its policy from disposal of federal lands to retention. The Progressive Movement held the view that government, using good scientific management practices, could better manage the land than what the Progressive reformers saw as chaotic and monopolistic private sector actors. Accordingly, they created new public agencies to manage or protect the land and to make the land productive by providing water for irrigation. Among these new agencies was the U.S. Bureau of Reclamation (USBR), created in 1902. In 1903, the first wildlife refuge was established. The Forest Service (FS) was created in 1905, and the National Park Service (NPS) in 1916. Although not created until 1946, the Bureau of Land Management (BLM), continued in this tradition.[3] In 1966, the National Wildlife Refuge System was created by aggregating all the wildlife refuges together under the administration of the Fish and Wildlife Service (FWS).[4]

The major federal land management agencies today include the Forest Service, located in the Department of Agriculture (USDA), and several additional agencies in the Department of Interior (DOI). These include the Bureau of Land Management, Fish and Wildlife Service, and the National Park Service. Together these agencies administer 614 million acres (95 percent) of federal land, mostly in the West and Alaska. These agencies also manage an additional 700 million onshore acres of subsurface mineral resources. The FS has charge of 173 million acres, BLM administers 247 million acres, FWS manages 89 million acres of which 77 million are in Alaska, and the NPS controls 85 million acres. The Department of Defense (DOD) manages an additional 19 million acres of bases and training areas. Federal lands also include 1.7 billion acres of offshore lands on the Outer Continental Shelf (OCS) administered by the Bureau of Ocean Energy Management (BOEM).[5]

Federal Legislation and Policies

There are numerous laws that govern the management and exploitation of public lands. Most establish fundamental ways in which public land may be used and to what commercial, recreational, or conservation purposes it is dedicated. Some also establish larger management systems, such as the Wild and Scenic River System or the National Wilderness Protection System. Other legislation and policies seek to protect wildlife.

Mining Law of 1872. The Mining Law of 1872 allowed for private individuals to mine and extract resources from public land. The act provided that if resources were found, the individual doing the mining could lay claim to those resources and mine without having to purchase the land or pay royalties. The act, however, does require that those wanting to mine in any manner greater than "casual use" be required to file a Mining Plan of Operation with the BLM. This plan must include anticipated environmental impacts. If the plan meets with BLM environmental standards, the plan will be approved, and the mining can take place.[6] This law is still in effect and guides mining operations on federal land.

The Bald and Golden Eagle Protection Act of 1940 (BGEPA). The symbol of the U.S., the Bald Eagle, was adopted by Congress in 1782. In an effort to protect the national symbol, Congress passed, and several times amended the BGEPA.[7] The act prohibits anyone without a permit from taking an eagle or an eagle's parts, nest, or eggs. The law provides criminal penalties for those who "pursue, shoot, shoot at, poison, wound, kill, capture, trap, collect, molest, or disturb" eagles. To disturb an eagle means to injure, interfere with its normal activities, or to cause an eagle to abandon its nest.[8]

Multiple Use Sustained Yield Act of 1960. Forests were traditionally thought to be managed to protect land, preserve water flows, and provide timber. The Multiple Use Sustained Yield Act expanded the uses of forest lands to include recreation, grazing, and wildlife and fish habitat. In 1964, the management objective of preserving wilderness was added. The FS was expected to manage the forests in a sustainable manner so that future generations would be able to depend upon these uses indefinitely. Two subsequent laws, the Forest Rangeland Renewable Resources Planning Act of 1974 and the National Forest

Management Act of 1976, again supported multiple use sustained yield and directed the FS to undertake long range planning efforts to assure those uses across the forest system. Achieving each of these outcomes can sometimes result in conflict within the agency as priorities are set and decisions are made.[9]

Wilderness Act of 1964. The Wilderness Act of 1964 and the Eastern Wilderness Act of 1974, which clarified some of the provisions of the original act, established the system of preserving wilderness areas in the United States. The Wilderness Act defined wilderness as land that retains its original primeval character, lacks human habitation or improvement, and has opportunities for solitude and primitive recreation.[10] The act addresses only lands managed by the FS, the FWS, and the NPS. In doing this Congress left out 66 percent of public lands managed by the BLM. It would take another 12 years, with the passage of the Federal Land Policy Management Act of 1976, before some of the BLM's land would be able to fall under wilderness designation.[11]

Wild and Scenic Rivers Act of 1968. This act established the National Wild and Scenic River System which was designed to preserve rivers and their banks in their natural free-flowing state.[12] Under the act, specific rivers or segments of rivers and their tributaries can be designated by Congress or the Secretary of Interior to become part of the system. These rivers are managed either by a federal or state agency. Federal agencies involved with the system include the FS, the FWS, the NPS, and the BLM. The activities of the agencies are coordinated by the Interagency Wild & Scenic Rivers Coordinating Council. Under the system, rivers are designated as wild, scenic, or recreational. Wild rivers are those that are undammed and generally inaccessible except by trail. These rivers are primitive, and their waters are unpolluted. Scenic rivers are similarly undammed, unpolluted, and have shorelines that remain mostly undeveloped but are accessible by road. Recreational rivers are readily accessible by rail or road, may have developed shorelines, and may have been diverted or dammed in the past. By 2014, the system protected over 12,000 miles of 208 rivers in 40 states. This system is small in comparison to the total number of rivers in the country, representing only one fourth of one percent of the nation's rivers. Numerous rivers in the U.S. are dammed. The country has more than 75,000 large dams affecting over 600,000 miles of rivers.[13]

National Environmental Policy Act of 1969 (NEPA). In addition to creating the Council on Environmental Quality (CEQ), NEPA provides the broad framework for protecting the environment by assuring that all federal government agencies give consideration to how their projects or actions might affect the environment prior to making decisions. Agencies are required to provide Environmental Assessments (EA) and Environmental Impact Statements (EIS) for all proposed projects that might affect the quality of the environment. NEPA requirements are raised when infrastructure projects are proposed, when land purchases are considered, or when public land designation is under review.[14] NEPA is a powerful tool for environmental protection for local communities because NEPA creates transparency when the federal government wants to fund or build a project that might impact that community.

Marine Mammal Protection Act of 1972 (MMPA). The Marine Mammal Protection Act passed as a bipartisan measure in Congress. During the period of time when it was passed, there was considerable public concern over the state of marine mammals, many of which were nearing extinction levels. Marine mammals of great concern included dolphins, whales, porpoises, manatees, and walruses. In passing the act, Congress sought to maintain appropriate numbers of animals to assure the species future survival and to put in place emergency measures to alleviate immediate, severe impacts that threatened species survival.[15] The MMPA has two essential goals: to identify the "optimum sustainable population" needed for marine mammals to survive and to maintain their role as a functioning part of the ecosystem. The optimum sustainable population was to be defined by the National Marine Fisheries Service (NMFS), otherwise known as the National Oceanic and Atmospheric Administration (NOAA) Fisheries. The other agency that plays a role in implementation is the FWS, which manages polar bears, sea otters, manatees, and walruses.[16]

Endangered Species Act of 1973 (ESA). The Endangered Species Act seeks to recover threatened and endangered species, that is, to bring the species back to the threshold at which protection will not be needed. Species with a high probability of future extinction may be listed as endangered or threatened under Section 4 of the act. Once listed, the FWS or NOAA Fisheries prepares a recovery plan to return the species to health. The largest threats to wildlife are loss of habitat and invasive species so recovery plans are devised to manage these risks. But the ESA has not been very effective in achieving its goals. Of the 1,260 species listed since 1973, only 13 have been recovered and another 22 species have moved from endangered to threatened.[17] Section 9 of the ESA prohibits a "take" of any listed species by any person. Section 7 prohibits federal agencies from taking actions that might harm a listed species or its critical habitat.

The ESA has been a controversial law, in large part because in the U.S. wildlife has always been considered publicly owned. Historically, lack of protections for various species, such as the buffalo, turkeys, and deer led to the formation of state game agencies to manage and recover these populations. Recovery efforts focused on hunting licenses, hunting seasons, and limitations on take. Private landowners can prohibit hunters from hunting on their land, however, land owners do not own the wildlife that roam on their lands.[18] When the FWS and NOAA Fisheries joined in the task of species protection under the ESA, protection of species on private land grew controversial as many recovery plans restricted the actions of private landowners. As the ESA began to be applied to the broader notion of protection of biodiversity rather than the more narrow construct of individual species protection, opposition to the ESA grew.[19] The ESA remains controversial both in terms of the restrictions it may place on private land use and the potential cost to jobs.

Federal Land Policy Management Act of 1976 (FLPMA). The Federal Land Policy Management Act of 1976 set the foundation for how public land should be managed in the United States. It formally ended the practice of the disposal of federal lands. Congress instead asserted in the law that federal lands should remain under federal ownership, unless land use planning procedures established by Title II of the act determine that disposal of a specific parcel was in the national interest. It established that the BLM must manage the land to achieve sustained yield of the multiple uses including livestock grazing, timber harvesting, mineral deposit extraction, recreation, watershed protection, wildlife and fish habitat protection, and conservation. Further, the act requires the BLM to periodically inventory its holdings as part of its land use management process.[20] The FLPMA extended wilderness protections to lands managed by the BLM and required the agency to inventory its lands and make recommendations for wilderness designation.[21]

National Forest Management Act of 1976 (NFMA). The NFMA amended the earlier Forest and Rangeland Renewable Planning Act of 1974 (RPA) by establishing standards for how the FS manages national forests and grasslands and requiring them to periodically update those standards. It requires the FS to compile studies on the status of renewable resources on the public and private lands and to develop a Land Management Plan, also known as a Forest Plan, for the land it manages. The Land Management Plan is to be based on current and anticipated future uses and demand for renewable resources from both public and private lands. NFMA also provides for public participation in the development of plans.[22]

Surface Mining Control and Reclamation Act of 1977 (SMCRA). This act established the Office of Surface Mining Reclamation and Enforcement (OSMRE) within the DOI and gave that office authority to regulate surface coal mining operations and to reclaim abandoned mines. The act requires the OSMRE to work in partnership with the states to accomplish these goals.[23]

Outer Continental Shelf Lands Act of 1978 (OCSLA). OCSLA placed the 1.7 billion acres of land off the shores of the U.S. under the control of the Bureau of Mineral Management Services (MMS). MMS was replaced by BOEM in 2010 after the *Deepwater Horizon* oil spill. The law requires BOEM to manage offshore oil and gas leases and to hold periodic sales of those leases.[24]

Alaska National Interest Lands Conservation Act of 1980 (ANILCA). This act resolved the status of various lands that were under federal control by providing them with final land designations. It designated nearly 80 million acres of refuge land in Alaska to different system designations, including National Parks, National Wildlife Refuge, Wild and Scenic Rivers, National Wilderness Preservation System, and National Forests. This act added more than 27 million acres to the wilderness system.[25]

The Lacey Act. Originally passed in 1900, Congress amended the Lacey Act in 2008 to strengthen its provisions against illegal logging. The amendment banned the importation or sale in the U.S. of any timber cut in violation of a law of any foreign country or the U.S. Violations of the law result in fines or criminal prosecution.[26]

Omnibus Public Lands Management Act of 2009. This act added two million acres of land to the National Wilderness Preservation System in 9 states, added thousands of miles to the National Wild and Scenic Rivers System, added trails to the National Trails System, and made three additions to the National Park System.[27]

Public Land Designations

Public lands have many different designations. Some of these designations limit certain activities that can take place on the lands, while other designations order the land agency with management authority to manage the land for multiple purposes.

National System of Public Lands. The National System of Public Lands is the formal designation for BLM lands which include grasslands, forests, mountains, arctic tundra, and deserts. The BLM has the authority to acquire, dispose of, and exchange lands.[28] About 156 million acres of BLM land are available for grazing. Twenty seven million acres are in BLM's *National Landscape Conservation System.* The BLM also manages about 700 million acres of subsurface land with the dedicated use for mineral extraction.[29] The BLM must comply with the limits set in the Federal Land Policy Management Act and the National Environmental Policy Act before exchanging land with private parties. The exchange may take place only if the BLM certifies that it is in the public interest to make such an exchange.[30]

National Wilderness Preservation System. Established by the Wilderness Act, the National Wilderness Preservation System contains 662 wilderness areas, encompassing 106 million acres. Of these, 48 million acres are located in the continental U.S., while 58 million are in Alaska.[31] Wilderness lands are to be managed to preserve them in their original condition in perpetuity. After the original designation of 9 million acres of wilderness in 1964, wilderness designation slowed due to the complicated study process required. However, after the courts ruled in 1971 that the Wilderness Act required the FS to study roadless areas adjacent to land that might be designated as wilderness, NEPA played a critical role in enlarging wilderness designations. This was because after the FS conducted two Roadless Area Review and Evaluations (RARE I and II) and recommended which land should be designated as wilderness, the courts ruled that the FS could not allow development on lands not recommended for wilderness status based on NEPA grounds. This injunction protected these lands from development. During the 1980s and 1990s, the amount of wilderness designations more than doubled and the courts continued to interpret NEPA in a way that protected from development lands that had wilderness potential but had not yet achieved wilderness designation.[32]

When FLPMA passed in 1976, BLM lands came under consideration for wilderness status. This law required the BLM to conduct inventories of land and recommend wilderness designations. The law also required the BLM to maintain the undeveloped characteristics of land it considered for wilderness status but did not recommend, so that Congress could later reconsider those areas for designation. Thus, these Wilderness Study Areas (WSAs) were placed under protections from road building, resource extraction, and development. Congress designated the first BLM wilderness lands in

1978. Since then, Congress has rarely made additional wilderness designations on the BLM's 253 million acres. Only 8.7 million acres of BLM land, or 3 percent, has wilderness designation. The BLM also manages 24 million acres in WSA status, but millions of more acres have wilderness potential. Conflicts over which lands should receive wilderness designation, how the BLM should protect those lands under review for wilderness designation, and which lands should be designated for multiple use sustained yield have persisted since the passage of FLPMA.[33]

National Wildlife Refuge System. In 1903, the first land was designated as a wildlife refuge. After that date, many more areas received that designation. In 1966, all of these areas were gathered together into the National Wildlife Refuge System, overseen by the FWS. The system today contains about 89 million acres, of which nearly 90 percent are in Alaska. These lands are to be managed with a focus on conservation of flora and fauna. Other uses such as recreation, timber cutting, and grazing are allowed if the FWS determines they are compatible with the needs of species.[34]

National Park System. The National Park System consists of nearly 400 areas designated by Congress or the president. Entities within the system are given a wide variety of names including national park, national preserve, national seashore, national recreation area, national battlefield, national historic site, national monument, national memorials, national reserves, national lakeshore, national trails, national parkways, and national rivers and wild and scenic rivers. Congress established the National Wild and Scenic River System to keep free-flowing rivers in their natural undammed state and to protect the lands that surround them.[35] The National Park System is comprised of 85 million acres of land, of which nearly two thirds are in Alaska. The NPS manages these lands with a dual mission which includes preservation of the parks and to provide public enjoyment. The National Park System lands typically receive a higher level of protection than do the lands managed by the BLM or the FS.[36]

Funding for Federal Land

The federal land management agencies receive funding in the form of appropriations and those funds are used to manage their land holdings and other assets. However, all of the federal land agencies have long lists of differed maintenance on their many assets including roads, buildings, water systems, and bridges. The combined maintenance backlog of the FWS, the NPS, the BLM, and the FS in 2016 was estimated at $18.62 billion. The NPS accounts nearly 60 percent, or over $10 billion, of the maintenance backlog. This backlog is a problem because maintenance deferred is costlier than maintenance done in a timely manner.[37]

Funding decisions for public land also involves consideration of state and local government units housing the land. Local governments near federal lands receive compensation from the federal government under a variety of programs. The most common of these programs is the "Payment in Lieu of Taxes" (PILT) program. Under PILT, counties with NPS lands receive payments. The FS and the BLM have programs that provide payments to states and localities based on the commercial activities they undertake including timber harvesting, oil and gas development, and mineral extraction. The FWS has a compensation program associated with some of its refuge land.[38]

The Land and Water Conservation Fund (LWCF) was established in in1965. This funding has allowed the federal land management agencies to purchase additional lands to serve the public as recreational areas and to provide grants to states wishing to enlarge their public recreational areas. Nearly all of the funds in LWCF come from oil and gas leases in the OCS.[39]

Disputes over Federal Land and Species Protection

The Sagebrush Rebellion. One of the earliest movements against federal control of land management in the West was the Sagebrush

Rebellion, which emerged as a response to the reversal of land disposition policy that was made law in Federal Land Policy and Management Act of 1976. Some Westerners saw this law as a violation of a long-held trust that western lands would eventually be turned over to the states for disposal. Many Westerners had long followed a pattern of grazing their animals on their private land during the winter but letting them graze on public land in the summer months. Many ranchers passed their grazing permits down to their heirs as they did their private property. A court case won by the National Resources Defense Council (NRDC) in the 1970s forced the BLM to more strictly control damage to public lands by eliminating overgrazing. Subsequent actions taken by the BLM drew the anger of Westerners. In 1979, Nevada passed a law calling for the state to take over all unappropriated land in the state. A conference attended by other western state leaders encouraged the same action across the West.[40] While the initial Sagebrush Rebellion fizzled out, tension over public land continues.

The Bundy Family. This tension can be seen in the standoff between the Bundy family and the BLM. In 2014, the BLM took action to round up Cliven Bundy's cattle which had been grazing on public land illegally for decades. Cliven Bundy owed the government more than $1 million in grazing fees. The conflict did not go well. Bundy's ranch in Bunkerville, Nevada was occupied by protesters who supported Bundy. When BLM rangers used force against one of Bundy's sons and the video spread over the Internet, many more armed protesters flocked to the ranch. Local police negotiated a truce to end the violent standoff and the BLM said it would handle the matter administratively.[41] Some of the supporters were eventually charged and convicted of threatening and assaulting a federal officer, but several defendants were acquitted. Two years later, in January 2016, Ammon Bundy and followers took armed control over the Malheur National Wildlife Refuge in Oregon. When tried for gun charges and conspiracy related to the takeover of the refuge, a sympathetic jury found them not guilty.[42] These conflicts demonstrate that many Westerners continue to hold the view that federal government ownership of land is an overreach of power that should be reversed.

Wilderness. The debate over wilderness preservation has existed in the U.S. since the early debates between conservation and preservation emerged. Preservation seeks protection of nature from use, while conservation seeks the proper use of nature.[43] Preservation is most closely associated with John Muir, a naturalist and friend of President Theodore Roosevelt. Muir, founder of the Sierra Club, led the crusade that resulted in the creation of Yosemite National Park in 1890.[44] Conservation, in contrast, was championed by Gifford Pinchot, the chief forester in the FS. Pinchot, in his 1910 book *The Fight for Conservation* argued for practical use of the forests to allow for sustained distribution of timber and other natural resources for urban development. Pinchot called for scientific management of forest resources to assure a continued flow of resources for future generations.[45] While most land policy in the United States generally flows from the concepts elaborated by Pinchot, in 1964 the U.S. became the first country in the world to designate land for protection as wilderness. In the half century since the original declaration, the U.S. has more than 109 million acres, mostly in the West, protected as wilderness. In recent years, wild lands designation has emerged as a partisan political issue, with bitter divides between the Republicans and Democrats regarding the restrictions on these lands. Many states in the West strongly wish these lands to be exploited for commercial activities.[46]

In the 1990s, the Democratic Clinton administration put in place policies to protect wilderness areas from exploitation. These efforts resulted in litigation from several states. Before the courts could act, the successor Republican Bush administration tried to reverse Clinton's policy agenda. Bush's actions resulted in a backlash from environmental groups who filed law suits. The Obama administration issued a "wild lands policy" in 2010 which promised a return to Clinton's policies, but this was immediately challenged by the

Republican majority in the House that denied funding for such efforts.[47]

An ongoing debate over wilderness has included the designation of the Arctic National Wildlife Refuge (ANWR) as protected. ANWR was established by the Alaska National Interest Lands Conservation Act of 1980. Congress deferred the decision on the management of the 1.5 million acres in the northernmost coastal plain of ANWR, area 1002, because it was thought to have large supplies of oil and gas while at the same time it was also known to be highly sensitive to animal populations. U.S. Geological Survey (USGS) scientists studied the area to estimate its oil and gas reserves and issued a report to Congress in 1987 and again in 1998. The 1998 study estimated that the 1002 region of ANWR holds between 4.3 and 11.8 billion barrels of oil.[48] The debate over whether to develop area 1002 by opening it for drilling has been long and bitter, with Republicans generally favoring opening the area for drilling but Democrats arguing to keep the area off limits. In 2015, the Obama administration released a new fifteen-year management plan that called for managing area 1002 as wilderness.[49] The opening of area 1002 in the Arctic National Wildlife Refuge for potential drilling in 2017 added another policy shift to a forty-year debate over protecting the region. The Trump administration had a provision written into the Tax Cuts and Jobs Act of 2017 that required the government to hold at least two oil and gas lease sales before 2027. Opponents, however, are likely to resist this policy change.[50]

One of the early actions of the Trump administration was to issue an executive order to review presidential designations under the Antiquities Act. The executive order instructed Interior Secretary Ryan Zinke to review any national monuments created after January 1996, some of which are wilderness lands. The Trump administration also indicated it was eager to change the boundaries of several protected areas by reducing their size. These efforts would reverse land protections made during the Clinton, Bush, and Obama administrations and are widely rejected by the Democrats but generally supported by Republicans.[51]

Endangered Species Protections. Many high-profile conflicts over the ESA have applied to public land. These include the conflict over the snail darter in Tennessee and the northern spotted owl in the Pacific Northwest. In the snail darter case, the Tennessee Valley Authority's (TVA) Tellico Dam was under construction and nearly complete when the snail darter was found in the Little Tennessee River. A lawsuit was filed that argued that completion of the dam would alter the habitat thus killing the snail darter. The case was eventually heard by the Supreme Court, which upheld the ESA's absolute prohibition against federal agencies jeopardizing protected species. However, eventually the ESA was amended to allow exceptions. Jimmy Carter signed the bill allowing the Tellico Dam to be completed in 1979. Before the dam was finished, the many snail darters were moved to another river, where they began recovery.[52] In the case of the northern spotted owl, after the 1960s the habitat for the owl began to shrink as loggers cut timber from the ancient forests on public lands in the Pacific Northwest. The owl was placed on the endangered species list in 1990, and this resulted in closing public forest lands to logging. Loggers consequently suffered from unemployment and could not find jobs with comparable pay and benefits elsewhere. Under a court order, the FWS designated nearly 7 million acres of Pacific Northwest forests as critical habitat for the owl's survival. This order also served to preserve the ancient forest ecosystem. Lawsuits were also filed again the BLM.[53] The controversy was bitter between loggers, saw mills, and environmentalists. The timber industry argued that overprotection of the owl had cost many jobs. Environmentalists, however, saw protection of the owl as a larger issue of protecting old-growth forests. The Northwest Forest Plan of 1994 was developed to protect the owl while also allowing reduced timber sales. The FWS issued a recovery plan in 2008 and revised it in 2011. The recovery plan continued the compromise between continued reduced timber harvest and protection of trees in areas the spotted owl preferred. As of 2017, the spotted owl remained on the endangered species list.[54]

While both the spotted owl and the snail darter controversies resulted from protection of species on public lands, the ESA applies to both public and private land and the majority of endangered species are on private lands. Further, the U.S. Supreme Court in *Babbitt v. Sweet Home* upheld the FWS' interpretation of "takes" to include habitat alteration that kills or injures wildlife, thus creating the application of the ESA as a land use regulation. For some private land holders whose land may be habitable to an endangered species, but which does not currently hold such a species, the incentive exists for the owner to modify the land in such a manner as to make it unattractive to endangered species and thus avoid potentially costly land use restrictions. Such actions, though, work to defeat the spirit of the ESA by reducing suitable habitat. One example of this behavior can be seen in the actions of landowners in North Carolina, who destroyed potential habitat of the red-cockaded woodpecker by preventing the establishment of old-growth pine forest by premature harvest of timber.[55] Studies have shown that many landowners consider the requirement that private landowners must protect endangered or threatened species on their land without compensation from the government vastly unfair. Many landowners manage their land to minimize the chance that an endangered species will seek to occupy it.[56]

GLOBAL CONSIDERATIONS

Global land and species protection include several international agreements. Among these are the Migratory Bird Treaty Act, the Convention on International Trade in Endangered Species of Wild Fauna and Flora, the Convention on Biological Diversity, and the Antarctic Treaty. These are discussed below.

Many countries have created their own domestic national parks, which play a significant role in both protecting land and species. The creation and management of transboundary parks also play a significant role in global conservation. National parks worldwide and the role of transboundary parks in international conservation are discussed below.

International Treaties

The Migratory Bird Treaty Act (MBTA). The MBTA was a response to the extinction of the previously vast number of passenger pigeons that had been wiped out for their feathers.[57] The MBTA was passed by Congress in 1918 to address the threat posed to all north American birds that migrated between the U.S. and Canada. Subsequent parties to the treaty included Mexico, Japan, and the former Soviet Union (now the Russian Federation). The MBTA makes it illegal to hunt, kill, or capture any listed migratory species without a permit (currently issued by the FWS). Prosecutions under MBTA in this early period were primarily for illegal hunting. When the environmental movement gained public support during the 1970s, prosecutions expanded to unintentional bird deaths due to agriculture, industrial activities, and habitat destruction.[58]

While the FWS lists guidance to help reduce incidental take,[59] many birds listed for protection under MBTA lose large numbers of individuals through unintentional take. For instance, each year wind turbines kill 33 thousand birds, communication towers kill nearly 5 million, cats kill 39 million, pesticides kill 72 million, electrical transmission lines kill over 170 million, and window and building collisions kill 900 million birds.[60] The current court interpretation of who should be prosecuted under these unintentional takes of birds is ambiguous, leaving advocates to urge for the renegotiation of the treaty to modernize it.

The Convention on International Trade in Endangered Species of Wild Fauna and Flora (CITES). CITES is an international treaty that prohibits the trade of endangered animals and plants or their parts. It is administered by the United Nations Environment Programme (UNEP) under a secretariat in Geneva, Switzerland. Parties to the convention are required to establish both a management authority and a scientific authority. The management authority issues permits that allow for the trading of plants or animals or their parts legally under the terms of the treaty. The scientific authority decides if trade of a particular plant or animal might endanger that species. Over 35,000 species are protected by CITES. Species threatened with extinction, Appendix I listed species, are given the highest level of protection, which typically includes restrictions on international trade for commercial purposes. The second level of protection is awarded to those species that are not currently threatened with extinction but may become so. They are listed in Appendix II. Trade in these species is allowed with a permit. A third list, Appendix III, is of species for which the home country provides domestic protection and askes other parties to assist with protection by controlling international trade. Every two or three years the member countries come together in a Conference of Parties (COP) to make changes to the protections of the listed species.[61] CITES works by imposing sanctions on countries that violate the trade agreement. Listing decisions are often controversial because they require member states to enact trade restrictions. These may save endangered species, but they also impose restrictions on activities that may harm poor countries.[62]

Three species—elephants, rhinoceroses, and tigers—are of particular interest for CITES as proposals for legalizing some trade for them continue to be forthcoming. All are under severe threat from poaching although they also suffer from habitat loss. Most of the subpopulations of these species are given the highest level of protection and thus a ban from commercial trade exists. For elephants and tigers, the commercial demand is for parts of the animal that can only be obtained through killing the animal. For elephants, the demand is for their ivory tusks. For tigers, the demand is for their skin and bones. For rhinos, the demand is for their horns, which might be removed without killing the animal if done by someone with the expertise, however, poachers kill rhinos to get the horns. Despite being listed in Appendix I, some legal trade has been allowed for elephants, tigers, and rhinos. For elephants, there have been several sales of state-controlled stockpiled ivory. White rhinos were moved to Appendix II and thus offered a lower level of protection. Siberian Tigers, which are listed in Appendix I, still had some allowable Chinese domestic trade of captivity-bred tigers that died in captivity.[63] At the 17th COP in 2016, further protections were put in place for elephants and a near total ban on commercial ivory sales was put into effect.[64] Some domestic sales of rhino and tiger parts continue, and poaching remains a major threat to elephants, tigers, and rhinos.

The Convention on Biological Diversity (CBD). The CBD was submitted for signature at the Rio Earth Summit in 1992 and it entered into force the following year. The CBD seeks to ensure that biodiversity is preserved by adopting social and economic development procedures that are both sustainable and equitable. Each country is required to provide financial resources within their ability to do so to preserve biological diversity. Recognizing the costs may be a burden for developing countries, developed countries are required to provide additional financial resources to assist developing countries to preserve biodiversity within their borders.[65]

Despite its lofty goals, the CBD has been largely unsuccessful in reversing the biodiversity losses that the world has seen since the 20th century. The pressures of climate change increase the threats to biodiversity with extinctions occurring many times faster than the expected rate. The CBD seeks to address this loss by incentivizing the protection of species and equitable sharing of the benefits that come from genetic resources. Critics suggest that the CBD needs major change if it is to be successful. In particular, critics argue that the failure of the U.S. to become a party to the treaty in large part to protect domestic intellectual property rights of the biotechnology industry has weakened the CBD.[66] The crisis of continuing biodiversity loss remains a critical failure for international environmental policy.

The Antarctic Treaty. Passed in 1961, the Antarctic Treaty sought to protect the environment of Antarctica, facilitate cooperative scientific research, and to prohibit any nation from staking a territorial claim. The treaty was amended in 1991 with the signing of the Protocol on Environmental Protection to the Antarctic Treaty. The 26 states that joined the agreement strengthened environmental protections for the continent. The U.S. ratified the treaty and in addition passed the Antarctic Science, Tourism, and Conservation Act of 1997 which brought the U.S. into compliance with the strengthened environmental protections of the Protocol.[67]

National Parks Worldwide and Transboundary Protected Areas

The idea of national parks originated in the United States with the founding of Yellowstone in 1872. By the time Theodore Roosevelt left the White House, the U.S. had established 8 national parks, 9 national monuments, and a number of national forests. By the 19th century, visitors were coming from around the world to view these parks. When they returned home, many decided to create their own national parks. For instance, a former New Zealand premier traveled to California's Hot Springs in 1873 and on return home he started a movement to preserve New Zealand's hot springs. In 1887, Canada started its national park system with the creation of Banff National Park. Australia was soon to follow. In the 1920s, a British Lord visited 3 American parks and 2 Canadian parks. Upon return to the U.K. he pushed for the creation of the British national park system. The idea kept spreading and being adopted in country after country. Today there are more than 200,000 parks and protected areas in virtually every nation in the world.[68]

While many of these are solely national parks, some are international. International parks fall under the names of peace parks, transboundary protected areas (TBPAs), or transfrontier conservation areas (TFCAs). Some were established for the purpose of conservation in regions where the ecosystem needing protection spanned national boundaries. Many are the result of abutting national protected areas.[69] For instance, in 1910, the U.S. established Glacier National Park in Montana, directly across the border from Canada's Waterton Lakes Park. This became a "peace park" spanning both sides of the border in 1926 as a gesture to the friendly relationships and on-going peace between the two nations.[70]

But other peace parks have been established specifically for the purpose of settling on-going interstate disputes such as the Cordillera del Condor which serves as part of the border between Peru and Ecuador. The creation of the park settled a 160-year dispute between the nations that resulted in 3 separate border wars. Between 1946 and 1969, 121 TBPA were established. In the 1970s, 240 new parks were established. This growth continued in the 1980s and 1990s and was promoted by the International Union for Conservation of Nature (IUCN), the Peace Parks Foundation, U.S. Agency for International Development (USAID), and the World Bank. Research suggests that these parks have been successful in promoting peace in Asia, Africa, and the Middle East.[71]

Peace parks also have been criticized for creating situations that promote poaching and that end in escalating violence. For instance, the Greater Limpopo Transfrontier Park (GLTP) between South Africa, Mozambique, and Zimbabwe has become the center of the rhino poaching crisis that began in 2013 when more than 1,000 rhinos were killed. Kruger National Park in South Africa is one of the main components of the GLTP and it holds the world's largest population of rhinos. Many Mozambicans, displaced by the creation of the GLTP, are thought to be the main group both comprising poachers and the key target for recruitment by poachers. High levels of poaching have resulted in militarized anti-poaching efforts on the part of Kruger Park rangers. In 2014 alone, more than 77 poachers were killed in Mozambique and the violence continues to spread threatening the peace of the peace park.[72]

Border disputes can also be based in surrounding waters. For instance, in 1994 Israel and Jordan agreed to the establishment of the Bilateral Red Sea Marine Peace Park to protect the coral reef in the Gulf of Aqaba as part of the Middle East peace talks.[73] In other areas around the world, marine-based disputes can be settled by establishment of marine peace parks. For instance, disputes over the Piran Bay in the Northern Adriatic Sea has led to conflicts between Slovenia and Croatia. A proposed solution to the dispute was the establishment of the Piran-Savudrija International Marine Peace Park.[74] International Marine Peace Parks have also been explored as an option for promoting peace in the South China Sea.[75]

CONCLUSION

The U.S., the world's third largest country, holds about 640 million acres as public land located primarily in the West. This public land was acquired in pieces over time. Some was acquired by purchase, some by war, and some by treaty. The policy goal of the federal government from the beginning of the country until the early 1900s, was to dispose of these lands. The U.S. changed its policy from disposal of federal lands to retention in the beginning of the 20th century when political changes were put in place by leaders of the Progressive Movement. They created new public land management agencies including the USBR, the FS, and the NPS. In the 1940s, the BLM was added and in the 1960s the FWS was also added.

There are many laws that govern the management and use of federal land. Most of these laws determine what commercial, recreational, or conservation purposes are allowed. Some legislation established larger land management systems, such as the Wild and Scenic River System or the National Wilderness Protection System. Other legislation and policies sought to protect wildlife. Among the most important of these laws are the Multiple Use Sustained Yield Act of 1960, the Wilderness Act of 1964, the Wild and Scenic Rivers Act of 1968, the National Environmental Policy Act of 1969, the Endangered Species Act of 1973, and the Federal Land Policy Management Act of 1976. This law formally ended the practice of the disposal of federal lands and declared retention of federal land in perpetuity.

Public lands have many different designations which restrict activities that can take place on them. Among these are the BLM's National System of Public Lands, the National Wilderness Preservation

System, the National Wildlife Refuge System, the National Park System, and the National Wild and Scenic River System.

The federal land management agencies receive funding in the form of annual appropriations to manage their land and assets, however, together the federal land agencies have over $18 billion of differed maintenance. Local and state governments proximate to public lands receive compensation from the federal government under several programs including the Payment in Lieu of Taxes program as well as programs that provide payments to states and localities based on timber harvesting, oil and gas development, and mineral extraction. The Land and Water Conservation Fund allows the federal land management agencies to purchase additional recreational lands and to provide grants to states to expand their public recreational areas.

There have been several high-profile controversies over federal ownership and control of public lands. One of the earliest, the Sagebrush Rebellion, was a response to the reversal of land disposition policy that was made formal in FLPMA. Led by Nevada, several western states demanded the federal government return all federal land to the states. While this movement failed, tensions over public land persist, and the more recent saga of the Bundy family shows. The debate over how much land should be protected as wilderness is an on-going dispute. While most public land is managed under the concepts set out in multiple use sustained yield policy, the U.S. has more than 100 million acres protected as wilderness. Many states in the West hold a strong preference for these wilderness lands to be exploited for commercial activities. This debate over wilderness protection can be seen most clearly in the partisan and bitter fight over ANWR. Many high-profile conflicts have also arisen over ESA protections on public land. Two of the most prominent of these were the snail darter and the northern spotted owl. Controversies have also resulted from application of the ESA to private land since the courts have interpreted take to include changing habitat, thereby allowing the law to control private land use. Attempts on the part of private land owners to circumvent the law have resulted in considerable dysfunction in the protection of species.

Global land and species protection policies consist of a number of international agreements including the MBTA, CITES, CBD, and the Antarctic Treaty. MBTA covers only birds that migrate between the U.S. and Canada, Mexico, Japan, and Russia. CITES and the CBD are broader treaties seeking to protect threatened or endangered species as well as biological diversity as a whole. The Antarctic Treaty protects the environment of Antarctica and seeks to facilitate cooperative scientific research.

While national parks originated in the United States, most nations in the world now have domestic national parks and protected areas. In addition to national parks, there are hundreds of peace parks and transboundary protected areas. Some were established for the purpose of conservation, but others were established specifically for the purpose of ending disputes between nations. These peace parks have been able to maintain harmony in many regions, although they are not without critics. Some suggest that peace parks may actually provide the opportunity for poachers to operate and that they have resulted in the militarization of environmentalists in an effort to ward off poaching.

---

[1] "The Largest Countries in the World," World Atlas, accessed September 25, 2017, http://www.worldatlas.com/articles/the-largest-countries-in-the-world-the-biggest-nations-as-determined-by-total-land-area.html.

[2] "Federal Land Ownership by State," Ballotpedia, accessed September 25, 2017, https://ballotpedia.org/Federal_land_ownership_by_state.

[3] Robert H. Nelson, "Our Languishing Public Lands," *Policy Review* (February & March 2012): 45–46.

[4] Katie Hoover, "Federal Lands and Natural Resources: Overview and Selected Issues for the 113th Congress," *Congressional Research Service Report 7-5700, R43429* (2014): 5.

[5] Hoover, "Federal Lands and Natural Resources," 3–6.

[6] Waldron, "*Center for Biological Diversity v. Department of Interior*: Proper Deference," 722.

[7] Roberto Iraola, "The Bald and Golden Eagle Protection Act," *Albany Law Review* 68 (2005): 973.

[8] "Bald and Golden Eagle Protection Act," FWS, accessed August 10, 2018, https://www.fws.gov/midwest/MidwestBird/EaglePermits/bagepa.html.

[9] Hoover, "Federal Lands and Natural Resources," 4.

[10]   Rosenberger, Sperow, and English, "Economies in Transition and Public Land-Use Policy," 267.

[11]   Olivia Brumfield, "The Birth, Death, and Afterlife of the Wild Lands Policy: The Evolution of the Bureau of Land Management's Authority to Protect Wilderness Values," *Environmental Law* 44 (2014): 250.

[12]   Comay, "National Park System," 3.

[13]   "About the WSR Act," Wild & Scenic Rivers Council, accessed October 4, 2017, https://www.rivers.gov/wsr-act.php.

[14]   "Summary of the national Environmental Policy Act," EPA, accessed October 2, 2017, https://www.epa.gov/laws-regulations/summary-national-environmental-policy-act.

[15]   Stephanie Dodson Dougherty, "The Marine Mammal Protection Act: Fostering Unjust Captivity Practices Since 1972," *Journal of Land Use* 28, no.2 (2013): 337.

[16]   Joe Roman et. al, "The Marine Mammal Protection Act at 40: Status, Recovery, and Future of U.S. Marine Mammals," *Annals of the New York Academy of Sciences* 1286 (2013): 29.

[17]   J. Michael Scott et al., "Recovery of Imperiled Species Under the Endangered Species Act: The Need for a New Approach," *Frontiers in Ecology and Environment* 3, no. 7 (2005): 383–384.

[18]   Samuel P. Hays, *A History of Environmental Politics Since 1945* (Pittsburgh: University of Pittsburgh Press, 2000), 80–83.

[19]   Timothy H. Tear, et al., "Status and Prospects for Success of the Endangered Species Act: A Look at Recovery Plans," *Science* (November 12, 1993): 976.

[20]   "The Federal Land Policy and Management Act of 1976, As Amended," BLM, accessed October 31, 2016, https://www.blm.gov/or/regulations/files/FLPMA.pdf.

[21]   Michael C. Blumm and Andrew B. Erickson, "Federal Wild Lands Policy in the Twenty-First Century: What a Long, Strange Trip It's Been," *Colorado Natural Resources, Energy, & Environmental Law Review* 25(2014): 31.

[22]   "National Forest Management Act of 1976." FS, accessed October 18, 2017, https://www.fs.fed.us/emc/nfma/includes/NFMA1976.pdf.

[23]   "Surface Mining Control and Reclamation Act," OSMRE, accessed October 18, 2017, https://www.osmre.gov/lrg.shtm.

[24]   Hoover, "Federal Lands and Natural Resources," 6–7.

[25]   "Digest of Federal Resource Laws of Interest to the U.S. Fish and Wildlife Service," FWS, accessed August 10, 2018, https://www.fws.gov/laws/lawsdigest/nwracts.html.

[26]   Yijin J. Lee, "The Lacey Act Amendments of 2008: The World's First Ban on Illegal Logging Combats Deforestation but Gets Stumped by Foreign Laws," *San Diego Journal of Climate & Energy Law* 5 (2013–14): 188.

[27]   "Public Law 111-11-Mar. 30, 2009," GPO, accessed October 18, 2017, https://www.gpo.gov/fdsys/pkg/PLAW-111publ11/pdf/PLAW-111pobl11.pdf.

[28]   Hoover, "Federal Lands and Natural Resources," 5.

[29]   Hoover, "Federal Lands and Natural Resources," 5.

[30]   Maya Waldron, "Center for Biological Diversity v. Department of Interior: Proper Deference," *Ecology Law Quarterly* 37 (2010): 722.

[31]   Randall S. Rosenberger, Mark Sperow, and Donald B.K. English, "Economies in Transition and Public Land-Use Policy: Discrete Duration Models of Easter Wilderness Designation," *Land Economics* 84, no.2 (2008): 267.

32 Michael C. Blumm and Lorena M. Wisehart, "The Underappreciated Role of the National Environmental Policy Act in Wilderness Designation and Management," *Environmental Law* 44 (2014): 324–325.

33 Blumm and Erickson, "Federal Wild Lands Policy in the Twenty-First Century," 31–37.

34 Hoover, "Federal Lands and Natural Resources," 5.

35 Laura B. Comay, "National Park System: What Do the Different Park Titles Signify?" Congressional Research Service Report 7-5700, R41816 (2013): 1–4.

36 Hoover, "Federal Lands and Natural Resources," 6.

37 Carol Hardy Vincent, "Deferred Maintenance of Federal Land Management Agencies: FY2007-FY2016 Estimates and Issues," Congressional Research Service Report 7-5700, R43997 (2017): 1.

38 Hoover, "Federal Lands and Natural Resources," 9.

39 "Land and Water Conservation Fund," NPS, accessed August 10, 2018, https://www.nps.gov/subjects/lwcf/index.htm.

40 Trudle Olson, "The Sagebrush Rebellion," *Rangelands* 2, no.5 (1980): 195–196.

41 Marshall Swearingen, "Arms on the Range," *High Country News*, February 8, 2016, 22–23.

42 Kristi Turnquist, "FBI Agents Posed as Filmmakers to Infiltrate the Bundy Family, 'Frontline' Documentary," *The Oregonian*, May 15, 2017, Newspaper Source Plus, 2W61362759646.

43 "Conservation vs Preservation and the National Park Service," NPS, accessed October 20, 2017, https://www.nps.gov/klgo/learn/education/classrooms/conservation-vs-preservation.htm.

44 Peter Carlson, "TR Goes Camping with John Muir," *American History* (June 2016): 14–15.

45 Jason R. Holley, "Gifford Pinchot and the Fight for Conservation: The Emergence of Public Relations and the Conservation Movement, 1901–1910," *Journalism History* 42, no.2 (2016): 91.

46 Blumm and Erickson, "Federal Wild Lands Policy in the Twenty-First Century," 4–5.

47 Blumm and Erickson, "Federal Wild Lands Policy in the Twenty-First Century," 6.

48 "Arctic National Wildlife Refuge, 1002 Area, Petroleum Assessment, 1998, Including Economic Analysis," USGS, accessed October 23, 2017, https://pubs.usgs.gov/fs/fs-0028-01/fs-0028-01.htm.

49 Stephen Haycox, "Battleground Alaska: Antistatism and Environmental Protection in America's Las Wilderness," *The Western Historical Quarterly* 48 (Summer 2017): 115.

50 Elizabeth Hardball, "Arctic National Wildlife Refuge Battle Ends, But Drilling Not A Given," National Public Radio, December 21, 2017, accessed December 29, 2017, https://www.npr.org/2017/12/21/572439797/arctic-national-wildlife-refuge-battle-ends-but-drilling-not-a-given.

51 Juliet Eilperin, "Trump Orders Review of National Monuments, Vows to 'End These Abuses and Return Control to the People," *The Washington Post*, April 26, 2017, https://www.washintonpost.com/news/energy-environment/wp/2017/05/25/zinkw-to-review-large-national-monuments-created-since-1996-to-make-sure-the-people-have-a-voice/?utm_term=.d3c5724f5a44.

52   Zygmunt J. B. Plater, "A Jeffersonian Challenge from Tennessee: The Notorious Case of the Endangered "Snail Darter" Versus TVA's Tellico Dam—And Where Was the Fourth Estate, the Press?" *Tennessee Law Review* 80 (2013): 522–527.

53   Jeb Boyt, "Struggling to Protect Ecosystems and Biodiversity Under NEPA and NFMA: The Ancient Forest of the Pacific Northwest and the Northern Spotted Owl," *Pace Environmental Law Review* 10 (1993): 1009.

54   "Northern Spotted Owl," FWS, accessed October 20, 2017, https://www.fws.gov/oregonfwo/articles.cfm?id=149489595.

55   Dean Lueck and Jeffrey A. Michael, "Preemptive Habitat Destruction Under the Endangered Species Act," *Journal of Law and Economics* XLVI (2003): 27–28.

56   Andrea Olive, "It is Just Not Fair: The Endangered Species Act in the United States and Ontario," *Ecology and Society* 21, no.3 (2016): 13, accessed October 18, 2017, doi:10.5751/ES-08627-210313.

57   Samuel J. Panarella, "A Bird in the Hand: Shotguns, Deadly Oil Pits, Cute Kittens, and the Migratory Bird Treaty Act," *Virginia Environmental Law Journal* 35 (2017): 166.

58   Andrew W. Minikowski, "A Vision or a Waking Dream: Revising the Migratory Bird Treaty Act to Empower Citizens and Address Modern Threats to Avian Populations," *Vermont Journal of Environmental Law* 16 (2014): 153–155.

59   "Incidental Take," FWS, accessed October 25, 2017, https://www.fws.gov/birds/policies-and-regulations/incidental-take.php.

60   Minikowski, "A Vision or a Waking Dream," 156.

61   "International Affairs," FWS, accessed August 10, 2018, https://www.fws.gov/international/cites/index.html.

62   Thomas Gehring and Eva Ruffing, "When Arguments Prevail Over Power: The CITES Procedure for the Listing of Endangered Species," *Global Environmental Politics* 8, no.2 (2008): 123.

63   Annecoos Wiersema, "Uncertainty and Markets for Endangered Species Under CITES," *Review of European Comparative & International Environmental Law* 22, no. 3 (2013): 240–241.

64   "What Can I Do With My Ivory?" FWS, accessed October 25, 2017, https://www.fws.gov/international/travel-and-trade/ivory-ban-questions-and-answers.html.

65   Cesare Costantino and Emanuela Recchini, "Environmental-Economic Accounts and Financial Resource Mobilization for Implementation of the Convention on Biological Diversity," *Statistika* 95, no.4 (2015):17–19.

66   Catherine Klein, "New Leadership Needed: The Convention on Biological Diversity," *Emory International Law Review* 31(2016): 135–140.

67   J. Timothy Ensminger, Lance N. McCold, and J. Warren Webb, "Environmental Impact Assessment Under the National Environmental Policy Act and the Protocol on Environmental Protection of the Antarctic Treaty," *Environmental Management* 24, no. 1 (1999): 13.

68   Tim Murphy, "The Radically International History of America's Best Idea," *Foreign Policy* (May/June 2017): 68–69.

69   Lawrence S. Hamilton, "Review of: Transboundary Protected Areas: The Viability of Regional Conservation Strategies," *Mountain Research and Development* 24, no. 2 (2004): 187.

70   Murphy, "The Radically International History of America's Best Idea," 70.

71   Karina Barquet, Paivi Lujala, and Jan Ketil Rod, "Transboundary Conservation and Militarized Interstate Disputes," *Political Geography* 42 (2014): 1–2.

72   Bram Buscher and Maano Ramutsindela, "Green Violence: Rhino Poaching and the War to Save Southern Africa's Peach Parks," *African Affairs* 115/458 (2015): 3–4.

73   Israel Ministry of Foreign Affairs, "Binational Red Sea Marine Peace Park," Israel Environment Bulletin 20, no.4 (1997), accessed November 5, 2017, http://www.mfa.gov.il/mfa/pressroom/1997/pages/binational%20red%20sea%20marine%20peace%20park%20-öct-97.aspx.

74   Peter Mackelworth, Drasko Holcer, and Bojan Lazar, "Using Conservation as a Toll to Resolve Conflict: Establishing the Prian-Savudrija International Marine Peace Park," *Marine Policy* 39 (2013): 112.

75   James Borton, "Marine Peace Park Plan Offers Promise for South China Sea," Geopolitical Monitor October 25, 2015, accessed November 5, 2017, https://www.geopolitical monitor.com/marine-peace-park-plan-offers-promise-for-south-china-sea/.

CHAPTER 9

The Oceans

INTRODUCTION

Oceans are vast saltwater bodies that cover over 70 percent of the Earth's surface. The oceans are divided into the Atlantic, Pacific, Indian, Southern, and Arctic. Small water areas, partially enclosed by land, include gulfs, seas, and bays. The oceans are essential for life on the planet. They absorb sunlight and this heat is transferred to the atmosphere through the ocean's currents, creating Earth's weather and climate. The oceans are home to most of the planet's plants and animals. They are the source of considerable food for the world's human population.[1] The oceans transport about 90 percent of global commerce and provide about one third of fossil fuel supplies as well as new sources of wave, wind, and tidal power.[2] Yet ecosystems of the oceans are threatened by overfishing, pollution, and global warming.

The oceans are affected by actions of individual counties as well as by international agreements among nations regarding the treatment of the oceans and marine life. Nations have long understood the necessity for standardization of regulations to assure safety for vessels as well as the rules for behavior in international waters and have established several international agreements and organizations to accomplish those goals. This chapter begins by exploring U.S. domestic laws and policy that govern treatment of the oceans and marine life. The international agreements and organizations that dictate the behavior of party nations towards the oceans are explored. Finally, discussion of the key issues that confront the oceans and marine life both near to the U.S. shore and in the high seas are detailed. In particular, discussion centers on restoration of the Gulf of Mexico in the aftermath of the *Deepwater Horizon* oil spill, ocean warming and acidification, sea-level rise, marine pollution, and the Great Pacific Garbage Gyre and other ocean garbage dumps.

DOMESTIC CONSIDERATIONS

Nearly 40 percent of the U.S. population lives near the oceans. These coastal areas are vital to the U.S. economy, contributing more than $6.6 trillion each year.[3] The U.S. and its coastal states exercise jurisdiction over vast amounts of submerged land. This is the result both of the vast shoreline of the United States and also because of U.S. territories and holdings in the Caribbean and South Pacific. The resulting U.S. Exclusive Economic Zone, described below, is larger than that held by any other country in the world, presenting challenges for effective ocean management and protection of marine resources. There are more than 20 federal agencies and 35 state or territorial agencies operating under a fragmented system of laws and management plans controlling fisheries, coastal and ocean habitats, wetlands and estuaries, and the exploitation of energy resources.[4] There are many critical ocean policies and laws to consider when trying to understand U.S. ocean policy.

Federal Legislation and Policies

Management of the Exclusive Economic Zone (EEZ) and the Territorial Seas of the United States. The establishment of EEZs worldwide was the result of the passage of the United Nations Convention on the Law of the Sea (UNCLOS III) which was opened for signature in 1982 and came into force in 1994.[5] UNCLOS III is discussed in detail later in the chapter, but one of its main functions was to provide definition for ocean zones which consist of territorial seas, EEZs, and high seas. Under the agreement, territorial seas of a nation extend out 12 miles from shore and in this zone nations have sovereignty. EEZs extend

200 nautical miles beyond the territorial sea and in this zone the nation has exclusive economic rights to all resources. Beyond the EEZ are international waters of the high seas where all nations have the right of free navigation and overflight.

The United States, however, never ratified UNCLOS III, despite its support by both the business community and the military. Initial opposition to UNCLOS III was tied to provisions in the treaty related to deep seabed mining. Revisions to the treaty have largely resolved these problems, nevertheless, ratification has not been forthcoming, despite support for ratification by every administration since Ronald Reagan's in the 1980s.[6] Continued opposition to UNCLOS III stems from the political right which argues that joining it could cede U.S. sovereignty to international organizations and tribunals.[7]

However, national interest in defining and protecting the U.S. EEZ is significant. The U.S. possesses the largest EEZ in the world, one that is nearly twice the size of the continental U.S.[8] The United States declared control over its EEZ by presidential action. By issuing Proclamation 5030, entitled the Exclusive Economic Zone of the United States of America, Ronald Reagan established a U.S. EEZ in 1983. The U.S. declaration is consistent with the terms of UNCLOS III, that is, that territorial waters over which the U.S. has sovereignty extend from the baseline, or average low water line, out 12 nautical miles. The EEZ extends out from the baseline to 200 nautical miles. President Reagan's proclamation established that area for exclusive American natural resource exploitation.[9] Within the EEZ, 8 regional fishery management councils (RFMCs) regulate ocean fishery resources. Additionally, the National Oceanic and Atmospheric Administration (NOAA), which was created in 1970 following publication of the first national study of oceans, provides scientific support for the oceans and the atmosphere. NOAA's National Marine Fisheries Service (NMFS), also known as NOAA Fisheries, regulates U.S. flag ships beyond the 200-mile EEZ, or on the high seas, and fisheries within the EEZ in coordination with the RFMCs.[10]

Within the 12-mile territorial sea, the federal government shares jurisdiction with coastal states, typically granting the states control over the 3 nautical miles closest to their shores. Texas, Florida, and Puerto Rico, however, have pursued claims to submerged land that extends out to 9 miles. This was done primarily through the Submerged Lands Act of 1953. Another law, the Outer Continental Shelf Lands Act of 1953 (OCSLA), was adopted to allow the federal government to arrange for the sale of leases to provide for the orderly development of resources in the outer continental shelf (OCS). The outer continental shelf is submerged land that lies between a continent and the deep ocean. The complications of managing resources in the territorial sea divided between the states and the federal government lead to the Coastal Zone Management Act of 1972 (CZMA). CZMA encouraged the states to implement plans for the development of coastal areas, provided federal funds to assist with such development efforts consistent with the national interest, and assured that federal actions will be consistent with state plans to the greatest extent possible.[11]

The Marine Protection, Research, and Sanctuaries Act of 1972 (Ocean Dumping Act). The definition of dumping is intermittent deposit of waste into the sea as opposed to continuous disposal from land-based pipelines or other sources. Two kinds of ocean dumping occur: containerized waste deposited on the ocean floor and wastes released for the purpose of dilution and dispersion.[12] Historically, the U.S. dumped dredged material, industrial wastes, radioactive wastes, and sewage sludge. The ocean dumping of dredged materials from harbor entrance channels was the most common type of dumping, accounting for nearly 90 percent of material dumped into the ocean. Prior to 1972 the only regulation of ocean dumping was to control its interference with navigation.[13]

The Ocean Dumping Act regulates dumping by preventing or strictly limiting the dumping of material that would harm human health, the marine environment, ecological systems, or the economic potential of the seas. Regulation is implemented using a permit system which both controls what is dumped and where it is dumped. Under provisions of the act, the Environmental Protection Agency (EPA) is required to research materials that may become problematic if dumped and to keep records on what materials are actually dumped. The law was passed at the same time as the London Convention of 1972 (discussed below) and many of the provision of that international treaty were included in the U.S. law.[14]

The Ocean Dumping Act was amended in 1988 largely in response to a number of events beginning in the summer of 1987 in which numerous beach closures and dolphin deaths occurred along the New York and New Jersey shores. Medical wastes and sewage washed up on many beaches causing public concern. Under the amendments, all municipalities were required to end the practice of dumping sewage sludge and industrial waste into the oceans by 1992.[15] Title IV of these amendments created the Shore Protection Act of 1988 (SPA). The SPA prohibits the transport of waste in coastal waters by ships without a permit. The EPA, in cooperation with the Coast Guard, is tasked with developing regulations to prevent spills of wastes from these vessels.[16]

Magnuson-Stevens Fishery Conservation and Management Act of 1976 (MSFCMA). The MSFCMA is the primary marine fisheries management program for the U.S. EEZ. The act was passed in response to concerns about foreign nations fishing just off American shores. After the end of World War II, 3-mile territorial waters were generally recognized as the norm. Fishing fleets rapidly increased in the aftermath of the war, seeking new sources of food to compensate for the devastated farmlands in war-torn regions. By the 1960s, the operations of foreign fishing fleets close to American shores gained attention and complaints grew from America's fishing industry. Congress responded with the passage of the Bartlett Act of 1964, which made it illegal for any foreign ship to fish in the territorial waters of the U.S. The act was amended in 1966 to extend American territorial waters to 12 nautical miles. By the 1970s, U.S. ocean policy had shifted to a protective position, largely in response to the vast amount of fish being taken by foreign fleets within 200 nautical miles of U.S. coasts. U.S.

policy embraced the concept of a 200-mile fishery conservation zone along with a 12-mile territorial sea.[17]

The MSFCMA established 8 Regional Fishery Management Councils responsible for drafting Fishery Management Plans (FMPs) for their areas of jurisdiction within the EEZ. The act was amended and reauthorized in 1996, with the passage of the Sustainable Fisheries Act (SFA), which emphasized conservation and sought to end overfishing. The act was again reauthorized in 2007 to put in place annual catch caps determined by coastal states to protect the fisheries from overfishing. NOAA Fisheries, the agency responsible for managing U.S. fisheries, has established the National Fishery Management Program (NFMP) in accord with provisions of the MSFCMA. Its goals are to prevent overfishing, to restore overfished stocks, to ensure conservation, to protect fish habitats, and to realize the sustainable future of the nation's fisheries through implementation of good management practices.[18]

Deep Seabed Hard Mineral Resources Act of 1980 (DSHMRA). This law was passed to provide a domestic legal framework for deep seabed mining in the high seas. The U.S. is not a party to UNCLOS III and will not accept the regulatory authority of the International Seabed Authority established by UNCLOS III. DSHMRA established NOAA as the agency that can authorize U.S. companies to explore and commercially exploit deep seabed sources of minerals.[19] NOAA has issued a number of exploratory permits to pursue sources of gold, nickel, copper, cobalt, manganese, zinc, and other valuable rare earth minerals in the seabed of international waters. U.S. interests, such as OMCO Seabed Exploration LLC, have been permitted to explore in the Clarion-Clipperton Zone (CCZ), a location in the Pacific about midway between Hawaii and Mexico. While these permits have been challenged in court due to the potential environmental harm mining might incur in such regions, businesses remain interested in pursuing deep seabed mining due to the potential value of such deposits.[20]

Oil Pollution Act of 1990 (OPA). This law authorizes natural resource trustees, which consist of several federal agencies, states, and Indian tribes, to evaluate the effects of oil spills, to seek compensation for damages, and to plan and implement restoration efforts.[21] The law was passed in response to the 1989 *Exxon Valdez* disaster in Alaska. The *Exxon Valdez* oil tanker sank after hitting Bligh Reef and released 11 million gallons of oil into Prince William Sound. The OPA gave the Coast Guard and the EPA authority to use the previously established Oil Spill Liability Trust Fund to initiate a first response while the Coast Guard investigated to identity responsible parties. The law was intended to respond to oil tanker spills, so it established regulation over tankers and dates by which all oil tankers must have a double hull.[22] The law also established a better mechanism for funding the Oil Spill Liability Trust Fund, initially through a tax on oil. Congress also provided for the creation of an emergency fund within the Oil Spill Liability Trust Fund that was available to the Coast Guard and the EPA for emergency removal costs and to the natural resource trustees for initiating damage assessments. This fund was set at $50 million each year and unspent amounts were allowed to carry over into future years.[23]

Domestic Ocean Issues of Importance

Restoring the Gulf of Mexico. The British Petroleum (BP) *Deepwater Horizon* accident was one of the worst environmental disasters in U.S. history. On April 20, 2010, the *Deepwater Horizon* oil drilling platform exploded, killing 11. After the initial explosion, the rig burned and eventually sank in 5,000 feet of water more than 40 miles off the Louisiana coast. The pipe that connected the drilling rig to the ocean floor broke, initiating the largest oil spill in U.S. history. Oil poured into the Gulf of Mexico for 86 days[24] due to the failure of the rig's blowout preventer. Initially, BP estimated the volume of oil spilled to be 1,000 barrels per day however U.S. government officials estimated that the volume may have been as great as 60,000 barrels per day.[25] By the time the well was plugged, nearly 5 million barrels of oil, or over 200 million gallons, had been released into the Gulf of Mexico.[26]

NOAA's Office of Response and Restoration, as the primary science agency for coastal oil spills, was involved with initial emergency response and later became a key actor in the damage assessment and restoration plan. NOAA's scientists investigated short-term impacts on fish, wildlife, and habitat in the immediate aftermath of the spill. Long-term impacts remain under investigation. Under provisions established by the Oil Pollution Act, the *Deepwater Horizon* Natural Resource Damage Assessment Trustees were assembled immediately after the spill. The trustee groups included federal agencies and the states of Alabama, Florida, Louisiana, Mississippi, and Texas. In 2010, the trustees released the damage assessment and restoration plan for the Gulf of Mexico, calling for BP to pay up to $8.8 billion for restoration.[27] The trustees justified this sum by finding that the spill had widely affected wildlife, habitat, and the ecology of the Gulf of Mexico and had also negatively impacted recreational activities including boating, fishing, and beach going.[28] In 2016, BP settled in court for natural resources injury to the Gulf of Mexico due to the spill agreeing to the damage assessment of the trustees.[29]

Other Ocean Concerns. Like the rest of the world, U.S. policy toward the oceans revolves around a number of issues associated with climate change. These include ocean acidification, ocean warming, loss of coral reefs, sea-level rise, and the impacts of severe weather events on coastal communities. The U.S. is also concerned with issues of sustainability including creating and maintaining sustainable fisheries in international waters. Additionally, the U.S. is attentive to the use of natural resources located in international waters, including mining the deep seabed. These issues are discussed below in an international context.

GLOBAL CONSIDERATIONS

The Challenges the Oceans Face

Sea-Level Rise. The oceans are rising both from glacial ice melt and through thermal expansion. The world's oceans have absorbed over 90 percent of the heat coming from climate change since the middle of the 20th century. This heat has warmed the oceans, resulting in thermal expansion. Global average sea levels have risen by 7 to 8 inches since the 1900s. About 3 inches of that rise has occurred since 1993. Rising seas threaten coastal cities globally. The threat comes from various causes. The occurrence of daily tidal flooding is increasing. Storm surges will increase in severity with higher seas. Global sea-level rise is expected to continue. Seas will rise at least several more inches in the next 15 years and by between 1 and 4 feet by 2100. Scientists warn that the possibility of sea-level rise by as much as 8 feet cannot be ruled out, given emerging research regarding the Antarctic ice sheet.[30]

While the melting of sea ice will have no effect on sea-level rise, the melting of land-based ice will have a major impact. Much of that land-based ice is on the enormous continent of Antarctica. Two of Antarctica's largest and fastest melting glaciers, the Pine Island and the Thwaites, could contribute to significant sea-level rise if they collapse into the ocean. As the world warms, it is clear that these glaciers will melt, but how fast they will melt is a critical question.[31] To answer that question, climatologists, Robert DeConto and David Pollard used the theory of marine cliff ice instability, suggesting that when a high enough temperature is reached, glaciers that extend into the sea will begin to melt from both the top and the bottom. Thus weakened, the glacier rapidly collapses into the sea. Their models predicted that Antarctica's collapsing glaciers alone could contribute as much as a meter of sea-level rise by 2100.[32] Such a significant increase in sea-level rise would flood many major world cities. Additional scientific research suggests that by 2100 the collapse of Antarctica's glaciers could contribute to the submerging of land that was home to 153 million people in 2017.[33]

The Arctic is also of particular importance for sea-level rise. A NOAA-sponsored report, the Arctic Report Card, stated that in 2017 the warming trend that is changing the Arctic continued. The Arctic in 2017 experienced the second warmest air temperatures, loss of sea ice, and above average ocean temperatures. The Arctic Report Card is an annual study undertaken by dozens of scientists in many nations. Now in its 12th year, the report consistently documents the changes in the Arctic. Among the findings reported from the 2017 study are that Arctic temperatures continue to rise at twice the rate of global temperatures. Global sea ice decline is greater than at any time in the last 1,500 years and the sea ice is getting thinner.[34] Arctic warming threatens Greenland's ice sheets, further contributing to sea-level rise.

Marine Pollution. The oceans suffer from two serious pollution issues: nutrient pollution and marine debris. It is estimated that 80 percent of the pollution in the ocean originates on land. Nutrient pollution comes from many sources including agricultural runoff, sewage and wastewater releases. This discharge floods the marine ecosystem with nitrogen, phosphorous, and other nutrients which cause algal blooms. As the algae decompose, they consume oxygen, creating dead zones where marine life cannot survive. An estimated 500 dead zones exist in the world. Marine debris is trash and other solid material that washes into the ocean. This debris may include plastics, garbage bags, nets, and other solid material that washes into the seas as a result of poor trash management practices on land.[35]

Ocean Garbage Patches. Located about halfway between California and Hawaii, and containing about 140,000 tons of plastic, the Great Pacific Ocean Garbage Patch or the North Pacific Gyre, is the largest garbage patch in the oceans. Estimates on its size vary from twice the size of the U.K., to the size of Texas, to twice the size of Texas. Over 8 million tons of plastic litter flows from the land to the sea each year. Once it enters the oceans, tides move it around. Ultraviolet radiation and movement of the sea breaks the plastic down into small particles that can be mistaken for food by marine life. Marine life can also become tangled in or snarled by larger pieces. At least a million sea birds and hundreds of thousands of marine mammals die each year from the plastic.[36]

The North Pacific Gyre is only one of several accumulations of small floating plastic particles in the North Pacific Ocean. The accumulating tiny plastic debris zones were first discovered in 1972. Since then, there have been many reports mostly from the North Atlantic or North Pacific. Graduate students from Scripps spent weeks in the North Pacific Gyre in 2009 and their water samples revealed many small plastic particles in the water. Similar findings have been reported by researchers in the Atlantic where water samples revealed high counts of small bits of plastic. Other patches have been predicted in the Indian Ocean, the South Pacific, and the South Atlantic.[37]

Sustainable Fisheries. Sustainable fisheries are based on the concept of harvesting a limited number of fish so that there are adequate populations left to reproduce and maintain a healthy population. However, by the 1990s, unregulated overfishing left many species on the brink of collapse.[38] The technology available to the commercial fishing industry enables such heavy catches that it is estimated that nearly a third of commercial fisheries globally may have already collapsed.[39]

Overfishing and destruction of marine habitat has been a persistent problem for more than a half century. Despite the international agreements seeking to protect fish stocks, they remain threatened. To address this problem, the United Nations (UN), for the first time, included maintaining sustainable fisheries as part of its 2030 agenda. Sustainable Development Goal 14 calls on the community of nations to "conserve and sustainably use the oceans, seas and marine resources for sustainable development."[40] This recognition by the UN points to the urgent need to protect fish stocks and to prevent overfishing.

Ocean Acidification. Absorption of carbon dioxide from the atmosphere causes the oceans to become more acidic. Many marine species are unable to adapt to the more acidic water. By 2014, the ocean had become 30 percent more acidic than it was before the Industrial Revolution.[41] Scientists have shown that changes in ocean chemistry, like acidification, can interfere with species' ability to sense and respond to predators. This is particularly a problem near coral reefs where the population of predators and prey are densely packed. Changes in acidity can have catastrophic consequences for the entire ecosystem.[42]

Ocean acidification also negatively impacts reef-building corals. The acidification, when combined with other stressors such as heat or cold, can have an interactive effect further harming the species.[43] Coral reefs provide a number of ecosystems services including protection of fisheries, shoreline protection and reduction of erosion, nitrogen fixation, and tourism and leisure opportunities. But coral reefs are in danger because ocean acidification harms the corals' ability to build reefs.[44] Coral bleaching events signal the stress of these creatures. Bleaching occurs when coral lose the algae that they depend upon for food. The reef turns white or very pale and becomes very susceptible to disease. Coral can recover from bleaching events, but if the stress is prolonged, the coral will die.[45]

International Treaties and Policies

There are a number of international and regional treaties that seek to manage and protect the oceans. These treaties seek to define the extent and uses of territorial seas and the high seas, to conserve and protect marine life, and to prevent pollution of ocean waters. Four Conventions were adopted as the outcome of the first United Nations Convention on the Law of the Sea (UNCLOS I) in 1958; these include the Convention on Territorial Sea and the Contiguous Zone (CTS), the Convention on the High Seas (CHS), the Convention on Fishing and Conservation of Living Resources of the High Seas (CFCLR), and the Convention on the Continental Shelf (CCS). These first attempts to codify international law regarding the oceans were later reworked and replaced in 1982 with the current UNCLOS III. The earlier conventions remain binding only on those state that were parties to the earlier conventions but did not become party to the 1982 Convention—the United States, Colombia, Israel, and Venezuela.[46]

Convention on Territorial Sea and the Contiguous Zone. CTS is one of the four conventions that were adopted after UNCLOS I. CTS entered into force in 1964, however it failed to address one significant issue— the extent of the territorial sea. While UNCLOS III would later set the range at 12 miles, CTS left this distance unresolved. Yet CTS did provide the main rules to define baselines, bays, delimitations between nations whose coasts face each other, and the contiguous zone. CTS also provided the rule of unrestricted innocent passage of vessels in straights used for international navigation that fall within the territorial seas of other nations.[47] The treaty established the contiguous zone as a band of water that extends out from the territorial sea to a distance of 24 nautical miles from the baseline in which a coastal state may exercise control over activities that might infringe on its customs or laws.[48]

Convention on the High Seas. CHS went into force in 1962. It defined the high seas as all parts of the ocean not including territorial seas. CHS provides provisions for freedom of the high seas, the right of nations to have ships flying their flags and the obligations of those states, the definitions of piracy, and the right to lay cables and pipelines. CHS also provided early environmental rules regarding the discharge of oil and radioactive substances.[49]

Convention on Fishing and Conservation of Living Resources of the High Seas. Originally drafted in 1958 under UNCLOS I, this convention attempted to deal with the problems of overfishing and to negotiate an arrangement by which nations might exercise conservation controls over fisheries and vessels traveling in international water. It had been clear since the late 19th century that uncontrolled commercial fishing could devastate fisheries. The idea that there should be some cooperative conservation efforts put in place to prevent such behavior is embodied in the convention. The convention declared that all states have the right to fish in international seas but that all states also have the obligation to conserve living resources in international waters.

Conservation was defined by the treaty to mean maintaining maximum possible sustained yield. The treaty lays out various scenarios for fishing. In one scenario, only a single nation's people are engaged in fishing a particular area of the high seas. In this case, the treaty declares it is the obligation of that nation to impose conservation programs on its own citizens if they are deemed necessary to conserve the living resources in the area. If two or more nations are fishing the same area and conservation programs are considered necessary, the nations are to enter into negotiations. If no agreement is arrived at within a year, any of the parties may initiate arbitration. The treaty specifies that once a conservation program is in place, other nations should respect it. Finally, the treaty recognizes that a coastal state has a special interest in protecting the living resources in the waters off its coast and therefore it has a right to be part of all negotiations, even if its citizens do not fish in that location.[50]

Convention on the Continental Shelf. CCS established as a sovereign right of a coastal state to the outer continental shelf off its shores even if the OCS exceeds beyond its territorial seas. The convention also established the rule that the rights of a coastal state to economic exploitation of its OCS do not require the state to proclaim its rights or to occupy the OCS.[51]

UN Convention on the Law of the Sea III. UNCLOS III, in its current form, replaced two prior treaties and the conventions attached to them (UNCLOS I and UNCLOS II) to define the rights of nations in regard to international waters or high seas, territorial seas, and outer continental shelves. UNCLOS I and UNCLOS II were negotiated in 1956 and 1960, respectively.[52] UNCLOS III is a comprehensive treaty that established the worldwide convention for the peaceful uses of the oceans and ocean resources. UNCLOS III was opened for signature in 1982 and immediately 115 nations signed the agreement. It finally came into force in 1994 when an adequate number of nations had ratified the agreement. UNCLOS III established different maritime zones including territorial seas, EEZs, and high seas. Under the agreement, the territorial seas of a nation extend 12 nautical miles from the nation's baseline, or average low water line. Nations have sovereignty over their territorial seas and foreign ships are allowed only "innocent passage" in these waters, meaning passage must be peaceful and not threaten the security of the coastal state. EEZs extend out from the territorial sea to 200 nautical miles from the baseline. In the EEZ, the coastal nation has the right to all economic exploitation of resources including fish, minerals, and energy. In the EEZ, other nations have the right of navigation and overflight. These rights of free navigation and overflight also extend to the high seas.[53]

There is some ambiguity under UNCLOS III regarding the rights of maritime powers to conduct military operations in the EEZ of other nations without prior permission. Article 58 of UNCLOS III states that maritime ships may engage in "other internationally lawful uses of the sea related to these freedoms, such as those associated with operation of ships, aircraft and submarine cables and pipelines, and compatible with the other provisions of the Convention." This language has been interpreted by the United States, Italy, Germany, the Netherland, and the United Kingdom to mean that naval operations are permitted because they fall under the "operation of ships" provision. Other nations disagree and have made statements regarding the need for foreign nations to obtain permission for naval operations in their EEZs. Among these nations are Brazil, Bangladesh, Cape Verde, Malaysia, India, and Pakistan.[54]

UNCLOS III underscored the principle of the freedom of the seas, guaranteeing every country's right to navigate and fish on the high seas. At the same time, UNCLOS III imposed conservation duties on nations to take actions to protect marine life and habitat on the high seas. UNCLOS III requires states that are fishing for the same resources in the same areas to create regional fisheries management organizations (RFMO) to provide coordination as had earlier conventions under UNCLOS I.[55]

Part XI of UNCLOS III established a system for the mining of the deep seabed, that is, in waters outside any nation's EEZ. The treaty

created an international organization, the International Seabed
Authority, to regulate deep seabed mining in international waters
through authorizing permits to explore and drill. The Authority also
has the obligation to collect and distribute royalties from such activities.
UNCLOS III designated the deep seabed to be managed under the
principle of "common heritage of mankind" (CHM). Such a
designation imposes restrictions on the management of deep seabed
resources including concerns for intergenerational sustainability of
resources as well as equity in benefit sharing especially with developing
nations.[56] It was this provision of the agreement that caused the United
States to object to the treaty, seeing this provision not in its economic
interest. In 1994, this part of UNCLOS III was modified to allow
greater flexibility and to encourage the participation of the U.S. in the
agreement, however, the U.S. remains a non-party.[57]

The London Convention. The London Convention of 1972, otherwise
known as The Convention on the Prevention of Marine Pollution by
Dumping of Wastes and Other Matter of 1972, is one of the first
international agreements for protection of the marine environment.
Beginning in the 1950s, several nations became concerned with the
effects on the marine environment given the virtually uncontrolled
dumping of waste into oceans. Parties to the London Convention
agreed to control dumping by implementing regulatory programs. The
London Convention requires parties to issue permits for the dumping
of wastes and to restrict some hazardous material from dumping. In
1996, parties to the London Convention negotiated a new agreement,
called the London Protocol, to update the original treaty. The London
Protocol entered into force in 2006. It prohibits incineration at sea and
restricts the material that may be dumped. Material that may be
dumped includes dredged material, sewage sludge, fish waste, vessels
and platforms, organic material of natural origin, bulky items made
from unharmful materials such as steel or concrete, and carbon dioxide
to be stored in seabed geological formations.[58]

*International Convention on Prevention of Pollution from Ships
(MARPOL).* Adopted in 1973 and subsequently revised in 1978 after a

number of tanker accidents, the MARPOL Convention went into effect in 1983. The convention was again modified and updated in 1997 and these changes came into force in 2005. The goal of the agreement is to minimize or prevent pollution from ships. Ships pollute through their normal operations as well as through accidental releases of pollutants. The agreement includes 6 annexes that address specific pollutants including oil, noxious liquid substances carried in bulk, harmful substances, sewage, garbage, and air pollution (in particular SO_x and NO_x).[59] The International Maritime Organization, discussed below, played a critical role in drafting this agreement.[60]

The Convention on the Conservation of Antarctic Marine Living Resources (CCAMLR). Adopted in 1980, CCAMLR is closely tied to the Antarctic Treaty (discussed in chapter 8) but focuses only on marine life. CCAMLR is one of 3 treaties adopted under the framework of the Antarctic Treaty, the others being the Convention on the Conservation of Arctic Seals of 1972, which entered in to force in 1978, and the Protocol on Environmental Protection to the Antarctic Treaty which entered into force in 1998. CCAMLR specified protection of Antarctic marine life while at the same time it allowed for some taking of marine life as long as it was deemed "rational." CCAMLR applies to all marine life in Antarctica except whales and seals. Seals are protected under the Convention on the Conservation of Arctic Seals and whales fall under the terms of the 1946 International Convention for the Regulation of Whaling. CCAMLR is different from many other treaties in that it was the first to incorporate ecosystem and precautionary approaches. It does this by requiring that parties maintain the ecological relationship between marine life harvested and those species that are dependent for survival on the species being harvested so that their populations may not be reduced. The precautionary approach is incorporated by requiring that harvesting be restricted to levels that can be reversed within decades if problems emerge.[61]

Regional Ocean Policies

United Nations Environment Programme (UNEP) Regional Seas Program.
Established in 1974, this program's initial concerns were with
transboundary pollution, conservation, ocean dumping, and scientific
research. As the program matured, greater emphasis came to be on
human activities in coastal areas that cause harm to the environment.[62]
The program currently focuses its efforts on marine litter, land-based
hazards that may wash into the ocean, coral reefs, coastal zone
management, small island developing states, and biodiversity in areas
beyond national jurisdiction (BBNJ). Under the BBNJ programs, the
secretariat oversees several regional agreements, including the
Convention for the Protection of the Marine Environment of the
North-East Atlantic (OSPAS Convention); the Convention on the
Protection of the Natural Resources and Environment in the South
Pacific Region (Noumea Convention); the Convention for the
Conservation of Antarctic Marine Living Resources (CCAMLR
Convention); the Convention for the Protection of the Mediterranean
Sea Against Pollution (Barcelona Convention); the Cenvenio para la
Proteccion del Medio Marino y la Zona Costera del Pacifico Sudeste
(Lima Convention); the Nairobi Convention for the Protection,
Management, and Development of the Marine and Coastal
Environment of the Western Indian Ocean; and the Abidjan
Convention for Cooperation in the Protection, Management, and
Development of the Marine and Coastal Environment of the Atlantic
Coast of the West, Central and Southern Africa Region.[63] The program
seeks to address the degradation of the world's oceans by engaging
neighboring countries to take specific actions to protect their own or
shared marine environments.[64]

European Union (EU) Integrated Maritime Policy (IMP). The European
Union has an extensive coastline that borders its member states and
relies on the oceans for their considerable contribution to the EU's
economy. Its resources include fisheries, aquaculture, energy, tourism,
and shipping. Historically, each nation developed and implemented its

own maritime policy. The development of the IMP began with the publication of a Green Paper on Maritime Policy in 2006 and was followed by a year of discussions among stakeholders about the benefits of an integrated marine policy. Based upon these discussions, the European Commission proposed the Integrated Maritime Policy in 2007.[65] The goals of the IMP are both to environmentally protect the coastal areas of the EU as well as to spur sustainable development and job creation.

International Ocean Management Organizations

International Hydrographic Organization (IHO). IHO is an intergovernmental consultative organization dedicated to support the safety of navigation and the environmental protection of the oceans. IHO was initially formed in 1921 under the name the International Hydrographic Bureau but was renamed to IHO in 1970. IHO's goals are to promote coordination among coastal states, uniformity in nautical charts, and advancement of the science of oceanography. Each member country sends a representative to IHO Assembly, which meets every three years to review the progress made by committees and working groups addressing issues of mutual agreement. The Assembly also may add new issues to the IHO's agenda. The IHO has a secretariat located in Monaco.[66]

International Maritime Organization (IMO). The IMO was established by the United Nations as a specialized agency, that is, an agency that is independent of the UN but works closely with it through special agreements. The organization was originally called the Inter-Governmental Maritime Consultative Organization (IMCO) but its name was changed in 1982. The IMO has two purposes: to improve safety and security of shipping involved in international trade and to control marine pollution. The IMO is made up of an Assembly and a Council. The Assembly is comprised of representatives of all member states and has the authority to adopt resolutions and pass them on to member states as recommendations. The Assembly can also amend conventions and pass those amendments to member states for ratification. The Assembly elects the Council, which has executive functions, and approves the appointment by the Council of the IMO Secretary, the lead administrator of the organization. The IMO has a secretariat located in London.[67]

The IMO's first job, after meeting for the first time in 1959, was to modify the International Convention for the Safety of Life at Sea (SOLAS), a treaty dealing with maritime safety. After completing this task, the IMO began its work facilitating international shipping traffic, providing guidance on the transport of dangerous cargo, and promoting a new system for measuring tonnage of ships. Safety remains the primary mission of IMO, but after the massive oil spill that occurred with the Torrey Canyon disaster of 1967, IMO began to turn its efforts to introduction of measures to prevent oil tanker accidents. The most important of these was the MARPOL agreement of 1973. In the 1970s, IMO modified the global search and rescue system by launching the International Mobile Satellite Organization and in the 1990s the Global Maritime Distress and Safety System. In 1998, IMO put in place the International Safety Management Code, which regulated passenger vessels, oil and chemical tankers, and large cargo ships. Agreements to protect the marine environment were put in place in the 2000s as were efforts to prevent crimes at sea.[68]

International Whaling Commission (IWC). Created in 1946, the IWC's purpose was to assure that whales did not become extinct and to promote the whaling industry. The IWC's own scientific committee never recommended that commercial whaling be prohibited but due to public outcry, largely driven by nonprofit organizations like Save the Whales, an introduction of a moratorium on commercial whaling began in 1986. Several countries continue to allow or promote whaling. Prominent among them are Norway and Japan.[69] The IWC continues to set catch limits for native subsistence whaling and focuses most of its attention on the protection of cetaceans. The IWC is particularly concerned with threats to whales coming from entanglement with nets, ship strikes, marine debris, and climate change.[70]

International Seabed Authority (ISA). ISA was established in 1994, when UNCLOS III was modified to make allowances for U.S. difficulties with the original agreement. ISA is an autonomous intergovernmental organization that answers to its member states. ISA has an Assembly which includes representatives of all member states. The role of the Assembly is to make policy recommendations. ISA has exclusive authority to manage the mineral resources in the deep seabed outside of any national jurisdiction. It also is responsible for collecting and distributing royalty revenues to developing countries in a manner consistent with the treaty. ISA's main effort to promote development of minerals has been through the crafting of mining code regulations and the approval of 26 exploratory missions sponsored by 20 states and private companies. The ISA has also developed policies for environmental protections and requires environmental impact assessments before it will consider applications for contracts for exploration.[71]

International Tribunal on the Law of the Sea (ITLOS). The Tribunal was established as part of the 1982 UNCLOS III agreement and came into force in 1994. The 168 parties to the convention can submit disputes to the Tribunal that arise out of differences in interpretation of UNCLOS III. The port city of Hamburg, Germany is the home of the Tribunal. The Tribunal is an independent judicial body that maintains close ties to the United Nations and has observer status in the General Assembly. The Tribunal is comprised of 21 judges who are elected by member states for a term of 9 years. The Tribunal has several chambers designated for different areas of disputes. These include the Seabed Dispute Chamber, the Chamber for Summary Procedure, the Chamber for Fisheries Disputes, the Chamber for Marine Environment Disputes, and the Chamber for Maritime Delimitation Disputes. As of 2017, the Tribunal had heard 25 cases dealing with disputes over release of vessels and crews captured by other states, freedom of navigation, coastal state jurisdiction in its maritime zones, the marine environment, and conservation of fish stocks. The Tribunal is only one court parties may use in dispute resolutions. UNCLOS III also permits resolutions through the International Court of Justice (ICJ), or an arbitral tribunal.[72]

CONCLUSION

U.S. domestic concerns over the sea are rooted in the fact that much of the American population lives near the oceans. Ocean regions in the U.S. contribute much to American prosperity from industries such as fishing, shipping, energy extraction, and tourism. The U.S. has a complex system in place to control its vast maritime zones which are larger than those held by other nations. The expansive EEZ presents many management challenges. Several federal agencies and a number of state or territorial agencies share jurisdiction over the EEZ and manage ocean resources under a disjointed system of laws and management plans.

The formation of EEZs globally resulted from the third United Nations Convention on the Law of the Sea which was negotiated in 1982. The U.S. is not a party to UNCLOS III and so domestic measures were undertaken to establish the U.S. EEZ. The United States declared control over its EEZ when Ronald Reagan issued a proclamation establishing it in 1983. Reagan's declaration was consistent with the terms of UNCLOS III in establishing territorial waters to 12 nautical miles and an EEZ to 200 nautical miles. The U.S. system for ocean and natural resource management within the EEZ includes 8 regional fishery management councils, as well as NOAA Fisheries, and the environmental and regulatory organizations of the coastal states and territories. The federal government shares jurisdiction with coastal states and territories in the territorial sea, typically granting states and territories control over the 3 nautical miles closest to their shores. Texas, Florida, and Puerto Rico are exceptions, claiming control out to 9 miles, under provisions of the Submerged Lands Act. The Outer Continental Shelf Lands Act allows the federal government to sell leases for energy resources in the OCS. The Coastal Zone Management Act provides for cooperation between the states, territories, and the federal agencies.

The U.S. regulates what can be dumped into the oceans through the Ocean Dumping Act. Prior to the passage of this act in 1972, the largest quantity of dumping came from dredged materials associated with clearing harbors for navigation. Later dumping included sewage, industrial waste, and radioactive substances. The Ocean Dumping Act established a permit system to control what and where materials could be dumped into the ocean. Instances of medical waste and sewerage washing up on New York and New Jersey beaches in 1987, resulted in an amendment to the law which forbade cities from dumping sewage and industrial wastes. The amendment also prohibited the transport of waste in coastal waters by ships without a permit and provided for cooperation between the EPA and the Coast Guard to prevent spills from these ships.

Control over fisheries in the U.S. EEZ was established by the Magnuson-Stevens Fishery Conservation and Management Act. The law set up 8 Regional Fishery Management Councils and required them to put in place Fishery Management Plans. These actions were strengthened by the 1996 amendment called the Sustainable Fisheries Act which sought to end overfishing. NOAA Fisheries is responsible for managing U.S. fisheries in a sustainable manner.

The Deep Seabed Hard Mineral Resources Act was passed to provide a domestic legal framework for deep seabed mining in the high seas. This law was necessary since the U.S. is not a party to UNCLOS III, which established the rules for deep seabed mining for party nations. The law gave NOAA the authority to allow U.S. companies to explore and commercially mine deep seabed minerals.

Provisions for dealing with oil spills and compensating communities harmed by those spills were provided in the Oil Pollution Act which was passed in the aftermath of the *Exxon Valdez* oil spill in Prince William Sound, Alaska. The law allowed for an emergency response by the Coast Guard in the event of a spill until the responsible party could be identified, required oil tankers to have double hulls, and established a trust fund to finance cleanups and restoration activities.

The major near-coast ocean issue affecting the U.S. in recent years is restoring the Gulf of Mexico after the *Deepwater Horizon* accident of 2010. This event was the largest oil spill in U.S. history and one of the worst environmental disasters ever to occur. Oil poured uncontrolled into the Gulf for 86 days releasing nearly 5 million barrels of oil. NOAA's scientists investigated short-term impacts on fish, wildlife, and habitat in the immediate aftermath of the spill. Long-term impacts remain under scientific investigation. In 2016, BP settled in court for the damages it caused and agreed to for cleanup and restoration.

Coastal regions of the U.S. are experiencing and will continue to experience effects from climate change. These include flooding associated with sea level rise, strong storm surge associated with more extreme storm events, instances of heavy precipitation and flooding, coastal erosion, bleaching and loss of coral reefs. Coastal regions and cities are seeking solutions by implementing resiliency strategies.

The international framework for continued freedom of the high seas while also providing nations with the right to commercially exploit ocean resources close to their shores is contained in the United Nations Convention on the Law of the Sea. Three such conventions have been held. UNCLOS I, in 1958, resulted in the creation of four conventions, including the Convention on Territorial Sea and the Contiguous Zone, the Convention on the High Seas, the Convention on Fishing and Conservation of Living Resources of the High Seas, and the Convention on the Continental Shelf. UNCLOS II was largely unsuccessful. These first attempts to codify international ocean law were later reworked and replaced in 1982 with the current UNCLOS III. However, the earlier conventions remain binding for those states, like the United States, that were parties to the earlier conventions but did not become party to the UNCLOS III.

UNCLOS III established the rights of nations in regard to peaceful uses of the oceans and their resources in international waters, territorial seas, outer continental shelves, and EEZs. UNCLOS III was opened for signature in 1982 and came into force in 1994 after hundreds of nations had ratified the agreement. Under the agreement, the territorial seas of a nation were determined to extend 12 nautical miles from the nation's baseline. Countries have full sovereignty over their territorial seas although foreign vessels are allowed peaceful passage in other nation's territorial seas. UNCLOS III also established that a nation's EEZ extends out to 200 nautical miles, and in this space the nation has sole right to all commercial activities.

UNCLOS III underscored the principle of the freedom of the seas while at the same time required party nations to conserve ocean resources. Fish stocks were to be conserved by requiring nations that fish in the same waters to coordinate fishing and control overfishing through regional fisheries management organizations. UNCLOS III established a system for mineral extraction from the deep seabed. The International Seabed Authority was established to approve permits to explore and drill and to collect and distribute royalties.

While UNCLOS III provides the overall rules on the use of the oceans, a number of other treaties address more specific concerns. Ocean dumping is the focus of the London Convention. Parties to the convention agreed to control dumping by implementing regulatory programs whereby each nation would institute a permit system for ocean dumping of substances considered safe to dispose of at sea. Harmful substances were restricted. In 1996, the treaty was updated by the London Protocol, which prohibits incineration at sea and further restricted the material that may be dumped. To reduce pollution to the oceans coming from ships, the MARPOL Convention and its later amendments were negotiated. Six annexes are included in the agreement to control oil, noxious liquid substances, harmful substances, sewage, garbage, and air pollution. The Convention on the Conservation of Antarctic Marine Living Resources protects Antarctic marine life. It applies to all marine life in Antarctica, except whales and seals that are separately protected under the Convention on the Conservation of Arctic Seals and the International Convention for the Regulation of Whaling.

In addition to these agreements, a few regional ocean agreements are of importance. The UNEP's Regional Seas Program emphasizes reducing marine waste and land-based sources of pollution, protection of coral reefs, coastal zone management, and biodiversity. It works by arranging partnerships between regional nations for conservation and pollution reduction. The EU also has a program, called the Integrated Maritime Policy, that seeks to provide environmental protection to the coastal nations of the EU.

A number of international organizations, loosely tied to the United Nations, have been organized to manage one or more aspect of global ocean policy. The International Hydrographic Organization is concerned with providing standardized maritime charts and promoting safety of shipping. The International Maritime Organization focuses on shipping safety and pollution prevention. The International Whaling Commission supervises commercial and indigenous whaling, with its recent efforts directed at imposing a moratorium on commercial whaling. The International Seabed Authority operates the global system of permitting for mining in international waters. The International Tribunal for the Law of the Sea resolves disputes that arise from UNCLOS III.

While the international agreements and organizations have been successful to some degree in creating and implementing global ocean policy, several critical issues still confront the world's oceans. These issues include sea-level rise, the existence of ocean garbage patches such as the North Pacific Great Garbage Patch, the persistence of extensive marine nutrient and debris pollution, overfishing and the lack of sustainable fisheries, and ocean acidification.

---

[1] "Oceans," National Geographic, accessed November 13, 2017, https://www.national geographic.com/environment/habitats/ocean/.

[2] "The Global Oceans Regime," Council on Foreign Relations, accessed November 13, 2017, http://cfr.org/report/global-oceans-regime.

[3] "Oceans and Coasts," NOAA, accessed November 13, 2017, http://www.noaa.gov/oceans-coasts.

4   Mary Turnipseed et al., "The Silver Anniversary of the United States' Exclusive Economic Zone: Twenty-Five Years of Ocean Use and Abuse, and the Possibility of a Blue Water Public Trust Doctrine," *Ecology Law Quarterly* 36 (2009): 1–3.

5   Jing Geng, "The Legality of Foreign Military Activities in the Exclusive Economic Zone Under UNCLOS," *Merkourios* 28, no. 74 (2012): 23.

6   Rachael E. Salcido, "Law Applicable on the Outer Continental Shelf and in the Exclusive Economic Zone," *The American Journal of Comparative Law* 58 (2010): 409.

7   Iosif Sorokin, "The UN Convention on the Law of the Sea: Why the U.S. Hasn't Ratified it and Where it Stands Today," *Berkeley Journal of International Law Blog* (March 30, 2015): 1, accessed November 27, 2017, http://berkeleytravaux.com/un-convention-law-sea-u-s-hasnt-ratified-stands-today/.

8   Salcido, "Law Applicable on the Outer Continental Shelf and in the Exclusive Economic Zone," 408.

9   "Proclamation 5030—Exclusive Economic Zone of the United States of America," Federal Register, accessed November 27, 2017, https://www.archives.gov/federal-register/codification/proclamations/05030.html.

10   Kathryn J. Mengerink, "The Pew Oceans Commission Report: Navigating a Route to Sustainable Seas," *Ecology Law Quarterly* 31 (2004): 693–694.

11   Salcido, "Law Applicable on the Outer Continental Shelf and in the Exclusive Economic Zone," 410.

12   Gunnar E. B. Kullenberg, "Ocean Dumping Sites," *Ocean Management* 2 (1974–75): 189.

13   T. A. Wastler, "Ocean Dumping Permit Program Under the London Dumping Convention in the United States," *Chemosphere* 10, no. 6 (1981): 659.

14   R. H. Burroughs, "Ocean Dumping: Information and Policy Development in the USA," *Marine Policy* (April 1988): 96–97.

15   Steven J. Moore, "Troubles in the High Seas: A New Era in the Regulation of U.S. Ocean Dumping," *Environmental Law* 22 (1992): 913.

16   "Summary of the Shore Protection Act," EPA, accessed December 4, 2017, https://www.epa.gov/laws-regulations/summary-shore-protection-act.

17   James P. Walsh, "The Origins and Early Implementation of the Magnuson-Stevens Fishery Conservation and Management Act of 1976," *Coastal Management* 42 (2014): 412–414.

18   Andrea Dell'Apa, Lisa Schiavinato, and Roger A. Rulfson, "The Magnuson-Stevens Act (1976) and its Reauthorizations: Failure or Success for the Implementation of Fishery Sustainability and Management in the US?" *Marine Policy* 36 (2012): 674.

19   "Seabed Management," NOAA, accessed December 4, 2017, http://www.gc.noaa.gov/gcil_seabed_management.html.

20   "Landmark Lawsuit Challenges U.S. Approval of Deep-sea Mineral Mining," Center for Biological Diversity, accessed December 4, 2017, https://www.biologicaldiversity.org/news/press_releases/2015/deep-sea-mining-05-13-2015.html.

21   "Gulf Spill Restoration," NOAA, accessed November 29, 2017, http://www.gulfspillrestoration.noaa.gov/co-trustees.

22   Garry A. Gabison, "Limited Solution to a Dangerous Problem: The Future of the Oil Pollution Act," *Ocean and Coastal Law Journal* 18, no. 2 (2013): 223–234.

23   David H. Sump, "The Oil Pollution Act of 1990: A Glance in the Rearview Mirror," *Tulane Law Review* 85 (2011): 1111.

[24]   Sam Kalen et al., "Lingering Relevance of the Coastal Zone Management Act to Energy Development in our Nation's Coastal Waters?," *Tulane Environmental Law Journal* 24 (2010): 74.

[25]   Richard Pallardy, "Deepwater Horizon Oil Spill of 2010," in *Encyclopedia Britannica,* last modified December 15, 2017, https://www.britannica.com/event/Deepwater-Horizon-oil-spill-of-2010.

[26]   "Deepwater Horizon Oil Spill," NOAA, accessed November 29, 2017, https://response.restoration.noaa.gov/oil-and-chemical-spills/significant-incidents/deepwater-horizon-oil-spill.

[27]   "A Comprehensive Restoration Plan for the Gulf of Mexico," NOAA, accessed November 29, 2017, http://www.gulfspillrestoration.noaa.gov/restoration-planning/gulf-plan/.

[28]   "How We Restore," NOAA, accessed November 29, 2017, http://www.gulfspill restoration.noaa.gov/how-we-restore.

[29]   "Deepwater Horizon Oil Spill," NOAA, accessed November 29, 2017, https://response.restoration.noaa.gov/oil-and-chemical-spills/significant-incidents/deepwater-horizon-oil-spill.

[30]   D. J. Wuebbles et al., "Climate Science Special Report: Fourth National Climate Assessment, Volume I," *U.S. Global Change Research Program* (2017): 12–34, doi:10.7930/J0DJ5C TG.

[31]   "Ice Apolcalypse," Grist, accessed December 15, 2017, https://grist.org/article/antarctica-doomsday-glaciers-could-flood-coastal-cities/.

[32]   Robert M. DeConto and David Pollard, "Contribution of Antarctica to Past and Future Sea-level Rise," *Nature* 531 (2016): 591.

[33]   Robert E. Kopp et al., "Evolving Understand of Antarctic Ice-Sheet Physics and Ambiguity in Probabilistic Seal-Level Projections," *Earth's Future* 5 (2017): 1, accessed December 15, 2017, doi: 10.1002/2017EF000663.

[34]   "Arctic Saw 2nd Warmest Year, Smallest Sea Ice Coverage on Record in 2017," NOAA, accessed December 14, 2017, http://www.noaa.gov/media-release/arctic-saw-2nd-warmest-year-smallest-winter-sea-ice-coverage-on-record-in-2017.

[35]   "Marine Pollution," U.S. Department of State, accessed December 20, 2017, https://www.state.gov/e/oes/ocns/opa/ourocean/248163.htm.

[36]   Christine Evans-Pughe, "All At Sea: Cleaning up the Pacific Garbage," *Engineering & Technology* (February 2017): 52–55.

[37]   Jocelyn Kaiser, "The Dirt on Ocean Garbage Patches," *Science* 328, no. 5985 (2010): 1506.

[38]   "Healthy Fish for a Healthy Ocean," Ocean Conservancy, accessed December 18, 2017, https://oceanconservancy.org/sustainable-fisheries/.

[39]   "Working for Sustainable Fishing," WWF Global, accessed December 18, 2017, www.panda.org/sustainablefishing.

[40]   Karmenu Vella, "Maintaining Healthy Ocean Fisheries to Support Livelihoods: Achieving SDG 14 in Europe," *UN Chronicle* 54, no.1/2 (2017): 1.

[41]   U.S. Department of State, " 'Our Oceans' Conference Outcomes: Charting a Path Toward a Global Ocean Policy," *Congressional Digest* September (2014): 11.

[42]   D. L. Dixson, "Lost at Sea," *Scientific American* 316, no 6. (2017): 43.

[43]   Javid Kavousi, John Everett Parkinson, and Takashi Nakamura, "Combined Ocean Acidification and Low Temperature Stressors Cause Coral Mortality," *Coral Reefs* 35 (2016): 903.

44   Carla I. Elliff and Iracema R. Silva, "Coral Reefs as the First Line of Defense: Shoreline Protection in Face of Climate Change," *Marine Environmental Research* 127 (2017): 151.

45   "What is Coral Bleaching?" NOAA, accessed December 20, 2017, https://ocean service.noaa.gov/facts/coralreef-climate.html.

46   Tullio Treves, "1958 Geneva Conventions on the Law of the Sea," *Audiovisual Library of International Law,* accessed December 12, 2017, http://legal.un.org/avl/ha/gclos/gclos.html.

47   Treves, "1958 Geneva Conventions on the Law of the Sea."

48   "Maritime Zones and Boundaries," NOAA, accessed December 12, 2017, http://www. gc.noaa.gov/gcil_maritime.html#territorial.

49   Treves, "1958 Geneva Conventions on the Law of the Sea."

50   William W. Bishop, Jr., "The 1958 Geneva Convention on Fishing and Conservation of the Living Resources of the High Seas," *Columbia Law Review* 62, no. 7 (1962): 1217.

51   Treves, "1958 Geneva Conventions on the Law of the Sea."

52   Sorokin, "The UN Convention on the Law of the Sea," 1.

53   Geng, "The Legality of Foreign Military Activities in the Exclusive Economic Zone under UNCLOS," 23–24.

54   Geng, "The Legality of Foreign Military Activities in the Exclusive Economic Zone under UNCLOS," 24–25.

55   Michaela Young, "Then and Now: Reappraising Freedom of the Seas in Modern Law of the Sea," *Ocean Development & International Law* 47, no.2 (2016): 168.

56   Aline Jaeckel, Kristina M. Gjerde, and Jeff A. Ardron, "Conserving the Common Heritage of Humankind—Options for the Deep-Seabed Regime," *Marine Policy* 78 (2017): 150.

57   Aline Jaeckel, "Deep Seabed Mining and Adaptive Management: The Procedural Challenges for the International Seabed Authority," *Marine Policy* 70 (2016): 206.

58   "Ocean Dumping: International Treaties," EPA, accessed August 30, 2017, https:// www.epa.gov/ocean-dumping/ocean-dumping-international-treaties.

59   "International Convention for the Prevention of Pollution from Ships (MARPOL)," IMO, accessed December 4, 2017, http://www.imo.org/en/about/conventions/listof conventions/pages/international-convention-for-the-prevention-of-pollution-from-ships-(marpol).aspx.

60   "Brief History of IMO," IMO, accessed December 13, 2017, http://www.imo.org/en/ About/HistoryOfIMO/Pages/Default.aspx.

61   Adriana Fabra and Virginia Gascon, "The Convention on the Conservation of Antarctic Marine Living Resources (CCAMLR) and the Ecosystem Approach," *The International Journal of Marine and Coastal Law* 23 (2008): 573–575.

62   Peter C. Schroder, "UNEP's Regional Seas Programme and the UNCED Future: Apres Rio," *Ocean & Coastal Management* 18 (1992): 101.

63   "Regional Seas," UNEP, accessed December 13, 2017, http://web.unep.org/ regionalseas/about/what-we-do/conservation-biodiversity-areas-beyond-national-jurisdiction-bbnj.

64   "Who We Are," UNEP, accessed December 13, 2017, http://web.unep.org/regional seas/about/who-we-are/overview.

65   Angela Carpenter, "The EU and Marine Environmental Policy: A Leader in Protecting the Marine Environment," *Journal of Contemporary European Research* 8, no. 2 (2012): 255.

[66] "About IHO," IHO, accessed December 13, 2017, https://www.iho.int/srv1/index.php?option=com_content&view=article&id=298&Itemid=297&lang=en.

[67] Felicity Attard, "IMO's Contribution to International Law Regulating Maritime Security," *Journal of Maritime Law & Commerce* 45, no. 4 (2014): 481.

[68] "Brief History of IMO," IMO, accessed December 13, 2017, http://www.imo.org/en/About/HistoryOfIMO/Pages/Default.aspx.

[69] Mihoko Wakamatsu et al., "Can Bargaining Resolve the International Conflict Over Whaling?," *Marine Policy* 81 (2017): 312.

[70] "The International Whaling Commission," IWC, accessed December 13, 2017, https://iwc.int/history-and-purpose.

[71] Caitlyn Antrim, "The International Seabed Authority Turns Twenty," *Georgetown Journal of International Affairs* (Winter/Spring 2015): 190.

[72] "General Information," International Tribunal for the Law of the Sea, accessed December 14, 2017, https://www.itlos.org/en/general-information/.

CHAPTER 10

Fossil Fuels

INTRODUCTION

Coal, natural gas, and oil provide the overwhelming majority of domestic and international energy. This chapter begins with a discussion of the current use and production of fossil fuels in the U.S. The environmental impacts associated with the use of fossil fuels are explored. A primary concern for U.S. policy, especially in the aftermath of several restrictions on the flow of international sources of oil to the U.S., is maintaining energy security. How and what the United States does to assure energy security is discussed. While fossil fuel policy in the U.S. tends to rely heavily on actions of the private sector, several federal laws and policies have exerted influenced. These and the underlying politics are discussed.

The chapter also discusses the global use and production of fossil fuels, as well as the consequences for the world's environment from such use. Global policies toward fossil fuels are explored beginning with the second anniversary of the 2015 Paris Agreement on climate change, in which every nation on the Earth considered its use of fossil fuels and how they impact global warming. Other proposed policies to reduce reliance on fossil fuels are reviewed, including proposed bans on internal combustion engines, national decisions to leave oil in the ground, disinvestment in fossil fuels, and attempts on the part of oil exporting countries like Saudi Arabia to diversify their economies.

DOMESTIC CONSIDERATIONS

U.S. Use of Fossil Fuels

The U.S. uses vast amounts of coal, oil, and natural gas. In 2016, the U.S. consumed 97.4 quadrillion (quads) British thermal units (Btu) of energy, and fossil fuels accounted for nearly 81 percent of that consumption, or 78.7 quads. Coal supplied 15 percent of U.S. energy needs, natural gas provided 29 percent, and oil provided 37 percent.[1]

Coal. Coal was formed from the deposits of plant material that fell into swamps and bogs many millions of years ago. The plants decomposed into peat which was covered by mud and sand. These mud and sand deposits formed the mudstone and sandstone formations found above coal seams that exist today. Over thousands of years, the peat was compressed until it turned into the coal which is extracted today. Coal is ranked based on the amount of carbon it contains. The higher the carbon content, the higher the energy content, or Btu per pound. Lignite contains as little as 30 percent carbon and the lowest energy content. Next highest in rank are subbituminous and bituminous. Anthracite, which is comprised of 90 percent carbon, has the highest ranking and the highest energy content.[2]

The U.S., like much of the rest of the world's industrialized nations, shifted from wood to coal as the primary fuel around 1850.[3] Widespread coal use declined in the aftermath of World War II as cheap oil and natural gas were introduced and the pipe network necessary for easy use of these fuels was developed. Reduced coal use also occurred because by the 1950s railroads shifted to diesel and electric locomotives, replacing their coal-fired steam locomotives.[4]

The overwhelming use of coal in the U.S. today is for production of electricity. In 2016, 91 percent of the coal used in the U.S. went to the electric power generation sector. Industry used about 8 percent of the coal burned and less than 1 percent was used by the residential and commercial sectors.[5]

Oil. Crude oil is a mixture of hydrocarbons that formed millions of years in the past when plants and animals died. It exists underground in liquid pools, within tiny holes in sedimentary rocks, and at the surface of the Earth in tar or oil sands. Crude oil needs to be refined to separate its several petroleum products, including gasoline and distillates, which consist of diesel fuel and heating oil, jet fuel, waxes, lubricating oil, asphalt, kerosene, and petrochemical feedstocks.[6]

While the use of oil dates back to ancient Egypt and Babylonia, the first commercial oil well was drilled in Titusville, Pennsylvania in 1859. Its use was primarily for replacing whale oil with kerosene for lighting.[7] Prior to the invention of the automobile in 1892, gasoline was not considered useful and was considered superfluous waste. After the growth of the automobile industry, gasoline became the primary product desired from crude oil refining. By the 1920s, over 9 million gasoline-powered automobiles were in use and gas stations began to appear across the country.[8]

Today the U.S. consumes more energy from oil than from any other source. In 2016, the U.S. consumed 19.7 million barrels of oil per day, accounting for 37 percent of overall U.S. energy use.[9] The largest use of oil in the U.S. in 2016 was transportation. The transportation sector consumed 71 percent of the oil used by the economy. Industry used 23 percent of the oil consumed in the U.S., the residential and commercial sectors consumed 5 percent, and the electric power generation sector used 1 percent of the oil consumed.[10]

Natural Gas. Natural gas exists deep within the Earth and is comprised of mostly methane. It was formed millions of years ago when plants and animals died, forming deep layers of organic material that was later covered with sand and dirt. After thousands of years under pressure it formed into natural gas. In some places the gas collected under layers of overlying rock. In other places, it collected in the tiny holes in some rocks, such as shale, and is called shale gas or tight gas. It also may have formed in coal deposits and if so is called coal bed methane.[11]

Natural gas was first exploited in the U.S. in 1821 when a well was dug in Freedonia, New York. For the industry to widely expand, though, pipeline infrastructure was necessary. After World War II, high-pressure pipelines were laid across the country creating the network needed for widespread use of natural gas. Between 1950 and 1970, natural gas use quadrupled. The introduction of price controls in the 1970s slowed growth but deregulation in the 1980s once again boosted the growing industry.[12] The application of hydraulic fracturing, or fracking, after 2005 revolutionized access to natural gas (and later oil) found in shale plays. With the use of ever improving techniques, U.S. production and use of natural gas increased rapidly.[13]

The use of natural gas in 2016 was roughly evenly divided between three sectors with industry consuming 34 percent, the residential and commercial sector consuming 27 percent, and the electric power generation sector consuming 36 percent. Transportation used a small amount of natural gas but accounted for only 3 percent of the total usage.[14]

U.S. Production of Fossil Fuels

The U.S. produces enormous amounts of fossil fuels. In 2016, the U.S. produced 65.6 quads of fossil fuels.[15] While this is a huge amount of production, it is important to note that U.S. consumption of fossil fuels in 2016 exceeded domestic production. However, because of improving fracking techniques, the U.S. is projected by the late 2020s to become a net exporter of both oil and natural gas.[16]

Coal. The U.S. holds 25 percent of the world's coal, or about 270 billion tons. In comparison, Western Europe holds a total of 36 billion tons, China holds about 126 billion tons, and India and Australia both have less than China. Only Russia, with 176 billion tons, comes close to the amount of recoverable coal reserves that the U.S. has. This enormous amount of coal has earned the U.S. the status of the "Saudi Arabia of coal."[17]

The amount of coal produced in any one year, however, depends on demand. Demand for U.S. coal is tightly coupled to coal-fired electricity production. In 2016, the U.S. produced 739 million short tons of coal, the lowest level of coal production since 1978. This decline is largely due to cheap and abundant supplies of natural gas over the period and especially since the development of shale gas through fracking. The electric power sector accounted for more than 90 percent of the coal used in the U.S. in 2016, and coal's share of electricity generation decreased between 2008 and 2016, leading to natural gas surpassing coal for electricity power generation for the first time in 2016.[18]

Oil and Natural Gas. The Energy Information Administration (EIA) estimated that the U.S. became the world's largest producer of oil and natural gas, or total petroleum hydrocarbons, in 2012. This massive increase in production was owed to ever-improving fracking technology, which more cost effectively was able to get at previously uneconomical supplies of gas and oil. In 2017, the International Energy Agency (IEA), which tracks energy for 29 countries around the world, predicted that the U.S. would move from being an oil importing nation to an oil and gas exporting nation by the late 2020s.[19] The U.S. became the world's largest producer of natural gas in 2009 when U.S. production exceeded that of Russia. The U.S. is poised to become the number two producer of crude oil in 2018, surpassing Saudi Arabia and approaching Russia's production levels.[20]

Fracking involves the use of directional drilling and the use of fracking fluids to get at unconventional sources of oil and gas stored in rocks. The application of the technique, and continuous improvements in its application, resulted in a reversal of America's oil and gas energy future. Rather than continuing to experience dwindling supplies of natural gas and oil, the U.S. began to produce in higher and higher amounts.[21]

Environmental Impacts of Fossil Fuel Use

Coal. Coal is a dirty fuel. Coal burns very uncleanly, emitting vast amounts of carbon dioxide (CO_2) into the atmosphere. CO_2 is a major contributor to climate change. Coal releases more carbon dioxide into the atmosphere per unit of heat energy than any other fossil fuel. The emissions vary based upon the type of coal and where it is mined, however, EIA analysis provides data for average U.S. coal emissions by coal type. Anthracite emits the most followed by lignite, subbituminous, and bituminous. In terms of pounds of carbon dioxide per million Btu of heat produced, U.S. anthracite emits 227.4 pounds, lignite 216.3, subbituminous 211.9, and bituminous 205.3.[22]

Emissions of carbon dioxide by the U.S. electric power generating sector show the impact of burning coal. In 2016, those plants burning coal emitted 1,241 million metric tons of CO_2 or 68 percent of the total, while those burning natural gas emitted 546 million metric tons or 30 percent of the total. The electric power generating sector in 2016 was 35 percent of total U.S. energy related CO_2 emissions of 5,171 million metric tons.[23]

Coal also releases conventional pollutants and is linked to many diseases including asthma, cancer, pulmonary diseases, and neurological problems. Burning coal also produces acid precipitation which is harmful to wildlife, forests, crops, and even buildings. When coal is burned it releases mercury, sulfur dioxide, nitrogen oxides, and particulate matter or soot. Coal also releases heavy metals including lead, cadmium, and other toxic heavy metals. Coal emits volatile organic compounds which form ozone in the lower atmosphere.[24]

Coal deposits in the U.S. are most often extracted by surface mining. Surface mining uses huge machines to remove the top layers of soil and rock to expose the coal seam. The coal is then removed and after the operation is complete, the area is supposed to be restored to pre-mine conditions, however, opponents suggest this is rarely accomplished. Strip mining is a commonly used surface mining technique. In the American West, where the land is generally flat, soil and rock are removed in narrow bands, or strips, to get to the coal. In the Appalachian region, contour mining is used because of the mountainous terrain. In contour mining soil and rock is removed and placed along the edge of the mine, where it eventually forms a high wall. Mountaintop removal mining, also common in Appalachia, is an extreme form of surface mining that involves removing as much as 1,000 feet of mountaintop to expose the coal. The soil and rock debris are typically dumped into valleys, were they destroy terrain and clog waterways. Mountaintop removal is very destructive to the land, which can never be restored to pre-mine conditions. It is controversial because of this topographical destruction and because of the environmental impact it may have on valleys where debris is dumped.[25]

When coal burns it puts off particulate matter, called coal ash, which must be collected so that it is not released into the atmosphere. Coal ash is dangerous because it contains heavy metals and other chemicals such as arsenic, selenium, cadmium, and chromium that are known to harm human health. The coal ash is typically collected and then mixed with water to form a slurry. The slurry is put in a pond, where it awaits further treatment. The nation has experienced a number of coal ash spills that have resulted in contamination of the surrounding lands. In 2008, a particularly spectacular one occurred at the Tennessee Valley Authority (TVA) Kingston Fossil Plant, when a dike failed, and 5.4 million cubic yards of coal ash was released, contaminating more than 300 acres. The site was declared a Superfund site.[26] The following year, the Environmental Protection Agency (EPA) released a list of 44 coal-fired power plants that it considered a high hazard because failure of an ash enclosure would likely result in loss of human life.[27]

Oil and Natural Gas. Oil and natural gas also pose environmental risks. While natural gas and common petroleum products release less carbon dioxide than coal when burned, they do release some. Natural gas is by far the cleanest burning fossil fuel, releasing 117 pounds of CO_2 per million Btu of energy. By contrast, the most common petroleum product, gasoline (without ethanol), releases 157.2 pounds per million Btu of energy. Diesel fuel and heating oil release 161.3

pounds, while propane releases 139 pounds.[28] Burning fossil fuels is the main anthropogenic contribution to climate change.

Besides releasing carbon dioxide, the natural gas and oil industry is also a significant source of methane emissions. Methane is a potent climate change gas with 25 times the warming potential of carbon dioxide. Burning oil or natural gas produces volatile organic compounds which contribute to the formation of ozone. These volatile organic compounds also contain a number of air toxics, including benzene, which are known carcinogens.[29]

Oil and natural gas also pose environmental risks through their retrieval and transport. Oil spills are common with thousands occurring in waters of the U.S. each year. Most, however, are small in size and spill less than a barrel of oil. Since the 1969 oil spill off the coast of Santa Barbara, California, there have been at least 44 oil spills of more than 10,000 barrels (420,000 gallons) that have impacted U.S. waters. The largest was the *Deepwater Horizon* in the Gulf of Mexico (discussed in Chapter 9).[30] Land-based spills from oil and gasoline pipelines are also common. Since 2010, there have been over 20 spills ranging from the lower amount of just under 187,000 gallons of gasoline spilled in Helena, Alabama in 2016 to the largest spill of just over 865,000 gallons of crude oil spilled in Mountrail County, North Dakota in 2013. In 2017, the controversial TransCanada's Keystone pipeline spilled 210,000 gallons of crude oil in South Dakota.[31]

Fracking for oil and natural gas poses environmental risks. Concerns include contamination of drinking water sources by pollutants[32] and the thousands of chemicals used in the fracking process, many of which are known to be carcinogens or endocrine disruptors.[33] Air pollution is also a fear. Pollutants such as hydrogen sulfide, nitrogen oxides, benzene and formaldehyde, particulate matter, sulfur dioxide, and ground level ozone have been shown to be released at most stages of fracking and extraction of oil and gas. Diesel exhaust from trucks is also a concern for air quality.[34]

Energy Security and Early Policy Responses

The concept of energy security for the U.S. dates back to the two energy crises of the 1970s. The first of these occurred in October of 1973, when the Organization of Arab Petroleum Exporting Nations (OAPEC) instituted an oil embargo on the U.S. and other nations that were supporters of Israel. This came in the wake of the Yom Kippur War between Israel and a coalition of Arab states led by Egypt and Syria. The embargo, along with general production cuts, changed world oil prices. Oil went from $2.90 a barrel to $11.65 by January 1974. Disagreements within OAPEC resulted in the lifting of the embargo by March of 1974 but the higher oil prices continued.[35] The second oil shock was also tied to Middle Eastern events, in particular, the Iranian Revolution of 1978–1979. Iranian oil production plummeted during the war by 4.8 million barrels a day (7 percent of the world's total production at the time). The shortages of oil and widespread panic buying spurred price increases that raised the cost of a barrel of oil to nearly $40, caused long lines at U.S. gas stations, and imparted considerable disruption to the U.S. economy.[36]

The political response to these oil shocks constituted the first bold U.S. attempt at achieving energy security. Political response to the 1973 oil shock resulted in the world's largest economies coming together to create the International Energy Agency to monitor energy markets and to provide coordinated action in times of crisis. The U.S. Congress mandated a 55-mile per hour speed limit to conserve fuel through the passage of the Emergency Highway Energy Conservation Act of 1974 (later rescinded). Congress also passed the Energy Policy and Conservation Act of 1975 which created Corporate Average Fuel Economy (CAFE) standards for new automobile fleets. The law allowed the Nixon administration to put oil price controls in place. It banned the export of crude oil, except to Canada (rescinded in 2015). Finally, the law allowed the U.S. to fulfill obligations to the newly created IEA by creating the Strategic Petroleum Reserve. The political response to the 1978 oil shock resulted in the Carter administration creating the Department of Energy (DOE) and in Congress passing the National Energy Act of 1978.[37] The National Energy Act had five key components. One of them, implemented under the title The National Gas Policy Act, tried to make natural gas more competitive.[38]

One definition of energy security typically used is the availability of ample supplies at affordable prices. To achieve this, however, several dimensions must be considered. The first of these is physical security, which includes protecting energy assets, infrastructure, trade routes, and supply chains. Also included in physical security is the ability to quickly recover or replace assets and infrastructure when lost or damaged. The second is providing access to energy supplies. This aspect assumes maintaining functioning energy companies to explore, contract, and acquire energy supplies. The third is the structure created by nations and international institutions established to secure functioning energy systems. The last is investment, to secure long-term provision of energy supplies.[39]

The U.S. has long made energy security a national priority. From the presidency of Harry Truman on, every U.S. president has held Middle Eastern oil security vital to U.S. interests. Jimmy Carter made that relationship explicit when he created the Carter Doctrine in 1979. In it Carter pledged, "An attempt by any outside force to gain control of the Persian Gulf region will be regarded as an assault on the vital interests of the United States, and such an assault will be repelled by any means necessary, including military force."[40]

Energy Laws, Policies, and Politics After Carter

When Ronald Reagan entered the White House, energy policy changed rapidly. Rather than a continued emphasis on shortages and perceived insecurity, Reagan shifted policy to reflect his conservative deregulatory approach. Reagan ideologically did not believe that government should be involved in energy markets, and so his policy was to leave energy to the private sector. During the 1980s and 1990s, energy prices were reasonably stable, and the federal government took little role in fossil fuel policy. But in 2000, when George W. Bush came to power, a series of events shifted the federal government back into an activist role on energy policy. One factor driving change was that energy prices were rising, due in part to the demand that China and India were putting on supplies. California experienced an energy crisis when a poorly managed deregulatory effort resulted in months of electric power interruptions. The terrorist attack on the World Trade Center on September 11, 2001 focused attention on the politically unstable Middle East. Fear of shortages compelled a new round of political discussions about energy. A National Energy Policy planning committee was formed as the vehicle for discussions. What came out of the National Energy Policy planning committee were recommendations that Congress passed into two major laws.[41]

The Energy Policy Act of 2005 continued prior policies (such as subsidies and low taxes) that encouraged heavy reliance on fossil fuels. It contained provisions to increase federal subsidies for exploration and production of gas and oil on federal lands and on the outer continental shelf (OCS). The law also contained a provision to increase the use of the then reasonably new technique of fracking by restricting the EPA from regulating fracking operations under the Safe Drinking Water Act.[42] The act also sought to increase the number of coal-fired electric power generating plants through the Clean Air Coal program which allocated $3 billion for commercial deployment of advanced coal-based power.[43] The Energy Independence & Security Act of 2007 had little to do with fossil fuels, however, it did seek to provide a future for the coal industry by promoting the development of carbon capture and sequestration.[44]

When the Obama administration took office, the nation was in deep recession and efforts were focused primarily on the economy. While most of the energy provisions in the American Recovery and Reinvestment Act of 2009 (AR&R) were aimed at increasing renewables, the law did include $3.4 billion for carbon capture and sequestration research and development (R&D) to assist the coal industry.[45] The Obama administration generally followed a green agenda, however, the application of fracking during the years Obama was in office vastly increased the amount of gas and oil produced in the U.S. The Obama administration's determination to take policy actions to address climate change, however, meant taking deliberate actions to curtail the burning of coal.

The shift back to emphasizing fossil fuels came swiftly in the Trump administration. Among the first actions taken by the administration was the decision to take steps to reverse the Clean Power Plan (CPP). The CPP was the Obama administration's key policy on climate change that sought to reduce greenhouse gas emissions, largely from coal-fired power plants. Trump had campaigned on reversing this plan and to withdraw from the Paris Agreement, both of which Trump argued were a war against coal.[46] Trump announced in June of 2017 that he intended to withdraw from the Paris Agreement, saying it would impose unfair environmental standards on American businesses. Formal withdrawal, however, cannot occur before 2020.[47]

The Trump administration encouraged more coal mining on federal lands by reversing an Obama ban on new coal leases on public land. The administration also promoted increased exploitation of oil and natural gas on public lands. To assist in this effort, the administration reduced protected wilderness and historic areas.[48] The opening of area 1002 in the Arctic National Wildlife Refuge (ANWR) for potential drilling extended a forty-year debate over protecting the porcupine caribou mating and migration land. This was accomplished in the 2017 Tax Cuts and Jobs Act, which contained provisions calling for the federal government to hold at least two oil and gas lease sales before 2027.[49] The administration rescinded proposed rules to control fracking and other oil and gas drilling practices on federal land. The rules, developed under the Obama administration, would have required companies to disclose the chemicals they use in fracking.[50] In April of 2017, the Trump administration signed an executive order to expand offshore oil and gas drilling in the Arctic and Atlantic Oceans, reversing an Obama-era executive order that withdrew millions of offshore acres from drilling.[51] At the very end of 2017, Trump proposed to reduce the safety requirements for offshore drilling that were put in place after the 2010 *Deepwater Horizon* accident.[52]

The U.S. fossil fuel industry benefits from favorable federal tax breaks and has since the early 20th century. Producers of fossil fuels received $4.76 billion in tax breaks in 2016 alone. Four of the largest tax breaks are tax breaks for costs associated with drilling new oil and gas wells, a deduction for domestic production of fossil fuels, a lower tax rate than most other industries, and accelerated amortization for geological and geophysical expenses.[53] Advocates of these tax incentives argue that fossil fuel production is central to the economy and so should receive favorable tax advantages. Environmentalists tend to argue that this level of subsidization of fossil fuels is harmful to the environment and discourages transition to clean energy sources.

GLOBAL CONSIDERATIONS

Global Use of Fossil Fuel

Coal. According to the International Energy Agency, in 2013, coal provided 29 percent of the world's energy supply and produced 41 percent of the world's electricity. The world's appetite for coal is large and growing. Global coal consumption increased more than 70 percent between 2000 and 2013. China consumes about half of the world's coal, but their consumption of coal will decline as China moves away from heavy industry toward services. China's shift away from coal will occur, not only because of economic shifts, but also because of commitments made to the Paris Agreement as well as concerns over local air pollution.[54]

Coal is used worldwide primarily to generate electricity, but it also plays an important role in the production of steel, the refining of aluminum, and the manufacture of paper. Coal by-products are used in the production of some chemicals, for instance, refined coal tar is used to make creosote oil, phenol, and benzene. The ammonia gas retrieved from coke ovens is used make ammonia salts, nitric acid and some fertilizers. Many other products have some coal components, including activated carbon used in water and air filters and carbon fiber used as a light weight reinforcement material in construction.[55]

Oil and Natural Gas. In 2013, oil provided for 31 percent of the world's energy supply.[56] In 2016, the world consumed 96 million barrels of oil per day, or more than 35 billion barrels per year. IEA projects continued rise in consumption, with the world surpassing the 100 million barrels per day threshold after 2020.[57] Consumption of natural gas worldwide is expected to increase from 120 trillion cubic feet in 2012 to 203 trillion cubic feet by 2040. Natural gas is a key source of fuel for both the electricity production sector and for industry. Natural gas use for industry and electric power generation worldwide is expected to increase annually by 1.7 percent and 2.2 percent, respectively. Consumption will increase more rapidly in the developing world than among developed nations as many locations in the developing world acquire necessary infrastructure.[58]

Global Production of Fossil Fuel

Coal. There are estimates that the world has one trillion tons of recoverable coal resources.[59] Coal resources are widely dispersed around the globe. Since the start of the 21st century, production of coal has been the fastest growing energy source. Coal production worldwide is expected to increase through 2020.[60]

Natural Gas and Oil. In November of 2017, the International Energy Agency released its annual forecast of energy supplies. It predicted that because of increased U.S. production, international energy markets will experience major changes. The IEA predicts that the U.S. will account for 80 percent of the increases in global oil supply by 2025, and that global energy demand will rise 30 percent by 2040, triggered largely by increased consumption by India. IEA also predicts that China will become the world's largest oil consumer.[61]

Demand for natural gas will also increase and producers of natural gas will increase their production by nearly 60 percent between 2012 and 2040. Total natural gas production in China, the U.S., and Russia will account for nearly half of the overall increase in world production. Use of fracking to release unconventional sources will drive production increases, especially in the U.S., China, and Canada. Liquefied natural gas (LNG) is also projected to account for a growing share of traded natural gas worldwide. The amount of LNG is projected to double between 2012 and 2040.[62]

Unlike coal deposits, oil and gas tend to be found in relatively few nations. Gas tends to be located in North America, Russia, and the Caspian region. Proven reserves of conventional oil are predominantly in the Middle East, with Saudi Arabia alone possessing 20 percent of the world's total. Such distribution poses geopolitical questions for availability of oil and gas to those that want it. However, the increasing impact of unconventional sources of gas and oil has changed the scenario to a significant extent.[63]

Global Environmental Impacts from Fossil Fuel Use

The worldwide consequences of fossil fuel use stem from extracting, transporting, and burning coal, oil, and natural gas.[64] Extraction is a significant source of pollution. Unregulated mining is a source of release of harmful materials into the air, land, and water. As more mines open in countries with weak environmental control structures in place, the likelihood of such releases increase.[65] As global energy demand rises, worldwide gas and oil drilling will become more invasive. The environmental impacts of extraction include acid mine drainage, ecosystem damage from strip and surface mines, oil spills at the point of extraction, land degradation and loss of habitat for many species.[66]

The transport of oil has resulted in many devastating spills across the world. One of the world's largest oil spills was also the first. In

1967, the first big supertanker, the *Torrey Canyon*, hit ground off the coast of the U.K. dumping between 25 and 36 million gallons of oil that spread into a 270-square mile slick. In 1972, 35 million gallons were dumped into the Gulf of Oman when the *Sea Star* collided with the *Horta Barbosa*. In 1988, over 40 million gallons were spilled off the coast of Nova Scotia, Canada. Forty five million gallons were spilled into the Mediterranean when an oil tanker sunk off the coast of Genoa, Italy. The ship sank but continued to leak oil for 12 years. In 1991, between 51 and 81 million gallons of oil spilled off the coast of Angola, creating an 80-square mile slick. In 1978, 69 million gallons spilled off the coast of Portsall, France after the *Amoco Cadiz* was caught in a winter storm. In 1983 alone, 79 million gallons spilled off the coast of South Africa, 80 million gallons leaked into the Persian Gulf off the coast of Iran when an oil tanker collided with an oil platform, and 84 million gallons spilled into the Kolva River in Russia when a pipeline ruptured. In 1979, off the coast of Mexico, 140 million gallons spilled when a Pemex well experienced a blowout. In 2010, the BP's *Deepwater Horizon* exploded in the Gulf of Mexico, spilling over 200 million gallons.[67] These spills have all been environmental calamities.

The worst oil spill in history occurred as part of a deliberate act during the First Gulf War, in 1991, when Iraqi forces tried to prevent invading U.S. Marines from landing by opening valves at an offshore oil terminal and releasing 6 million barrels of oil into the Persian Gulf. As Saddam Hussein was chased out of Kuwait, he had his forces set fire to almost 800 oil wells. The resulting fire, with temperatures as high as 3,000 degrees, resulted in massive air pollution and extensive environmental damage.[68]

The burning of fossil fuels is the primary source of air pollution worldwide. Burning fossil fuels releases particulates, mercury, nitrogen dioxide, sulfur dioxide, and carbon monoxide. Ozone is created by chemical reaction when volatile organic compounds, carbon monoxide, and nitrogen dioxide bake in sunlight. Each of these has been tied to poor health outcomes. The World Health Organization (WHO) argues that air pollution is the greatest single environmental health risk. In

2012, WHO reported that about 3.7 million deaths worldwide could be tied to ambient air pollution and another 3.7 million deaths to household air pollution. The burning of fossil fuels results in the release of carbon dioxide, the main anthropogenic cause of climate change. Low-income populations and children are the groups most harmed by both pollution and climate change, which adds consideration of inequity to the burning of fossil fuels.[69]

Fossil Fuel Use in a Warming World

The acceleration of climate change has added another consideration to energy security. Potential threats to energy security are no longer just connected with availability, accessibility, and affordability. The acceptability of specific fuels has now become part of the discussion between and among nations. Using this perspective, energy security is thought of in a different light by including the threat of climate change and the need to consider shifting sources of fuels to reach climate change policy goals.[70]

Many governments, international organizations, and corporations have reconsidered energy security to include this dimension. For instance, France's parliament passed a law in 2017 to ban the production of oil and gas by 2040 in mainland France and its overseas territories. While largely symbolic, since France imports most of its fossil fuel, the move nevertheless signals a clear change in sentiment. France also plans to ban the sale of diesel and gasoline engine cars by 2040.[71] France is not alone in this policy direction. The U.K. said in 2017 that it would ban new gasoline and diesel cars beginning in 2040 and that by 2050 all cars in the U.K. will need to be zero emission vehicles. India also announced in 2017 that every vehicle sold after 2030 should be electric. Norway's transportation plan states that all new passenger cars sold after 2025 should be zero emission vehicles. At least 8 other countries have set targets for electric car sales including Austria, Denmark, Ireland, Japan, the Netherlands, Portugal, Korea and Spain. While Germany has not set a date for a ban, political leaders have suggested that moving toward electric vehicles makes sense.[72]

Even automakers are joining the movement. For instance, Toyota announced that it planned to stop making gasoline-powered cars by 2050.[73]

Divestment from fossil fuels is also gaining attention. For instance, in 2017, New York Governor Cuomo called on New York State's Common Fund, a $200 billion retirement fund and the third largest in the U.S., to stop investing in all entities with significant fossil fuel-related activities.[74] In December 2017, at the second anniversary of the Paris Agreement, President Emmanuel Macron of France arranged the One Planet conference to bring together businesses and governments to strategize about how to meet their Paris goals. At the conference, France's Axa, the world's third largest insurance company, has pledged to divest 2.4 billion Euros in coal assets and 700 million Euros in tar sands. Additionally, it has put in place a policy of not investing in companies with more than 30 percent of their revenue or power coming from coal. Many local governments signed the One Planet charter, which requires local governments to use their purchasing decisions to move away from fossil fuels. Nearly 2,000 nongovernmental organizations (NGOs) from 60 countries called on the World Bank to end its financing of fossil fuel projects and for all governments to end their subsidies for fossil fuels. More than 50 companies, including Adidas, Alliance, H&M, and Phillips signed a declaration calling for fossil fuels to be phased out.[75]

Even Saudi Arabia is taking policy action to address the issue of fossil fuels. In 2016, Saudi Arabia approved a diversification plan, called Saudi Vision 2030, to move the Kingdom away from its oil dependence.[76] It remains to be seen if this plan will be successful, but that fact that a country with a fifth of the world's proven reserves of oil senses an urgency to no longer be so dependent on oil sales says much about the shifting views towards fossil fuels in the era of climate change.

CONCLUSION

More than 80 percent of American energy use relies on fossil fuels. Coal, which is very abundant in the U.S., has been a fuel in use since the 1850s. After 1945, coal use somewhat declined when the U.S. shifted to oil and natural gas as alternative fuels. The primary use for coal today is for the production of electricity. By 2016, more than 90 percent of the coal used was for electric power generation.

The first American oil well was drilled in Titusville, Pennsylvania in 1859. Its primary value was the kerosene it provided for lighting. After the growth of the automobile industry in the early 1900s, gasoline became a main product from crude oil refining. The U.S. gets 37 percent of its energy from oil, more than from any other single source. In 2016, that consumption amounted to more than 19 million barrels of oil per day. Transportation remains the main use of oil in the U.S. today, consuming over 70 percent of all the oil used in the economy.

Natural gas was first used in the U.S. in the early 1820s but did not become widely used until after World War II, when a network of pipelines was laid across the country. After that infrastructure was in place, the use of natural gas vastly increased. Natural gas is used by industry, residential and commercial sectors, and the electric power generating sector. The application of hydraulic fracturing and directional drilling after 2005 revolutionized access to the U.S.'s massive supply of unconventional gas and oil.

One quarter of the world's coal, or about 270 billion tons, is in the U.S. The amount of coal produced in the U.S., however, depends on demand and, since over 90 percent of coal is used by the electric generating sector, demand for U.S. coal is mostly set by that use. In recent years, coal production in the nation has been declining due in large part to cheap and abundant supplies of fracked natural gas.

The EIA reported that the U.S. became the world's largest producer of total petroleum hydrocarbons in 2012, and it has continued to maintain its number one slot since then. The U.S. became the world's largest producer of natural gas in 2009, when U.S. production surpassed that of Russia. The U.S. is likely to become the world's number two producer of crude oil in 2018, surpassing Saudi Arabia and rivaling Russia's production levels. The huge increase in production is due to constant innovation in fracking technology and capability. Because of this revolutionary technology, the IEA predicts that the U.S. would move from being an oil importing nation to an oil and gas exporting nation by the late 2020s.

The use of fossil fuels has many environmental consequences. When coal burns, it emits vast amounts of carbon dioxide into the atmosphere, which drives continued global warming. Coal releases more carbon dioxide into the atmosphere per unit of energy produced than any other fossil fuel. Coal also harms the environment when it is extracted from the ground. Coal is most often removed by surface mining which uses giant machines to remove the top layers of soil and rock to expose the coal. Strip mining and mountaintop removal mining are common. Both ways of extracting the coal are destructive of land, habitat, and water.

Coal emits conventional pollutants including mercury, sulfur dioxide, nitrogen oxides, particulate matter, heavy metals, and volatile organic compounds which form ozone in the lower atmosphere. Air pollution coming from coal combustion is linked to many diseases including asthma, cancer, pulmonary diseases, neurological problems. Burning coal also produces acid rain, associated with the sulfur and nitrous oxides released. Coal ash, created when coal is burned, contains heavy metals and other harmful chemicals. America has experienced a number of coal ash spills that have resulted in contamination of the surrounding lands. The massive coal ash spill of TVA's Kingston Fossil Plant caused EPA to identify more than 40 other potentially hazardous facilities.

While natural gas and oil release less carbon dioxide than coal when burned, they still pose environmental risks. Burning fossil fuels is the main anthropogenic contribution to climate change. Oil and natural gas release methane into the atmosphere, which is 25 times more powerful than carbon dioxide as a global warming gas. Burning oil and gas releases volatile organic compounds that help to produce ground-level ozone pollution. Combustion of oil and gas releases carcinogens, including air toxics such as benzene. Oil and natural gas also pose environmental risks through their retrieval and transport. Oil spills are common and while most spills are small, some are quite large. Since 1969 there have been at least 44 large oil spills in U.S. waters. Fracking for oil and natural gas poses environmental risks of drinking water contamination from the chemicals in the fracking fluid. Air pollutants such as methane, hydrogen sulfide, nitrogen oxides, benzene, formaldehyde, particulate matter, and sulfur dioxide are released as a result of fracking activities.

The energy crises of the 1970s renewed within the U.S. political system a fear of energy insecurity. The political response to the 1973 oil shock resulted in the creation of the IEA, the 55-mile per hour speed limit, CAFE standards, oil price controls, a ban on the export of crude oil, and creation of the Strategic Petroleum Reserve. The political response to the 1978 oil shock resulted in establishing the DOE and efforts to make natural gas more competitive.

Since the end of World War II, every U.S. president has considered Middle Eastern oil security a vital U.S. interest. The Carter Doctrine pledged the use of American military force should any nation attempt to control oil shipments in the Persian Gulf. After the election of Ronald Reagan, energy policy shifted away from government action to a deregulatory approach. During the 1980s and 1990s, stable energy prices and adequate supply kept the federal government out of fossil fuel policy. After the September 11, 2001 attacks, policy shifted back to concern for energy security and the National Energy Policy planning committee was established. Its recommendations resulted in the Energy Policy Act of 2005 and the Energy Independence & Security Act of 2007.

The Obama administration used provisions in the American Recovery and Reinvestment Act of 2009 to increase renewables but also funded carbon capture and sequestration R&D to assist the U.S. coal industry. The wide spread use of fracking during the Obama years massively increased the amount of gas and oil produced in the U.S. Policy actions taken to address climate change resulted in efforts to reduce the burning of coal during the Obama years.

The swing back to emphasizing fossil fuels, especially coal, came quickly in the Trump administration. Efforts included steps to reverse the Clean Power Plan, withdrawal from the Paris Agreement, and increased exploitation of coal, oil, and natural gas on public lands, including offshore. The opening of area 1002 in ANWR reversed a forty-year ban on drilling.

Since the beginning of the 20th century, the U.S. fossil fuel industry has benefited from favorable tax breaks. Producers of fossil fuels received many billions in annual tax breaks in recent years. Supporters of theses tax incentives justify them based upon the importance of the fossil fuel industry to the overall economy. Opponents claim that these polluting industries should get no special tax treatment, rather, they should be made to pay the full cost of the environmental damage their industries produce.

The world relies heavily on fossil fuels. Coal provides about one third of the world's energy supply and is heavily used to produce the world's electricity. There has been an enormous increase in the use of coal worldwide since the turn of the century. China now consumes about half of the world's coal. Oil provides another third of the world's energy supply, and that consumption is expected to increase. It is likely that by 2020 the world will be consuming 100 million barrels of oil per day. Consumption of natural gas worldwide is also expected to increase and will likely nearly double in use by 2040.

The estimated one trillion tons of recoverable coal resources in the world are widely distributed among the nations. That is not the case for oil and natural gas which are found in relatively few nations. Natural gas reserves are in North America, Russia, and the Caspian region. Proven reserves of conventional oil are mainly in the Middle East. Because of increased U.S. production since 2012, international energy markets are experiencing major changes. One of those major changes will be when the U.S. shifts from being an importer of oil to an exporter of both oil and natural gas.

The extraction, transport, and burning of fossil fuels have major environmental global impacts. Extraction is an important source of pollution, releasing harmful materials into the air, land, and water. As global energy demand grows, worldwide fossil fuel extraction is becoming more intensive and destructive. Shipping oil around the world has resulted in many devastating spills. Oil spills and environmentally damaging oil fires have also resulted from the First Gulf War. Burning fossil fuels causes air pollution from particulates, mercury, nitrogen dioxide, sulfur dioxide, and carbon monoxide. The burning of fossil fuels releases carbon dioxide, the main cause of climate change.

Global warming has added another concern to energy security. Nations can no longer just consider availability, accessibility, and affordability of energy supplies. They must also now add consideration of the acceptability of specific fuels, in particular, the acceptability of fossil fuels given their contribution to climate change. Many governments, NGOs, and businesses are in the process of thinking about and dealing with the acceptability of fossil fuels. This reconsideration has resulted in several nations setting a date for the phaseout of gasoline and diesel-powered vehicles. Deliberation has also turned to divestment from fossil fuels and diversification of national economies so that they are no longer dependent on fossil fuels.

---

[1] "U.S. Primary Energy Consumption by Source and Sector, 2017," EIA, accessed August 10, 2018, https://www.eia.gov/totalenergy/data/monthly/pdf/flow/css_2017_energy.pdf.

[2] Roger A. Hinrichs and Merlin Kleinbach, *Energy: Its Use and the Environment* (Fort Worth: Harcourt College Publishers, 2002), 221–222.

[3]   Samuel P. Hays, *A History of Environmental Politics Since 1945* (Pittsburg: University of Pittsburg Press, 2000), 11.

[4]   Hinrichs and Kleinbach, Energy, 222.

[5]   "U.S. Primary Energy Consumption by Source and Sector, 2016."

[6]   "Crude Oil and Petroleum Products Explained," EIA, accessed December 27, 2017, https://www.eia.gov/energyexplained/index.cfm?page=oil_home.

[7]   Hinrichs and Kleinbach, Energy, 206.

[8]   "Gasoline Explained," EIA, accessed December 28, 2017, https://www.eia.gov/energyexplained/index.cfm?page=gasoline_history.

[9]   "Oil: Crude and Petroleum Products Explained," EIA, accessed January 4, 2018, https://www.eia.gov/energyexplained/index.cfm?page=oil_use.

[10] "U.S. Primary Energy Consumption by Source and Sector, 2016."

[11] "Natural Gas Explained," EIA, accessed December 27, 2017, https://www.eia.gov/energyexplained/index.cfm?page=natural_gas_home.

[12] Hinrichs and Kleinbach, Energy, 218.

[13] Dianne Rahm, "Regulating Hydraulic Fracturing in Shale Gas Plays: The Case of Texas," *Energy Policy* 39 (2011): 2975.

[14] "U.S. Primary Energy Consumption by Source and Sector, 2016."

[15] "Primary Energy Production by Source," EIA, accessed December 28, 2017, https://www.eia.gov/totalenergy/data/monthly/pdf/sec1_5.pdf.

[16] "U.S. Leads World in Oil and Gas Production, IEA Says," BBC News, accessed December 28, 2017, http://www.bbc.com/news/business-41988095.

[17] Jeff Goodell, *Big Coal: The Dirty Secret Behind America's Energy Future* (Boston: Houghton Mifflin Company, 2006), xvi.

[18] "U.S. Coal Production and Coal-Fired Electricity Generation Expected to Rise in Near Term," EIA, accessed December 28, 2017, https://www.eia.gov/todayinenergy/detail.php?id=29872.

[19] "U.S. Leads World in Oil and Gas Production, IEA Says.".

[20] Christopher Alessi and Alison Sider, "U.S. Oil Output Expected to Surpass Saudi Arabia, Rivaling Russia for Top Spot," *Wall Street Journal*, January 19, 2018, accessed January 24, 2018, https://www.wsj.com/articles/u-s-crude-production-expected-to-surpass-saudi-arabia-in-2018-1516352405.

[21] Rahm, "Regulating Hydraulic Fracturing in Shale Gas Plays," 2975.

[22] "Carbon Dioxide Emission Factors for Coal," EIA, accessed December 29, 2017, https://www.eia.gov/coal/production/quarterly/co2_article/co2.html.

[23] "How Much of U.S. Carbon Dioxide Emissions are Associated with Electricity Generation?," EIA, accessed December 29, 2017, https://www.eia.gov/tools/faqs/faq.php?id=77&t=11.

[24] "Coal and Air Pollution," Union of Concerned Scientists, accessed January 5, 2018, https://www.ucsusa.org/clean-energy/coal-and-other-fossil-fuels/coal-air-pollution#.Wk_PjkxFzL8.

[25] "Coal Production Using Mountaintop Removal Mining Decreases by 62% Since 2008," EIA, accessed August 10, 2018, https://www.eia.gov/todayinenergy/detail.php?id=21952.

[26] "EPA Response to Kingston TVA Coal Ash Spill," EPA, accessed December 29, 2017, https://www.epa.gov/tn/epa-response-kingston-tva-coal-ash-spill.

[27] Renee Schoof, "EPA List Shows Dangerous Coal Ash Sites Found in 10 States," *McClatchy Newspapers*, June 29, 2009, accessed December 29, 2017, http://www.mcclatchydc.com/news/nation-world/national/article24543913.html.

[28] "How Much Carbon Dioxide is Produced When Different Fuels are Burned?," EIA, accessed December 29, 2017, https://www.eia.gov/tools/faqs/faq.php?id=73&t=11.

[29] "Controlling Air Pollution from the Oil and Gas Industry," EPA, accessed January 5, 2018, https://www.epa.gov/controlling-air-pollution-oil-and-natural-gas-industry/basic-information-about-oil-and-natural-gas.

[30] "Largest Oil Spills Affecting U.S. Waters Since 1969," NOAA, accessed December 29, 2017, https://response.restoration.noaa.gov/oil-and-chemical-spills/oil-spills/largest-oil-spills-affecting-us-waters-1969.html.

[31] Associated Press, "Top 20 Onshore U.S. Oil and Gas Spills Since 2010," *USA Today*, November 17, 2017, accessed December 29, 2017, https://www.usatoday.com/story/news/nation/2017/11/17/top-20-onshore-oil-and-gas-spills/876390001/.

[32] Martha Powers et al., "Popular Epidemiology and "Fracking": Citizens' Concerns Regarding the Economic, Environmental, Health and Social Impacts of Unconventional Natural Gas Drilling Operations," Journal of Community Health 40 (2015): 534.

[33] Christopher D. Kassotis, et al., "Endocrine-Disrupting Chemicals and Oil and Natural Gas Operations: Potential Environmental Contamination and Recommendations to Assess Complex Environmental Mixtures," *Environmental Health Perspectives* 124, no. 3 (March 2016): 256.

[34] M.L. Finkel and A. Law, "The Rush to Drill for Natural Gas: A Five-Year Update," *American Journal of Public Health* 106, no. 10 (2016): 1729.

[35] "Oil Shock of 1973–74," Federal Reserve History, accessed December 30, 2017, https://www.federalreservehistory.org/essays/oil_shock_of_1973_74.

[36] "Oil Shock of 1978–79," Federal Reserve History, accessed December 30, 2017, https://www.federalreservehistory.org/essays/oil_shock_of_1978_79.

[37] "Oil Dependence and U.S. Foreign Policy," Council on Foreign Relations, accessed December 30, 2017, https://www.cfr.org/timeline/oil-dependence-and-us-foreign-policy.

[38] Michael E. Kraft, *Environmental Policy and Politics* (New York: Routledge, 2018), 209.

[39] Daniel Yergin, *The Quest: Energy, Security, and the Remaking of the Modern World* (New York: Penguin Books, 2012), 269.

[40] Yergin, *The Quest*, 129.

[41] Walter A. Rosenbaum, *American Energy: The Politics of 21st Century Policy* (Los Angeles: Sage/CQ Press, 2015), 41–42.

[42] "The Halliburton Loophole," *New York Times*, November 2, 2009, accessed January 2, 2018, http://www.nytimes.com/2009/11/03/opinion/03tue3.html.

[43] Rosenbaum, *American Energy*, 102.

[44] "Summary of the Energy Independence and Security Act," EPA, accessed January 2, 2018, https://www.epa.gov/laws-regulations/summary-energy-independence-and-security-act.

[45] Rosenbaum, *American Energy*, 110.

[46] Coral Davenport, et al., "What is the Clean Power Plan and How Can Trump Repeal It?" *New York Times*, October 10, 2017, accessed January 2, 2018, https://www.nytimes.com/2017/10/10/climate/epa-clean-power-plan.html.

[47] Michael D. Shear, "Trump Will Withdraw U.S. From Paris Climate Agreement," *New York Times*, June 1, 2017, accessed January 2, 2018, https://www.nytimes.com/2017/06/01/climate/trump-paris-climate-agreement.html.

[48] Eric Lipton and Barry Meier, "Under Trump, Coal Mining Gets New Life on Public Lands," *New York Times*, August 6, 2017, accessed January 2, 2018, https://www.nytimes.com/2017/08/06/us/politics/under-trump-coal-mining-gets-new-life-on-us-lands.html.

[49] Elizabeth Hardball, "Arctic National Wildlife Refuge Battle Ends, But Drilling Not A Given," National Public Radio, December 21, 2017, accessed December 29, 2017, https://www.npr.org/2017/12/21/572439797/arctic-national-wildlife-refuge-battle-ends-but-drilling-not-a-given.

[50] Mead Gruver, "Trump Administration Rescinding Rules for Oil, Gas Drilling," USA Today, December 29, 2017, accessed January 2, 2018, https://www.usatoday.com/story/news/politics/2017/12/28/trump-administration-oil-gas-drilling/989066001/.

[51] Alessandra Potenza, "Trump Signs Executive Order to Expand Offshore Oil and Gas Drilling in Arctic and Beyond," *The Verge*, April 28, 2017, accessed January 2, 2018, https://www.theverge.com/2017/4/28/15451652/donald-trump-executive-order-offshore-oil-gas-drilling-climate-change.

[52] Zahra Hirji, "Trump Delivers Two More Wins for Oil and Gas Companies in 2017," *Buzzfeed News*, December 29, 2017, accessed January 2, 2018, https://www.buzzfeed.com/zahrahirji/trump-delivers-two-more-wins-for-oil-gas-in-2017?utm_term=.pwQYLyD3m#.yeYAmPnJq.

[53] Mark J. Perry, "Does the Oil-and-Gas Industry Still Need Tax Breaks?" *Wall Street Journal*, November 13, 2016, accessed January 3, 2018, https://www.wsj.com/articles/does-the-oil-and-gas-industry-still-need-tax-breaks-1479092522.

[54] "Coal," IEA, accessed January 3, 2018, https://www.iea.org/about/faqs/coal/.

[55] "Uses of Coal," World Coal Association, accessed January 4, 2018, https://www.worldcoal.org/coal/uses-coal.

[56] "Coal," IEA, accessed January 3, 2018, https://www.iea.org/about/faqs/coal/.

[57] "Oil," IEA, accessed January 3, 2018, https://www.iea.org/about/faqs/oil/.

[58] "Natural Gas," IEA, accessed January 4, 2018, https://www.eia.gov/outlooks/ieo/pdf/nat_gas.pdf.

[59] Goodell, *Big Coal*, xv.

[60] "Coal," IEA, accessed January 3, 2018, https://www.iea.org/about/faqs/coal/.

[61] "U.S. Leads World in Oil and Gas Production, IEA Says."

[62] "Natural Gas," IEA, accessed January 4, 2018, https://www.eia.gov/outlooks/ieo/pdf/nat_gas.pdf.

[63] Yergin, *The Quest*, 288.

[64] "The Hidden Costs of Fossil Fuels," Union of Concerned Scientists, accessed January 4, 2018, https://www.ucsusa.org/clean-energy/coal-and-other-fossil-fuels/hidden-cost-of-fossils#.Wk5050xFzL8.

[65] "Environmental Risks of Mining," Mission 2016, accessed January 4, 2018, http://web.mit.edu/12.000/www/m2016/finalwebsite/problems/mining.html.

[66] "What Are the Environmental Impacts from Mining & Drilling," *Sciencing*, accessed August 10, 2018, https://sciencing.com/environmental-impacts-mining-drilling-19199.html.

67 "The 13 Largest Oil Spills in History," Mother Nature Network, accessed January 4, 2018, https://www.mnn.com/earth-matters/wilderness-resources/stories/the-13-largest-oil-spills-in-history.

68 Yergin, *The Quest*, 11.

69 Frederica P. Perera, "Multiple Threats to Child Health from Fossil Fuel Combustion: Impacts of Air Pollution and Climate Change," *Environmental Health Perspectives* 125, no.2 (2017): 142.

70 Gavin Bridge, "Energy (In)Security: World-Making in an Age of Scarcity," *The Geographical Journal* 181, no. 4 (2015): 335.

71 "France Bans Fracking and Oil Extraction in all of its Territories," *The Guardian*, December 20, 2017, accessed August 10, 2018, https://www.theguardian.com/environment/2017/dec/20/france-bans-fracking-and-oil-extraction-in-all-of-its-territories.

72 Alanna Petroff, "These Countries Want to Ban Gas and Diesel Cars," *CNN Money*, September 11, 2017, accessed January 5, 2018, http://money.cnn.com/2017/09/11/autos/countries-banning-diesel-gas-cars/index.html.

73 Leada Gore, "Toyota: We're Going to Quit Making Gas-Powered Vehicles," Al.com, October 15, 2015, accessed January 4, 2018, http://www.al.com/news/index.ssf/2015/10/toyota_were_going_to_quit_maki.html.

74 "Governor Cuomo Unveils 9th Proposal of 2018 State of the State; Calling on the NYS Common Fund to Cease All New Investments in Entities with Significant Fossil Fuel-Related Activities and Develop a De-Carbonization Plan for Divesting from Fossil Fuel," Governor's Press Office, December 19, 2017, accessed January 4, 2018, http://www.governor.ny.gov/news/govenor-cuomo-unveils-9th-proposal-2018-state-state-calling-nys-common-fund-cease-all-new.

75 Fiona Harvey, "Calls for Greater Fossil Fuel Divestment at Anniversary of Paris Climate Deal," *The Guardian*, December 12, 2017, accessed January 5, 2018, https://www.theguardian.com/environment/2017/dec/12/calls-for-greater-fossil-fuel-divestment-at-anniversary-of-paris-climate-deal.

76 Ian Black, "Saudi Arabia Approves Ambitious Plan to Move Economy Beyond Oil," *The Guardian*, April 25, 2016, accessed January 5, 2018, https://www.theguardian.com/world/2016/apr/25/saudi-arabia-approves-ambitious-plan-to-move-economy-beyond-oil.

CHAPTER 11

Nuclear Power

INTRODUCTION

The commercial U.S. nuclear industry arose from federal government efforts beginning in the 1950s to promote the new source of power. This chapter explores the birth and development of the nuclear industry in the United States. That development was not without difficulties. Four primary problems plagued and continue to weigh on the expansion of commercial nuclear power in the U.S. The first is the fear of accidents and other safety issues. This fear was largely responsible for vastly increasing the costs of nuclear power plant construction. The second is the unsolved issue of what to do with the nuclear waste. Nuclear waste includes both the spent fuel, created by civilian reactor operations, and the extensive waste left over from the nation's military weapons complex. A closely related issue is assuring the security of fissile materials. Finally, as nuclear facilities reach the end of their usability, the issue of safe decommissioning rises in urgency. Each of these is explored in this chapter.

As the United States adopted nuclear energy, President Eisenhower made it American policy to offer the technology to American allies. The Soviet Union independently developed its own nuclear power technology and spread it to its allies. As a result, nuclear energy began its worldwide expansion. The chapter explores the growth of the industry globally. Just as nuclear energy had domestic detractors, opposition to nuclear energy developed in many countries worldwide. The chapter describes this opposition. Nuclear power use presents the countries that adopt it the need to deal with safety issues and to devise strategies for spent fuel management. In a worldwide context, spent fuel management also includes some consideration of the enormous military waste associated with the former Soviet Union. Each of these is discussed in this chapter.

DOMESTIC CONCERNS

The U.S. entered the atomic age, and later the nuclear age, as a result of efforts to develop new weapons during the Second World War. In the aftermath of the war, experimental reactors at Oak Ridge and Idaho Falls National Laboratories demonstrated that nuclear power could produce electricity, in 1948 and 1951, respectively. President Eisenhower was determined to see the technology, that had ushered in the era of highly destructive weaponry, put to beneficial uses. In 1953, he gave his "Atoms for Peace" speech, which began a U.S.-led initiative to show how this technology could help the world's people. By 1955, development of nuclear power had advanced rapidly, leading Louis Strauss, the Chair of the Atomic Energy Commission, to forecast that nuclear power would soon be "too cheap to meter." In 1958, the Shippington plant, based on federal government research and development (R&D), began generating electricity, becoming the first commercial reactor in operation.[1]

The Development of the U.S. Nuclear Energy Industry

Nuclear power grew quickly in the 1960s and 1970s in large part because of heavy promotion of the industry by the federal government. Part of this promotion was the support provided by the Price-Anderson Act of 1957 and its later revisions. The act provided the industry with a cash pool from which they could draw to compensate the public in the event of a nuclear accident. The act limited total liability for the industry in the event of an accident. The Price-

Anderson Act was initially put in place to allow the nuclear industry to begin to develop by giving the young industry protections against claims they might have to pay out in the event of a serious nuclear accident. However, the Price-Anderson Act has been repeatedly extended, most recently through the Energy Policy Act of 2005 through 2025.[2]

Nuclear power plants use fission to split uranium atoms inside a reactor to create heat. The heat is used to produce steam which turns a turbine and produces electricity. Nuclear power generation produces no carbon dioxide, nitrogen oxides, or sulfur dioxide.[3] This clean air fact of nuclear power, however, did not mean that environmentalists embraced the new technology. Opposition to the industry coincided with the rise of the environmental movement in the 1960s and 1970s. Environmental groups were more concerned with the spent fuel, a by-product of nuclear energy production, that can cause serious environmental contamination if not handled appropriately. Despite this opposition, the industry grew rapidly in its early years due to federal government support. But this was to change rapidly in 1979 with the partial meltdown at Pennsylvania's Three Mile Island (TMI) plant.[4]

After the TMI accident, the American public became increasingly skeptical of nuclear power. However, 47 reactors that had been approved for construction before 1977 came on line in the late 1970s and 1980s.[5] But the TMI accident had an enormous impact on the industry. Some reactors under construction during 1979 were halted, while plans for another 124 reactors were cancelled.[6] The American public's doubt was further reinforced over the years by spectacular and devastating events occurring in foreign nations. In 1986, the catastrophic nuclear accident at Chernobyl, in Ukraine, reminded the public of the danger posed by nuclear power.[7]

By 2010, increased concern over climate change, along with new supportive federal government actions, caused many proponents of the industry to hope for a revitalization. The Energy Policy Act of 2005 signaled considerable Bush administration support for expansion of the nuclear industry. The act provided $18.5 billion in financial incentives for construction of advanced nuclear plants. In his 2010 State of the Union Address, Barack Obama endorsed growth of the nuclear industry. But all this momentum was rapidly reversed with the March 11, 2011 Fukushima Daiichi nuclear power plant accident in Japan.[8] The accident caused three meltdowns and significant radioactive releases, resulting in the evacuation of more than 160,000 people.[9]

The Trump administration also tried to provide assistance to the nuclear industry that found itself struggling in the wake of Fukushima and competition from cheap natural gas. Rick Perry, Secretary of Energy, proposed to subsidize any power plant that had a 90-day supply of fuel on site. The proposal was based on the argument that the electricity grid would be made more stable by saving the coal and nuclear plants that had plans to close in 2017. Eight nuclear plants had announced planned retirements. The subsidy would have cost taxpayers over $10 billion a year. Surprisingly, the Republican-controlled Federal Energy Regulatory Commission (FERC) unanimously rejected Perry's proposal, saying there was no evidence that the scheduled retirements of either coal of nuclear plants threatened grid stability.[10]

Despite the beleaguered history of the commercial nuclear industry, in 2017, the U.S. continued to operate 99 nuclear reactors, with two new plants under construction, and several more in the planning stage. These new plants are expected to come online by 2020 or soon thereafter. The licensing of these new plants marked the end of a 30-year period in which few reactors were built. In 2017, the U.S. was the world's largest producer of nuclear power, accounting for 30 percent of total world output.[11] Nuclear power, however, only contributes about 9 percent of the overall energy used in the U.S.[12]

Environmental Concerns and the U.S. Nuclear Industry

Safety. The Nuclear Regulatory Commission (NRC) publicly announced after the Fukushima disaster, that it did not have adequate information to determine the threat posed by earthquakes to the nation's nuclear plants. This is a serious matter for the industry because the key reason for cost escalation in the construction of new plants is fear of reactor safety. Despite efforts of advocates to streamline the permitting process to reduce costs, fear of public and environmental safety continues to keep the permitting process both lengthy and costly.[13]

In 2012, Allison Macfarlane, chair of the NRC, also noted that in a post-Fukushima world, nuclear plants need to consider more than just earthquakes. Other primary risks include flooding, tornadoes, and hurricanes. In the aftermath of Fukushima, NRC issued new orders and required new safety measures to assure that an event similar to Fukushima could not happen in the U.S. Plants were ordered to evaluate their vulnerability in terms of both floods and earthquakes.[14]

While some environmentalists favor nuclear energy because of its lack of contribution to climate change, many environmental groups are united in their opposition to the nuclear industry. They are particularly concerned with safety issues, calling attention to the possibility of an accident causing a large release of radioactivity. They also argue that even during normal operations, nuclear plants discharge radiation to the air and water. They are concerned that the culture of secrecy that surrounded the development of nuclear weapons was adopted by the commercial nuclear industry and that such a culture prevents revelation of routine discharges. Aging nuclear reactors are also considered a threat, as materials break down over time. Ohio's David-Besse reactor was an example of this safety concern. In 2002, the plant came very close to a catastrophe due to corrosion that had eaten a large hole in the reactor vessel. It was shut down for several years to make repairs.[15]

Commercial Nuclear Waste. The fuel assemblies in commercial nuclear reactors consist of long, narrow metal alloy tubes clustered together. They contain uranium oxide pellets. After several years of use, the fuel assemblies build up a large quantity of radioactive isotopes, including plutonium. Once enough of these isotopes accumulate, the fuel assemblies are termed spent fuel and need to be removed from the reactor. Once removed from the reactor, the spent fuel rods can be sent to a chemical separation, or reprocessing, facility where the plutonium is extracted, fabricated into MOX fuel, and burned in a suitable reactor. Alternatively, the spent fuel can be considered waste. In the U.S., most spent fuel has not been reprocessed and has accumulated since the 1950s. Spent fuel generates a large amount of heat and must be cooled. Since the initial construction of U.S. commercial nuclear power plants, spent fuel has been stored deep underwater in cooling ponds constructed adjacent to the power plants.[16] Eventually the waste needs to be deposited in a permanent repository, where it can be isolated from the environment for thousands of years.

When the commercial nuclear power industry began in the 1950s, the problem of waste disposal was not carefully considered and had a low priority. Scientists and engineers at the time viewed waste as a technological problem of secondary importance and put their full efforts into reactor design and development. Neither the Atomic Energy Commission (AEC) nor its successor organizations, the Energy Research and Development Administration (ERDA) and the Department of Energy (DOE), had been able to design a suitable disposal facility and so spent fuel waste remained on site at the power plants in cooling ponds. By the 1970s, however, anti-nuclear environmental activists began to focus on the issue. Their key concern was the potential effect a radioactive release could have on human health and the environment. In 1976, they succeeded on getting the issue on the ballot by linking power plant construction to the availability of a permanent waste disposal site. By 1978, more than 30 states had passed legislation dealing with radioactive waste and in many of those states the legislation they passed banned the construction of a disposal site in their state. Congress saw the need to put in place an orderly procedure to find a national geological repository for the permanent disposal of the nation's nuclear waste, and so passed the Nuclear Waste Policy Act of 1982 (NWPA).[17]

The NWPA required that the federal government take possession of the nation's commercial waste by 1998. Commercial power plants were to contribute to a Nuclear Waste Fund to pay for the costs of waste disposal. The act established a process by which DOE would recommend to the president a group of sites to become permanent repositories and the president would select two from that list. However, most states did not want to be under consideration for such a site and controversy ensued. As a result, in 1987, Congress abandoned the process specified in the NWPA, and simply named Yucca Mountain in Nevada to be the site for the first repository. This action was fought by the people and politicians of Nevada. That resistance slowed the process of actually establishing the disposal site, forcing the 1998 date to be revised. In 2002, the Bush administration pushed back the date to 2010, even though commercial power plants had already paid more than $3 billion in taxes (the tax was later struck down by the courts). Nevada sued, and the matter was relegated to court struggles until 2010, when DOE's Secretary Chu recommended to President Obama that the repository plan be terminated. The president subsequently took Yucca Mountain's line item out of the federal budget.[18] After 7 years of being off the table, Donald Trump's FY 2018 budget once again listed the line item. Republicans generally agree that failure to open the repository is one of the key problems stalling the development of the nuclear power industry.[19]

The time that the spent fuel waste has rested in cooling ponds has raised some concerns. The spent fuel in these ponds is tightly packed together and loss of water from one of these pools could result in a large radioactive release to the environment.[20] A secondary concern is that terrorists might be tempted to steal some of this nuclear material to use in a domestic attack. To discuss these concerns, a Blue Ribbon

Commission was formed. The 2012 Blue Ribbon Commission Report recommended that the government establish a series of geographically distributed federal government-run sites that could take the spent fuel from the cooling ponds. Once relocated, the spent fuel could be put into safer and stronger dry casks. This would not substitute for a national repository, but it would provide an interim alternative to the status quo. Dry casks are engineered to survive floods, fires, and even airplane impacts. They are 100-ton structures that are difficult to steal and require no cooling systems or power.[21]

Military Nuclear Waste. The U.S. produced atomic, and later nuclear, weapons beginning with the World War II Manhattan Project. To do so, the U.S. created the nuclear weapons complex, a series of sites dispersed across the U.S. each with a specific task in the many steps involved in making a nuclear device. Those steps included uranium mining and milling, uranium refining, uranium enrichment, uranium foundry, fuel and target fabrication, plutonium production reactors, chemical separation, nuclear components, assembly and testing. The complex has generated much nuclear waste and contamination. By the DOE's own accounting, the complex includes "unique radiation hazards, unprecedented volumes of contaminated water and soil, and a vast number of contaminated structures ranging from reactors to chemical plants for extracting nuclear materials to evaporation ponds."[22]

The largest portion of nuclear waste remaining from the production of nuclear weapons resulted from the production of plutonium and highly enriched uranium. Of all the steps in nuclear weapons production, chemical separation accounts for the majority of the waste and contamination. Chemical separation activities account for 85 percent of the radioactivity generated, 71 percent of the contaminated water, 33 percent of contaminated soil, and 24 percent of the contaminated surplus facilities.[23]

Most of the DOE's chemical separation activities took place at the Hanford Nuclear Reservation in Washington state. In its 177 aging steel tanks, stored underground for radiation shielding, rests more than 200,000 m³ of radioactive chemical waste. More than one third of these tanks have leaked, releasing vast amounts of radioactive materials into soil and groundwater flowing toward the Columbia River. By 2002, the federal government had spent more than $5 billion dollars to clean the site and in that year, the DOE believed it would have to spend another $40 billion to finish the cleanup.[24] That estimate proved optimistic. In 2016, the DOE concluded that it would take another $107.7 billion and the work would not be completed until 2060.[25]

In 2015, the National Governor's Conference issued a report to the nation's governors regarding the cleanup of the entire complex—which affects many states. The report said that the cleanup of the nuclear weapons complex is the single largest environmental cleanup effort in the world. The effort is expected to continue into 2070 and is expected to cost as much as $350 billion (in 2015 dollars).[26]

The Security of Fissile Materials. The U.S. has long thought about the security of fissile materials. The decision not to reprocess spent fuel was based largely on security concerns. Reprocessing, or chemical separation, strips the plutonium and uranium from the nuclear waste that comprises spent fuel rods. Once separated, the plutonium can be refabricated by mixing it with metal oxide and re-used as MOX fuel in reactors capable of burning it; or, the plutonium can be used to make nuclear weapons. In the 1970s, the U.S. decided that reprocessing would create too much of a risk for nuclear proliferation and decided to dispose of spent fuel after one-time use, eventually storing it in a national repository yet to be built. This decision was aligned with U.S. policy to prevent the spread of nuclear weapons through the Nuclear Non-Proliferation Treaty. In a post-September 11 world, terrorism is also a major concern. Less than 20 pounds of plutonium can make a simple nuclear weapon. If the plutonium is laced in spent fuel, it is far more difficult for a terrorist to steal than if it is separated through reprocessing.[27]

Decommissioning. When a nuclear power plant reaches the end of its useful life, the NRC requires it to be decommissioned. This involves removing all radioactive materials from the site including structures and their contents plus equipment as well as any radioactive soil or water on the site. The money for this operation comes from a financial instrument created before the plant was licensed, guaranteeing funds for end-of-life cleanup. Decommissioning is expensive, costing about half a billion dollars per plant. This amount of money may constitute as much as one quarter of the cost of building the plant in the first place. The NRC is concerned that companies have inadequate financial guarantees in place to pay for decommissioning.[28]

GLOBAL CONCERNS

The Birth and Development of the Global Nuclear Power Industry

As the U.S. entered the atomic and later nuclear age, so did the world. President Eisenhower's "Atoms for Peace" speech was followed with a 1955 conference held in Geneva that publicly displayed reactor technology, and during which the U.S. offered assistance to American allies to help them develop their own nuclear industries.[29] This conference, which at the time was the most widely attended gathering of scientists and engineers, confirmed to a large audience that nuclear energy was possible and helped drive adoption of the emerging technology. Cooperation across Europe was also driven by the Suez Crisis of 1956. Fearing loss of access to oil, the foreign ministers of France, Germany, and Italy set up a committee to set targets for installed nuclear power generation.[30]

The Soviet Union had done much work on atom bomb production during World War II, and by 1946 the Institute of Physics and Power Engineering was established to develop nuclear power technology. In 1954, the Soviet Union successfully operated the Atom Mirny (peaceful atom) reactor which produced electricity until it was repurposed as a research reactor in 1959.[31]

Also, in 1954, the first nuclear submarine, the *Nautilus*, was commissioned. It had been designed and developed under the leadership of U.S. Admiral Hyman Rickover. One of the key innovations was that it used a pressurized water reactor (PWR), which would become the model for civilian nuclear power reactor designs.[32] The Shippingport, Pennsylvania nuclear reactor which was started up in 1957, used the PWR designed by Rickover. In 1960, Westinghouse designed its first commercial nuclear PWR using Rickover's innovation. In addition, the boiling water reactor (BWR) was developed by Argonne National Laboratory and General Electric used this design for its first commercial nuclear reactor.[33]

Canada and Britain went in different directions, but both had commercial nuclear reactors in the 1950s. Canada used heavy-water as a coolant rather than light-water as did the U.S.'s PWRs and BWRs. Canada's CANDU reactor was the result. The British used gas rather than water as a coolant.[34] France used a gas-graphite design for their first nuclear reactor which launched in 1956 but later adopted the PWR. In 1964, two Soviet nuclear power plants were commissioned. In 1972, Kazakhstan produced the first commercial fast neutron reactor. But worldwide, most countries chose to adopt the U.S. light-water PWRs or BWRs.[35]

By the early 1960s, demonstration nuclear power plants were operating in most major industrial nations. In 1963, the U.S. introduced the idea of "turnkey" plants with a guaranteed fixed price that was more competitive than coal or oil plants. The result was that by 1967, U.S. utilities alone had ordered more than 50 plants. The problem was that each of these plants lost the manufacturer money due to aggressive low bidding to beat out oil and coal. Turnkey plants were soon abandoned slowing the growth of the industry. The rise of environmental apprehension associated with the new nuclear industry also slowed its development in the 1970s, both in the U.S. and across Europe. Green political parties grew in Europe in the 1970s and all were anti-nuclear. The TMI accident virtually ended orders for new plants in the U.S. by the end of 1970s and worldwide demand also slowed. In 1978, an

Austrian referendum rejected nuclear power, a similar referendum in Ireland stopped nuclear power there, and Sweden's voters approved a measure to phase out its nuclear power plants. Chernobyl broadened the opposition in the 1980s. Deregulation of electricity in the U.S. and Europe in the 1990s pushed prices down, making investment in expensive nuclear power plants risky. Nuclear power became very attractive to Asia and developing countries in the beginning in the 1990s, however, because energy demand growth was rapid and the need to deal with pollution coming from fossil fuel-fired plants was increasing in importance. China, India, Japan, and Korea all expanded their nuclear capacity rapidly, and that expansion continued into the 21st century.[36]

In 2017, nuclear power provided 11 percent of the world's electricity production and in several countries, nuclear power provided considerably more of their electricity, including France (72 percent), Slovakia (54 percent), Ukraine (52 percent), Belgium (51 percent), Hungary (51 percent), Sweden (40 percent), Slovenia (35 percent), Bulgaria (35 percent), Switzerland (34 percent), Finland (33 percent), Armenia (31 percent), South Korea (30 percent), and the Czech Republic (29 percent).[37] As of 2018, 31 countries worldwide were operating over 447 nuclear reactors and 60 new plants were under construction.[38] The regional discussion that follow shows the worldwide distribution of operating reactors in 2018 and expected growth of the nuclear industry.

North, South and Central America. The United States, with 99 nuclear reactors, had the most of any nation in 2018. The U.S. had 2 reactors under construction and another 4 on order or planned. Planned status indicates that approvals and funding have been assured, making operational capacity likely within 8 to 10 years. Canada had 19 functioning reactors and another 2 planned. South and Central America had several functioning nuclear reactors, with 3 in Argentina, 2 in Brazil, 2 in Mexico. In addition, Argentina had 3 under construction or planned, and Brazil had 5 under construction or planned.[39]

The future of nuclear power in the United States is unclear, in part because Westinghouse, the American nuclear power subsidiary of Toshiba, ended its nuclear plant construction business in 2017. The reasons may be attributed to several causes, including the slowing demand for electricity, cheap natural gas, and the availability of renewables. In the aftermath of Fukushima, safety issues are also on both the U.S. and Canadian public agenda.[40] Nuclear power in South and Central America is concentrated in only 3 countries and even in those countries that have nuclear power, it makes up only a small part of their energy generation. Like in the U.S. and Canada, post-Fukushima anxiety persists in South and Central America.[41]

Europe. A large region, with a large population, Europe had many nuclear reactors in 2018. Armenia had 1 operating reactor and 1 planned. Belarus had 2 under construction and 2 planned. Belgium had 7 operating reactors. Bulgaria had 2 operating reactors. The Czech Republic had 6 operating, and 2 planned. Finland had 4 operating reactors, 1 under construction, and 1 planned. France, with its heavy reliance on nuclear power, had 58 operating reactors and 1 under construction. Germany had 7 operating reactors. Hungary had 4 operating reactors and 2 planned. The Netherlands had 1 operating reactor. Poland had 6 planned reactors. Romania had 2 operating reactors and 2 planned. Slovakia had 4 operating reactors and 2 under construction. Slovenia had 1 operating reactor. Spain had 7 operating reactors. Sweden had 8 operating reactors. Switzerland had 5 operating reactors. Turkey had 4 planned reactors. Ukraine had 15 operating reactors and 2 planned. The United Kingdom had 15 operating reactors and 11 planned.[42]

The future of nuclear energy seems to be threatened in several European nations. Germany announced plans to phase out nuclear power in the wake of the Fukushima disaster, as have Switzerland, Spain, and Belgium. Under the leadership of Emmanuel Macron, even France is shifting to reduce its reliance on nuclear power. Macron seeks to bring down the share of electric generation from nuclear power to 50 percent. Italy, Austria, and Portugal have repeated their desire to stay nuclear-free. The U.K., in contrast, is adding nuclear capacity, as are Hungary and Turkey.[43]

Asia. Asia is a large, populous region with many nuclear reactors as of 2018. Bangladesh had 1 reactor under construction and 1 planned. China had a heavy reliance on nuclear power with 38 operating reactors, 20 under construction, and 39 planned. India had 22 operating reactors, 6 under construction, and 19 planned. Indonesia had 1 planned. Japan had 42 operating reactors, 2 under construction, and 9 planned. South Korea had 24 operating, 4 under construction, and 1 planned. Pakistan had 5 operating and 2 under construction. Russia had 35 operating reactors, 7 under construction, and 26 planned. Viet Nam had 4 planned reactors.[44]

Despite public concern over Fukushima, nuclear energy use continues to expand in Asia. After adopting comprehensive security policies in the wake of Fukushima, nuclear growth in China is ambitious. Projections suggest that by 2030, China will have 110 nuclear power plants in use, overtaking the U.S. for the largest number of reactors. India, also, is planning a wide expansion of nuclear energy but threats exist in some locations. Two of its plants are located on the southeast coast, which is prone to tsunamis. Pakistan also has plants operating in flood-prone and earthquake-prone areas. Nevertheless, Pakistan desires expansion of its nuclear power capacity. South Korea has a heavy reliance on nuclear power, but the public is growing concerned about expansion, not only because of Fukushima, but also because of 2012 and 2013 scandals over fake safety certificates.[45] Russia is working toward nuclear expansion, including deployment of advanced reactor designs. Russia also has a strategy that includes the export of nuclear goods and services to other countries.[46]

Middle East. In 2017, Egypt had 2 planned reactors. Iran had 1 operating reactor, and 4 planned. Jordan had 2 planned. The UAE had 4 reactors under construction.[47] At least part of the demand for these plants is driven by the need to desalinate water. The UAE, for instance, desalinates large amounts of water, with 96 percent of its water consumption coming from 70 desalinization plants in the country. If the fuel for desalinization efforts continues to come from fossil fuels, their contribution to climate change will be very great, especially as population increases and more water needs to be desalinated. Coupling nuclear power with desalination may be the only way to meet the regions vast need for clean water without extensive contribution to climate change.[48] Saudi Arabia, in 2017, continued to suffer from electricity shortages. This situation resulted in the adoption of a new nuclear policy, with the Kingdom deciding it will build 16 nuclear power plants over the next several decades. If the Kingdom implements this policy, it will be one of the next Middle Eastern nations to have a commercial nuclear industry.[49]

Africa. Only one country in Africa had nuclear power in 2017. That was South Africa, with 2 operating reactors.[50] However, at the general conference of the International Atomic Energy Agency (IAEA) in 2015, ten African nations revealed their desire to create nuclear power programs. However, the large upfront costs of nuclear power along with the safety and security issues may deter this development.[51]

Environmental Concerns and the Global Nuclear Industry

Safety. One of the worst nuclear disasters occurred on April 26, 1986, when a power surge during a reactor systems test resulted in a massive explosion that blew the roof off of unit 4 of the nuclear power station in Chernobyl, Ukraine. There was a massive radioactive release and fire. Emergency responders used helicopters to dump sand and boron onto the reactor debris to extinguish the fire and prevent further nuclear reactions. Within weeks after the accident, the remaining structure was covered in a concrete structure, called a sarcophagus, to limit the release of more radioactive material into the environment. The accident resulted in deaths from radiation exposure for workers and first responders. Twenty eight workers died from severe radiation exposure within a few months of the accident. More than another 100 workers suffered severe radiation sickness. Many of the cleanup workers also were exposed to elevated levels of radiation. The accident caused contamination to spread mainly across Belarus, Ukraine, and Russia.[52] Chernobyl remains uninhabited today, with continued high levels of radiation.

The destruction of the Fukushima Daiichi nuclear power plant occurred after a magnitude 9.0 earthquake on March 11, 2011. The earthquake caused a 15-meter tsunami that hit the plant. As a result of the tsunami, power was disrupted and so cooling of three of the plant's reactors could not be maintained. Within days, all three cores melted down, precipitating massive releases of radiation to both the air and water. More than 160,000 people were evacuated from their homes due to the accident.[53]

Environmental organizations point to a number of instances of commercial nuclear power plant problems that have not received the same attention as disasters like Chernobyl or Fukushima. For instance, in 1999, at Japan's Tokai-mura nuclear fuel plant, two workers died from radiation exposure. In 2000, it was revealed that safety data and inspections had been manipulated at more than 10 Japanese reactors to avoid expensive repairs. In 2006, Japanese courts ordered a nuclear reactor shut down when it was revealed that it could not withstand an earthquake. In 2003, French nuclear safety officials ordered the shutdown of two reactors sited on the Rhone River that were damaged due to flooding. In 2000, the Sellafield nuclear fuel processing facility in the U.K. was found to have fundamentally flawed safety procedures in place. The Sellafield MOX plant was also found to have violated safety standards.[54]

Spent Fuel Management. There are two ways to deal with spent fuel. The first strategy is the one that the U.S. uses, which is, to use the fuel once (once-through cycle) and consider it waste after the first use. This strategy requires cooling of the spent fuel in cooling ponds for 5 to 10 years, followed by disposal in a storage facility, which may be a temporary dry storage facility, but eventually must be a permanent high-level waste disposal facility. The second strategy involves reprocessing the spent fuel (twice-through cycle). This strategy requires initial cooling in cooling ponds, followed by transport to a reprocessing facility. Reprocessing is typically done using the PUREX (plutonium and uranium redox extraction) process, which separates the plutonium and uranium but leaves behind minor actinides and fission products. The minor actinides and fission products are stored in glass through a process called vitrification, and then handled as high-level waste. Eventually this vitrified waste will go to a permanent disposal facility. The extracted plutonium is recycled into fuel by mixing it with metal oxide at a MOX fuel fabrication plant. The resulting MOX fuel can be burned in reactors designed for MOX. In 2017, these reactors comprised about 10 percent of the world's reactors. The separated uranium can be reused after re-enrichment, however, it is more radioactive than naturally mined uranium, so using it would require reactors with extra shielding and the adoption of additional protection procedures. This makes reuse of the recovered uranium too expensive for reactors technology deployed in 2018, and so it is typically stored.[55]

Historically, the reason for development of reprocessing technologies was to recover the plutonium for weapons manufacture. The civilian use of reprocessing, along with the development of reactors that can burn MOX fuel, enables up to 30 percent more energy to be gained from the original mined uranium. The advantages of reprocessing, as opposed to direct disposal of spent waste, include reduced natural uranium use, decreased volume of high-level waste, and reduced radioactivity in the waste that is produced. Additionally, the radioactivity in reprocessed waste after about 100 years decreases much more rapidly than the radioactivity from once-through cycle waste. The disadvantages of reprocessing include the necessary addition of several processing steps, fuel transportation, increased risk of proliferation, and increased cost. As of 2017, about 100,000 tons of fuel from commercial nuclear reactors had been reprocessed in facilities in France, the U.K., Russia, India, and Japan.[56] However, many countries have reprocessed their spent fuel without building a reprocessing facility of their own, by shipping their waste to existing facilities. For example, Russia has agreements to reprocess and store nuclear waste from plants they have constructed or are constructing in other countries. These include Egypt, Turkey, Belarus, Hungary and Finland.[57]

Regardless of which strategy is used to manage spent fuel, the need for permanent disposal of waste remains. Over the years that the nuclear industry has existed, many final disposal methods have been considered. Some have been rejected due to political or safety issues, such as disposal in the deep seabed. Disposal in stable geological formations has been debated and generally approved by international organizations worldwide. The consensus among nations is that the most preferable final disposal method is for each nation to have a deep geological repository. The performance of such a deep geological repository depends on a multi-barrier concept to contain the radioactive material and isolate it from the environment for many thousands of years. Two kinds of barriers are generally considered. The first is a rock formation that serves as a natural geological barrier. The second is an engineered barrier, the purpose of which is to protect the radioactive material from intrusion by water, corrosion, and other predictable problems that might degrade the isolation.[58]

Nations began studying the construction and maintenance of deep geological repositories in the 1960s. The first investigations into using salt mines for permanent repositories were undertaken in U.S., in 1960, and in Germany, in 1965. Sweden explored using granite rock isolation in 1977. In 1980, Belgium studied using underground clay formations. In 1983, Switzerland considered the feasibility of using crystalline rock in the Alps for storage. Since then, many nations have undertaken studies of potential formations suitable for permanent storage of high-level waste. In the U.S., efforts to develop Yucca Mountain have stumbled, leaving the U.S. without a permanent repository. As of 2016, in Europe, only Finland had begun construction of a deep geological repository. Sweden had an application for a final repository under review. As of 2017, many of the nations most aggressively building their nuclear power industries have no firm plans for a repository. China will not build a laboratory to study the issue until 2020 but hopes to have a repository by 2050. India has not yet even settled on a methodology.[59]

Management of spent fuel also extends to military spent fuel and other contamination. Like the U.S., Russia has an enormous environmental legacy from its Cold War production of nuclear weapons. In an attempt to clean its nuclear weapons complex in the Arctic, the country is sending its spent fuel rods from Andreeva Bay to its Mayak reprocessing plant in Ozersk. Ozersk was the center of the U.S.S.R.'s nuclear weapon's program. Two shipments of spent fuel happened in 2017. This program is partially funded by Norway, Japan, and Europe since the mid-1990s. In 2017, 26,000 containers of spent fuel in northern Russia awaited reprocessing. In addition, there are thousands of containers of other nuclear waste, reactors, and decommissioned nuclear submarines still sitting in Arctic waters. Many documented releases of radioactive material have occurred. In 2014, Russia's Rosatom pledged to clean up Russia's nuclear waste within 25 years, but action has been slow due to lack of funding and lack of storage areas to hold the waste coming from the weapons complex. Russia has storage facilities in Siberia and in the Urals.[60]

CONCLUSION

Atomic weapons developed by the United States during the Second World War provided the foundation for the development of peaceful nuclear power in the 1950s. By 1958, the U.S. had developed commercial nuclear power. The U.S. industry grew rapidly in the 1960s and 1970s, helped by federal government subsidies and support.

Opposition to nuclear power overlapped with the rise of the environmental movement in the 1960s and 1970s. Environmental groups focused on the threats posed by spent fuel and the fear of an accident. Their fears were realized in 1979 with the partial meltdown at Three Mile Island plant. After the accident, American public opinion quickly turned against nuclear power. Despite the growing public sentiment, 47 reactors that had been approved for construction before the TMI accident came on line in the late 1970s and 1980s. But the accident profoundly affected the growth of the industry. Several reactors under construction were stopped and plans for others were pulled. Anti-nuclear public opinion was strengthened in the wake of Chernobyl in the mid-1980s. In America, the industry stagnated. Increased concern of climate change in the 21st century, along with new supportive federal government actions of the Bush and Obama administrations, caused many advocates of the industry to hope for a nuclear renewal. Their hopes were dashed with the Fukushima Daiichi nuclear power plant accident. Despite support from the Trump administration, competition from cheap natural gas makes investment in new nuclear facilities unlikely.

Environmental issues plague the industry. The chief concern is safety. The public fears the release of radioactive substances, should an accident occur. Three Mile Island, Chernobyl, and Fukushima cast a long shadow. Public demand for safety creates layers of permits and approvals, slowing new plant construction, and increasing cost. Additionally, many environmental groups call attention to the threats posed by aging plants, pointing to examples like Ohio's David-Besse plant, whose reactor vessel was nearly compromised by corrosion.

By far the clearest environmental complaint is tied to the question: What do you do with the waste? The issue of spent fuel was initially trivialized by a growing industry more concerned with reactor design and performance. The waste problem was not given much thought. By the 1970s, anti-nuclear environmental activists united around the concern, getting legislation passed in several states tying approval of new nuclear power plant construction to the availability of a permanent waste disposal site. Congress eventually acted, passing the Nuclear Waste Policy Act, to set up a process to site a national repository. The opposition of most states to being considered for housing such a repository resulted in bitter controversy. In the end, Congress abandoned the process for site selection it had set up, and selected Yucca Mountain, Nevada much to the chagrin of Nevadans. After many years of court battles, the Obama administration took the Yucca

Mountain line item out of the federal budget. The Trump administration, however, reintroduced it in the FY2018 budget. The future of Yucca Mountain remains uncertain.

Lacking a national repository, spent fuel waste has accumulated in cooling ponds, raising concerns. It is tightly packed in the cooling ponds and loss of water from one of these ponds could result in a large radioactive release to the environment. To remedy the situation, a 2012 Blue Ribbon Commission Report recommended the establishment of a number of regional federally run sites to receive the spent fuel from the cooling ponds and hold it in dry cask storage.

The U.S. also has a major problem associated with nuclear waste from the nuclear weapons complex. While the nuclear weapons complex's most contaminated site is the Hanford Nuclear Reservation in Washington state, the entire complex affects many states. The National Governor's Conference report of 2015 called the cleanup the single largest environmental effort in the world, with anticipated costs of $350 billion and a time frame expected to last more than another 50 years.

The threat of proliferation is another issue which looms large for the nuclear industry. The U.S. decision, made in the 1970s, against reprocessing was largely based on the fear that the separated plutonium could be used to spread nuclear weapons. Later the fear that terrorists could gain access to plutonium also became a concern.

Decommissioning nuclear power plants when they reach the end of their useful life is becoming more of an environmental issue as U.S. facilities age. Part of the concern is owed to the fact that few plant owners have set aside sufficient cash to pay for the removal of radioactive materials at the sites.

As the U.S. entered the atomic age, so did the world. President Eisenhower's policy elaborated in the "Atoms for Peace" speech served to spread the nuclear industry to American allies. The Soviet Union did the same for its allies. The result was that from the 1950s onward, many nations began to develop and use nuclear energy.

Within a decade of their initial appearance, nuclear power plants were operating in most major industrial nations. Utilities were ordering and building plants. The growth of environmental concerns associated with the new nuclear industry slowed its growth worldwide. The accident at Three Mile Island virtually ended growth in the U.S. Many European countries, including Austria, Ireland and Sweden, pushed back against nuclear power. Chernobyl widened the opposition to nuclear power in the 1980s. But at the same time nuclear power was becoming less popular in the U.S. and Europe, it became very attractive to Asia and developing countries. China, India, Japan, and Korea all expanded their nuclear industries quickly in the 1990s. Growth continued into the 21st century.

The future of the nuclear power industry worldwide varies from nation to nation. While the U.S. in 2017 had more nuclear power capacity than any other country, the future of nuclear power in the United States is unclear. Westinghouse filed for bankruptcy protection in 2017 due to the slowing demand for electricity, and the availability of cheap natural gas and renewables. Fukushima renewed safety concerns. The future of nuclear power in South and Central America is in question. It is concentrated in only 3 countries, where it contributes only a small part of their energy generation. The future of nuclear energy is threatened in several European nations, including Germany, Switzerland, Spain, and Belgium. Although France remains committed to nuclear energy, it is expected to reduce its heavy reliance on it. Italy, Austria, and Portugal continue to stay nuclear-free. The U.K., however, is growing its commercial nuclear industry, as are Hungary and Turkey. Asia is where the nuclear industry is likely to flourish in the future. China is expected to have 110 nuclear power plants operational by 2030, passing the U.S. for the largest number of reactors. India, Pakistan, and Russia are expanding their nuclear industry. Russia also plans to export nuclear goods and services to countries around the globe. The industry may also grow in the Middle East and Africa.

Two environmental concerns impact the nuclear industry and its growth worldwide. Safety remains a key issue for the nuclear industry worldwide, as two of the worst nuclear accidents, Chernobyl and Fukushima, continue to remind the world's people of the seriousness of a nuclear accident. Spent fuel management and the need to build national repositories for permanent disposal of waste provide challenges moving into the future.

---

[1]   Larry Kaufmann, "Prospects for Nuclear Power in the U.S.," *Geopolitics of Energy* (August 2017): 2.

[2]   "The Price Anderson Act," Center for Nuclear Science and Technology Information, accessed January 10, 2018, http://cdn.ans.org/pi/ps/docs/ps54-bi.pdf.

[3]   "FAQ About Nuclear Energy," Nuclear Energy Institute, accessed January 10, 2018, https://www.nei.org/Knowledge-Center/FAQ-About-Nuclear-Energy.

[4]   Kauffmann, "Nuclear Power," 2.

[5]   "Nuclear Power in the USA," World Nuclear Association, accessed January 10, 2018, http://www.world-nuclear.org/information-library/country-profiles/countries-t-z/usa-nuclear-power.aspx.

[6]   Kauffmann, "Nuclear Power," 2.

[7]   "Background on Chernobyl Nuclear Power Plant Accident," NRC, accessed January 10, 2018, https://www.nrc.gov/reading-rm/doc-collections/fact-sheets/chernobyl-bg.html.

[8]   Walter A. Rosenbaum, *Environmental Politics and Policy* (Thousand Oaks: Sage/CQ Press, 2017): 290–293.

[9]   "Fukushima Accident," World Nuclear Association, accessed January 10, 2018, http://www.world-nuclear.org/information-library/safety-and-security/safety-of-plants/fukushima-accident.aspx.

[10]   Joanna Walters, "Energy Agency Rejects Trump Plan to Prop Up Coal and Nuclear Power Plants," *The Guardian*, January 8, 2018, accessed January 11, 2018, https://www.the guardian.com/environment/2018/jan/08/donald-trump-coal-industry-plan-rejected-rick-perry.

[11]   "Nuclear Power in the USA," World Nuclear Association, accessed January 10, 2018, http://www.world-nuclear.org/information-library/country-profiles/countries-t-z/usa-nuclear-power.aspx.

[12]   "U.S. Primary Energy Consumption by Source and Sector, 2016," EIA, accessed December 27, 2017, https://www.eia.gov/totalenergy/data/monthly/pdf/flow/css_2016_energy.pdf.

[13]   Walter A. Rosenbaum, *American Energy: The Politics of 21st Century Policy* (Los Angeles: Sage/CQ Press, 2015): 126.

[14]   "What's Next for the NRC? A Conversation with Allison Macfarlane," *Bulletin of the Atomic Scientists* 68, no. 6 (2012): 4.

[15]   "Cracks in Nuclear Power Plant," Greenpeace International, accessed January 11, 2018, http://www.greenpeace.org/international/en/campaigns/nuclear/safety/.

[16]   Gordon R. Thompson, "The U.S. Effort to Dispose of High-Level Radioactive Waste," *Energy & Environment* 19 no. 3+4 (2008): 392–393.

[17]   Bruce B. Clary, "The Enactment of the Nuclear Waste Policy Act of 1982: A Multiple Perspectives Explanation," *Policy Studies Review* 10, no. 4 (Winter 1991/92): 90.

[18]   Rosenbaum, *American Energy*, 128–130.

[19]   John Siciliano, "Yucca Mountain Funding a Bright Spot for Republicans Trump's Budget," *Washington Examiner,* June 20, 2017, accessed January 11, 2018, http://www.washingtonexaminer.com/yucca-mountain-funding-a-bright-spot-for-republicans-trumps-budget/article/2626544.

[20]   Thompson, "The U.S. Effort to Dispose of High-Level Radioactive Waste," 392.

[21]   Robert Rosner and Rebecca Lordan, "Why America Should Move Toward Dry Cask Consolidated Interim Storage of Used Nuclear Fuel," *Bulletin of the Atomic Scientists* 70, no.6 (2014): 48.

[22]   Office of Environmental Management, "Closing the Circle on the Splitting of the Atom: The Environmental Legacy of Nuclear Weapons production in the United States and What the Department of Energy is Doing About It," *Department of Energy DOE/EM-0266* (1996): 4.

[23]   Office of Environmental Management, "Linking Legacies: Connecting the Cold War Nuclear Weapons Production Processes to the Environmental Consequences," *Department of Energy DOE/EM-0319* (1997): 6.

[24]   Thomas C. Perry and Christopher R. Abraham, "Money for Nothing: After $5 Billion, Still No Solution to Hanford's Nuclear Waste Woes," *IEEE Spectrum* (July 2002): 12.

[25]   Annette Cary, "$107.7 Billion Needed to finish Hanford Cleanup," *Tri-City Herald*, February 22, 2016, accessed January 11, 2018, www.tri-cityherald.com/news/local/hanford/article61912837.html.

[26]   Andrew Kambour, Jerry Boese and Ryann Child, "Cleaning Up America's Nuclear Weapons Complex: 2015 Update for Governors," *National Governors Association* (2015): 3, accessed August 10, 2018, https://www.nga.org/center/publications/cleaning-up-americas-nuclear-weapons-complex-2015-update-for-governors/.

[27]   "Nuclear Reprocessing: Dangerous, Dirty, and Expensive," Union of Concerned Scientists, accessed January 11, 2018, https://www.ucsusa.org/nuclear-power/nuclear-plant-security/nuclear-reprocessing#.Wle1KExFzL8.

[28]   Rosenbaum, *American Energy*, 132.

[29]   Kauffmann, "Nuclear Power," 2.

[30]   "50 Years of Nuclear Energy," IAEA, accessed January 12, 2018, https://www.iaea.org/About/Policy/GC/GC48/Documents/gc48inf-4_ftn3.pdf.

[31]   "Online History of Nuclear Energy," World Nuclear Association, accessed January 12, 2018,   http://www.world-nuclear.org/information-library/current-and-future-generation/outline-history-of-nuclear-energy.aspx.

[32]   Daniel Yergin, *The Quest: Energy, Security, and the Remaking of the Modern* World (New York: Penguin, 2012): 366–369.

[33]   "Online History of Nuclear Energy."

[34]   Yergin, *The Quest*, 366.

[35]   "Online History of Nuclear Energy."

[36]   "50 Years of Nuclear Energy."

[37] "World Statistics," Nuclear Energy Institute, accessed January 12, 2018, https://www.nei.org/Knowledge-Center/Nuclear-Statistics/World-Statistics.

[38] "Nuclear Power in the World Today," World Nuclear Association, accessed January 12, 2018, http://www.world-nuclear.org/information-library/current-and-future-generation/nuclear-power-in-the-world-today.aspx.

[39] "World Nuclear Power Reactors & Uranium Requirements," World Nuclear Association, accessed January 12, 2018, http://www.world-nuclear.org/information-library/facts-and-figures/world-nuclear-power-reactors-and-uranium-requireme.aspx.

[40] Diane Cardwell, "The Murky Future of Nuclear Power in the United States," *New York Times*, February 18, 2017, accessed January 12, 2018, https://www.nytimes.com/2017/02/18/business/energy-environment/nuclear-power-westinghouse-toshiba.html.

[41] Santiago Miret, "Nearly Forgotten—Nuclear Power in Latin America," *Berkeley Energy & Resources Collaborative*, November 14, 2015, accessed January 14, 2018, http://berc.berkeley.edu/nearly-forgotten-nuclear-power-in-latin-america/.

[42] "World Nuclear Power Reactors & Uranium Requirements."

[43] Viktor Katona, "The Slow Death of Nuclear Power in Europe," *Oilprice.com*, August 30, 2017, accessed January 12, 2018, https://oilprice.com/Alternative-Energy/Nuclear-Power/The-Slow-Death-Of-Nuclear-Power-In-Europe.html.

[44] "World Nuclear Power Reactors & Uranium Requirements."

[45] Thomas Latschan, "Nuclear Energy Booming in Asia," *dw.com,* November 3, 2016, accessed January 14, 2018, http://www.dw.com/en/nuclear-energy-booming-in-asia/a-1911 0848.

[46] "Nuclear Power in Russia," World Nuclear Association, accessed January 14, 2018, http://www.world-nuclear.org/information-library/country-profiles/countries-o-s/russia-nuclear-power.aspx.

[47] "World Nuclear Power Reactors & Uranium Requirements."

[48] Caline Malek, Nuclear Power Vital to Meet Middle East's Water Demand," *The National*, June 20, 2017, accessed January 14, 2018, https://www.thenational.ae/uae/environment/nuclear-power-vital-to-meet-middle-east-s-water-demand-1.92384.

[49] Leonard Hyman and William Tilles, "Nuclear Power's Resurgence in the Middle East," *Oilprice.com,* December 18, 2017, accessed January 14, 2018, https://oilprice.com/Alternative-Energy/Nuclear-Power/Nuclear-Powers-Resurgence-In-The-Middle-East.html.

[50] "World Nuclear Power Reactors & Uranium Requirements."

[51] David Thomas, "Going Nuclear: Africa's Energy Future?" *African Business*, January 31, 2017, accessed January 14, 2018, http://africanbusinessmagazine.com/sectors/energy/going-nuclear-africas-energy-future/.

[52] "Background on Chernobyl Nuclear Power Plant Accident."

[53] "Fukushima Accident."

[54] "Cracks in Nuclear Power Plant."

[55] Laura Rodriguez-Penalonga and B. Yolanda Moratilla Soria, "A Review of the Spent Nuclear Fuel Cycle Strategies and the Spent Nuclear Fuel Management Technologies," *Energies* 10 (2017): 1237–1238.

[56] "Processing of Used Nuclear Fuel," World Nuclear Association, accessed January 15, 2018, http://www.world-nuclear.org/information-library/nuclear-fuel-cycle/fuel-recycling/processing-of-used-nuclear-fuel.aspx.

[57] Eurasianet, "Russia Takes Action to Clean Up Soviet Era Nuclear Waste," *Oilprice.com*, December 2, 2017, accessed January 14, 2018, https://oilprice.com/Alternative-Energy/Nuclear-Power/Russia-Takes-Action-To-Clean-Up-Soviet-Era-Nuclear-Waste.html.

[58] Rodriguez-Penalonga and Soria, "A Review of the Spent Nuclear Fuel Cycle Strategies," 1243.

[59] Boris Faybishenko, Jens Birkholzer, David Sassani, and Peter Swift, "International Approaches for Deep Geological Disposal of Nuclear Waste: Geological Challenges in Radioactive Waste Isolation," *Lawrenece Berkeley National Laboratory LBNL-1006984* (2016): 1.1–1.15.

[60] "Russia Takes Action to Clean Up Soviet Era Nuclear Waste."

CHAPTER 12

Renewable Energy

INTRODUCTION

Renewable energy is the name given to those sources of energy that are seen to be inexhaustible and are typically environmentally friendly. The sources of renewable energy are several. Hydropower uses the power of water to drive turbines to generate electricity. Hydropower is one of the oldest forms of renewable energy. Wind, one of the fastest growing sources, uses tall wind turbines usually arrayed in wind farms to generate electricity. Solar power, another of the fast-growing sources, either uses photovoltaics (PVs) to directly transform sunlight into electricity or uses mirrors to concentrate sunlight to create steam to drive turbines, generating electricity. Solar power also includes passive solar, used in green buildings, to take advantage of the natural habitat to reduce energy consumption and increase energy efficiency. Biomass includes wood, waste, and other plant material that can be burned in a power plant to produce electricity or heat. Biomass also includes dung, that is widely burned in developing countries to provide home heating and cooking. Biofuels include ethanol, biodiesel, and other advanced biofuels made from algae, cellulose, and other raw materials. Geothermal power comes from hot water or steam naturally occurring underground in hot springs that can be pumped to the surface to turn a turbine and generate electricity.[1] This chapter looks at each of these sources of energy production and examines their use in the U.S. The environmental consequences of using each of the sources of renewable energy are considered. The federal, state, and local legal and policy approaches are explored. On the global level, renewables play a critical role. The chapter explores the use of each of these renewables worldwide.

DOMESTIC CONSIDERATIONS

Renewable Energy Use in the U.S.

In 2016, renewables accounted for 10 percent of energy produced and consumed in the U.S. About 55 percent of that energy was used to generate electricity, 23 percent was used by industry, 14 percent was used in the transportation sector, and 8 percent was used by the residential and commercial sectors.[2] In 2016, renewables accounted for about 15 percent of total U.S. electricity generation.[3] One of the largest sources of renewable energy is hydroelectric, which accounts for 24 percent of all the renewable energy produced in the U.S. Biomass also produces 24 percent. Biofuels produce 22 percent. Wind follows, producing 21 percent. Solar accounts for 6 percent and geothermal produces the remaining 2 percent.[4]

Hydropower. The use of renewable energy in the U.S. dates back to colonial times, when many individuals and settlements depended on running water to power facilities, such as gristmills for grinding grain. By the late 1800s, hydropower was being used sporadically to generate electricity. The first hydroelectric plant was opened in Wisconsin in 1882. Niagara Falls, New York was the site of another early hydroelectric plant. Like other early sites, it was a direct current plant used to power arc and incandescent lighting.[5] George Westinghouse's alternating current would eventually win out over direct current, and Samuel Insull's meter would allow the use of electricity to spread.[6] During World War I, the U.S. Bureau of Reclamation (USBR) engaged in building dams, primarily in the American West, that also produced electricity. However, it would not be till the 1930s when USBR launched its largest projects, including the Grand Coulee Dam on the Columbia River, the Hoover Dam on the Colorado, and the Central

Valley Project in California. The U.S. Army Corps of Engineers (USACE) also built many dams during this time. Throughout World War II, electricity demand sored. Hydropower provided much of the electricity needed to produce the ships, tanks, airplanes, and munitions necessary to win the war.[7]

The Tennessee Valley Authority (TVA) began dam construction on the Tennessee River system shortly after its creation in 1933. TVA was one of the early federal hydroelectric production authorities serving Tennessee, Alabama, Georgia, Mississippi, Kentucky, North Carolina, and Virginia. Building the facility was not without controversy, as dam construction displaced many thousands of families. By the 1940s, TVA was constructing a dozen hydroelectric plants to help with the war effort. TVA provided electricity for the Oak Ridge plant's efforts in the Manhattan project.[8]

After the war, American cities grew and so did their demand for electricity. During the Truman administration, 13,000 miles of transmission lines were laid to get the electricity from where it was generated to where it was consumed. During the Eisenhower years, new hydro plants came online. In the 1960s, private utilities in the American West integrated their production and distribution systems with the federal government's hydroelectric power system. Initial efforts to do this had occurred in the 1930s, when the Bonneville Power Administration was created to market electricity from the Grand Coulee Dam and the Bonneville Dam as well as future dams that would be built in the Columbia River basin. Because California needed power, and the Pacific Northwest generated more power than could be used in that location, Congress approved the Pacific Northwest/Pacific Southwest Intertie. Eventually this would link the federal hydropower system with the Los Angeles Department of Water and Power, Pacific Gas and Electric Company, the Southern California Edison Company, and San Diego Gas and Electric Company. In 1977, the Western Area Power Administration was created to supervise energy marketing and transmission in all areas of the West not overseen by the Bonneville Power Administration.[9]

The New Melones Powerplant in California was the last large dam built in the American West by USBR. It was operational in 1979. By this time, sites for locating new dams in the American West had largely been exhausted and so the frenzy of dam building by USBR and the Army Corps ended. These agencies put their efforts into increasing the capacity of existing hydroelectric plants through modernization efforts. By 2014, USBR had modernized 41 of its 53 hydroelectric plants, increasing their electric generation by 20 percent.[10]

Dam construction also came to end at TVA in 1979. Its last large dam, the Tellico Dam, had become controversial because of the endangered status of the snail darter. TVA's Tellico Dam was under construction and nearly complete when the snail darter was found in the Little Tennessee River. A lawsuit was filed, arguing that completion of the dam would alter the habitat thus killing the snail darter. Construction was halted until President Carter signed the bill allowing the Tellico Dam to be completed in 1979.[11] But that marked the end to large dam construction for TVA. In 2017, TVA's hydroelectric system consisted of 29 dams and a pumped-storage plant near Chattanooga.[12] In pumped storage hydroelectric plants, water is pumped to high reservoirs when excess electricity is available and when demand is high it is released to a lower reservoir, producing electricity on the way down.[13]

Hydroelectric power is widely distributed across the U.S. Most states use some amount of hydro, although states with mainly flat terrain, such as Florida and Kansas, produce very little hydro. States in the Pacific Northwest, including Oregon, Washington, and Idaho, use hydro as their main power source. The ranking of hydro production for the high-producing states in the U.S. is Idaho, Oregon, Washington, South Dakota, Maine, Montana, California, Colorado, Alaska, and Nevada.[14]

Wind. The power of wind to generate electricity was first used in the U.S. in 1887 in Cleveland, Ohio. Charles Brush built a windmill and connected it to a dynamo and a network of batteries to light his home.

While most urban areas in the U.S. drew their electric power from centrally connected grids that were not powered by wind, the rural U.S. used wind to generate electricity. Marcellus Jacobs, a South Dakotan, developed blades adopted from the design of the small planes he flew. Jacobs marketed his windmills to farmers across the country, eventually selling over 30,000 wind turbines. His efforts were joined by other manufacturers spreading thousands of wind turbines across rural America in the early 1900s. The New Deal's rural electrification program eventually spread centrally powered electricity across rural areas in the 1930s, reducing the use of independent wind turbines for several decades.[15]

In the 1940s, Palmer Putnam installed a 175-foot tall wind turbine on a mountain near Rutland, Vermont. Unlike earlier independent turbines, Putnam connected his turbine to the already established grid. In doing so, Putnam showed that wind energy could be integrated with established grids. While his turbine only operated into 1945 before being damaged, the concept of grid-integrated wind power was established. The crisis created by the oil embargo in 1973 led the federal government to fund large wind energy projects to convince the utilities that wind was feasible. These early projects were generally not successful and with federal funding cuts of the Reagan administration, most federally-funded wind projects ended. But California, under the leadership of Governor Jerry Brown, continued to subsidize investments in wind and under the Public Utilities Regulatory Policy Act (PURPA) (described below), continued to provide high rates to independent generators of electricity. The result was a California wind frenzy, which gave birth to the modern wind industry. Another innovation helped define the shape of the emerging industry. Rather than putting up single large turbines, California entrepreneurs installed smaller turbines, networked together by computers, and clustered in what came to be called wind farms. California's intense winds soon proved troublesome for their unstable turbines and they turned to sturdy Danish technology for a solution. By the mid-1980s, almost all of California's wind turbines were imported from Denmark.[16]

In 1992, Texas became a net importer of oil and natural gas as its supplies of conventional reservoirs declined. This caused the governor to commission the Sustainable Energy Development Council to advance a strategic plan to exploit the state's renewable resources. In 1999, Texas passed the Texas Public Utility Regulatory Act and shortly thereafter the Texas Public Utility Commission put in place rules which required that, beginning in 2002, utilities in competitive areas of the state (80 percent of the state) were required to include in their energy portfolios an increasing portion of renewables, with wind favored. At the time of its adoption, this renewable portfolio standard (RPS) was ambitious (RPS are discussed below). It launched Texas' wind power industry.[17]

The early wind industry had its ups and downs associated with changes in leadership and lapsing of federal wind production tax credits. The Energy Policy Act of 1992 (discussed below) returned wind production tax credits. By 2000, General Electric decided to move heavily into wind energy to serve the European market which was growing rapidly. With the Energy Policy Act of 2005 and the development of renewable portfolio standards in multiple states, the wind industry began growing again in the U.S. Between 2005 and 2009, installed wind capacity in the U.S. grew at an average annual rate of 40 percent, or the equivalent of adding about 9 new nuclear reactors, annually.[18]

Wind power in the U.S. is not evenly distributed. The central plains states and the west coast states tend to have the largest capacity for wind production. By 2015, the single largest producer was Texas, with production of over 20 gigawatts. Next in production was Iowa, with production of almost 7 gigawatts, followed by Oklahoma, California, Kansas, Illinois, Minnesota, Oregon, Washington, and Colorado.[19]

Solar Power. The solar power industry emerged in the U.S. as a result of a number of separate breakthroughs. In 1891, Clarence Kemp, a Baltimore inventor, patented the first commercial solar water heater.

In 1905, Albert Einstein published a paper, explaining the photoelectric effect. In 1908, William Bailley of the Carnegie Steel Company invented a solar collector with copper coils and an insulated box, which was basically the design of modern day solar collectors. During World War II, passive solar buildings in the U.S. were in great demand due to the energy scarcity of the war years. In 1954, the first silicon PV cell was built in Bell Labs and the following year Western Electric began selling commercial licenses for PV technologies. In the mid-1950s, the first office building using solar water heating and solar passive design was built in the U.S. NASA launched the first spacecraft that used PVs in 1964. In the1960s and 1970s, PVs were becoming more efficient and less costly.[20]

In 1979, President Jimmy Carter held a press conference on the roof of the White House to highlight the installation of a solar hot water heater. Two years earlier, he had urgently called on the nation to end its reliance on imported oil and transform the energy sector, calling such efforts the 'moral equivalent of war.'[21] Carter created the Department of Energy (DOE) and Congress appropriated money for research and development (R&D). The Carter administration also established a new national laboratory, the Solar Energy Research Institute. In 1978, the Carter administration pushed through the Public Utilities Regulatory Policy Act, which created financial incentives for the expansion of the solar industry. However, things would turn around rapidly. The Iranian Revolution created a second oil shock and Carter responded by shifting his energy policy to emphasize creating synthetic liquid fuels from coal. Reagan's defeat of Carter in 1980 marked the end to Carter's brief renewable energy push.[22]

Reagan did not share Carter's enthusiasm for government intervention in markets. During the Reagan years, the federal government did little to promote solar or other renewables. But even without federal government support, the solar industry made advances. Utility-scale solar—both PV and solar thermal—first came on line in the 1980s.[23] In 1982, the first PV power station went online in Hisperia, California. By 1983, ARCO Solar built a 120-acre PV plant for Pacific

Gas & Electric that provided power for more than 2,000 homes. In the 1980s, nine solar thermal plants were built in California. The design used rows of mirrors that concentrated the sun's light onto a system of pipes filled with oil. The heat was used to produce steam, which powered a turbine to generate electricity.[24]

In 1991, President George W. Bush broadened the mission of the Solar Energy Research Institute and renamed it the National Renewable Energy Laboratory. The lab continued doing R&D on solar and, in 1994, developed a solar cell that exceeded 30 percent efficiency for the first time. The renaming of the lab was part of a general shift in the country at the time where the word solar was replaced with renewables. The change was precipitated by the anti-solar rhetoric of the Reagan years.[25] When Bill Clinton came to office, his administration talked about expanding the federal role in energy policy. In particular, Clinton promised to alter government R&D priorities to promote renewables, including solar.[26] Clinton's attitude was not hostile to solar or renewables in general, but his attention was often with non-environmental matters. Nevertheless, solar advancement continued. In 1999, construction was completed on 4 Times Square, the tallest skyscraper in New York at the time. It incorporated building-integrated PVs on the 37th through 43rd floors and on the south and west-facing outside walls that provided power to the building.[27]

In the 2000s, solar technologies continued to improve and spread. The Bush administration was concerned with energy security, especially in the aftermath of the September 11, 2001 attacks on the Pentagon and the World Trade Center. While most of the energy policy capsulized in the 2005 Energy Policy Act was focused on promoting fossil fuels, there was a provision for a solar tax credit.[28] The Obama administration expanded solar through federal support for 16 new solar plants.[29] In the first year of the Trump administration, the president called repeatedly for a border wall and at one point said that the wall should include solar panels to generate electricity to pay for the wall. But when the prototypes of the proposed wall appeared, none had solar panels.[30] Nevertheless, the solar industry continued to expand. As of

2016, utility-scale solar power plants made up 2 percent of the U.S.'s electricity generating capacity. Between 2010 and 2017, these plants grew at a rate of 72 percent per year. California had the highest amount of utility-scale solar, followed by North Carolina, Arizona, Nevada, Georgia, Utah, and Texas.[31] Residential solar also grew at a rapid pace, although the rate of new installations slowed in 2017 primarily because the utility sector attempted to stifle independent electricity generation.[32]

In 2018, Donald Trump approved four years of tariffs on imports of solar panels. The tariffs were structured to slowly decline from 30 percent to 15 percent over four years. The introduction of these tariffs may slow the expansion of the solar industry in the U.S., an industry that depends on equipment made abroad for 80 percent of its supply. While the tariff favors American manufacturers, most of the solar industry in 2018 was based on installation and service. Most U.S. solar installations rely on imported equipment coming from Asia. The tariffs are expected to increase the cost of large solar farms by 10 percent and about 3 percent for residential systems. The tariff will likely curtail plans for some solar installation, particularly in 2018 and 2019.[33] A challenge to these tariffs is likely in the World Trade Organization (WTO).

Biomass and Biofuels. Historically in the U.S., biomass was drawn from three sources: wood, waste, and alcohol fuels. In the last several decades, corn has become a primary source for the production of biofuels. Wood energy is used in the U.S in wood stoves and fireplaces for residential home heating or as an additional source of space heating. Waste, such as municipal solid waste, manufacturing waste, or landfill gas is used in waste-to-energy plants.[34]

Biofuels include ethanol and biodiesel that are made from biomass materials and are typically blended with petroleum but can be used on their own. Using biofuels reduces the need for gasoline and diesel. Biofuels are also cleaner burning than oil products. Ethanol is an alcohol made from sugars found in many plants, including potatoes, sugar cane, and corn. Ethanol can also be made from woody crops such as switchgrass, however, as of 2018, the process had not yet been widely commercialized. Almost all of the gasoline sold in the U.S. in 2018 was blended with 10 percent ethanol. Only flexible-fuel vehicles can run on higher blends of ethanol. Biodiesel is a fuel made from fats, vegetable oils, or greases and can be used in diesel engines. Most biodiesel is blended with diesel fuel at a 20 percent rate.[35]

Biofuels have a long history of use in the U.S. In the 1700s, vegetable oils and fats lit lights, and alcohol burning stoves were a source of indoor heat. By the 1800s, whale oil was widely used. In the 1900s, the U.S. took policy action to further the use of biofuels. This began in 1906, when Teddy Roosevelt led the repeal of the Distilled Spirits Tax of 1862. However, alcohol production slowed as the prohibition movement took hold. Fear of oil shortages during World War I led Henry Ford to produce a Model T and farm tractors that could run on alcohol as well as gasoline. Henry Ford developed ethanol for blending with gasoline in a Kansas plant, but it went bankrupt in 1939 in large part due to opposition from the oil industry. Ethanol plants reopened for the war effort but cheap oil in the decades after World War II reduce the demand for the alternative fuel.[36]

The oil shocks of the 1970s changed the future of oil alternatives. In the U.S., the focus was on corn-based ethanol. The 40 cents per gallon subsidy provided by the Energy Policy Act of 1978 launched the U.S. industry. The act also put in place a protective tariff against imported ethanol.[37] In the 1980s, farmers began producing ethanol to add value to their corn. Ethanol's use to control carbon monoxide emissions encouraged increased production in the 1990s. In 2005, the first renewable fuel standard (RFS) was put in place by the Energy Policy Act and it required ethanol production of 4 billion gallons in 2006 rising to 7.5 billion gallons by 2012. The Energy Independence and Security Act of 2007 included a second RFS which required renewable fuel use to increase to 36 billion gallons by 2022.[38]

Geothermal. The U.S. has large geothermal resources, located mostly in the American West. Nationally, geothermal accounted for very little of the electricity produced in the U.S., but in states with excellent geothermal potential, like California, geothermal produced 5 percent of the state's total power generation. In 2011, the U.S. had geothermal plants operating in Oregon, Idaho, Wyoming, California, Nevada, Utah, Colorado, Arizona, Alaska, and New Mexico. To use geothermal power, a well is typically drilled into an underground aquifer of hot water, releasing steam, which drives a turbine to produce electricity. Buildings can also be heated directly by circulating the hot water from geothermal sites through closed loop pipeline systems.[39] In 2018, the U.S. had 64 geothermal plants and two of the largest in the world. The largest geothermal plant in the world is Geysers Geothermal Complex, located just north of San Francisco, California. The complex is made up of eighteen power plants and has an installed capacity of over 1,500 megawatts (MW). The site began producing power in 1960 and is continuing to add capacity. The Salton Sea Geothermal Plant in southern California is comprised of a complex of power plants and is the fifth largest geothermal plant in the world.[40]

Environmental Consequences of Renewable Energy Use

Hydropower. While there are no air emissions associated with hydro, there are environmental impacts. In the 1960s and 1970s, increasing awareness from the growing environmental movement resulted in people taking another look at hydroelectric power. They concluded that there were large environmental costs, mostly associated with loss of habitat for wildlife and fish. For instance, the Grand Coulee Dam had blocked the natural migration paths for salmon to their spawning grounds in the upper Columbia River basin. The water reservoirs created by the federal dam system also significantly altered the natural landscape and flooded archeological sites. Creation of these reservoirs also forced whole communities to relocate as their towns went under water. These issues were at the core of the decade-long conflict surrounding the building of the New Melones dam in California. The construction of that dam destroyed a popular location for white water recreation, flooded archeological sites, and the West's deepest limestone canyon.[41]

Wind. Wind is a clean power source, contributing no pollution to the air. Wind power does have adversaries who raise concerns over noise, aesthetic impacts, and most importantly bird and bat deaths. Noise is associated with the turning of the turbine blades. Early model wind turbines were nosier than newer models, which have been improved by better designs and insulating materials. Visual impacts are a complaint of detractors, because wind turbines are typically sited in highly visible locations. Offshore wind turbines have been heavily criticized for ruining the sea view. The most important concern, however, is avian and bat mortality resulting from collision with rotating blades. Conservation groups have raised these concerns. Studies have been undertaken to monitor bird and bat deaths, as well as to investigate possible ways to mitigate such deaths.[42]

Solar Power. While solar power does not contribute to toxic air emission when in operation, there are potential environmental impacts. The first of these is based in land use. Utility-scale solar farms can result in land degradation and habitat loss, depending on siting. Utility-scale PV farms take between 3.5 to 10 acres per megawatt. The manufacture of PV components also uses considerable amounts of water, and concentrating solar thermal plants require water for cooling. The PV manufacturing process uses several hazardous materials including hydrochloric acid, sulfuric acid, nitric acid, hydrogen fluoride, acetone, and trichloroethane. Inhalation of silicon dust may pose a hazard to workers. Thin-film PV also contains more toxic materials than those used in traditional silicon PVs that must be handled and disposed of carefully to avoid environmental contamination. Air emissions of greenhouse gases does occur during manufacturing, transport, installation, maintenance, and decommissioning.[43]

Biomass and Biofuels. Biomass can pollute the air when combusted. Residential fireplaces and wood stoves can have considerable negative impacts on local air quality. Waste-to-energy power plants must be carefully monitored to assure they do not emit hazardous substances.[44] The World Health Organization (WHO) reports that over three billion people worldwide cook and heat their homes with open fires or simple stoves that are fueled by animal dung, crop waste, wood or charcoal. These practices produce severe indoor air pollution and result in more than four million premature deaths, over half of which are among children.[45]

Ethanol is non-toxic, biodegradable, and burns much cleaner than gasoline. However, ethanol does have much higher evaporative emissions from tanks or pumps which contribute to ozone formation. Gasoline also requires additional refining before being blended with ethanol. Burning ethanol reduces carbon dioxide emissions, because the plants used to make ethanol absorb carbon dioxide as they grow and that offsets the carbon dioxide they release when burned. Critics of ethanol raise issues associated with the full life cycle assessment of ethanol, which includes growing, transporting, and processing the feedstock in order to manufacture the ethanol. Under some of these assessments, corn ethanol has been shown to be a significant contributor to carbon dioxide (CO_2) emissions. Biodiesel burns much cleaner than petroleum-based diesel, producing fewer harmful air emissions including particulates, carbon monoxide, and sulfur dioxide. However, biodiesel may produce slightly higher emissions of nitrogen oxide. Burning biodiesel is also carbon-neutral.[46]

Geothermal. Geothermal plants can have environmental impacts on water. Water from geothermal plants may have elevated levels of sulfur, salt, and minerals. If such water escapes, it may cause contamination. Water is also used in geothermal plants for cooling, and this can require a considerable amount of water. Most geothermal plants reinject water drawn from the reservoir back into the reservoir, however, some is lost to steam, and so outside water must be used for reinjection to maintain a constant volume of water in the reservoir. This water does not necessarily have to be potable water. Treated waste-water can be used. Closed loop geothermal plants have few air emissions, but open loop plants emit hydrogen sulfide, which changes to sulfur dioxide in the atmosphere. Some geothermal plants also produce mercury emissions, which must be controlled. Geothermal plants may also have a large land footprint.[47]

Federal Law and Policy

One of the earliest pieces of legislation to address the issue of renewable energy was the National Energy Act of 1978. The National Energy Act had five key components, and one of them came under the title the Public Utilities Regulatory Policy Act. PURPA helped to expand the number of independent generators of electricity and was especially helpful to solar and wind power. Other provisions of the act focused on improving energy efficiency and conservation. Congress wrote provisions into the law that allowed tax credits for home insulation, created guidelines for appliance energy efficiency standards, and imposed a tax on gas-guzzler automobiles.[48] The act also attempted to create a strong biofuel sector by providing a subsidy for blenders and placing a tariff on imported ethanol.[49] In 1980, Carter signed the Energy Security Act into law. It included incentives for development of renewables and established the U.S. Synthetic Fuels Corporation to produce liquid fuel from coal to replace oil.[50]

When Ronald Reagan took office, he moved away from the policies of Nixon, Ford, and Carter. Within a few years of entering office, he was successful in ending many of the programs created to address the oil crises of the 1970s. He also used his budget cuts to eliminate funding for much of the energy R&D supporting renewables.[51] By the 1990s, some concern about energy independence once again emerged and the result was the Energy Policy Act of 1992. The act's purpose was to promote the use of renewable energy and to encourage energy efficiency and conservation in buildings by requiring states to certify its codes for residential and commercial buildings met the Council of American Building Officials Model Energy Code. It also amended PURPA by requiring electric utilities to set rates so that outlay for demand side management were as profitable as were outlays for new generation.[52]

By the time the George W. Bush administration came into office, energy was once again becoming an issue of intense national concern. This was so in large part because of the attack of September 11, 2001, and concern over rising instability in the Middle East. The result was two energy policy laws that had several provisions for renewables and energy efficiency.

The Energy Policy Act of 2005, while primarily focused on fossil fuels, did have provisions for renewables and energy efficiency. It required increased use of ethanol and biofuels to be blended with gasoline between 2006 and 2012. It also provided a subsidy for blenders and protected them by imposing a tariff on imported ethanol.[53] The act created a number of programs that were intended to appeal to renewable energy proponents. These programs included more than $14 billion in tax incentives to be available for conservation and efficiency, a solar investment tax credit, and support for R&D on biofuels and hydrogen fuel cells.[54]

The Energy Independence and Security Act of 2007 sought to move the U.S. toward energy independence and security in large part through the increased use of renewable energy and improved efficiency. In particular, the law put restrictions on the use of energy by federal government agencies, thus attempting to improve efficiency. The law increased the Corporate Average Fuel Economy standards. It tried to promote a strong biofuel sector by mandating an increase in required use of domestically produced biofuels to 36 billion gallons annually by 2022. This was a massive increase to the Renewable Fuel Standard set in the 2005 Energy Policy Act.[55] By 2017, the U.S. ethanol industry had experienced considerable growth, largely through production of corn-based ethanol.[56]

When the Obama administration came to White House, the country was in a deep recession. Obama, however, used the $775 billion American Recovery and Reinvestment Act of 2009 (AR&R) to partially fulfill his green agenda. By the mid-2013, the Obama administration had invested more in renewable energy than any other administration.

The administration massively increased federal support for development of renewables on public land. Between 2008 and 2010 these investments included 16 new solar projects, 4 wind farms, and 7 geothermal facilities. More than 2,600 private renewable energy projects received subsidies under the AR&R. Developers of renewable projects were allowed to receive up to 30 percent of the cost of their projects from this program.[57] In 2013, Obama signed into law the Hydropower Regulatory Efficiency Act and the Bureau of Reclamation Small Conduit Hydropower Development and Rural Jobs Act. Both of these sought to increase the development of small hydropower projects.[58]

State and Local Law and Policy

Renewable Portfolio Standards. Among the most significant state-level policy measures are the renewable portfolio standards. RPS require a certain set percentage of a state's electricity to come from renewable sources. Typically, the state legislature will require private utilities to demonstrate that they are using a fixed percent of hydro, wind, solar, biomass, or geothermal. By 2018, 37 states had passed RPS. The first wave of RPS were enacted between the mid-1990s and 2002 as part of electricity deregulation. The second wave came after electricity deregulation had largely stopped, after the California crisis. The last mandatory RPS was passed in 2009 by Kansas, although several states have enacted non-binding voluntary RPS. RPS were drivers of the adoption of wind power in states like Texas, the nation's single largest producer of wind energy.[59]

Net-metering and Other Solar Incentives. Another significant state-based policy measure was net-metering under which consumers pay only for the net cost of electricity used minus the electricity generated by their rooftop PV. Net-metering standards were passed in 43 states, setting the rules and regulations for paying independent producers of electricity flowing onto the grid. Net-metering rules were a boon to rooftop PV by allowing utility customers with PVs to sell their excess generation to the utility, thus minimizing the cost of rooftop systems.

Generous net-metering laws, like California's 1995 law, set the stage for solar PV to expand quickly by allowing customers to be paid a retail rate for the electricity they generated. After California adopted net-metering, another 16 states rapidly followed, passing a series of laws to promote residential PV between 1997 and 1999. In the 1990s, however, residential PV was very expensive and rapid industry growth did not occur. The later passage of the investment tax credit, combined with the shift in the solar industry from selling rooftop PV to leasing them, would have the desired impact. The 2005 Energy Policy Act included a 30 percent investment tax credit for residential and commercial solar PV. It was only supposed to last for a few years but was extended until 2008. In that year, the financial crisis opened another opportunity, and the tax credit was extended again through 2016. In 2016, the newly created solar leasing companies were successful in lobbying for a long-term extension of the tax credit in the Consolidated Appropriation Act of 2015. As of 2018, the investment tax credit is due to expire in 2021.[60]

Green Power Purchasing. Green pricing is an optional program provided for customers of utilities to encourage the production of renewable energy. Customers voluntarily purchase a percent of their energy use from renewables. In many cases, cities, counties, and public universities enter into such agreements to assure that they support the renewable energy sector.[61]

Public Benefit Funds (PBF). Also referred to as a system benefit charge, PBF are state-level programs created during electricity restructuring as a policy to assure adequate funding for renewables and energy efficiency. Most PBF mandate demand-side management programs and low-income assistance programs. PBF programs exist in 20 states and the District of Columbia. Six other states allow utilities to add a charge to utility bills to collect money to support renewable energy or energy efficiency programs.[62]

Grants, Loans, Rebates, and Tax Expenditures. Many states and localities provide an assortment of grants, loans, and rebates to subsidize renewable energy and energy efficiency. Tax expenditures typically include corporate tax credits, personal tax credits, property tax credits, sales tax credits, or direct industry support for the support of renewables and energy efficiency.[63]

GLOBAL CONSIDERATIONS

The Use of Renewables Globally

Hydropower. Hydropower has been used worldwide since ancient times. The Chinese first harnessed the power of water by constructing water wheels to grind grain, break ore, and assist in paper making dating back to 200 BCE. Water power use has been historically linked to economic growth, for instance, the use of water-driven cotton mills in England in the early 1700s. It is widely believed that water power started the British industrial revolution.[64]

The world's first commercial hydroelectric plants were operational in the 1880s in the U.S and Canada. Germany launched a plant in 1891 followed by Australia in 1895. By the turn of the 20th century, the technology was spreading worldwide. China built its first hydroelectric plants in 1905 in Taipei followed rapidly by plants in mainland China. The U.S. and Canada dominated hydroelectric engineering in the first half of the 20th century. From the 1960s through the 1980s, the largest plants were built in Canada, the Soviet Union, and Latin America. Brazil and China took leadership for hydroelectric engineering after the 1980s. The world's second largest dam was built in 1984 between Brazil and Paraguay. The world's largest dam is China's Three Gorges Dam, which was operational in 2008.[65]

Hydroelectric power produces 19 percent of the world's total electricity and about 25 countries depend on hydro for 90 percent or more of their electricity needs. In Norway, hydro provides virtually all the country's electricity.[66] China is the largest producer of hydroelectricity. Next in rank come Canada, Brazil, the U.S., Russia, Norway, India, Venezuela, Sweden, and Japan.[67]

Wind. The power of wind was first used to sail ships. On land, the use of windmills goes back thousands of years. Windmills were used both for grinding grain and to pump water for consumption, irrigation, or drainage. Windmills were used in Persia as far back as the 10th century. They spread throughout the Islamic world and then into China. In medieval England, windmills were used to replace water wheels, which were held as a monopoly by the church and the nobility as a source of power and wealth. Windmills spread across Europe by the 12th century. Across Europe, windmills came to be used for industrial purposes, including grinding olives, making gun powder, and powering the bellows of blast furnaces. Between the 13th century and the beginning use of steam and coal in the 19th century, windmills powered much of Europe's industrial activities.[68]

The modern wind industry developed in Europe, led by Denmark, during World War I and World War II when they depended on wind to fill in for electricity disruptions. After the Second World War, wind power could not compete with cheap electricity coming from fossil fuels and so the industry lost momentum. After the oil embargo of 1973, though, wind had a rebirth. The Danes focused on building sturdy turbines that could withstand very high winds. The Vestas company built these machines and one of their first large customers was a California company, Zond. Thus, Danish technology helped build the American wind industry.[69]

Wind power grew steadily in Europe. This was owed primarily to development in Germany and Spain. Germany's Feed-In Tariff law passed in 1990, allowed small generators to feed electricity into the grid. The law specified how much they would be paid for their electricity. Generation from hydro, biogas, and landfill gas received 80 percent of the retail rate. Wind and solar received 90 percent. In 1991, there were 1,000 wind turbines in Germany. Within a decade, the amount of wind power increased ten-fold.[70] Spain also introduced a feed-in tariff in 1994, which decreed that by 1999 wind producers could either receive a fixed rate per kilowatt (KW) hour generated or the average hourly market price for electricity.[71]

Wind power spread worldwide in the 21st century, although it is not evenly distributed across the globe. Africa and the Middle East had relatively little installed capacity by 2016, producing less than 4,000 MW. By contrast, Asia produced over 200,000 MW, led by Chinese production of nearly 169,000 MW. In 2016, Europe produced 161,000 MW, led by Germany, with production of 50,000 MW and Spain, with production of 23,000 MW. Latin America and the Caribbean together produced just over 15,000 MW. North America produced over 97,000 MW, led by U.S. production of over 82,000 MW. Australia, New Zealand, and the Pacific Islands together produced under 5,000 MW. Global world installed capacity of wind power has grown enormously in the 21st century. In 2001, the world had just under 24,000 MW installed. By 2016, that number had grown to just under 487,000 MW. Much of the growth was due to China's massive investment in wind. By 2017, the top producers of wind power were China, the U.S., and Germany.[72]

Solar Power. Solar power has been used worldwide for thousands of years. Humans first used solar power by concentrating the sun's heat with glass or mirrors to light fires. The Roman bathhouses took advantage of passive solar through their large south facing windows. The Anasazi also used passive solar in their cliff dwellings. The first solar collector dates back to the 1700s. It was used to cook food. In 1839, the photoelectric effect was discovered by Edmond Becquerel, a French scientist, and by 1860, a French mathematician, August Mouchet, proposed the concept for making a solar-powered steam engine. In 1908, U.S. inventors developed the first solar collector. In 1954, Bell Labs in the U.S. built the first silicon PV cell. Improvements in efficiency and decreasing costs in the decades that followed enabled the solar industry to spread worldwide.[73]

China entered the solar equipment market in 2004 when demand was very high worldwide and especially in Europe. Chinese solar production rapidly expanded. After the 2008 financial crisis, the Chinese government strategically targeted solar with its economic stimulus plan and private investment followed. As a result, China became the leading producer of solar panels in the world by 2008. This growth precipitated a worldwide oversupply of solar panels that reduced costs and threatened the viability of solar companies elsewhere in the world, ending in the bankruptcies of Solyndra and Evergreen Solar. The strains placed on the U.S. producers of solar led to trade challenges. By 2010, the U.S. requested WTO intervention. In 2012, the U.S. imposed duties on Chinese solar cell manufacturers on the grounds that they received subsidies from the Chinese government. In 2014, the U.S. imposed anti-dumping measures against Chinese solar panel makers. The Chinese responded against the U.S. by investigating cleantech products from the U.S. that had received subsidies from state governments.[74] The trade dispute continued with the tariff on imports of solar power imposed by the Trump administration in 2018.[75]

In 2016, solar power added worldwide grew 50 percent with China and the U.S. both almost doubling the amount of solar they added in the prior year. In 2016, the new solar capacity installed worldwide was 76 gigawatts(GW), up massively from the 50 GW installed in 2015. By 2016, the world had 305 GW of solar power capacity, up from 50 GW in 2010. Solar growth was not even across all nations, as growth actually fell in the U.K. when the government cut incentives for households to install rooftop solar and cut subsidies to utility-scale solar farms. Despite the setback, the U.K. still led Europe for solar growth accounting for 29 percent of newly added capacity. Germany added 21 percent to its capacity and France slightly more than 8 percent. By 2017, Europe had 104 GW of solar installed. Worldwide the solar industry continues growing, although as of 2016, it only provided on average 4 percent of electricity demand.[76]

By 2017, 60 percent of the world's solar cells were made in China and Taiwan. China is also rapidly expanding its use of solar power. The world's largest solar farm, Longyangxia Dam Solar Park, is also located in China. China is also home to the world's largest floating solar farm, built in Huainan, Anhui Province, over an old coal mine that has filled with rain water.[77]

Biomass and Biofuels. Around the world, woody biomass is the primary biomass fuel. It is used for heating, cooking, and production of electricity. Woody biomass includes branches, twigs, wood chip, bark, and pellets made from sawdust and other residues. Wood is also the source of 52 million tons of charcoal used in many countries for cooking and smelting of metal ore. Biomass also comes from agricultural waste, such as straw, which is produced as a by-product of growing cereals. Similar feedstock includes stalks, seed husks, and foliage. As of 2016, biomass produced 14 percent of the world's total energy use from renewables. Estimates suggest future biomass use will increase and mature technologies will allow for efficient conversion to energy. Biomass is also changing from a traditional, local energy source to a mature, modern, and globally traded commodity. The international trade of biomass is primarily wood pellets, of which 27 million tons were traded in 2015. The use of biomass is different around the world. Biomass used in Africa and Asia is primarily dung, fuel wood, crop waste, and charcoal used for cooking and heating. In Europe, biomass from wood pellets and municipal solid waste is used for combined power and heating.[78]

Biofuels have been used in lamps to provide light since the 1700s all across Europe and whale oil was introduced in the 1800s. By the 1900s, Germany created the world's first large-scale biofuel industry under the leadership of Kaiser Wilhelm. The Kaiser supported the use of alcohol made from potatoes rather than oil, and by 1906, German distilleries produced over 27 million gallons. Across Germany, ethanol-fueled lights, heaters, and other home appliances were in use. By the 1920s, biofuels were becoming popular in other countries. Brazil built a biofuel plant in 1927 to make alcohol biofuels from sugarcane and by 1937, ethanol was 7 percent of Brazil's fuel consumption. By 1932, 30 industrial nations across Europe and in the tropics had mandatory ethanol blending policies. Interest in oil alternatives during the Second World War provided world demand for some ethanol production, but cheap oil after the war reduced demand. The oil shocks of the 1970s once again created demand for oil alternatives. This trend continued worldwide, with 40 nations having policies or mandates for biofuel development by 2012.[79]

The food versus fuel debate has dominated the global politics of biofuel for decades. In 2008, the United Nations general-secretary called for a reconsideration of biofuels in light of a worldwide hunger crisis. This called attention to the fact that arable land was being used to produce biofuels rather than food, increasing the threat that many may go hungry or starve because of such policies.[80] Conservation groups became concerned about the use of palm oil and sugar cane to make biofuels because growing such crops in mass could devastate rain forests. Also, the process of growing crops along with providing them with fertilizers and pesticides is energy intensive. Opponents argue that the ethanol energy derived from some crops, such as corn, is actually less than the energy needed to grow the crop. Further, they suggest that since the energy used to make fertilizers and pesticides comes primarily from oil and gas, biofuels do not displace as much fossil fuel use as suggested by proponents.[81]

Geothermal. Geothermal energy provides less than 1 percent of the world's electricity generation and an even smaller percent of overall world energy consumption. Nevertheless, by 2016, 24 countries had geothermal plants. The countries with the largest utilization of direct thermal heat in 2015 were China, Turkey, Iceland, Japan, Hungary, the U.S., and New Zealand.[82] The Philippines houses three of the ten largest geothermal plants in the world, followed by the U.S. with two, and Indonesia with two, and Italy, Mexico, and Iceland each with one.[83]

CONCLUSION

Renewables accounted for 10 percent of energy produced and consumed in the U.S. in 2016. More than half of the output of renewables was for electricity generation. U.S. renewables consist of hydro, biomass and biofuels, wind, solar, and geothermal.

The use of hydropower in the U.S. dates back to colonial times, when gristmills depended on running water. Hydroelectric emerged in the late 1800s, with small plants in Wisconsin, and Niagara Falls. The U.S. Bureau of Reclamation built the major hydroelectric facilities in the 1930s, including the Grand Coulee and Hoover Dams. The Army Corps of Engineers also became a dam building competitor of USBR. The 1930s also saw the creation of the TVA, which would come to provide electricity to most of the rural southeast. After the Second World War, demand for electricity mushroomed as did U.S. hydro capacity. By the 1960s, private utilities in the American West integrated their production and distribution systems with the federal government, creating the Pacific Northwest/Pacific Southwest Intertie. The era of high-dam building ended in the U.S. by 1980, as locations for new dam sites were non-existent. Hydroelectric power is widely distributed across the U.S. although states with flat geographies produce only small amounts.

Wind power has been used in the U.S. to produce electricity since the late 1880s, but wind was not centrally connected to the grid. Rather, wind was used to support farms and other independent operations across rural America. The ability to tie wind turbines to the grid had been demonstrated in the 1940s but it would take the oil embargo of 1973 before the modern wind industry would emerge. Wind power gained a hold first in California and Texas. The early wind industry was volatile due to the unstable production tax credit which repeated lapsed and was reinstated. The Energy Policy Act of 2005 and the development of RPS in the states helped the industry to stabilize and grow. Wind power in the U.S. is concentrated in the central plains states and on the West Coast. By 2015, the single largest producer of wind energy was Texas.

The modern solar industry developed in the U.S. after World War II and experienced its initial growth in the aftermath of the oil crises of the 1970s. The policies of Jimmy Carter and the passage of PURPA were important for its early growth. The election of Reagan marked a turning point. The federal government did little to promote solar during the Reagan years but even without federal government support, the industry made progress. Utility-scale solar came online in the 1980s.

The industry continued to experience growth for the next several decades although solar only contributed a small amount of power to American industry and residences. By 2016, utility-scale solar power plants made up only 2 percent of the U.S.'s electricity generating capacity.

U.S. biomass comes from wood, waste, alcohol fuels, and corn. Wood energy is used in wood-burning stoves and fireplaces. Waste, such as municipal solid waste, manufacturing waste, or landfill gas is used in waste-to-energy plants. The most common use of biomass in the U.S. is for the production of biofuels. Almost all of the gasoline sold in the U.S. today is blended with ethanol. The blending of biodiesel with petroleum-based diesel is also common. Like other renewables, the oil shocks of the 1970s changed the future of biofuels. The subsidy provided by the Energy Policy Act of 1978 launched the U.S. industry and subsequent laws that established or expanded the RFS helped it grow. By law, renewable fuel use will increase to 36 billion gallons annually by 2022.

The U.S. has large geothermal resources, located mostly in the American West, and the world's largest geothermal plant. The U.S. has 64 geothermal plants in total, but together they account for very little of the power generated in the country, although they are significant power generators in some states, particularly California.

Energy use has environmental consequences, and while renewables are much cleaner than fossil fuels they may still have impacts. Hydroelectric power is associated with loss of habitat for wildlife and fish, a significantly altered natural landscape, flooded archeological sites, and massive community relocations. Wind, while it does not contribute to air pollution, does raise concerns over noise, aesthetic impacts, and bird and bat deaths. While solar power does not contribute to toxic air emission when in operation, the manufacture and installation may. Large solar facilities may result in loss of habitat. Biomass can pollute the air when burned, significantly lowering air quality. Biofuels can contribute to ozone formation. Geothermal plants can have environmental impacts on water, air, and land.

Federal legislation for renewables includes several important laws, including the National Energy Act of 1978, which included the Public Utilities Regulatory Policy Act. PURPA was instrumental in expanding the number of independent generators of electricity and served to help the emergence of solar, biofuel, and wind power. The Energy Policy Act of 1992 promoted the use of renewable energy and to encouraged energy conservation in buildings. The Energy Policy Act of 2005, contained provisions for renewables and energy efficiency. It put in place a RFS for the promotion of ethanol. The Energy Independence and Security Act of 2007 expanded the RFS. The American Recovery and Reinvestment Act of 2009 provided an investment in renewable energy greater than that of any other administration.

State and local laws and policies are also of considerable importance. Renewable portfolio standards, net-metering, green power purchasing, public benefit funds, and an array of grants, loans, rebates and tax expenditures put in place by states and localities have all served to support the growth of renewables.

Just as the U.S. has seen large growth in the use of renewables, so too has the world. Hydroelectric power produces 19 percent of the world's total electricity. China is the largest producer of hydroelectricity with Canada, Brazil, the U.S., Russia, Norway, India, Venezuela, Sweden, and Japan following. Wind power spread worldwide in the 21st century, although its distribution is uneven. The big wind power producers include China, the U.S., and Germany. Solar power, invented in the U.S. in the 1950s, is now dominated by Chinese production. While solar power is growing worldwide at a rapid pace, it still only provides for 4 percent of the world's electricity demand. Globally, biomass produced 14 percent of the world's total energy use from renewables. Sources of biomass vary by region. In Africa and Asia biomass sources such as dung, fuel wood, crop waste, and charcoal are used for cooking and residential heating. The use of these without adequate ventilation is a serious health issue. In Europe, wood pellets are used for combined power and heating or municipal solid waste is burned in waste-to-energy power plants. The primary use of biomass in the U.S. is for biofuels. Geothermal energy, while important in some localities, provides less than 1 percent of the world's electricity generation.

1   Daniel Yergin, *The Quest: Energy, Security, and the Remaking of the Modern World* (New York: Penguin, 2012): 529–530.

2   "U.S. Primary Energy Consumption by Source and Sector, 2016," EIA, accessed December 27, 2017, https://www.eia.gov/totalenergy/data/monthly/pdf/flow/css_2016_energy.pdf.

3   "How Much of U.S. Energy Consumption and Electricity Generation Comes for Renewable Energy Sources?" EIA, accessed January 17, 2018, https://www.eia.gov/tools/faqs/faq.php?id=92&t=4.

4   "U.S. Energy Consumption by Energy Source, 2016," EIA, accessed January 17, 2018, https://www.eia.gov/energyexplained/index.cfm?page=renewable_home.

5   "Hydropower Program," USBR, accessed January 17, 2018, https://www.usbr.gov/power/edu/history.html.

6   Yergin, *The Quest,* 348–352.

7   "Hydropower Program."

8   "Hydroelectric," TVA, accessed January 17, 2018, https://www.tva.gov/Energy/Our-Power-System/Hydroelectric.

9   "Hydroelectric Power in the 20th Century and Beyond," NPS, accessed January 17, 2018, https://www.nps.gov/articles/7-hydroelectric-power-in-the-20th-century-and-beyond.htm.

10   "Hydroelectric Power in the 20th Century and Beyond."

11   Zygmunt J. B. Plater, "A Jeffersonian Challenge from Tennessee: The Notorious Case of the Endangered "Snail Darter" Versus TVA's Tellico Dam—And Where Was the Fourth Estate, the Press?" *Tennessee Law Review* 80 (2013): 522–527.

12   "Hydroelectric."

13   Roger A. Hinrichs, and Merlin Kleinbach, *Energy: Its Use and the Environment* (Fort Worth: Harcourt College Publishers, 2002): 377.

14   "Hydroelectric Power Water Use," USGS, accessed January 18, 2018, https://water.usgs.gov/edu/wuhy.html.

15   Yergin, *The Quest*, 599–600.

16   Yergin, *The Quest*, 602–603.

17   Dianne Rahm, "Renewable Energy in Texas," in *Sustainable Energy and the States: Essays on Politics, Markets, and Leadership*, ed. Dianne Rahm (Jefferson, NC: McFarland& Company, Inc. Publishers, 2006), 54–56.

18   Yergin, *The Quest*, 608.

19   "Today in Energy," EIA, accessed January 19, 2018, https://www.eia.gov/todayinenergy/detail.php?id=31032.

[20] "The History of Solar," DOE, accessed January 20, 2018, https://www1.eere.energy.gov/solar/pdfs/solar_timeline.pdf.

[21] Robert Y. Shum, "Where Constructivism Meets Resource Constraints: The Politics of Oil, Renewables, and a U.S. Energy Transition," *Environmental Politics* 24, no.3 (2015): 382.

[22] Yergin, *The Quest*, 533–536.

[23] "Utility-scale Solar has Grown Rapidly Over the Past Five Years," EIA, accessed January 20, 2018, https://www.eia.gov/todayinenergy/detail.php?id=31072.

[24] "The History of Solar."

[25] Yergin, *The Quest*, 545.

[26] Keith Schneider, "The Transition: Energy Policy; Clinton to Revamp Energy Dept. Role," *New York Times*, November 23, 1992, accessed January 20, 2018, http://www.nytimes.com/1992/11/23/us/the-transition-energy-policy-clinton-to-revamp-energy-dept-role.html?pagewanted=all.

[27] "The History of Solar."

[28] Walter A. Rosenbaum, *American Energy: The Politics of 21st Century Policy* (Los Angeles: Sage/CQ Press, 2015), 102.

[29] Rosenbaum, *American Energy*, 158–159.

[30] Tracy Jan, "Trumps Proposal for a 'Solar' Border Wall Now Appears Dead," *Washington Post*, October 26, 2017, accessed January 21, 2018, https://www.washingtonpost.com/news/wonk/wp/2017/10/26/trumps-proposal-for-a-solar-border-wall-now-appears-dead/?utm_term=.81807879ed00.

[31] "Utility-scale Solar has Grown Rapidly Over the Past Five Years."

[32] Ivan Penn, "Rooftop Solar Installations Rising but Pace of Growth Falls," *LA Times*, March 15, 2017, accessed January 21, 2018, http://www.latimes.com/business/la-fi-rooftop-solar-20170314-story.html.

[33] Brian Eckhouse, Ari Natter, and Chris Martin, "Trump's Tariff on Solar Mark Biggest Blow to Renewables Yet," *Bloomberg*, January 23, 2018, accessed January 23, 2018, https://www.bloomberg.com/news/articles/2018-01-22/trump-taxes-solar-imports-in-biggest-blow-to-clean-energy-yet?utm_content=tictoc&utm_campaign=socialflow-organic&utm_source=twitter&utm_medium=social&cmpid%3D=socialflow-twitter-tictoc.

[34] "Biomass," Institute for Energy Research, accessed January 22, 2018, https://www.instituteforenergyresearch.org/?encyclopedia=biomass-2.

[35] "Biofuels: Ethanol and Biodiesel Explained," EIA, accessed January 22, 2018, https://www.eia.gov/energyexplained/index.cfm?page=biofuel_home.

[36] "Biofuel—Biodiesel History," Energy-101, accessed August 8, 2018, http://www.energy-101.org/renewable-energy/biofuelsbiomass-facts/biofuel-biodiesel-facts/biofuel-biodiesel-history.

[37] Wallace E. Tyner, "The U.S. Ethanol and Biofuel Boom: Its Origins, Current Status, and Future Prospects," *Bioscience* 58, no.7 (July 2008): 646.

[38] "Energy," North Dakota State University Energy Publications, accessed January 22, 2018, https://www.ag.ndsu.edu/energy/biofuels/energy-briefs/history-of-ethanol-production-and-policy.

[39] "Today in Energy," EIA, accessed January 22, 2018, https://www.eia.gov/todayinenergy/detail.php?id=3970.

40 Praven Duddu, "The Top 10 Biggest Geothermal Power Plants in the World," *Power Technology*, November 11, 2013, accessed January 22, 2018, https://www.power-technology.com/features/feature-top-10-biggest-geothermal-power-plants-in-the-world/.

41 "Hydroelectric Power in the 20th Century and Beyond."

42 "Wind Energy Development," BLM, accessed January 19, 2018, http://windeis.anl.gov/guide/concern/index.cfm.

43 "Environmental Impacts of Solar Power," Union of Concerned Scientists, accessed January 21, 2018, https://www.ucsusa.org/clean_energy/our-energy-choices/renewable-energy/environmental-impacts-solar-power.html#.WmTnbkxFzL8.

44 "Biomass."

45 "Household Air Pollution and Health," World Health Organization, accessed January 22, 2018, http://www.who.int/mediacentre/factsheets/fs292/en/.

46 "Biofuels: Ethanol and Biodiesel Explained."

47 "Environmental Impacts of Geothermal Energy," Union of Concerned Scientists, accessed January 22, 2018, https://www.ucsusa.org/clean_energy/our-energy-choices/renewable-energy/environmental-impacts-geothermal-energy.html#.WmYzJExFzL8.

48 Michael E. Kraft, *Environmental Policy and Politics* (New York: Routledge, 2018): 209.

49 Walter A. Rosenbaum, *American Energy: The Politics of 21st Century Policy* (Los Angeles: Sage/CQ Press, 2015): 79.

50 "Oil Dependence and U.S. Foreign Policy," Council on Foreign Relations, accessed December 30, 2017, https://www.cfr.org/timeline/oil-dependence-and-us-foreign-policy.

51 Walter A. Rosenbaum, *American Energy: The Politics of 21st Century Policy* (Los Angeles: Sage/CQ Press, 2015): 40.

52 "H.R. 776 (102nd): Energy Policy Act of 1992," Govtrack, accessed January 2, 2018, https://www.govtrack.us/congress/bills/102/hr776.

53 "Summary of the Energy Policy Act," EPA, accessed January 2, 2018, https://www.epa.gov/laws-regulations/summary-energy-policy-act.

54 Rosenbaum, *American Energy*, 102.

55 "Summary of the Energy Independence and Security Act," EPA, accessed January 2, 2018, https://www.epa.gov/laws-regulations/summary-energy-independence-and-security-act.

56 Jason P.H. Jones et al., "Policy Uncertainty and the U.S. Ethanol Industry," *Sustainability* 9 (2017): 2056.

57 Rosenbaum, *American Energy*, 158–159.

58 "History of Hydropower," DOE, accessed January 17, 2018, https://energy.gov/eere/water/history-hydropower.

59 Leah C. Stokes and Hanna L. Breetz, "Politics in the U.S. Energy Transition: Case Studies of Solar, Wind, Biofuels and Electric Vehicles Policy," *Energy Policy* 113 (2018): 79.

60 Stokes and Breetz, "Energy Transition," 80–81.

61 "Green Power Pricing," EPA, accessed January 19, 2018, https://www.epa.gov/greenpower/green-power-pricing.

62 "Public Benefit Funds," Center for Climate and Energy Solutions, accessed January 19, 2018, https://www.c2es.org/document/public-benefit-funds/.

63 Sunjoo Park, "State Renewable Energy Governance: Policy Instruments, Markets, or Citizens," *Review of Policy Research* 32, no. 3 (2015): 277.

[64] "A Brief History of Hydro," International Hydropower Association, accessed January 18, 2018, https://www.hydropower.org/a-brief-history-of-hydropower.

[65] "A Brief History of Hydropower."

[66] "Hydroelectric Power in the 20th Century and Beyond."

[67] "Hydroelectric Power Water Use."

[68] Yergin, *The Quest*, 597–598.

[69] Yergin, *The Quest*, 604–605.

[70] "Germany Feed Law," Windworks.org, accessed January 19, 2018, www.wind-works.org/cms/index.php?id=190.

[71] "Feed-in Tariffs," IEA, accessed January 19, 2018, https://www.iea.org/policiesand measures/pams/spain/name-23929-en.php.

[72] Lauha Fried, "Global Wind Statistics 2016," *Global Wind Energy Council* (2017): 1–4.

[73] "The History of Solar."

[74] Ka Zeng, "Domestic Politics and U.S.-China Trade Disputes Over Renewable Energy," *Journal of East Asian* Studies 15 (2015): 431.

[75] Eckhouse, Natter, and Martin. "Trump's Tariff on Solar Mark Biggest Blow to Renewables Yet."

[76] Adam Vaughan, "Solar Power Growth Leaps by 50% Worldwide Thanks to US and China," *The Guardian*, March 7, 2017, accessed January 21, 2018, https://www.theguardian.com/environment/2017/mar/07/solar-power-growth-worldwide-us-china-uk-europe.

[77] Chris Baraniuk, "Future Energy: China Leads World in Solar Power Production," *BBC News*, June 22, 2017, accessed January 21, 2018, http://www.bbc.com/news/business-403 41833.

[78] Bharadwaj Venkata, "World Energy Resources: Bioenergy 2016," *World Energy Council* (2016): 4–6.

[79] "Biofuel—Biodiesel History."

[80] Julian Borger, "UN Chief Calls for Review of Biofuels Policy," *The Guardian*, April 4, 2008, accessed January 22, 2018, https://www.theguardian.com/environment/2008/apr/05/biofuels.food.

[81] "Biofuels," National Geographic, accessed January 22, 2018, https://www.national geographic.com/environment/global-warming/biofuel/.

[82] Ted Montague, "World Energy Resources: Geothermal 2016," *World Energy Council* (2016): 2.

[83] Duddu, "The Top 10 Biggest Geothermal Power Plants in the World."

The Ozone Layer

INTRODUCTION

The depletion of the protective ozone layer became an international concern in the 1970s, emerging as one of the early truly multilateral environmental policy issues. This was because nations realized that the only answer to the problem of depletion of the ozone layer would be to bring all nations in concert to implement a shared solution. Both industrialized nations and developing nations had to agree to a path forward to address the phenomenon. This was accomplished by designing an agreement that recognized the "common but differentiated responsibilities" of nations; a concept that, while elaborated earlier, was listed as Principle 7 of the Rio Declaration. The chapter discusses how this was accomplished.

Uncertainty in the science explaining ozone depletion existed at the time that initial discussions took place. This meant negotiating an agreement using the precautionary principle, which balances the costs of taking precautionary action against the risks of inaction, until scientific evidence can provide more certainty. The chapter explores the factors that led the negotiators to initially take a precautionary approach. The chapter also discusses how delegates later strengthened terms of the agreement and accelerated the phaseout of ozone depleting substances (ODS) once scientific evidence of the link between chlorofluorocarbons (CFCs) and ozone depletion was firmly established.

The Montreal Protocol, which provided the binding agreement to reduce and eventually eliminate ozone depleting substances, has been called one of the most successful multilateral environmental agreements (MEA) ever negotiated. Part of that success is attributed to the flexibility built into the ozone regime that allowed the protocol to be adjusted and amended when new scientific information became available, without having to renegotiate the entire agreement. Adjustments allowed for the strengthening and acceleration of phaseouts for substances already covered by the agreement. Amendments allowed for the addition of new substances to the list of controlled substances. The chapter discusses the structures that became part of the ozone secretariat that allowed for review of new scientific information and adjustment or amendment of the treaty. Each of the amendments is discussed in detail.

MULTILATERAL EFFORTS TO COMBAT OZONE DEPLETION

The Phenomenon of Ozone Depletion

The ozone layer is a concentration of ozone in the stratosphere, a part of the atmosphere that begins about 6 miles above Earth's surface and extends to about 31 miles. Ozone is concentrated in a layer between about 9 and 18 miles. Ozone absorbs ultraviolet (UV) radiation coming from the sun which is linked to several harmful effects including skin cancers, cataracts, crop and ecosystem damage. Ozone is constantly created and destroyed in the stratosphere, as a naturally occurring process, and remains at a stable volume if not acted upon by hostile agents. However, when chlorine and bromine atoms come into contact with ozone in the atmosphere, they destroy ozone molecules at a rate much faster than ozone can naturally recreate. One chlorine atom can, in fact, destroy over 100,000 ozone molecules. Some compounds, such as CFCs, release chlorine or bromine when exposed to sunlight in the stratosphere and thus are ODS.[1]

CFCs were developed beginning in the 1920s to replace hazardous substances commonly used for refrigerants, including ammonia, methyl chloride, and sulfur dioxide. A number of fatal accidents in the 1920s put pressure on industry to come up with safer refrigerants. Frigidaire, General Motors, and Du Pont collaborated on a replacement. General Motors first synthesized CFCs in 1928 to use in commercial applications. Frigidaire was issued a patent for CFCs in that same year. In 1930, Du Pont and General Motors formed Kinetic Chemical company to produce Freon, its tradename for CFCs. By 1935, Frigidaire and its competitors had sold over 8 million refrigerators using Freon in the U.S. In the same year, Carrier Corporation used Freon in the first home air conditioners. After the Second World War, CFCs came to be used as propellants for insecticides, paints, hair sprays, and other personal care products. By the 1950s and 1960s, CFCs were marketed internationally.[2]

In 1974, Mario Molina and F.S. Rowland published a paper linking ozone depletion to CFCs. They theorized that, while CFCs were inert in the lower atmosphere, as CFCs were exposed to intense sunlight in the stratosphere, they gave off significant numbers of chlorine atoms, leading to the destruction of stratospheric ozone.[3] The Molina and Rowland paper was a scientific bombshell, kicking off a worldwide debate. In 1976, the National Academy of Sciences confirmed the effects of CFCs on ozone, Congressional hearings were held, and the U.S. federal government began to explore banning CFC use, especially as propellants in aerosol cans. The chemical industry argued that the data were inconclusive, and no drastic actions should be taken.[4]

Activists began to mobilize on both sides. In the summer of 1975, Richard Scorer, a respected scientist from the U.K., toured the U.S. arguing that the Molina-Rowland theory was hyperbole. His tour was organized by a public relations firm hired by the chemical industry. The chemical industry also placed ads in publications urging that chemicals be given the benefit of the doubt until scientific proof was provided linking CFCs to ozone depletion. Opposition also mounted as environmental groups called for precautionary action, arguing that if the Molina-Rowland theory was right, severe degradation to the ozone layer could occur before proof was found. Friends of the Earth and Natural Resources Defense Council petitioned the Consumer Product Safety Commission (CPSC) for a ban on all nonessential uses of CFCs. Initially, nonessential use included use in aerosol products, pressurized dispensers, and foam products containing or manufactured with CFCs (but over time the classification of nonessential use would grow). In 1976, the Carter administration launched a task force to consider CFCs. The task force contained representatives from relevant federal agencies and it recommended precautionary action. A few weeks after the recommendation, the Food and Drug Administration (FDA) proposed to phase out all nonessential uses of CFCs in products under its authority. The Environmental Protection Agency (EPA) also announced a ban on all nonessential uses. By 1977, EPA, FDA, and CPSC jointly announced a timetable for the phaseout of CFCs.[5]

Anxiety over increases in skin cancers, cataracts, and possible plant and crop damage led the U.S., Canada, Norway, Denmark, and Sweden to ban CFCs as propellants in cans and other consumer products.[6] The United Nations Environment Programme (UNEP) held a conference in 1977, and at it adopted a World Plan of Action on the Ozone Layer. A coordinating committee was established to organize future UNEP actions on ozone depletion. Negotiations for a multilateral agreement to protect the ozone layer were begun by UNEP in 1981.[7]

The Discovery of the Ozone 'Hole'

In 1984, British scientists, working at Halley Bay Station in Antarctica, published a study reporting their measurements of ozone over Antarctica. Joseph Farman, Brian Gardiner, and Jonathan Shanklin found that each spring the amount of ozone found in the Southern Hemisphere had dropped sharply since the late 1970s, and that this was linked to a corresponding rise of CFCs measured in the atmosphere. Farman had no proof of causation, nevertheless, he organized news conferences seeking to popularize the finding. The following year, National Aeronautics and Space Administration (NASA) scientists published a reanalysis of their satellite data, confirming the presence of the ozone hole. The NASA data showed that the mid-October values for ozone had fallen 40 percent between 1975 and 1984.[8]

The discovery of the hole in the ozone layer was major news, attracting much public attention, and provoking an overwhelming sense of psychological dread in the public. The ozone hole was perceived to be globally catastrophic and its impacts were generally thought to severely threaten present and future generations. Fear of increased skin cancers and cataracts were viewed by the public as personally endangering and the peril appeared inescapable. The possibility of threats to crops raised concerns over potential food insecurity. Because the ozone hole was unfamiliar and high-risk, the public demanded action, regardless of the uncertainty of the science.[9]

Vienna Convention for the Protection of the Ozone Layer

The Vienna Convention, the framework convention for the Montreal Protocol, was adopted in 1985 and entered into force in 1988. The convention did not set up any binding requirements on parties, but it did seek to promote cooperation among nations in creating and maintaining a system of observations, research, and information exchange on how human activities effect the ozone layer. The Convention also sought to bring the parties together to negotiate a subsequent agreement that would put in place mandatory reductions of emissions that harm the ozone layer. The parties to the Vienna Convention meet once every three years to make decisions to administer the agreement. The Vienna Convention also established two funds. The Trust Fund for the Vienna Convention supports the ozone secretariat and the meetings of the conference of parties (COP), as well as providing assistance to developing countries so that they may attend the conference. The Trust Fund for Research and Systematic Observation provides monies to developing countries so that they may meet their obligations to research and provide observations. Research and monitoring activities of the parties are reviewed by the Ozone Research Managers (ORM) meeting with the goal of identifying any gaps in data. ORM recommendations are forwarded to the COP. An Advisory Committee coordinates with the ozone secretariat and the World Meteorological Organization (WMO).[10]

Further Scientific Investigation and Understanding

Seven international agencies joined together in 1985 to write an assessment of the state of the ozone layer. Their report warned that if CFCs in the atmosphere continued to rise, there would be dire consequences to the ozone layer. They hypothesized that chlorine atoms might react on the surfaces of stratospheric clouds in polar regions, thus accelerating ozone loss over Antarctica. In 1986, American scientists went to Antarctica to study the ozone hole. Their measurements and findings pointed to chlorine as the culprit, but there was still no proof. Later in 1986, NASA formed an International Ozone Trends Panel along with the UNEP, the Federal Aviation Administration (FAA), the National Oceanic and Atmospheric Administration (NOAA), and WMO.[11]

In 1986, Du Pont, the world's largest producer of CFCs, announced that within five years alternatives to CFCs could be widely available. Because of the growing concern over the impacts on the ozone layer, industry representatives acknowledged that there should be restrictions on the growth of CFC production. Du Pont's leadership went even further, calling for a global limit of CFC emissions.[12] Having an alternative to CFCs was essential to enable a successful reduction of CFCs. Du Pont and other chemical manufacturers were successful in creating hydrochlorofluorocarbons (HCFCs) and hydrofluorocarbons (HFCs) in the 1980s. These would later be adopted as alternatives for CFCs, although they still have negative impacts on the atmosphere. HCFCs destroy less ozone than CFCs. CFCs, HCFCs, and HFCs, however, are all potent global warming gases.[13]

In 1987, Margaret Kripke, a University of Texas skin cancer expert testified before the White House Domestic Policy Council that the world would definitely see an increase of skin cancers with the depletion of the ozone layer. She also underscored the point that there were other issues of global importance to consider, including possible harm to the global food supply and the potential spread of diseases due to the harmful effects of UV radiation on the human immune system. At a Senate hearing held in 1987, University of Maryland scientist, Alan Teramura, warned of undeniable crop damage that would result from a less protective ozone layer.[14] These warnings, and others like them coming from medical and scientific experts, made taking decisive action to prevent and reverse ozone depletion more urgent.

Montreal Protocol on Substances That Deplete the Ozone Layer

The Montreal Protocol was designed to reduce the production and consumption of ODS so that the ozone layer could repair itself. It was agreed to in 1987 and entered into force in 1989. The Montreal Protocol was designed for flexibility, allowing parties to respond quickly to new scientific information and to accelerate reductions of chemicals already covered by the Protocol through an adjustment process. Adjustments are automatically applicable to all parties to the agreement. Since its adoption, the Protocol has been adjusted 6 times. The Protocol can also be amended to enable the addition of new chemicals and to create new financial mechanisms to help developing nations comply with the agreement. Amendments need to be ratified by parties to the agreement before those changes apply to those parties. The annual meeting of parties (MOP) also results in decisions about the implementation of the Protocol.[15]

The Montreal Protocol established a number of organizations to support the decision making of the parties. These include the Technology and Economic Assessment Panel (TEAP), the Technical Options Committees (TOCs), and the Scientific Assessment Panel (SAP). TEAP is the main scientific and technical group and is made up of experts from both developed and developing countries. If the parties have questions, TEAP provides technical answers. Parties are not allowed to interfere with the working of TEAP. They can make political arguments only after TEAP releases its reports. Lack of interference increases the integrity of TEAP reports. The TOCs provide specialized expertise to evaluate requests from parties for exemptions and to work with the parties to assure the earliest possible phaseout of banned ODS. The SAP constantly monitors the ozone layer and the restoration actions taken. It makes recommendations on appropriate next steps for ozone layer recovery.[16] In addition, the Environmental Effects Assessment Panel (EEAP) monitors the photobiology and photochemistry of the ozone layer. Comprised mainly of scientists located in universities and research institutions, EEAP writes periodic assessments of the various effects of ozone layer depletion.[17] Through the use of these committees and panels, the Montreal Protocol stays informed of state-of-the-art science, as well as of parties' needs.

The Montreal Protocol at first introduced control measures for some CFCs and halons for developed countries, called non-Article 5 parties. Non-Article 5 parties were initially required to reduce CFCs use by 50 percent by 1999. Developing countries, called Article 5 parties, were granted a 10-year waiver period during which they could increase their use of ODS before they had to comply with reductions.[18] The inclusion of provisions to allow developing nations to adopt a less pressing schedule of reductions allowed developing nations to become part of the solution to the problem rather than a blocking coalition. The grace period allowed developing countries, like China and India, to continue to expand their use of air conditioning and cooling devices like refrigerators and freezers powered by cheap CFCs rather than their more expensive replacement compounds. These provisions helped these countries meet the demands of their growing middle-class citizens.[19]

Scientific Proof

In August and September of 1987, NASA managed a multi-institutional study of the atmosphere over Antarctica to explain the loss of ozone over the continent. Airborne samples were collected to obtain a database of chemicals, weather, and cloud formations associated with ozone loss. It was the largest data acquisition over Antarctica ever undertaken. The results of the study were presented at the Polar Ozone Symposium in Colorado in May of 1988 and published in a special two volume edition of the *Journal of Geophysical Research*. The data showed the lowest level of ozone ever recorded, the inverse correlation between ozone and chlorine, and proved that CFCs were responsible for depletion of the ozone layer.[20]

London Amendment of 1990

Based on this new scientific information, the Montreal Protocol was amended to call for a full phaseout of CFCs, halons, and other ODS.[21] At the second MOP, held in London in 1990, delegates augmented the schedule of phaseouts through an adjustment and added another 10 CFCs, carbon tetrachloride (CTC), and methyl chloroform to the list of ODS. The London Amendment changed the ODS phaseout schedule by requiring developed nations to completely eliminate CFCs, halons, and carbon tetrachloride by 2000 and by 2010 in developing countries. Methyl chloroform was to be phased out by 2005 in developed countries and by 2015 in developing countries.[22]

The London Amendment also established the Multilateral Fund (MLF), which provides funds to Article 5 countries to help with their obligations to phase out ODS. Article 5 countries are those with per capita consumption of ODS of less than 0.3 kg per year, or the developing countries. The MLF was the first financial mechanism to be formed as the result of an international environmental treaty. It follows the principle that would be formalized in the Rio Earth Summit in 1992 that countries have a "common but differentiated responsibilities" to protect the Earth's environment. The differentiation stems from those nations responsible for the pollution and those nations not responsible for it. In 1986, developed countries consumed more than 85 percent of ODS and they agreed to contribute to a fund to help Article 5 countries comply with the goals of the Montreal Protocol. The MLF funds only the additional or incremental costs incurred by developing nations in converting to non-ODS technologies. The MLF is managed by an Executive Committee that consists of delegates from 7 developed and 7 developing nations, elected annually at the MOP. The Executive Committee reports the status of its operations to the MOP. Financial assistance is given in the form of grants and loans coming from UNEP, the United Nations Development Programme (UNDP), the United Nations Industrial Development Organization (UNIDO), or the World Bank. Up to 20 percent of the contributions to the MLF can also be distributed by a contributing party directly to a bilateral partner through eligible projects. The MLF is replenished every three years by the donor nations.[23]

The creation of the MLF generated incentives for developing nations to agree to amendments that added new substances to the list of ODS. It also helped to assure that production of ODS would actually decline and not simply move from the developed world to the developing world as a result of Article 5 parties refusing to ratify amendments that added new substances to the treaty. The Montreal Protocol also put in place strong trade restrictions to prevent parties from importing controlled substances from non-party countries, thus reducing the potential benefits for Article 5 nations to leave the agreement.[24]

Copenhagen Amendment of 1992

This amendment, passed at MOP 4, again accelerated phaseout of ODS and added HCFCs to the list of chemicals that needed to be eliminated, for developed countries, by 2004. Developed countries were to end the use of CFCs, halons, carbon tetrachloride and methyl chloroform by 1996, and methyl bromide use was capped at 1991 levels.[25]

At MOP 4, delegates also agreed to put in place non-compliance procedures. An Implementation Committee was created that put in place dispute resolution measures. Actions that can be taken to resolve non-compliance include providing financial and technical assistance to help parties comply, issuing cautions, and suspension of specific rights under the Protocol. A party to the treaty can approach the Implementation Committee seeking assistance from other nations to meet their obligations. This created another opportunity for Article 5 nations to continue to be part of the Protocol. Parties are also required to submit reports with data on imports, exports, and production of controlled ODS to the Implementation Committee. This keeps the Implementation Committee appraised of activities in all countries.[26]

Montreal Amendment of 1997

This amendment expanded the phaseout of HCFCs to developing countries. Methyl bromide was to be phased out by developed countries by 2005 and by developing countries by 2015.[27] The amendment also required each country to establish a system for licensing the import and export of controlled substances.[28]

Beijing Amendment of 1999

This amendment tightened controls over production and trade of HCFCs. Bromochloromethane was added to the list of ODS and was to be phased out by 2004.[29]

MOP 21 Through MOP 28

After the Beijing Amendment, annual MOPs continued, and decisions were adopted on a wide variety of issues. In 2009, at MOP 21, initial consideration was given to the addition of HFCs to the Protocol. This was because HFCs have very high global warming potential (GWP). MOP 21 also adopted decisions on alternatives to

HCFCs and environmentally-sound management of methyl bromide and other ODS. MOP 22 adopted decisions on terms of reference for the TEAP study of MLF replenishment and evaluation of financial mechanisms. MOP 23, met in 2011 in Bali, Indonesia and adopted decisions on a $450 million USD replenishment of MLF for the 2012–2014 period. Again, delegates discussed two proposed amendments to add HFCs to the Protocol. MOP 24, met in Geneva, Switzerland in 2012 and MOP 25, met in Bangkok, Thailand in 2013. Both discussed but did not reach agreement on an HFC amendment. Decisions were adopted on procedural issues in TEAP. MOP 26 met in Paris, France, in 2014, and delegates debated ways to move the HFC amendment forward. They adopted decisions on the next wave of funding for the MLF. MOP 27 met in Dubai, UAE in 2015 and adopted decisions on avoiding imports of products containing or relying on HCFCs. Delegates adopted the Dubai pathway on HFCs, which was a roadmap for the HFC amendment.[30]

Kigali Amendment of 2016

At MOP 28, in Kigali, Rwanda, in 2016, delegates agreed to amend the Montreal Protocol to include HFCs and to set a phaseout schedule for the substances. The passage of the amendment marked years of debate about what to do with HFCs. The Montreal Protocol had paradoxically paved the way for widespread use of HFCs, by using HFCs to replace stronger ODS such as CFCs and HCFCs, both of which are greenhouse gases (GHGs). While HFCs deplete the ozone layer only a small amount, they are extremely powerful GHGs, with more global warming potential than CFCs or HCFCs. HFCs can be up to 10,000 times more powerful than carbon dioxide. The Montreal Protocol can be amended to ban any chemical, even those that only modestly affect the ozone layer such as HFCs.[31]

By phasing out HFCs, the Montreal Protocol can protect the ozone layer without worsening climate change. Estimates suggest that the Kigali Amendment will mitigate between 70 to 100 billion tons of carbon dioxide equivalent by 2050 and prevent up to 0.5 Celsius increase in global warming by 2100. Prioritizing adoption of energy efficient newer technologies could hypothetically double these mitigation improvements. Developed countries began to transition to HCFCs once CFCs were phased out. By 2009, 77 percent of shifts were from HCFCs to HFCs. The transition to HFCs also began shortly thereafter in developing countries.[32]

Several proposed HFC amendments were put forward in 2015. One was backed by Canada, the U.S., and Mexico. Its terms included a phaseout of HFCs, requiring developed nations to begin with a 10 percent reduction in 2019, scaling to a 35 percent reduction by 2024, a 70 percent reduction by 2030, and an 85 percent reduction by 2038. The corresponding schedule for A5 parties included a grace period of no reductions through 2021, followed by a 20 percent reduction by 2026, a 60 percent reduction by 2032, and an 85 percent reduction by 2046. Amendment proposals were also submitted by the European Union (EU), the Island States, and India. The EU and Island states wanted a quicker phaseout. India, however, wanted A5 nations to have more flexibility to continue to use HFCs for another several decades. India's concern was based on the higher expected cost of air conditioners, refrigerators, and other products using HFC alternatives. The U.S. responded by assuring A5 nations that the non-A5 nations would provide financial assistance to A5 nations as they transitioned to the newer products. This promise obtained consensus.[33]

The terms of the accepted compromise amendment include a freeze for A5 parties beginning in 2024 and a first 10 percent reduction for developed countries in 2019. The phaseout is rapid for developed countries which must reduce HFCs by 85 percent by 2036, relative to their baseline of 2011–2013. Most A5 countries, including China, follow a slightly less aggressive phaseout schedule, reaching a reduction of 80 percent of HFCs by 2045, relative to their baseline consumption levels in 2020–2022. A small number of A5 countries received an exemption and do not have to freeze until 2028. However, a group of private philanthropists and donor nations announced in 2017 that they would provide $80 million in support to A5 nations, with an initial freeze date of 2024, to help them accelerate their reduction schedules or to improve their energy efficiency.[34] These actions represent an acceptance of the "common but differentiated responsibilities" principle and the fact that developing nations require financial and technical assistance.

In addition, establishment of a licensing system for controlling import and export of HFCs needs to be in place by 2019 (or three months after the amendment is ratified by 20 countries).[35] The Kigali Amendment also requires regular reporting and review. Reviews will be undertaken every five years. TEAP will assess the newly available technologies and recommend adjustments to the MOP if they seem prudent.[36] As of January 22, 2018, 24 parties had ratified the Kigali Amendment a sufficient number to allow it to enter into force in 2019.[37]

U.S. PHASEOUT OF ODS

In the U.S., phaseout of ODS was implemented by EPA regulations issued under its Clean Air Act authority. The regulations comply with schedules set under the Montreal Protocol. Under U.S. law, CFCs are treated as Class I controlled substances while HCFCs are treated as Class II controlled substances. Class I substances have higher ozone depleting potential and as of 2018 have been completely phased out in the U.S. Class II substances were introduced as transitional substitutes for many Class I substances and, as of 2018, are being phased out.[38]

The EPA also introduced the Significant New Alternatives Program (SNAP) under its Clean Air Act authority to identify chemicals that might provide viable alternatives to ODS.[39] The EPA publishes a list of available acceptable alternative chemicals by industrial or commercial application, thus promoting the use of alternatives and a faster phaseout of ODS. The EPA review for each replacement chemical includes data on ozone depletion potential, global warming potential, local air quality impacts, occupation and consumer health and safety, toxicity, flammability, and ecosystem impacts. As of July 2015, the EPA also issued a final rule prohibiting the use of some HFC products where viable alternatives had been identified.[40]

FACTORS LEADING TO SUCCESS OF THE MONTREAL PROTOCOL

The Montreal Protocol and amendments is the only multilateral treaty negotiated in the history of the United Nations to receive universal ratification.[41] A large part of the reason for this success is the attention paid by delegates to both "common but differentiated responsibilities" and the need for financial and technical support to flow from the developed nations to the developing nations. By allowing A5 nations grace periods before phaseout of ODS needed to begin, the Protocol recognized the need for the developing countries to continue to add cheaper refrigeration, air conditioning, and other products still based on the older and more ozone depleting gases. By providing financial incentives to the developing countries to transition to the newer technologies, the developed nations also showed they understood the needs of the A5 countries. These mechanisms together resulted in cooperation, rather than conflict.

Using a 'start and strengthen' model, the Montreal Protocol has, over its 30-year history, been able to start modestly but gradually expand to control the production and consumption of many ODS. By 2010, the Montreal Protocol had successfully phased out nearly 100 of the worst ODS, avoiding adverse impacts expected from depletion of the ozone layer on humans, animals, crops, and other plants. Unfortunately, as climate was not considered in ozone deliberations until 2009, most of the worst ODS were replaced first with HCFCs and later with HFCs. With the addition of the Kigali Amendment, though, that situation changed and the threat of HFCs both to the ozone layer and to the climate was addressed.[42]

The Montreal Protocol was successful because there was political will to act on an issue that portended a global environmental disaster. Even before the scientists were able to confirm a causal link between CFCs and ozone depletion, public and political opinion sought precautionary action. Much of the willingness certainly was attributed to the fear associated with the ozone hole and the wide attention it received in the media.[43]

A good deal of the success of the Montreal Protocol is owed to the fact that alternatives to ODS were forthcoming. Du Pont had done considerable research and development (R&D) on alternatives to CFCs in the early 1980s. When restrictions seemed forthcoming, Du Pont redoubled its efforts. Between 1986 and 1988, the company poured $45 million into research on HCFCs and HFCs. Because these alternatives were more expensive than CFCs, Du Pont realized that only CFC regulation would make them marketable. Du Pont was also concerned about the harm CFC production was doing to its public image, given the public response to the ozone hole. Rather than blocking the regulation of CFCs, Du Pont saw a business opportunity in marketing alternative chemicals.[44] Similarly, when HCFCs and HFCs came under scrutiny, a number of companies took action to promote safer alternatives and technologies. Chemours announced its Opteon™ family of low global warming potential alternatives to HFCs, Daikin Industries publicized its commitment to eliminate fugitive HFC emissions from its production facilities worldwide, Demilec released its first hydrofluoroolefin alternative for blown spray foam, Dow Chemical publicized its commitment to elimination of high-global warming potential HFCs, and Honeywell announced its Solstice$_R$ line of low global warming potential products. Many other firms moved to position themselves for the transition away from HFCs.[45]

The organizational structure of the Montreal Protocol itself has promoted success. The three assessment panels, TEAP, SAP, and EEAP and the various technical committees, have provided independent scientific and technical information to the delegates, helping them to make science-based informed decisions. The periodic assessments carried out by the panels and their reporting requirements assure the unbiased functioning of the Montreal Protocol.[46]

CONCLUSION

The ozone layer is the name used to refer to the concentration of ozone in the stratosphere. Ozone absorbs the sun's harmful UV radiation, preventing it from reaching the surface of the Earth. If that UV radiation did hit the Earth's surface, humans and animals would suffer from many more skin cancers and cataracts. Widespread crop damage that might result in food shortages could also be anticipated. Plants, other than crops, would also be adversely affected. Ozone has a natural cycle of creation and destruction in the stratosphere that allows it to remain a stable, protective layer. However, the interaction of chlorine and bromine atoms with ozone results in the rapid destruction of ozone molecules at rates that prohibit natural regeneration. CFCs and HCFCs release chlorine or bromine when exposed to sunlight. Their presence in the upper atmosphere led to the start of the depletion of the ozone layer.

CFCs date to the 1920s. They were developed to replace hazardous substances commonly used for refrigerants after a number of fatal accidents occurred. Frigidaire, General Motors, and Du Pont each worked on creating replacement chemicals and each marketed CFCs. They were first used for refrigerants and air conditioners. Later they were marketed as propellants for paints, insecticides, hair sprays, and other personal care products. By the 1960s, CFCs were a global product.

In 1974, two U.S. scientists, Molina and Rowland, theorized that as CFCs were exposed to intense sunlight in the stratosphere, they gave off significant numbers of chlorine atoms, leading to the destruction of stratospheric ozone. Their paper attracted worldwide attention and concern but since it provided only speculation and no substantial scientific proof, the chemical companies producing CFCs fought any regulation. Nevertheless, nervousness over increasing numbers of skin cancers and cataracts, along with possible plant and crop damage led to several nations, including the U.S., to ban CFCs as propellants. UNEP organized a conference to consider the ozone issue in 1977, marking the beginnings of actions toward a new world treaty.

The shocking discovery of the ozone hole over Antarctica in 1984 provoked further public consternation. NASA's confirmation of the presence of the ozone hole guaranteed heavy press coverage. The phenomenon generated substantial uneasiness. The public viewed the ozone hole as a global environmental calamity. Government officials were moved to take action, even though scientific proof linking CFCs to ozone depletion had not yet been obtained.

Nations gathered in Vienna, Austria to draft the Vienna Convention, which became the framework convention for the Montreal Protocol. The Vienna Convention promoted cooperation among nations to put in place a system of observations, research, and information exchange on ozone layer depletion. As discussions were underway in Vienna, more scientific information was revealed. A group of international agencies provided assessment of the ozone layer that cautioned something needed to be done. American scientists went to Antarctica to study the ozone hole, finding further evidence of the destructive role of chlorine coming from CFCs. CFC manufacturers, including Du Pont, joined the worldwide discussion suggesting that their corporate R&D showed that CFC alternatives like HCFCs and HFCs were possible, albeit more expensive. Other scientists warned with great urgency of expected rates of skin cancers, cataracts, and crop damage likely to produce food shortages.

The Montreal Protocol provided binding reductions of ODS. It was designed to be flexible, allowing rapid response to new scientific information. It used two measures to provide this flexibility: adjustments and amendments. Adjustments, automatically applicable to all parties to the agreement, allowed for the ratcheting up of phaseouts of chemicals already covered by the Protocol. Amendments allowed for the addition of new ODS. The committees and panels created by the agreement also allowed for careful attention to scientific and technical changes as well as up to date information flows to delegates. The Montreal Protocol's implementation recognized the "common but differentiated responsibilities" of countries by creating grace periods and longer phaseout schedules for Article 5 parties. After the negotiation of the Montreal Protocol, a NASA coordinated study of the atmosphere over Antarctica provided proof of the use of CFCs and depletion of the ozone layer.

Based on this new scientific certainty, in 1990, the Montreal Protocol was amended by the London Amendment which implemented a more rapid phaseout of CFCs, halons, and other ODS. At the conference that was held in London, additional ODS were also added to the list of controlled substances. The London Amendment also established the MLF to provide financial assistance to Article 5 countries so that they could meet their obligations under the agreement. The Montreal Protocol was amended again in Copenhagen in 1992 accelerating the phaseout of ODS and adding HCFCs to the list of controlled chemicals. Further strengthening of the agreement would happen through the Montreal Amendment in 1997 and the Beijing Amendment in 1999.

Discussions about HFCs started in 2009 but many years of would pass before HFCs were added to the list of controlled substances. Finally, in 2016, delegates agreed to the Kigali Amendment which set a phaseout schedule for HFCs. This amendment marked a shift in the decision making of the ozone regime to include not only impacts on the ozone layer but on global warming as well. The Kigali Amendment, once implemented, will mitigate much carbon dioxide equivalent and prevent considerable increases in global warming.

The Montreal Protocol is often considered a model MEA. There are several reasons such claims have been made. The recognition that developing nations needed both more time and financial assistance to become partners with the developed nations in protecting the ozone layer was one. The 'start and strengthen' model allowed expansion of the list of controlled chemicals as scientific knowledge improved. Starting with just a handful of CFCs, by 2010, the Montreal Protocol had successfully phased out nearly 100 ODS. Political will to act to save the ozone layer, even before the scientists were able to confirm the tie between CFCs and ozone depletion, was another factor leading to success. The Montreal Protocol could not have succeeded if there were no viable replacement chemicals or technologies made available. Finally, the well-designed assessment panels and technical committees provide the delegates the accurate scientific and technical information they need to make informed science-based decisions.

[1]   "Basic Ozone Layer Science," EPA, accessed January 26, 2018, https://www.epa.gov/ozone-layer-protection/basic-ozone-layer-science.

[2]   "Chlorofluorocarbons (CFCs)," NOAA, accessed January 26, 2018, https://www.esrl.noaa.gov/gmd/hats/publictn/elkins/cfcs.html.

[3]   Mario J. Molina and F.S. Rowland, "Stratospheric Sink for Chlorofluoromethanes: Chlorine Atomcatalysed Destruction of Ozone," *Nature* 249 (1974): 810.

[4]   "Chlorofluorocarbons and Ozone Depletion," American Chemical Society, accessed January 26, 2018, https://www.acs.org/content/acs/en/education/whatischemistry/landmarks/cfcs-ozone.html.

[5]   Craig Collins, *Toxic Loopholes: Failures and Future Prospects for Environmental Law* (Cambridge: Cambridge University Press, 2010): 160–161.

[6]   Gary W. Ewart et al., "From Closing the Atmospheric Ozone Hole to Reducing Climate Change," *Annals of the American Thoracic Society* 12, no. 2 (February 2015): 247.

[7]   Kate Helfenstein-Louw, et al., "A Brief History of the Ozone Regime," *Earth Negotiations Bulletin* 19, no. 138 (2017): 1, accessed January 22, 2018, http://enb.iisd.org/ozone/cop11-mop29/.

[8]   Jonathan Shanklin, "Reflections on the Ozone Hole," *Nature* 465 (May 6, 2010): 34.

[9]   Collins, *Toxic Loopholes*, 170.

[10]   "The Vienna Convention for the Protection of the Ozone Layer," Ozone Secretariat, accessed August 10, 2018, https://unep.ch/ozone/pdfs/viennaconvention2002.pdf.

[11]   Stephen O. Andersen, Marcel L. Halberstadt, and Nathan Borgford-Parnell, "Stratospheric Ozone, Global Warming, and the Principle of Unintended Consequences: An Ongoing Science and Policy Success Story," *Journal of the Air & Waste Management Association* 63, no.6 (2013): 615.

[12]   Peter M. Morrisette, "The Montreal Protocol: Lessons for Formulating Policies for Global Warming," *Policy Studies Journal* 19, no. 2 (Spring 1991): 155.

[13]   "Hydrochlorofluorocarbons," Gale Encyclopedia of Science, accessed January 28, 2018, http://www.encyclopedia.com/history/historians-and-chronicles/historians-miscellaneous-biographies/hydrochlorofluorocarbons.

[14]   Andersen, Halberstadt, and Borgford-Parnell, "Stratospheric Ozone, Global Warming, and the Principle of Unintended Consequences," 616.

[15]   "The Montreal Protocol on Substances that Deplete the Ozone Layer," Ozone Secretariat, accessed August 10, 2018, http://web.unep.org/ozonaction/who-we-are/about-montreal-protocol.

[16]   Mark W. Roberts, "Finishing the Job: The Montreal Protocol Moves to Phase Down Hydrofluorocarbons," *Review of European, Comparative & International Environmental Law* 26 (2017): 222.

[17]   "Assessment Panels," UNEP, accessed August 10, 2018, http://ozone.unep.org/science.

[18]   Helfenstein-Louw, et al., "A Brief History of the Ozone Regime," 1.

[19]   "Ozone Depletion," Enviropedia, accessed January 28, 2018, http://www.ozone-hole.org.uk/17.php.

[20]   "NASA Airborne Antarctic Ozone Experiment," NASA, accessed January 27, 2018, https://geo.arc.nasa.gov/sge/jskiles/fliers/all_flier_prose/antarcticO3_condon/antarcticO3_condon.html.

[21]   Morrisette, "The Montreal Protocol," 155.

[22]   "International Treaties and Cooperation," EPA, accessed January 28, 2018, https://www.epa.gov/ozone-layer-protection/international-treaties-and-cooperation.

[23]   "Multilateral Fund," Multilateral Fund for the Implementation of the Montreal Protocol, accessed January 28, 2018, http://www.multilateralfund.org/aboutMLF/default.aspx.

[24]   Sean Cumberlege, "Multilateral Environmental Agreements: From Montreal to Kyoto—A Theoretical Approach to an Improved Climate Change Regime," *Denver Journal of International Law & Policy* 37, no. 2 (2009): 314–315.

[25]   "International Treaties and Cooperation."

[26]   Cumberlege, "Multilateral Environmental Agreements," 316.

[27]   "International Treaties and Cooperation."

[28]   "Licensing and Quota Systems," UNEP, accessed January 28, 2018, http://web.unep.org/ozonaction/what-we-do/licensing-and-quota-systems.

[29]   "International Treaties and Cooperation."

[30]   Helfenstein-Louw, et al., "A Brief History of the Ozone Regime," 2.

[31]   Lynn L. Bergeson, "The Montreal Protocol is Amended and Strengthened," *Environmental Quality Management* (Spring 2017): 137.

[32]   Roberts, "Finishing the Job," 220–221.

[33]   Bergeson, "The Montreal Protocol is Amended and Strengthened," 138.

[34]   Bergeson, "The Montreal Protocol is Amended and Strengthened," 139.

[35]   "Licensing and Quota Systems."

[36]   Bergeson, "The Montreal Protocol is Amended and Strengthened," 139.

[37]   "Status of Ratification," Ozone Secretariat, accessed August 10, 2018, http://ozone.unep.org/vienna-convention-protection-ozone-layer/94589.

[38]   "What is the Phaseout of Ozone-Depleting Substances?" EPA, accessed January 28, 2018, https://www.epa.gov/ods-phaseout/what-phaseout-ozone-depleting-substances.

[39]   "Significant New Alternatives Program," EPA, accessed January 28, 2018, https://www.epa.gov/snap.

[40]   Bergeson, "The Montreal Protocol is Amended and Strengthened," 139.

[41]   Bergeson, "The Montreal Protocol is Amended and Strengthened," 139.

42 Roberts, "Finishing the Job," 222.

43 Morrisette, "The Montreal Protocol," 155–156.

44 Collins, *Toxic Loopholes*, 196–197.

45 Bergeson, "The Montreal Protocol is Amended and Strengthened," 140.

46 "Assessment Panels."

CHAPTER 14

Climate Change Policy

INTRODUCTION

Climate change has been internationally recognized as an environmental problem since the 1980s, although scientists had long understood the relationship between the warming of the planet and atmospheric concentrations of greenhouse gases (GHGs). This chapter begins with a discussion of the greenhouse effect and how scientists came to understand that anthropogenic additions to the volume of GHGs in the atmosphere were causing the planet to warm.

Once human-induced global warming was suspected, world leaders began to organize internationally to better understand what role human activities had in contributing to this warming. Once enough was understood about human additions to the increasing levels of GHGs in the atmosphere, international meetings were organized to begin discussions on what actions could be taken to mitigate, or bring down, the volumes of GHGs.

Early agreements on the mitigation of climate change relied on several principles that had emerged from wider international discussions and agreements going back to the 1970s. One of these principles was the notion that nations have "common but differentiated responsibilities" to protect the planet. Another closely associated principle was that developing nations needed financial and technical assistance if they were to be able to join the developed countries as partners in mitigation efforts. These principles, and how they played out climate negotiations leading to the Kyoto Protocol, are explored.

The refusal of the U.S. to join the Kyoto Protocol had important consequences, both domestically and internationally. While the federal government played little part in attempts to mitigate GHGs before the Obama administration came to office, state- and local-based efforts did emerge. The chapter explores the efforts of states to organize regional compacts to reduce GHGs and efforts of localities to create green cities committed to climate change mitigation.

With the election of Barack Obama, U.S. federal policy had the possibility of changing. The Obama administration, primarily using executive action, put in place a number of policy initiatives to combat climate change. The Obama administration understood clearly that without the commitment of developing countries, especially China and India, to reducing their GHG emissions, the U.S. Congress would probably reject unilateral American efforts. Moreover, since China had overtaken the U.S. as the world's largest emitter of GHGs, and India's emissions were ready to rise dramatically, the Obama administration knew that any serious attempt to mitigate GHGs would require the full participation of developing countries. The Obama administration first worked with China to develop a bilateral agreement to reduce GHGs emissions. Having demonstrated willingness to provide international leadership once again, the Obama administration played a critical role in negotiation of a successor treaty to the Kyoto Protocol. The Paris Agreement is discussed in detail in the chapter.

America's commitment to international leadership on climate policy, however, would be reversed with the election of Donald Trump. The chapter explores efforts taken by the Trump administration to reverse Obama's climate legacy. The chapter closes with a discussion of the issues that loom large as climate change policy is implemented in the next several decades including the political will to act and the manageability of solutions given the dependence of modern society on fossil fuels. The chapter closes with a cautionary exploration of potential geoengineering solutions that may be used in the future.

MULTILATERAL EFFORTS TO COMBAT CLIMATE CHANGE

The Phenomenon of Climate Change

The greenhouse effect makes life on Earth possible. Without the warming provided by the greenhouse effect, the Earth would be quite cold. The sun's radiation includes its visible light, as well as ultraviolet (UV) and infrared radiation. When this solar energy hits the atmosphere, about one third is reflected back into space. The rest is absorbed by the Earth, especially by the oceans, heating the planet. The Earth reradiates some of the energy it has absorbed, mostly as heat in infrared radiation. Some naturally occurring GHGs allow visible light to escape back to space but trap some forms of infrared radiation. These include water vapor, methane, nitrous oxide, and carbon dioxide. Together they keep the planet about 60 °F warmer than it otherwise would be.[1]

Water vapor is the most abundant GHG, but it acts primarily as a feedback to the climate. As the climate warms, water vapor increases in the atmosphere. With increased water vapor, there are more clouds and precipitation. Carbon dioxide (CO_2) is the most important GHG. It is released by normal processes such as human and animal respiration and volcanic eruptions, but it is also released as a result of human activities such as the burning of fossil fuels and deforestation. Human activities have increased the amount of CO_2 in the atmosphere substantially since the beginning of the Industrial Revolution.[2] About 250 years ago, at the beginning of the Industrial Revolution, CO_2 levels in the atmosphere were about 280 parts per million (ppm). Since then, humans have been emitting CO_2 into the atmosphere in large volumes. By 2016, CO_2 levels had hit 400 ppm and continue to climb.[3] CO_2 stays in the atmosphere for a long time, depending on the process that is used to remove it. There are several processes that remove CO_2 from the air. About 60 to 85 percent of CO_2 in the atmosphere is dissolved into the oceans in a process that can stretch from 20 to 200 years. The rest is removed by other processes, such as rock formation and chemical weathering, that can take many thousands of years.[4] In 2014, CO_2 emissions accounted for 76 percent of global GHGs.[5]

Other GHGs include methane, nitrous oxide, and industrial chemicals containing chlorine or fluorine, such as chlorofluorocarbons (CFCs), hydrochlorofluorocarbons (HCFCs), and hydrofluorocarbons (HFCs). Methane is produced both as a natural process and as the result of human activities. Human activities that produce methane include the decomposition of wastes in landfills, rice cultivation, the digestion of ruminant animals (especially animals raised for human consumption), manure from livestock, and fugitive methane emissions from oil and gas production and refining operations.[6] Methane is primarily removed from the atmosphere by chemical reaction and persists in the air only about 12 years, but it is a much stronger GHG than CO_2.[7] In 2014, methane accounted for 16 percent of global GHG emissions.[8] In 2014, nitrous oxides comprised 6 percent of global emissions. Nitrous oxide is released into the atmosphere by fertilizers, fossil fuel combustion, biomass burning, and nitric acid production. Nitrous oxide remains in the atmosphere for over 100 years.[9] CFCs, HCFCs, and HFCs are synthetic chemicals used largely as refrigerants and are now regulated by the Montreal Protocol (discussed in chapter 13). CFCs, HCFCs, and HFCs consist of a wide family of compounds that vary in their atmospheric duration. Some last less than a year while others persist for many thousands of years.[10] In 2014, these gases made up 2 percent of the world's GHG emissions.[11]

Global surface air temperatures have increased about 1.8°F since 1900. The years between 1900 and 2016 have been the warmest in the history of modern civilization. In addition to warming, researchers worldwide have documented many other changes that have already occurred including changes of surface, atmospheric, and ocean temperatures; shrinking snow cover; melting glaciers; decreased sea ice;

rising sea levels; ocean acidification; an increase in extreme weather events; increased number and severity of heatwaves; and large forest fires.[12]

These changes will increase existing dangers and add additional risks to both natural and human systems. Moreover, these hazards will not be evenly distributed but will fall more harshly on poor and disadvantaged people worldwide. Poorer human populations will be unable to command the resources to adapt to life in a warmer world. Climate change is expected to have many negative effects on human, animal, and plant populations. For instance, climate change is projected to threaten food security for many. Climate change will also reduce renewable surface water and groundwater resources, thus increasing competition for water. Climate change is expected to lead to an increase in bad health outcomes for many, especially in developing countries. For the plant and animal world, a large number of species face the risk of extinction. Plants cannot readily shift their geographic ranges fast enough to keep up with the current rate of climate changes projected. Many animals, either land-based or marine, will also not be able to effectively deal with ecosystem shifts. Marine animals will face higher levels of ocean acidification.[13]

By 2050, lacking any change in human behavior that rapidly reduces the emission of GHGs, climate change will result in worsening drought conditions in many geographic locations worldwide, including the American Southwest, Southern Europe, and other regions around the world that are heavily populated or farmed, thus increasing food insecurity. Sea levels will likely rise by 1 foot by 2050 and by 4 feet by 2100, threatening massive flooding. The permafrost worldwide will thaw, releasing massive amounts of additional CO_2 and methane into the atmosphere, thus further exacerbating warming. Wildfires, especially in the northern boreal forests of Canada, Russia, and Alaska will release much stored CO_2 into the atmosphere, both from burning of the trees and because many of these forests are growing on permafrost or peatland. All of these outcomes will decrease the ability of ocean and land sinks to absorb more CO_2 emissions, causing a feedback loop that will intensify climate change. Superstorms will become more threatening, because warmer air can hold much more water and because atmospheric blocking patterns are holding storms stuck in place for lengthy periods of time.[14]

These and many other devastating effects are forecasted by the world's scientists if there is no effective action on GHG mitigation. Since the world's population and leaders learned of the potential for these catastrophic results, many individuals, groups, and political leaders worldwide have worked to put in place agreements that will reduce GHG emissions and thereby avoid the worst of these outcomes.

The Growing Awareness of the Global Warming

In 1896, a Swedish scientist, Svante Arrhenius, published a paper linking the burning of fossil fuels with increases in CO_2 in the atmosphere. Arrhenius showed that heat would transfer to outer space differently in air with greater concentrations of CO_2 than in air with lower concentrations. Air with higher levels of CO_2 retained heat. These calculations led Arrhenius to hypothesize the greenhouse effect. While his hand calculations lacked the rigor of later computer models, other scientists took up the investigation and began to explore the phenomenon. By the 1930s, there was a general realization that North America and the North Atlantic had warmed a great deal since the late 1800s. An amateur scientist, G.S. Callendar, argued that the warming was due to the greenhouse effect. In the 1950s, several scientists, funded by the U.S. Navy, looked deeper into Callendar's claims and supported his theories. Beginning in 1958, highly accurate measurements of CO_2 were taken by Charles Keeling in Mauna Loa, Hawaii. This data series also included evidence to allow scientists to separate CO_2 coming from the burning of fossil fuels from CO_2 coming from the natural carbon cycle. By the 1960s, scientists verified that the levels of CO_2 in the atmosphere were increasing annually. In that decade, scientists made advances in computer models allowing them to begin predictions of GHG concentrations. Scientists also developed techniques to use ancient pollens and fossil shells to determine age-old temperatures worldwide. By the end of the 1960s, scientists were able to predict that future temperatures would increase by several degrees within the coming century.[15]

The environmental movement was born in the late 1960s and came to full bloom in the 1970s. The American environmental movement was a bellwether for the world movement. In the 1970s, climate change was discussed in the U.S. Congress but mostly as an aside to the then larger issues of acid rain and ozone depletion. In 1977, climate change emerged as a key issue of discussion when the U.S. Congress held hearings on President Carter's proposed synthetic fuels program. The National Wildlife Federation testified that Carter's program would release massive amounts of CO_2 in the atmosphere, disrupting the climate. In 1980, Congress held hearings specifically on the effects of CO_2 levels rising in the atmosphere. In 1988, the dramatic testimony of the National Atmospheric and Space Administration's (NASA's) Dr. James Hansen confirming the onset of global warming and its consequences, raised the political profile of the issue.[16]

The first international response to the threat was the creation, in 1988, of the Intergovernmental Panel on Climate Change (IPCC) by the World Meteorological Organization (WMO) and the United Nations Environment Programme (UNEP). IPCC's initial role was to provide scientific evidence regarding climate change and its causes, as well as the socioeconomic and environmental impacts. The IPCC was made up of scientific experts from almost all of the world's countries. The IPCC was to draft periodic reports that summarized the current scientific understanding, providing the world's political leaders not only an assessment of the progression of climate change but also recommendations on adaptation and mitigation strategies. The First Assessment Report (FAR) was released in 1990. It had considerable influence over the development of the United Nations Framework Convention on Climate Change (UNFCCC).[17]

The United Nations Framework Convention on Climate Change

The FAR supported the establishment of the UNFCCC at the United Nations Conference on Environment and Development (UNCED), commonly called the Rio Earth Summit. The UNFCCC served as the framework treaty to begin worldwide negotiation for a binding treaty that would reduce GHG emissions. The UNFCCC set in motion a series of Conference of Parties (COP) in which delegates would negotiate a binding treaty.[18] While the UNFCCC did not itself impose mandatory GHG reductions, it did impose data gathering and reporting requirements on parties to the Convention, which include almost all countries in the world, including the U.S.

European countries led the effort to develop the Kyoto Protocol in the aftermath of the UNFCCC. The first achievement was adoption of the Berlin Mandate at the first COP in 1995. The Berlin Mandate, which called for negotiating binding GHG reductions, was accepted after the release of IPCC's Second Assessment Report (SAR) which underscored the anthropogenic nature of global warming and stressed the urgency of taking action. After another two years of negotiations, the Kyoto Protocol was finalized in Kyoto, Japan.[19]

The Kyoto Protocol

The Kyoto Protocol followed the logic of the Rio Declaration that had come out of the Rio meeting in 1992. Principle 7 of the Rio Declaration stated countries had "common but differentiated responsibilities" whereby the developed nations were to be held accountable for the pollution they had created, but developing nations were held to a different standard. The concept of different standards for developed and developing nations dated back as far as 1972, when the UN Stockholm Conference elaborated the importance of development for developing nations, suggesting that the cause of much environmental degradation in developing nations was due, in fact, to their failure to develop. Poverty reduces choices and many of the choices made in the circumstance of poverty are bad for the environment. It was generally accepted, therefore, that developing nations should seek development first. Once they had worked their way out of poverty they could focus, like the rest of the world's wealthier nations, on pollution reduction. That notion was written into the Kyoto Protocol, which held developed nations responsible for binding reductions in GHG emissions while allowing the developing nations to continue to develop without any binding GHG emission reductions.[20]

The Kyoto Protocol required 37 industrialized nations and the European Union (Annex I Parties) to commit to a specific percent reduction of GHGs relative to their 1990 levels by 2012. Percent reductions varied by nation. The U.S., the world's high emitter at the time of the negotiations, was required to reduce by 7 percent, Japan 6 percent, Germany 8 percent, Canada 6 percent, and the Russian Federation 0 percent. Developing nations (non-Annex I Parties) were allowed to increase their emissions. Non-Annex I parties included China, India, South Korea, Indonesia, and Mexico whose 1990 emissions were considerable. In 1990, China represented 11 percent of the world's emissions, India 3, South Korea 1, Indonesia 0.7, and Mexico 1. Because their emissions were allowed to increase, by 2012, these countries contributed much more to the climate change problem than in 1990. By 2012, China represented 28 percent of the world's emissions, India 6, South Korea 2, Indonesia 1, and Mexico 1.[21]

The Kyoto Protocol allowed Annex I nations flexible mechanisms to reach their target reductions. Three mechanisms were included in the agreement: international carbon emissions trading, the clean development mechanism (CDM), and joint implementation (JI). The emissions trading schema was modeled after the cap-and-trade program put in place in the U.S. as part of the 1990 Clean Air Act Amendments for sulfur dioxide. Each Annex I nation was given allowable emissions called assigned amount units (AAUs) which could be traded if not used. CDM allowed Annex I nations to get credits for emission reduction efforts undertaken in developing countries while JI allowed Annex I nations to get credits for emission reduction efforts undertaken in another Annex I nation.[22] Some of these flexibility measures came to be criticized as failures. For instance, "hot air" trading resulted from the excess credits possessed by Russia that did not reflect new emissions reductions. Critics also argued that projects undertaken under the CDM might have been undertaken anyway and thus actually represented emissions reduction loopholes for developed nations.

The Kyoto Protocol went into force after Russia ratified it in 2005 but the U.S. was never a party to the agreement. This proved problematic for the success of the Kyoto Protocol, as the world's largest emitter was not a party. The use of the principle of "common but differentiated responsibilities" was disliked by many American elected officials—particularly senators who would have the responsibility of ratifying the Kyoto Protocol. Then President Bill Clinton signed the Kyoto Protocol and brought it home for consideration, but the Senate sent the message via a straw vote that they would reject the treaty, thus President Clinton never submitted it for ratification. The reason many senators gave for rejecting the treaty was that it was unfair for the U.S. to have to undertake GHG emission reductions that might harm the economy if developing countries, particularly China, had no such obligation under the treaty. These same reasons persisted during the Bush administration, which never submitted the treaty for ratification.[23]

Negotiating a Successor Treaty to the Kyoto Protocol

The Kyoto Protocol was never intended to be a permanent solution to climate change. Subsequent negotiations were anticipated from the very beginning of the agreement. This is reflected in the initial compliance period provided by the Kyoto Protocol of 2008–2012, with compliance obligations in later years left for further negotiation.

There was much hope that the Copenhagen COP 15 in 2009 would result in a new binding treaty to replace Kyoto, but that did not happen. Several months before the meeting, the G8 countries had met and adopted the goal of limiting global warming to 2°C (3.6°F) by 2100. But the problem of bringing developing nations into a binding agreement continued to vex negotiations. China and India insisted that the developed nations agree to GHG emission reductions of 40 percent over the next decade. They, in turn, showed their willingness to engage by agreeing to increase use of renewable energy and to improve their energy efficiency. Negotiations in Copenhagen yielded only the Copenhagen Accord, a non-binding agreement calling for the extension of the Kyoto Protocol to 2020.[24]

A breakthrough on the equity issue came at COP 20 in Lima, Peru, in 2014. The Lima agreement solved the problem between developed and developing countries. The Lima agreement changed the basis for negotiation to Intended Nationally Determined Contributions (INDCs). Using this approach, each country proposes its own plan to reduce GHG emissions, thereby making sure that every country would be part of the system.[25]

The Paris Agreement

The Paris Agreement became the successor treaty to the Kyoto Protocol. It was agreed to in Paris on December 12, 2015 by 195 nations. The Paris Agreement elaborates several major goals and ways to achieve them. The text of the Paris Agreement contains two sections, the Paris Decision and the Paris Agreement. The Paris Decision section, comprised of 140 separate decisions, lists "Decisions to Give Effect to the Agreement" and is not legally binding. The Paris Agreement section lists the 29 Articles of the legally binding agreement. The three primary goals are specified in Article 2 of the agreement. Perhaps the most important goal is to limit the increase in global average temperature to "well below 2°C (3.6°F) above pre-industrial levels" and to try to limit that increase to 1.5 °C. The second goal is to help countries adapt to living in a warmer world. The third goal is to provide money for poorer countries to pursue "climate resilient development." How to achieve these goals is specified in more detail in the agreement.[26]

The initial INDCs, the result of the Lima COP, were the starting point of the Paris negotiations. As countries join the Paris Agreement, the INDCs become NDCs (nationally determined contributions). Preliminary analysis of the initial round of INDCs suggested that if all nations reached their stated goals, global average temperature would rise by 2.7°C, which is more than the goal stated in Article 2. Therefore, the agreement requires that all nations prepare a succession of NDCs, with each new NDC being an improvement over the last one submitted. NDCs are to be submitted in five-year intervals. The inclusion of all nations into the Paris Agreement through these voluntary national plans is an entirely new way to approach international climate talks. While the Paris Agreement still acknowledges that rich nations should proceed with more haste in reducing emissions than poor nations, nevertheless, all nations are to be held accountable for their actions.[27]

All nations are required to "conserve and enhance" all resources that act to absorb greenhouse gases, especially forests. The agreement allows use of the REDD+ process. REDD stands for Reducing Emissions from Deforestation and Forest Degradation and the + stands for conservation, sustainable management, and enhancements of forests.[28] The agreement specifically allows parties to fund reforestation efforts in developing countries and get credits (offsets) toward meeting their targeted goals in exchange. The agreement also supports an alternative approach preferred by some, called Joint Mitigation and Adaptation (JMA), which argues that by giving indigenous people strong legal rights to their land their communities will be strengthened, and, in turn, they will protect the forests.[29]

The agreement acknowledges that the poor nations need financial assistance if they are to reduce their emissions and adapt to a warmer world while continuing to work their way out of poverty. The Paris Agreement section says funding is expected to be "continuous and enhanced" over time while the Decision section acknowledges that $100 billion will be needed annually. The rich nations are expected to report, biennially, how their financing efforts are progressing. In addition to direct finance, the rich nations are expected to transfer technologies that might assist developing nations with adaptation and mitigation efforts, as well as to provide developing nations with capacity building to achieve these goals.[30]

All nations are required to account for their NDCs using measurement methods that are transparent, accurate, and comparable. All nations are required to report national anthropogenic greenhouse gas inventories using the good practices established by the Intergovernmental Panel on Climate Change. Nations are required to report both sources of gases and removals (sinks). These reports are to be done in such a way that they show progress in achieving the NDCs. Finally, periodically the parties to the agreement will meet and take stock of progress (called the "global stocktake"). The first global stocktake will occur in 2023 and every five years thereafter. The results of the global stocktake are to be used by parties to revise their NDCs so that the world makes its commitment to limit temperature increases to "well below 2°C." However, item 20 of the Decision section calls for an earlier "facilitative dialogue" to take place in 2018 and at that meeting countries are also supposed to update and improve their NDCs.[31]

THE ROLE OF U.S. CLIMATE CHANGE POLICY

Federal Actions

The federal government clearly has a mixed record on climate change policy. Since becoming a party to the UNFCCC, U.S. leadership has pivoted several times. While Clinton signed the Kyoto Protocol, he never submitted it to Congress for ratification. The U.S. remained outside the agreement during the Bush administration as well. The election of Barack Obama marked a shift to climate-friendly policies. Early in the Obama administration, there was an attempt to pass legislation aimed at climate change. The Waxman-Markey bill passed in the House but not the Senate. This failure resulted in the administration relying heavily on existing law (the Clean Air Act) to try to move forward. Also, recognizing the impasse associated with past climate negotiations, the Obama administration worked with China to produce a bilateral agreement in 2014 on emissions reductions. While this agreement allowed China's GHG emissions to rise until 2030 while America pledged to reduce its emissions between 26 and 28 percent of 2005 levels by 2025, it nonetheless was important because it brought China to the table and to a commitment.[32] These talks served as a precursor to the Paris negotiations and proved successful in assuring the participation of China in those negotiations. Since signing the Paris Agreement, China, as the world's largest emitter of GHGs, has taken critical steps to reduce its emissions including putting in place the world's largest emissions trading system for its nation's power generating plants. The system will be fully operational by 2019.[33]

To fulfill U.S. commitments under the Paris Agreement, the Obama administration took a number of actions. It increased fuel efficiency standards for vehicles, increased energy efficiency standards, and placed regulations on methane emissions coming from oil and gas production. The administration also relied heavily on the Clean Power Plan which was announced by the Obama administration in August of 2015. The purpose of the plan was to reduce carbon dioxide emissions, or carbon pollution, from power plants. Specifically, the plan demanded a reduction of carbon dioxide emissions by 32 percent from 2005 emission levels by 2030. Power plants account for over one third of the carbon dioxide released in the U.S. each year. The Environmental Protection Agency (EPA), under the authority given it by the Clean Air Act, established standards to reduce carbon emissions from new and existing power plants. Under the final rule published October 23, 2015, the EPA established performance standards that new and existing power plants must meet. The Clean Power Plan allowed states to determine their own plans to meet the standards. Each state was required to submit a plan to the EPA indicating how it would meet the performance standards specified in the Clean Power Plan given the mix of electricity generating units in the state.[34]

Almost immediately after the publication of the final rule that put the Clean Power Plan into force, a coalition of states filed a lawsuit arguing that the EPA was exceeding its lawful authority. The Supreme Court, in a separate suit, stayed the implementation of the plan. While the lawsuit was in process, the Trump administration took office. In 2017, EPA Administrator, Scott Pruitt, directed the agency to begin action to withdraw the Clean Power Plan.[35]

Trump, a long-standing global warming denier, repeatedly stated his opposition to taking action to mitigate climate change after his election to office. Trump called climate change a hoax devised by the Chinese to hurt the U.S. economy. The Trump administration's culture of climate denial is shared by virtually all his top appointees.[36] In 2017, the Trump administration announced the U.S. would withdraw from the Paris Agreement. This withdrawal, when competed in 2020, will make the U.S. the only nation on the planet that is not a party to the agreement.[37]

State and Local Actions

State and local governments have responded to the series of federal administrations opposing climate action by putting in place climate change policies themselves. By the time the Obama administration came to office, 16 states had adopted GHG reduction targets. In addition, 39 states had joined the national Climate Registry to monitor and report their emissions. Several states had also come together in regional partnerships to reduce GHG emissions. These regional partnerships include the Regional Greenhouse Gas Initiative (RGGI), made up of a coalition of eastern states, the Western Climate Initiative (WCI), and the Midwestern Greenhouse Gas Reduction Accord (MGGRA). Separately, California adopted a program for its transportation sector that was much stronger than federal standards and will lower GHG emissions while simultaneously cleaning the air. Twelve other states proposed following California's standards. California also regulates all emissions through a combination cap-and-trade system and by direct regulations.[38]

State governments continually adjust their climate policies in response to electoral shifts. Gubernatorial swings in Arizona, New Mexico, and Utah contributed to the scaling-down of WCI in 2011. With the withdrawal of several states, only California and several Canadian provinces remained in the partnership for the launch of its 2013 cap-and-trade program. The MGGRA also lost support from newly elected governors in the Midwest, who simply ignored the original memorandum of understanding that had underpinned the agreement. Even RGGI suffered losses as New Jersey withdrew after the election of a Republican Governor Chris Christie.[39] New Jersey, however, reentered RGGI in 2018 after the election of Governor Phil Murphy.[40]

In February of 2016, the governors of 17 states came together to sign a new agreement called the Governors' Accord for a New Energy Future. The states that joined the accord were California, Connecticut, Delaware, Hawaii, Iowa, Massachusetts, Michigan, Minnesota, Nevada, New Hampshire, New York, Oregon, Pennsylvania, Rhode Island, Vermont, Virginia, and Washington. The accord obligates these states to take action to promote "renewable, cleaner and more energy efficient solutions" to supply their state's energy needs. The agreement focuses on diversification of energy sources as well as deploying innovative technologies and ideas. The opening text of the document stresses that challenges that the states face necessitate new energy solutions. These challenges listed in the document are "extreme weather events, such as flood, droughts, wildfires and sea-level rise" which the governors argue can cause harm to their states electricity reliability as well as damage to the economy.[41]

Cities also have taken independent action given the stagnation and conflict that typifies federal climate policy. More than 1,000 municipalities, home to more than 30 percent of the nation's population, have pledged to reduce their GHG emissions. These actions are totally voluntary, as no state has required cities to undertake such reductions. While efforts to reduce GHGs come with costs, they also come with many benefits to local governments. Energy efficiency initiatives also save costs for fuel and electricity. Cutting energy use improves air quality. Innovative climate action plans may highlight a city as a good place to live and locate a business. These actions on behalf of cities are important because it is estimated that 30 to 40 percent of anthropogenic GHGs are emitted by cities.[42]

Cities are also leaders on other fronts. For instance, several California cities, including Oakland and San Francisco, initiated law suits against oil companies for damages resulting from climate change. In January of 2018, New York City also announced that it filed a lawsuit against five oil companies for climate change-related damages. The suit included BP, Chevron, ConocoPhillips, ExxonMobil, and Royal Dutch Shell. New York, like Oakland and San Francisco, is attempting to make the argument that the oil companies are responsible for the damage the city may suffer because of coastal flooding and sea-level rise. Also, in January, New York City's pension fund announced that within 5 years it would divest from its fossil fuel holdings. The city holds more than $5 billion in fossil fuel investments.[43] Other cities may follow this lead and take similar actions.

CLIMATE CHANGE POLICY'S UNCERTAIN FUTURE

The Political Will to Act

While most of the world has indicated a willingness to act, the failure of the U.S. to show leadership is problematic. The fact that the Trump administration has publicly committed to withdrawal from the

Paris Agreement will make other countries ask if their efforts are worthwhile. This is bad for climate cooperation. American withdrawal also means that American funding for developing nations' assistance will be removed, raising their costs for both mitigation and adaptation efforts. The cutting of funding for climate research in the U.S., that is also part of the Trump strategy, will further undermine the IPCC and its scientific integrity.[44]

Despite lack of leadership at the federal level, many U.S. efforts to reduce GHGs will endure at the state and local levels. The importance of the involvement of the civil sector should not be overlooked. The American civil sector climate change movement, begun in 1989 with the establishment of the Climate Action Network, continues to grow and participate in climate debates, both domestically and internationally. These efforts will continue.[45]

Managing a Solution Given Global Dependence on Fossil Fuels

While global negotiations in Paris were, at long last, able to get past the equity problems that proved a serious barrier to U.S. participation in the Kyoto Protocol, other considerable obstacles to GHG remediation remain. Perhaps the largest one is that fossil fuels drive the world's economy and this inherently raises issues of national competition.[46] The fossil fuel industry dominates political economies globally. Over 80 percent of the world's energy is provided by fossil fuels.[47] Transitioning to new fuels will involve decades of effort. It will require massive growth of alternative energy sources, and new technological breakthroughs. The transition will also happen at time when demand for energy, in particular electricity, is increasing. But to eliminate the main source of GHG emissions, fossil fuel use must transition to cleaner sources of energy. The difficulty of making such a transition to prevent the emission of GHGs into the atmosphere has moved some to consider other potential solutions. One of these is geoengineering.

Geoengineering

Early consideration of geoengineering was typically thought of in the realm of science fiction or fantasy, but in 2006 a Nobel Prize-winner, Paul Crutzen, published a paper in a respected academic journal thus bringing considerable credibility to the field. Crutzen's paper suggested seeding the atmosphere with sulfur to reflect sunlight back into space.[48]

Geoengineering approaches generally fall into two categories: Solar Radiation Management (SRM) and Carbon Dioxide Removal (CDR). Crutzen's approach, dispersing stratospheric aerosols, became one of the key ideas in SRM. The overall goal is to reflect a portion of the Sun's energy back into space. Other approaches include using space reflectors to block a portion of sunlight so that it cannot reach Earth's surface and albedo enhancement, such as increasing the reflectivity of clouds or the land surface, reflecting more sunlight back to space.[49] Critics of SRM techniques argue that while they would lower temperatures, they would not reduce carbon dioxide levels and would have no impact on ocean acidification.

Of the two approaches CDR is preferable since it would get at the root problem, carbon dioxide. CDR approaches include reforestation and widescale tree planting, charring biomass and burying it so that the carbon is stored in the soil, and burning biomass in equipment using carbon capture and sequestration technology. Another CDR approach is ambient air capture, which would involve using large filters to scrub carbon dioxide out of the air and then store it. Other proposed CDR approaches include ocean fertilization which involves adding nutrients to the oceans allowing the water to absorb more carbon dioxide. A similar approach is ocean alkalinity, which would involve grinding up rocks such as limestone and dispersing them in the ocean to increase the ocean's ability to absorb carbon dioxide and to reduce ocean acidification.[50]

Geoengineering is very contentious. Many consider it extremely dangerous, arguing that interfering with nature on the scale proposed by enthusiasts could be globally catastrophic. Nevertheless, serious academic programs both in the United States and worldwide are focusing programs, classes, and seminar series on geoengineering. Harvard University is actively studying the development of a stratospheric aerosol approach. In 2010, Oxford University's Oxford Martin School established the Oxford Geoengineering Program to "engage with society about the issues associated with geoengineering and conduct research into some proposed techniques." One of the first accomplishments of the program was to write the "Oxford Principles" which are proposed guidelines for the regulation of geoengineering. The guidelines insist on public participation in decision making, open disclosure of research and publication results, independent assessments of impacts, and "governance before deployment."[51]

The National Academy of Sciences (NAS) rejected the use of the term geoengineering in its 2015 report on the subject, proposing instead the use of the term 'climate intervention' arguing that the term 'engineering' implied more control than NAS thought likely. NAS also rejected the use of SRM, preferring 'albedo modification' again arguing that the term 'management' implies more control than such experiments would have. NAS favored the use of carbon removal strategies, suggesting they are safe albeit expensive. NAS rejected albedo modification strategies in general, arguing that the only solution to the effects of climate change is massive reductions in GHGs.[52]

CONCLUSION

Without the greenhouse effect, life on Earth would not be possible. But human releases of carbon dioxide from the burning of fossil fuels since the beginning of the Industrial Revolution have resulted in dangerous anthropogenic additions to GHG levels. While carbon dioxide is the main GHG, methane, nitrous oxide, CFCs, HCFCs, and HFCs all contribute to global warming. The Earth's surface air temperatures have increased nearly 2°F since the turn of the 20th century. This warming has resulted in increases in land, air, and ocean temperatures which, in turn, have led to less snow cover, retreating glaciers, less sea ice, rising sea levels, ocean acidification, heavy precipitation events, intense storms, droughts, heatwaves, and massive forest fires. These changes increase risks to human settlements and the ecology. Poor and disadvantaged people worldwide will be less likely to be able to adapt to life in a warmer world. Climate change threatens food and water security for many. It will result in poor health for many, especially in developing countries. Plant and animal face risks of extinction if they cannot adapt to rapid ecosystem shifts. Without changes in human behavior to reduce GHG emissions, these and many other life-threatening events are likely.

The understanding that the burning of fossil fuels correlates with increases in atmospheric carbon dioxide dates to before 1900, although the first extensive annual data series was not begun until 1958. Keeling's data series substantiated that the levels of CO_2 in the atmosphere were increasing annually. By the end of the 1960s, computer models predicted that temperatures would increase by several degrees by the end of the century. Concern about global warming and its consequences spread to the growing environmental movement in America and worldwide in the 1970s and 1980s. Congressional testimony by NASA's James Hansen, in 1988, verifying that global warming and its consequences had already begun, raised public awareness and concern.

As concerns over climate change and its potential negative impacts grew, the international community created the IPCC to keep the world's leaders informed of new scientific evidence as well as the socioeconomic and environmental impacts. The IPCC's First Assessment Report, released in 1990, had substantial influence over the organization of the UNFCCC. The UNFCCC was a framework treaty that began a series of COPs with the first goal of negotiating a binding treaty to reduce GHG emissions.

The Kyoto Protocol required Annex I Parties to commit to a specific percent reduction of GHGs relative to their 1990 levels by 2012 while Non-Annex I Parties were allowed to increase their emissions. Three flexible mechanisms were included in the treaty to allow Annex I nations to reach their targeted reductions, including international carbon emissions trading, the CDM, and JI. The Kyoto Protocol went into force in 2005, after Russian ratification. While President Clinton signed the document, he never submitted it for ratification. This was due to the fact that many Senators thought the provisions allowing developing nations increases in their emissions while the U.S. faced decreases, was unfair. These criticisms continued during the Bush administration, keeping the U.S. out of the agreement. This proved to be a great failure of the Kyoto Protocol.

World leaders were aware of the reason for U.S. opposition. Moreover, by 2012, China was no longer a small contributor to climate change, making its active participation in a global treaty to succeed the Kyoto Protocol essential for success. The Lima agreement in 2014 solved the problem between developed and developing countries by changing the basis for negotiation to INDCs. Using this approach, each country presented its own plan to reduce GHG emissions, keeping every country in the agreement.

The Paris Agreement, based on NDCs, became the successor treaty to the Kyoto Protocol. The Paris Agreement elaborated three goals: to limit the increase in global average temperature to well below 2°C, to assist countries to adapt to living in a warmer world, and to finance poorer countries so that they could achieve climate resilient development. The agreement requires that each nation submit an improved NDC every five years. The active presence of all nations in the Paris Agreement through these voluntary national plans was an important innovation. Yet the Paris Agreement continued to acknowledge the needs of developing countries for financial assistance and a slower pace of emission reductions.

The U.S. government's climate change policy has shifted with successive presidential administrations. After becoming a party to the UNFCCC, under George H.W. Bush, U.S. leadership has variously supported and refused to support international climate mitigation action. The U.S. remained a non-party to the Kyoto Protocol during the administrations of Clinton and Bush. Obama's administration marked a shift to climate-friendly policies and under his leadership the U.S. joined the Paris Agreement. One of the key ways in which the Obama administration sought to meet its promised emission reductions, was through the Clean Power Plan. The plan, however, never went into effect, having been blocked by the courts. Under the Trump administration, EPA Administrator, Scott Pruitt, began action in 2017 to withdraw the Clean Power Plan. Trump, a global warming denier, began the swing back to refusal to support international action to mitigate climate change. In 2017, the Trump administration announced its intent to withdraw from the Paris Agreement by 2020.

U.S. state and local governments have been active players in climate change policy. By 2009, 16 states had adopted GHG reduction targets, 39 states had joined the national Climate Registry, and several states had also come together in regional partnerships to reduce GHG emissions. With electoral shifts after 2009, several states withdrew from climate actions previous governors had committed them to. However, later electoral shifts resulted in a second reversal and states recommitting to climate efforts. By 2016, 17 governors signed the Governors' Accord for a New Energy Future to decrease reliance on fossil fuel and thus address the climate crisis. Cities also have taken independent action with more than 1,000 municipalities pledging to reduce their GHG emissions.

The future of climate change policy is uncertain. Though the world's nations have committed to action, the failure of the U.S. to take leadership poses challenges. If the U.S. does formally withdraw from the Paris Agreement, other countries might question their own commitments, especially costly obligations. If American withdrawal also means less funding for necessary climate science and assistance to developing nations, this will further undermine international cooperation. Despite lack of leadership at the federal level, however, many U.S. efforts to reduce GHGs will persist at the state and local level. An active American civil sector, focused on climate change, will continue to participate in climate policy development both domestically and internationally.

A large uncertainty moving forward is how to manage the transition to a non-carbon-based international economy. With the vast majority of the world's energy coming from fossil fuels, transitioning to new fuels will take decades. This shift will require explosive growth of alternative energy sources and technological innovation. The difficulty of making such a transition, and the lack of success in past multilateral efforts to reduce GHGs, has moved some to consider other potential solutions, including geoengineering. Many consider geoengineering approaches to solar radiation management, through activities such as distributing stratospheric aerosols, placing space reflectors, or other attempts at albedo enhancement, controversial if not dangerous. Geoengineering carbon dioxide reduction efforts are less controversial, depending on the method employed, but slow and expensive. Nevertheless, failure to make meaningful headway on reducing the levels of GHGs in the atmosphere makes consideration of implementing these potential solutions more likely.

---

[1]   Joseph Romm, *Climate Change: What Everyone Needs to Know* (Oxford: Oxford University Press, 2016), 1.

[2]   "Global Climate Change," NASA, accessed February 2, 2018, https://climate.nasa.gov/evidence/.

[3]   Romm, *Climate Change,* 1–2.

[4]   Duncan Clark, "How Long Do Greenhouse Gases Stay in the Air?," *The Guardian*, January 16, 2012, accessed August 10, 2018, https://www.theguardian.com/environment/2012/jan/16/greenhouse-gases-remain-air.

[5]   "Global Emissions by Gas," EPA, accessed February 4, 2018, https://www.epa.gov/ghgemissions/global-greenhouse-gas-emissions-data.

[6]   "Global Climate Change."

[7]   Clark, "How Long Do Greenhouse Gases Stay in the Air?"

[8]   "Global Emissions by Gas."

[9]   "Global Climate Change."

[10]   Clark, "How Long Do Greenhouse Gases Stay in the Air?"

[11]   "Global Emissions by Gas."

[12]   D. J. Wuebbles et al., "Climate Science Special Report: Fourth National Climate Assessment, Volume I," *U.S. Global Change Research Program* (2017): 12–34, doi:10.7930/J0DJ5CTG.

[13] R.K. Pachauri and L.A. Meyer, eds., "Climate Change 2014: Climate Change Synthesis Report," *Fifth Assessment Report of the Intergovernmental Panel on Climate Change* (2015): 13–15.

[14] Romm, *Climate Change,* 73–96.

[15] Dianne Rahm, *Climate Change Policy in the United States: The Science, the Politics and Prospects for Change* (Jefferson, NC: McFarland & Company, Inc. Publishers, 2010), 11.

[16] Robert J. Brulle, "The US National Climate Change Movement," in *Changing Climate Politics: U.S. Policies and Civic Action*, ed. Yael Wolinsky-Nahmias (Thousand Oaks, CA: CQ Press, 2015), 146–148.

[17] Rahm, *Climate Change Policy in the United States*,15–16.

[18] Walter A. Rosenbaum, *Environmental Politics and Policy* (Thousand Oaks, CA: Sage/CQ Press, 2017), 359–360.

[19] Yael Wolinsky-Nahmias, "Introduction: Global Climate Politics," in *Changing Climate Politics: U.S. Policies and Civic Action*, ed. Yael Wolinsky-Nahmias (Thousand Oaks, CA: CQ Press, 2015), 5–6.

[20] Rahm, *Climate Change Policy in the United States*, 74–75.

[21] Wolinsky-Nahmias, "Introduction: Global Climate Politics," 6–7.

[22] Rahm, *Climate Change Policy in the United States*, 81–83.

[23] Rahm, *Climate Change Policy in the United States*, 77.

[24] Wolinsky-Nahmias, "Introduction: Global Climate Politics," 9–11.

[25] "Lima to Paris," UNFCCC, accessed February 3, 2018, http://newsroom.unfccc.int/lima/lima-call-for-climate-action-puts-world-on-track-to-paris-2015/.

[26] "Adoption of the Paris Agreement," UNFCCC, accessed February 3, 2018, http://unfccc.int/resource/docs/2015/cop21/eng/l09.pdf.

[27] "Adoption of the Paris Agreement."

[28] "REDD+ Platform," UNFCCC, accessed February 3, 2018, http://redd.unfccc.int/.

[29] "Adoption of the Paris Agreement."

[30] "Adoption of the Paris Agreement."

[31] "Adoption of the Paris Agreement."

[32] Mark Lander and Jane Perlez, "Rare Harmony as China and U.S. Commit to Climate Deal," *New York Times*, September 3, 2016, accessed February 3, 2018, https://www.nytimes.com/2016/09/04/world/asia/obama-xi-jinping-china-climate-accord.html.

[33] Fiona Harvey, "China Aims to Drastically Cut Greenhouse Gas Emissions Through Trading Scheme," *The Guardian*, December 19, 2017, accessed February 4, 2018, https://www.theguardian.com/environment/2017/dec/19/china-aims-to-drastically-cut-greenhouse-gas-emissions-through-trading-scheme.

[34] EPA, "Carbon Pollution Emission Guidelines for Existing Stationary Sources: Electric Utility Generating Units," *Federal Register* 80, no 205 (October 23, 2015): 64662.

[35] Brady Dennis and Juliet Eilperin, "Scott Pruitt Says EPA Will Repeal Clean Power Plan Tuesday: 'The War on Coal is Over," *Washington Post*, October 9, 2017, accessed February 3, 2018, https://www.washingtonpost.com/news/energy-environment/wp/2017/10/09/pruitt-tells-coal-miners-he-will-repeal-power-plan-rule-tuesday-the-war-on-coal-is-over/?utm_term=.962bf8fbe88c.

[36] Georgina Gustin, "Climate Denial Pervades the Trump White House, Bit It's Hitting Some Limits," *Inside Climate News*, January 8, 2018, accessed February 4, 2018, https://inside

climatenews.org/news/08012018/climate-change-denial-trump-hoax-2017-year-review-pruitt-tillerson-endangerment-finding.

[37] Michael D. Shear, "Trump Will Withdraw U.S. From Paris Climate Agreement," *New York Times*, June 1, 2017, accessed February 3, 2018, https://www.nytimes.com/2017/06/01/climate/trump-paris-climate-agreement.html.

[38] Rosenbaum, *Environmental Politics and Policy*, 368–369.

[39] Barry G. Rabe, "A New Era in States' Climate Policies?," in *Changing Climate Politics: U.S. Policies and Civic Action*, ed. Yael Wolinsky-Nahmias (Thousand Oaks, CA: CQ Press, 2015), 64.

[40] Dustin Racioppi, "Murphy Directs New Jersey to Re-Enter Regional Greenhouse Gas Initiative," *northjersey.com*, January 29, 2018, accessed February 4, 2018, https://www.northjersey.com/story/news/new-jersey/governor/2018/01/29/murphy-directs-new-jersey-re-enter-regional-greenhouse-gas-initiative/1074921001/.

[41] "The Accord," Governors' Accord for a New Energy Future, accessed February 4, 2018, http://www.governorsnewenergyfuture.org/the-accord/.

[42] Rachel M. Krause, "Climate Policy Innovation in American Cities," in *Changing Climate Politics: U.S. Policies and Civic Action*, ed. Yael Wolinsky-Nahmias (Thousand Oaks, CA: CQ Press, 2015), 82–83.

[43] Justine Calma, "New York City is Taking BP, Chevron, ConocoPhillips, ExxonMobil, and Royal Dutch Shell to Court," *Grist*, January 10, 2018, accessed January 14, 2018, http://grist.org/briefly/new-york-city-is-taking-bp-chevron-conocophillips-exxon-mobil-and-royal-dutch-shell-to-court/?utm_medium=email&utm_source=newsletter&utm_campaign=daily.

[44] Hai-Bain Zhang, et al., "U.S. Withdrawal from the Paris Agreement: Reasons, Impacts, and China's Response," *Advances in Climate Change Research* 8 (2017): 220.

[45] Brulle, "The US National Climate Change Movement," 152–153.

[46] Sean Cumberlege, "Multilateral Environmental Agreements: From Montreal to Kyoto—A Theoretical Approach to an Improved Climate Change Regime," *Denver Journal of International Law & Policy* 37, no. 2 (2009): 316–317.

[47] Daniel Yergin, *The Quest: Energy, Security, and the Remaking of the Modern World* (New York: Penguin Books, 2012), 720.

[48] Paul Crutzen, "Albedo Enhancement by Stratospheric Sulfur Injections: A Contribution of Resolve a Policy Dilemma?," *Climatic Change* 77 (2006): 211–219.

[49] "What is Geoengineering?," Oxford University, accessed February 4, 2018, http://www.geoengineering.ox.ac.uk/what-is-geoengineering/what-is-geoengineering/.

[50] "What is Geoengineering."

[51] "Oxford Geoengineering Programme," Oxford University, accessed February 4, 2018, http://www.geoengineering.ox.ac.uk/.

[52] Romm, *Climate Change*, 163–164.

Bibliography

Abbott, Kenneth W., and Steven Bernstein. "The High-Level Political Forum on Sustainable Development: Orchestration by Default and Design." *Global Policy* 6, no.3 (2015): 222–233.

Abel, Guy J., Bilal Barakat, Samir KC, and Wolfgang Lutz. "Meeting the Sustainable Development Goals Leads to Lower World Population." *Proceedings of the National Academy of Sciences* 113, no. 50 (2016): 14294–14299.

Adler, Robert W. "Clean Water Act." In *Encyclopedia of Science and Technology Communication,* edited by Susanna Hornig Priest, 139–141. Thousand Oaks: Sage Publications, Inc., 2010.

Alessi, Christopher, and Alison Sider. "U.S. Oil Output Expected to Surpass Saudi Arabia, Rivaling Russia for Top Spot." *Wall Street Journal*, January 19, 2018. Accessed January 24, 2018. https://www.wsj.com/articles/u-s-crude-production-expected-to-surpass-saudi-arabia-in-2018-1516352405.

Alwaeli, Mohamed. "Cost and Cost-Effectiveness of Recycling of Municipal Solid Waste." In *Recycling: Processes, Costs and Benefits*, edited by Charlene J. Nielsen, 1–52. New York: Nova Science Publishers, Inc., 2011.

American Chemical Society. "Chlorofluorocarbons and Ozone Depletion." Accessed January 26, 2018. https://www.acs.org/content/acs/en/education/whatischemistry/landmarks/cfcs-ozone.html.

Andersen, Stephen O., Marcel L. Halberstadt, and Nathan Borgford-Parnell. "Stratospheric Ozone, Global Warming, and the Principle of Unintended Consequences: An Ongoing Science and Policy Success Story." *Journal of the Air & Waste Management Association* 63, no.6 (2013): 607–647.

Andresen, Steinar. "The Effectiveness of UN Environmental Institutions." *International Environmental Agreements: Politics, Law and Economics* 7, no. 4 (2007): 317–336.

Antrim, Caitlyn. "The International Seabed Authority Turns Twenty." *Georgetown Journal of International Affairs* (Winter/Spring 2015): 188–196.

Aquifer Guardians in Urban Areas. "Welcome to AGUA." Accessed November 16, 2016. www.aquiferguardians.org.

Associated Press. "Top 20 Onshore U.S. Oil and Gas Spills Since 2010." *USA Today*, November 17, 2017. Accessed December 29, 2017. https://www.usatoday.com/story/news/nation/2017/11/17/top-20-onshore-oil-and-gas-spills/876390001/.

Attard, Felicity. "IMO's Contribution to International Law Regulating Maritime Security." *Journal of Maritime Law & Commerce* 45, no. 4 (2014): 479–565.

Atwood, Donald, and Claire Paisley-Jones. "Pesticides Industry Sales and Usage 2008–2012 Estimates." *Biological and Economic Analysis Division, Office of Pesticide Programs, office of Chemical Safety and Pollution Prevention, EPA* (2017): 1–32.

Ballotpedia. "Federal Land Ownership by State." Accessed September 25, 2017. https://ballotpedia.org/Federal_land_ownership_by_state.

Baraniuk, Chris. "Future Energy: China Leads World in Solar Power Production." *BBC News*, June 22, 2017. Accessed January 21, 2018. http://www.bbc.com/news/business-40341833.

Barquet, Karina, Paivi Lujala, and Jan Ketil Rod. "Transboundary Conservation and Militarized Interstate Disputes." *Political Geography* 42 (2014): 1–11.

Barroso, Carmen. "Beyond Cairo: Sexual and Reproductive Rights of Young People in the New Development Agenda." *Global Public Health* 9, no. 6 (2014): 639–646.

BBC News. "U.S. Leads World in Oil and Gas Production, IEA Says." Accessed December 28, 2017. http://www.bbc.com/news/business-41988095.

Betsill, Michele M. "International Climate Change Policy." In *The Global Environment: Institutions, Law, and Policy*, edited by Regina S. Axelrod and Stacy D. VanDeveer, 234–258. Los Angeles: Sage/CQPress, 2015.

Berck, Peter, Amnon Levy, and Khorshed Chowdhury. "An Analysis of the World's Environment and Population Dynamics with Varying Carrying Capacity, Concerns and Skepticism." *Ecological Economics* 73 (2012):103–112.

Bergeson, Lynn L. "The Montreal Protocol is Amended and Strengthened." *Environmental Quality Management* (Spring 2017): 137–141.

Biermann, Frank, and Bernd Siebenhuner. "The Role and Relevance of International Bureaucracies." In *Managers of Global Change: The Influence of International Environmental Bureaucracies,* edited by Bernd Siebenhuner and Frank Biermann, 1–14. Cambridge, MA: The MIT Press, 2009.

Bishop, William W., Jr. "The 1958 Geneva Convention on Fishing and Conservation of the Living Resources of the High Seas." *Columbia Law Review* 62, no. 7 (1962): 1206–1229.

Black, Ian. "Saudi Arabia Approves Ambitious Plan to Move Economy Beyond Oil." *The Guardian*, April 25, 2016. Accessed January 5, 2018. https://www.theguardian.com/world/2016/apr/25/saudi-arabia-approves-ambitious-plan-to-move-economy-beyond-oil.

BLM. "About the BLM." Accessed August 10, 2018. https://www.blm.gov/about.

BLM. "The Federal Land Policy and Management Act of 1976: As Amended." Accessed August 10, 2018. https://www.blm.gov/or/regulations/files/FLPMA.pdf.

BLM. "Wind Energy Development." Accessed January 19, 2018. http://windeis.anl.gov/guide/concern/index.cfm.

Blumm, Michael C., and Andrew B. Erickson. "Federal Wild Lands Policy in the Twenty-First Century: What a Long, Strange Trip It's Been." *Colorado Natural Resources, Energy, & Environmental Law Review* 25 (2014): 1–59.

Blumm, Michael C., and Lorena M. Wisehart. "The Underappreciated Role of the National Environmental Policy Act in Wilderness Designation and Management." *Environmental Law* 44 (2014): 323–372.

BOEM. "About BOEM." Accessed October 31, 2016. http://www.boem.gov/About-BOEM/.

BOEM. "Office of Budget and Program." Accessed November 7, 2016. https://www.boem.gov/BOEM-FY-2017-Budject-Justification/.

Borger, Julian. "UN Chief Calls for Review of Biofuels Policy." *The Guardian*, April 4, 2008. Accessed January 22, 2018. https://www.theguardian.com/environment/2008/apr/05/biofuels.food.

Borton, James. "Marine Peace Park Plan Offers Promise for South China Sea." *Geopolitical Monitor*, October 25, 2015. Accessed November 5, 2017. https://www.geopoliticalmonitor.com/marine-peace-park-plan-offers-promise-for-south-china-sea/.

Boyt, Jeb. "Struggling to Protect Ecosystems and Biodiversity Under NEPA and NFMA: The Ancient Forest of the Pacific Northwest and the Northern Spotted Owl." *Pace Environmental Law Review* 10 (1993): 1009–1050.

Bowen, William M., and Michael V. Wells. "The Politics and Reality of Environmental Justice: A History and Considerations for Public Administrators and Policy Makers." *Public Administration Review* 62, no.6 (2002): 688–698.

Bridge, Gavin. "Energy (In)Security: World-Making in an Age of Scarcity." *The Geographical Journal* 181, no. 4 (2015): 328–339.

Brown, George F. "United Nations International Conference on Population, Mexico City, 6–13 August 1984." *Studies in Family Planning* 15, no. 6 (1984): 296–302.

Brulle, Robert J. "The US National Climate Change Movement." In *Changing Climate Politics: U.S. Policies and Civic Action*, edited by Yael Wolinsky-Nahmias, 146–170. Thousand Oaks, CA: CQ Press, 2015.

Brumfield, Olivia. "The Birth, Death, and Afterlife of the Wild Lands Policy: The Evolution of the Bureau of Land Management's Authority to Protect Wilderness Values." *Environmental Law* 44 (2014): 249–284.

BSEE. "Budget Justification." Accessed November 7, 2016. https://www.bsee.gov/sites/bsee.gov/files/budget-justifications//bsee-fy-2017-budget.pdf.

BSEE. "History." Accessed October 31, 2016. http://www.bsee.gov/who-we-are/history.

Burroughs, R.H. "Ocean Dumping: Information and Policy Development in the USA." *Marine Policy* (April 1988): 96–104.

Buscher, Bram and Maano Ramutsindela. "Green Violence: Rhino Poaching and the War to Save Southern Africa's Peach Parks." *African Affairs* 115/458 (2015): 1–22.

California Environmental Protection Agency Air Resources Board. "Key Events in the History of Air Quality in California." Accessed August 10, 2018. https://ww2.arb.ca.gov/about/history.

Calma, Justine. "New York City is Taking BP, Chevron, ConocoPhillips, ExxonMobil, and Royal Dutch Shell to Court." *Grist*, January 10, 2018. Accessed January 14, 2018. http://grist.org/briefly/new-york-city-is-taking-bp-chevron-conocophillips-exxon-mobil-and-royal-dutch-shell-to-court/?utm_medium=email&utm_source=newsletter&utm_campaign=daily.

Cardwell, Diane. "The Murky Future of Nuclear Power in the United States." *New York Times*, February 18, 2017. Accessed January 12, 2018. https://www.nytimes.com/2017/02/18/business/energy-environment/nuclear-power-westinghouse-toshiba.html.

Carlson, Peter. "TR Goes Camping with John Muir." *American History* (June 2016): 14–15.

Carpenter, Angela. "The EU and Marine Environmental Policy: A Leader in Protecting the Marine Environment." *Journal of Contemporary European Research* 8, no. 2 (2012): 248–267.

Carter, Nicole T., Stephen P. Mulligan, and Clare Ribando Seelke. "U.S. Mexican Water Sharing: Background and Recent Developments." *Congressional Research Service Report 7-5700, R43312* (2017): 1–22.

Cary, Annette. "$107.7 Billion Needed to finish Hanford Cleanup." *Tri-City Herald*, February 22, 2016. Accessed January 11, 2018. www.tri-cityherald.com/news/local/hanford/article61912837.html.

Census Bureau. "U.S. and World Population Clock." Accessed July 27, 2017. https://www.census.gov/popclock/.

Center for Biological Diversity. "Landmark Lawsuit Challenges U.S. Approval of Deep-sea Mineral Mining." Accessed December 4, 2017. https://www.biologicaldiversity.org/news/press_releases/2015/deep-sea-mining-05-13-2015.html.

Center for Climate and Energy Solutions. "Public Benefit Funds." Accessed January 19, 2018. https://www.c2es.org/document/public-benefit-funds/.

Center for Nuclear Science and Technology Information. "The Price Anderson Act." Accessed January 10, 2018. http://cdn.ans.org/pi/ps/docs/ps54-bi.pdf.

CEWEP. "Confederation of European Waste-to-Energy Plants." Accessed August 4, 2017. www.cewep.eu/.

City of Chicago. "What is Single Stream Recycling." Accessed August 10, 2018. https://www.cityofchicago.org/content/dam/city/depts/doe/general/RecyclingAndWasteMgmt_PDFs/Multi Unit/FAQs.pdf.

Clark, Duncan. "How Long Do Greenhouse Gases Stay in the Air?" *The Guardian*, January 16, 2012. Accessed August 10, 2018. https://www.theguardian.com/environment/2012/jan/16/greenhouse-gases-remain-air.

Clary, Bruce B. "The Enactment of the Nuclear Waste Policy Act of 1982: A Multiple Perspectives Explanation." *Policy Studies Review* 10, no. 4 (Winter 1991/92): 90–102.

Clayton, Carol, H. David Gold, Brent Gurney, Mark Kalpin, and Alexander White. "Minimizing Risk Under the Clean Water Act." *Energy Law Journal* 36, no. 69 (2015): 69–94.

Cleland, John. "World Population Growth; Past, Present and Future." *Environmental and Resource Economics* 55, no. 4 (2013): 543–554.

Collins, Craig. *Toxic Loopholes: Failures and Future Prospects for Environmental Law.* Cambridge: Cambridge University Press, 2010.

Comay, Laura B. "National Park System: What Do the Different Park Titles Signify?" *Congressional Research Service Report 7-5700, R41816* (2013): 1–14.

Costantino, Cesare, and Emanuela Recchini. "Environmental-Economic Accounts and Financial Resource Mobilization for Implementation of the Convention on Biological Diversity." *Statistika* 95, no.4 (2015): 17–28.

Cotruvo, Joseph A. "The Safe Drinking Water Act: Current and Future." *Journal of the American Water Works Association* 104, no.1 (2012): 57–62.

Corso, Phaedra S., Michael H. Kramer, Kathleen A. Blair, David G. Addiss, Jeffrey P. Davis, and Anne C. Haddix. "Costs of Illness in the 1993 Waterborne Cryptosporidium Outbreak, Milwaukee, Wisconsin." *Emerging Infectious Diseases* 9, no. 4 (2003): 426–431.

Council on Foreign Relations. "Oil Dependence and U.S. Foreign Policy." Accessed December 30, 2017. https://www.cfr.org/timeline/oil-dependence-and-us-foreign-policy.

Council on Foreign Relations. "The Global Oceans Regime." Accessed November 13, 2017. http://cfr.org/report/global-oceans-regime.

Crow, Deserai A., and Andrea Lawlor. "Media in the Policy Process: Using Framing and Narratives to Understand Policy Influences." *Review of Policy Research* 33, no. 5 (2016): 472–489.

Crow, Deserai A., Elizabeth A. Albright, and Elizabeth Koebele. "Environmental Rulemaking Across States: Process, Procedural Access, and Regulatory Influence." *Environment and Planning C: Government and Policy* 34, no.7 (2016): 1222–1240.

Crutzen, Paul. "Albedo Enhancement by Stratospheric Sulfur Injections: A Contribution of Resolve a Policy Dilemma?" *Climatic Change* 77 (2006): 211–219.

Cumberlege, Sean. "Multilateral Environmental Agreements: From Montreal to Kyoto—A Theoretical Approach to an Improved Climate Change Regime." *Denver Journal of International Law & Policy* 37, no. 2 (2009): 303–329.

Daly, Herman E. "Toward Some Operational Principles of Sustainable Development." *Ecological Economics* 2 (1990): 1–6.

Davenport, Coral, Jonathan Ellis, Lisa Friedman, Brad Plumer and Tatiana Schlossberg. "What is the Clean Power Plan and How Can Trump Repeal It?" *New York Times,* October 10, 2017. Accessed January 2, 2018. https://www.nytimes.com/2017/10/10/climate/epa-clean-power-plan.html.

DeConto, Robert M., and David Pollard. "Contribution of Antarctica to Past and Future Sea-level Rise." *Nature* 531 (2016): 591–597.

DeGarmo, Denise K. *International Environmental Treaties and State Behavior: Factors Influencing Cooperation.* New York: Routledge, 2005.

Dell'Apa, Andrea, Lisa Schiavinato, and Roger A. Rulfson. "The Magnuson-Stevens Act (1976) and its Reauthorizations: Failure or Success for the Implementation of Fishery Sustainability and Management in the US?" *Marine Policy* 36 (2012): 673–680.

Dennis, Brady, and Juliet Eilperin. "Scott Pruitt Says EPA Will Repeal Clean Power Plan Tuesday: 'The War on Coal is Over." *Washington Post*, October 9, 2017. Accessed February 3, 2018. https://www.washingtonpost.com/news/energy-environment/wp/2017/10/09/pruitt-tells-coal-miners-he-will-repeal-power-plan-rule-tuesday-the-war-on-coal-is-over/?utm_term=.962bf8fbe88c.

Dinham, Barbara, and Satinath Sarangi. "The Bhopal Gas Tragedy 1984 to ? The Evasion of Corporate Responsibility." *Environment & Urbanization* 14, no. 1 (2002): 89–99.

Dixson, D. L. "Lost at Sea." *Scientific American* 316, no 6. (2017): 42–45.

DOE. "Department of Energy: FY 2017 Congressional Budget Request." Accessed November 7, 2016. http://www.energy.gov/sites/prod/files/2016/02/f29/FY2017BudgetinBrief_0.pdf.

DOE. "History of Hydropower." Accessed January 17, 2018. https://energy.gov/eere/water/history-hydropower.

DOE. "Mission." Accessed October 31, 2016. http://www.energy.gov/mission.

DOE. "The History of Solar." Accessed January 20, 2018. https://www1.eere.energy.gov/solar/pdfs/solar_timeline.pdf.

DOI. "Who We Are." Accessed October 31, 2016. http://www.doi.gov/whoweare/Mission-Statement.

DOT. "Municipal Solid Waste and Construction and Demolition Debris." Accessed August 4, 2017. https://www.bts.gov/archive/subject_areas/freight_transportation/faf/faf4/debris.

Dougherty, Stephanie Dodson. "The Marine Mammal Protection Act: Fostering Unjust Captivity Practices Since 1972." *Journal of Land Use* 28, no.2 (2013): 337–367.

Duddu, Praven. "The Top 10 Biggest Geothermal Power Plants in the World." *Power Technology*, November 11, 2013. Accessed January 22, 2018. https://www.power-technology.com/features/feature-top-10-biggest-geothermal-power-plants-in-the-world/.

Eckhouse, Brian, Ari Natter, and Chris Martin. "Trump's Tariff on Solar Mark Biggest Blow to Renewables Yet." *Bloomberg*, January 23, 2018. Accessed January 23, 2018, https://www.bloomberg.com/news/articles/2018-01-22/trump-taxes-solar-imports-in-biggest-blow-to-clean-energy-yet?utm_content=tictoc&utm_campaign=socialflow-organic&utm_source=twitter&utm_medium=social&cmpid%3D=socialflow-twitter-tictoc.

EIA. "Biofuels: Ethanol and Biodiesel Explained." Accessed January 22, 2018. https://www.eia.gov/energyexplained/index.cfm?page=biofuel_home.

EIA. "Carbon Dioxide Emission Factors for Coal." Accessed December 29, 2017. https://www.eia.gov/coal/production/quarterly/co2_article/co2.html.

EIA. "Coal Production Using Mountaintop Removal Mining Decreases by 62% Since 2008." Accessed August 10, 2018. https://www.eia.gov/todayinenergy/detail.php?id=21952.

EIA. "Crude Oil and Petroleum Products Explained." Accessed December 27, 2017. https://www.eia.gov/energyexplained/index.cfm?page=oil_home.

EIA. "Gasoline Explained." Accessed December 28, 2017. https://www.eia.gov/energyexplained/index.cfm?page=gasoline_history.

EIA. "How Much Carbon Dioxide is Produced When Different Fuels are Burned?" Accessed December 29, 2017. https://www.eia.gov/tools/faqs/faq.php?id=73&t=11.

EIA. "How Much of U.S. Carbon Dioxide Emissions are Associated with Electricity Generation?" Accessed December 29, 2017. https://www.eia.gov/tools/faqs/faq.php?id=77&t=11.

EIA. "How Much of U.S. Energy Consumption and Electricity Generation Comes for Renewable Energy Sources?" Accessed January 17, 2018. https://www.eia.gov/tools/faqs/faq.php?id=92&t=4.

EIA. "Natural Gas Explained." Accessed December 27, 2017. https://www.eia.gov/energyexplained/index.cfm?page=natural_gas_home.

EIA. "Oil: Crude and Petroleum Products Explained." Accessed January 4, 2018. https://www.eia.gov/energyexplained/index.cfm?page=oil_use.

EIA. "Primary Energy Production by Source." Accessed December 28, 2017. https://www.eia.gov/totalenergy/data/monthly/pdf/sec1_5.pdf.

EIA. "Today in Energy." Accessed January 19, 2018. https://www.eia.gov/todayinenergy/detail.php?id=31032.

EIA. "Today in Energy." Accessed January 22, 2018. https://www.eia.gov/todayinenergy/detail.php?id=3970.

EIA. "U.S. Coal Production and Coal-Fired Electricity Generation Expected to Rise in Near Term." Accessed December 28, 2017. https://www.eia.gov/todayinenergy/detail.php?id=29872.

EIA. "U.S. Energy Consumption by Energy Source, 2016." Accessed January 17, 2018. https://www.eia.gov/energyexplained/index.cfm?page=renewable_home.

EIA. "U.S. Primary Energy Consumption by Source and Sector, 2017." Accessed August 10, 2018. https://www.eia.gov/totalenergy/data/monthly/pdf/flow/css_2017_energy.pdf.

EIA. "Utility-scale Solar has Grown Rapidly Over the Past Five Years." Accessed January 20, 2018. https://www.eia.gov/todayinenergy/detail.php?id=31072.

Ehrlich, Paul R., and Anne H. Ehrlich. "The Population Bomb Revisited." *The Electronic Journal of Sustainable Development* 1, no. 3 (2009): 1–13. Accessed February 6, 2017, www.ejsd.org.

Eilperin, Juliet. "Trump Orders Review of National Monuments, Vows to 'End These Abuses and Return Control to the People." *The Washington Post*, April 26, 2017. https://www.washintonpost.com/news/energy-environment/wp/2017/05/25/zinkw-to-review-large-national-monuments-created-since-1996-to-make-sure-the-people-have-a-voice/?utm_term=.d3c5724f5a44.

Elliff, Carla I., and Iracema R. Silva. "Coral Reefs as the First Line of Defense: Shoreline Protection in Face of Climate Change." *Marine Environmental Research* 127 (2017): 148–154.

Energy-101. "Biofuel—Biodiesel History." Accessed August 8, 2018 http://www.energy-101.org/renewable-energy/biofuelsbiomass-facts/biofuel-biodiesel-facts/biofuel-biodiesel-history.

Ensminger, J. Timothy, Lance N. McCold, and J. Warren Webb. "Environmental Impact Assessment Under the National Environmental Policy Act and the Protocol on Environmental Protection of the Antarctic Treaty." *Environmental Management* 24, no. 1 (1999): 13–23.

Environment California. "About Us." Accessed November 16, 2016. www.environmentcalifornia.org.

Environment Canada, UNEP, and University of Joensuu. *MEA Negotiator Handbook*. Joensuu, Finland: University of Joensuu-UNEP Course Series 5, 2007.

Enviropedia. "Ozone Depletion." Accessed January 28, 2018. http://www.ozone-hole.org.uk/17.php.

EPA. "Advancing Sustainable Materials Management: Facts and Figures." Accessed July 26, 2017. https://www.epa.gov/smm/advancing-sustainable-materials-management-facts-and-figures#USState.

EPA. "Background on Drinking Water Standards in the Safe Drinking Water Act (SDWA)." Accessed August 10, 2018. https://www.epa.gov/dwstandardsregulations/background-drinking-water-standards-safe-drinking-water-act-sdwa.

EPA. "Basic Information About Landfills." Accessed July 31, 2017. https://www.epa.gov/landfills/basic-information-about-landfills#whattypes.

EPA. "Basic Ozone Layer Science." Accessed January 26, 2018. https://www.epa.gov/ozone-layer-protection/basic-ozone-layer-science.

EPA. "Carbon Monoxide (CO) Pollution in Outdoor Air." Accessed May 25, 2017. https://www.epa.gov/co-pollution/basic-information-about-Carbon-Monoxide-co-outdoor-air-pollution.

EPA. "Carbon Pollution Emission Guidelines for Existing Stationary Sources: Electric Utility Generating Units." *Federal Register* 80, no. 205 (October 23, 2015): 64662.

EPA. "Clean Water Laws, Regulations, Executive Orders." Accessed July 20, 2017. https://www.epa.gov/cwa-404/clean-water-laws-regulations-executive-orders.

EPA. "Cleaning Up Sites." Accessed August 27, 2017. https://www.epa.gov/superfund.

EPA. "Controlling Air Pollution from the Oil and Gas Industry." Accessed January 5, 2018. https://www.epa.gov/controlling-air-pollution-oil-and-natural-gas-industry/basic-information-about-oil-and-natural-gas.

EPA. "Criteria for the Definition of Solid Waste and Solid and Hazardous Waste Exclusions." Accessed August 10, 2018.

https://www.epa.gov/hw/criteria-definition-solid-waste-and-solid-and-hazardous-waste-exclusions.

EPA. "Defining Hazardous Waste: Listed, Characteristic and Mixed Radiological Wastes." Accessed August 22, 2017. https://www.epa.gov/hw/defining-hazardous-waste-listed-characteristic-and-mixed-radiological-wastes#listed.

EPA. "Energy Recovery from the Combustion of Municipal Solid Waste (MSW)." Accessed July 31, 2017. https://www.epa.gov/smm/energy-recovery-combustion-municipal-solid-waste-msw.

EPA. "Environmental Justice." Accessed August 28, 2017. https://www.epa.gov/environmentaljustice.

EPA. "EPA History: Water—The Challenge of the Environment: A Primer on EPA's Statutory Authority." Accessed July 14, 2017. https://archive.epa.gov/epa/aboutepa/epa-history-water-challenge-environment-primer-epas-statutory-authority.html.

EPA. "EPA Response to Kingston TVA Coal Ash Spill." Accessed December 29, 2017. https://www.epa.gov/tn/epa-response-kingston-tva-coal-ash-spill.

EPA. "Global Emissions by Gas." Accessed February 4, 2018. https://www.epa.gov/ghgemissions/global-greenhouse-gas-emissions-data.

EPA. "Green Power Pricing." Accessed January 19, 2018. https://www.epa.gov/greenpower/green-power-pricing.

EPA. "Greenhouse Gas Emissions." Accessed May 26, 2017. https://www.epa.gov/ghgemissions/inventory-us-greenhouse-gas-emissions-and-sinks.

EPA. "Ground Water and Drinking Water: National Primary Drinking Water Regulations." Accessed July 17, 2017. https://epa.gov/ground-water-and-drinking-water/national-primary-drinking-water-regulations.

EPA. "Guide for Industrial Waste Management." Accessed July 27, 2017. https://www.epa.gov/sites/production/files/2016-03/documents/industrial-waste-guide.pdf

EPA. "Highlights of Key Provisions in the Frank R. Lautenberg Chemical Safety for the 21st Century Act." Accessed August 10, 2018. https://www.epa.gov/assessing-and-managing-chemicals-under-tsca/highlights-key-provisions-frank-r-lautenberg-chemical.

EPA. "International Cooperation." Accessed May 26, 2017. https://www.epa.gov/international-cooperation/persistent-organic-pollutants-global-issue-global-response.

EPA. "International Cooperation: Cleaning Up Electronic Waste (E-Waste)." Accessed August 22, 2017. https://www.epa.gov/international-cooperation/cleaning-electronic-waste-e-waste.

EPA. "International Treaties and Cooperation." Accessed January 28, 2018. https://www.epa.gov/ozone-layer-protection/international-treaties-and-cooperation.

EPA. "Landfills." Accessed July 31, 2017. https://www.epa.gov/landfills.

EPA. "Lead Air Pollution." Accessed May 25, 2017. https://www.epa.gov/lead-air-pollution/basic-information-about-lead-air-pollution.

EPA. "Learn the Basics of Hazardous Waste." Accessed August 10, 2018. https://www.epa.gov/hw/learn-basics-hazardous-waste.

EPA. "Municipal Solid Waste Landfills: Economic Impact Analysis for the Proposed New Subpart to the New Source Performance Review." Accessed August 5, 2017. https://www3.epa.gov/ttnecas1/regdata/EIAs/LandfillsNSPSProposalEIA.pdf.

EPA. "National Pollution Discharge Elimination System." Accessed August 10, 2018. https://www.epa.gov/npdes.

EPA. "Nitrogen Dioxide (NO₂) Pollution." Accessed May 25, 2017. https://www.epa.gov/no2-pollution/basic-information-about-no2.

EPA. "Ocean Dumping: International Treaties." Accessed August 30, 2017. https://www.epa.gov/ocean-dumping/ocean-dumping-international-treaties.

EPA. "Organizational Chart." Accessed November 7, 2016. https://www.epa.gov/aboutepa/epa-organizational-chart.

EPA. "Our Nation's Air." Accessed November 6, 2017. https://gispub.epa.gov/air/trendsreport/2017/#highlights.

EPA. "Ozone Layer Protection." Accessed May 25, 2017. https://www.epa.gov/ozone-layer-protection.

EPA. "Ozone Pollution." Accessed May 25, 2017. https://www.epa.gov/ozone-pollution/ozone-basics.

EPA. "Particulate Matter (PM) Pollution." Accessed May 25, 2017. https://www.epa.gov/pm-pollution/particulate-matter-pm-basics.

EPA. "Pesticide Registration Fees and Fee Waivers." Accessed August 26, 2017. https://www.epa.gov/pesticide-registration/pesticide-registration-fees-and-fee-waivers.

EPA. "Planning Budget Results." Accessed August 10, 2018. https://www.epa.gov/planandbudget.

EPA. "Recycling Basics." Accessed August 2, 2017. https://www.epa.gov/recycling/recycling-basics.

EPA. "Regulatory Information by Topic: Waste." Accessed August 22, 2017. https://www.epa.gov/regulatory-information-topic/regulatory-information-topic-waste.

EPA. "Resource Conservation and Recovery Act (RCRA) Overview." Accessed July 26, 2017. https://www.epa.gov/rcra/resource-conservation-and-recovery-act-rcra-overview.

EPA. "Safe Drinking Water Act Requirements for Six-Year Reviews." Accessed July 17, 2017. https://epa.gov/dwsixyearreview/safe-drinking-water-act-requirements-six-year-reviews.

EPA. "Significant New Alternatives Program." Accessed January 28, 2018. https://www.epa.gov/snap.

EPA. "Sulfur Dioxide Basics." Accessed May 25, 2017. https://www.epa.gov/so2-pollution/sulfur-dioxide-basics.

EPA. "Summary of the BEACH Act." Accessed July 19, 2017. https://www.epa.gov/laws-regulations/summary-beach-act.

EPA. "Summary of the Emergency Planning & Community Right-to-Know Act." Accessed August 27, 2017. https://www.epa.gov/laws-regulations/summary-emergency-planning-community-right-know-act.

EPA. "Summary of the Energy Independence and Security Act." Accessed January 2, 2018. https://www.epa.gov/laws-regulations/summary-energy-independence-and-security-act.

EPA. "Summary of the Energy Policy Act." Accessed January 2, 2018. https://www.epa.gov/laws-regulations/summary-energy-policy-act.

EPA. "Summary of the Federal Insecticide, Fungicide, and Rodenticide Act." Accessed August 26, 2017. https://www.epa.gov/laws-regulations/summary-federal-insecticide-fungicide-and-rodenticide-act.

EPA. "Summary of the Food Quality Protection Act." Accessed August 26, 2017. https://www.epa.gov/laws-regulations/summary-food-quality-protection-act.

EPA. "Summary of the National Environmental Policy Act." Accessed October 2, 2017. https://www.epa.gov/laws-regulations/summary-national-environmental-policy-act.

EPA. "Summary of the Pollution Prevention Act." Accessed August 28, 2017. https://www.epa.gov/laws-regulations/summary-pollution-prevention-act.

EPA. "Summary of the Shore Protection Act." Accessed December 4, 2017. https://www.epa.gov/laws-regulations/summary-shore-protection-act.

EPA. "Superfund History." Accessed August 27, 2017. https://www.epa.gov/superfund/superfund-history.

EPA. "Sustainable Management of Construction and Demolition Materials." Accessed August 10, 2018. https://www.epa.gov/smm/sustainable-management-construction-and-demolition-materials.

EPA. "Sustainable Management of Food." Accessed August 10, 2018. https://www.epa.gov/sustainable-management-food.

EPA. "Toxic Release Inventory (TRI) Program." Accessed August 28, 2017. https://www.epa.gov/toxics-release-inventory-tri-program/learn-about-toxics-release-inventory.

EPA. "Types of Pesticide Ingredients." Accessed August 10, 2018. https://www.epa.gov/ingredients-used-pesticide-products/types-pesticide-ingredients.

EPA. "What Are Hazardous Air Pollutants?" Accessed May 26, 2017. https://www.epa.gov/haps/what-are-hazardous-air-pollutants.

EPA. "What is a Municipal Solid Waste Landfill?" Accessed August 10, 2018. https://www.epa.gov/landfills/municipal-solid-waste-landfills#whatis.

EPA. "What is Acid Rain." Accessed May 25, 2017. https://www.epa.gov/acidrain/what-acid-rain.

EPA. "What is the Phaseout of Ozone-Depleting Substances?" Accessed January 28, 2018. https://www.epa.gov/ods-phaseout/what-phaseout-ozone-depleting-substances.

Ercin, A. Ertug, and Arjen Y. Hoekstra. "Water Footprint Scenarios for 2050: A Global Analysis." *Environment International* 64 (2014): 71–82.

Eurasianet. "Russia Takes Action to Clean Up Soviet Era Nuclear Waste." *Oilprice.com* December 2, 2017. Accessed January 14, 2018. https://oilprice.com/Alternative-Energy/Nuclear-Power/Russia-Takes-Action-To-Clean-Up-Soviet-Era-Nuclear-Waste.html.

European Commission. "Batteries & Accumulators." Accessed August 30, 2017. http://ec.europa.eu/environment/waste/batteries/index.htm.

European Commission. "Guidelines on the Interpretation of the R1 Energy Efficiency Formula for Incineration Facilities Dedicated to the Processing of Municipal Solid Waste According to Annex II of Directive 2008/98/EC on Waste." Accessed August 4, 2017. www.ec.europa.eu/environment/waste/framework/pdf/guidance.pdf.

European Commission. "International Issues: Multilateral Environmental Agreements." Accessed January 25, 2017. http://ec.europa.eu/environment/international_issues/agreements_en.htm.

European Commission. "Polychlorinated Biphenyls and Polychlorinated Terphenyls (PCBs/PCTs)." Accessed August 30, 2017. http://ec.europa.eu/environment/waste/pcbs/index.htm.

European Commission. "REACH." Accessed August 30, 2017. http://ec.europa.eu/environment/chemicals/reach/reach_en.htm.

European Commission. "The RoHS Directive." Accessed August 10, 2018. http://ec.europa.eu/environment/waste/rohs_eee/index_en.htm.

European Commission. "Waste Oils." Accessed August 10, 2018. http://ec.europa.eu/environment/waste/oil_index.htm.

Evans-Pughe, Christine. "All At Sea: Cleaning up the Pacific Garbage." *Engineering & Technology* (February 2017): 52–55.

Ewart, Gary W., William N. Rom, Sidney S. Braman, and Kent E. Pinkerton. "From Closing the Atmospheric Ozone Hole to Reducing Climate Change." *Annals of the American Thoracic Society* 12, no. 2 (February 2015): 247–251.

Fabra, Adriana, and Virginia Gascon. "The Convention on the Conservation of Antarctic Marine Living Resources (CCAMLR) and the Ecosystem Approach." *The International Journal of Marine and Coastal Law* 23 (2008): 567–598.

Farkas, Rachel. "Recent Developments: The Bush Administration's Decision to Defund the United Nations Population Fund and Its Implications for Women in Developing Nations." *Berkeley Women's Law Journal* 18, no. 1 (2003): 237–253.

Faybishenko, Boris, Jens Birkholzer, David Sassani, and Peter Swift. "International Approaches for Deep Geological Disposal of Nuclear Waste: Geological Challenges in Radioactive Waste Isolation." *Lawrence Berkeley National Laboratory LBNL-1006984* (2016): 1.1–25.11.

Federal Register. "Proclamation 5030—Exclusive Economic Zone of the United States of America." Accessed November 27, 2017. https://www.archives.gov/federal-register/codification/proclamations/05030.html.

Federal Reserve History. "Oil Shock of 1973–74." Federal Reserve History. Accessed December 30, 2017. https://www.federalreservehistory.org/essays/oil_shock_of_1973_74.

Federal Reserve History. "Oil Shock of 1978–79." Accessed December 30, 2017. https://www.federalreservehistory.org/essays/oil_shock_of_1978_79.

Fewell, Brent. "The Failure of Cooperative Federalism in Flint, Michigan." *Journal of the American Water Works Association* 108, no. 3 (2016): 12–14.

Fiorino, Daniel J. "Environmental Protection Agency." In *A Historical Guide to the U.S. Government,* edited by George T. Kurian, 203–210. Oxford: Oxford University Press, 1998.

Finkel, M.L., and A. Law. "The Rush to Drill for Natural Gas: A Five-Year Update." *American Journal of Public Health* 106, no. 10 (2016): 1728–1729.

Finkle, Jason L., and C. Alison McIntosh. "United Nations Population Conferences: Shaping the Policy Agenda for the Twenty-First Century." *Studies in Family Planning* 33, no. 1 (2002): 11–23.

Fowler, Luke. "Assessing the Framework of Policy Outcomes: The Case of the U.S. Clean Air Act and Clean Water Act." *Journal of Environmental Assessment Policy and Management* 16, no. 4 (2014):1–20. Accessed May 18, 2017. doi:10.1142/S1464333214500343.

"France Bans Fracking and Oil Extraction in all of its Territories." *The Guardian*, December 20, 2017. Accessed August 10, 2018. https://www.theguardian.com/environment/2017/dec/20/france-bans-fracking-and-oil-extraction-in-all-of-its-territories.

Fried, Lauha. "Global Wind Statistics 2016." *Global Wind Energy Council* (2017): 1–4.

FS. "About the Agency." Accessed October 31, 2016. http://www.fs.fed.us/about-agency.

FS. "National Forest Management Act of 1976." Accessed October 18, 2017. https://www.fs.fed.us/emc/nfma/includes/NFMA1976.pdf.

Funk and Wagnalls New World Encyclopedia. "Solid Waste Disposal." 2016. EBSCO*host* (Accession number: SO144000).

FWS. "About the U.S. Fish and Wildlife Service." Accessed August 10, 2018. https://www.fws.gov/help/about_us.html.

FWS. "Bald and Golden Eagle Protection Act." Accessed August 10, 2018. https://www.fws.gov/midwest/MidwestBird/EaglePermits/bagepa.html.

FWS. "Conserving the Nature of America." Accessed October 31, 2016. https://www.fws.gov.

FWS. "Digest of Federal Resource Laws of Interest to the U.S. Fish and Wildlife Service." Accessed August 10, 2018. https://www.fws.gov/laws/lawsdigest/nwracts.html.

FWS. "Incidental Take." Accessed October 25, 2017. https://www.fws.gov/birds/policies-and-regulations/incidental-take.php.

FWS. "International Affairs." Accessed August 10, 2018. https://www.fws.gov/international/cites/index.html.

FWS. "Northern Spotted Owl." Accessed October 20, 2017. https://www.fws.gov/oregonfwo/articles.cfm?id=149489595.

FWS. "What Can I Do With My Ivory?" Accessed October 25, 2017. https://www.fws.gov/international/travel-and-trade/ivory-ban-questions-and-answers.html.

Gabison, Garry A. "Limited Solution to a Dangerous Problem: The Future of the Oil Pollution Act." *Ocean and Coastal Law Journal* 18, no. 2 (2013): 223–254.

Gale Encyclopedia of Science. "Hydrochlorofluorocarbons." Accessed January 28, 2018. http://www.encyclopedia.com/history/historians-and-chronicles/historians-miscellaneous-biographies/hydrochlorofluorocarbons.

Gehring, Thomas, and Eva Ruffing. "When Arguments Prevail Over Power: The CITES Procedure for the Listing of Endangered Species." *Global Environmental Politics* 8, no.2 (2008): 123–148.

Geng, Jing. "The Legality of Foreign Military Activities in the Exclusive Economic Zone Under UNCLOS." *Merkourios* 28, no. 74 (2012): 22–30.

Gerlak, Andrea K. "Federalism and U.S. Water Policy: Lessons for the Twenty-First Century." *Publius: The Journal of Federalism* 36, no.2 (2005): 231–257.

Gilland, Bernard. "World Population and Food Supply: Can Food Production Keep Pace with Population Growth in the Next Half-Century?" *Food Policy* 27, no. 1 (2002): 47–63.

Glastmeyer, Susan T., Edward T. Furlong, Dana W. Kolpin, Angela L Batt, Robert Benson, J. Scott Boone, Octavia Conerly, Maura J. Donohue, Dawn N. King, Mitchell S. Kostich, Heath E. Mash, Stacy L. Pfaller, Kathleen M. Schenck, Jane Ellen Simmons, Eunice A. Varughese, Stephen J. Vesper, Eric N. Villegas, and Vickie S. Wilson. "Nationwide Reconnaissance of Contaminants of Emerging Concern in Source and Treated Drinking Waters of the United States." *Science of the Total Environment* 501–502 (2017): 909–922.

Global Water System Project. "The Bonn Declaration on Global Water Security." Accessed July 18, 2017. www.gwsp.org/fileadmin/documents_news/Bonn_Water_Declaration_final.pdf.

Goodall, Jeff. *Big Coal: The Dirty Secret Behind America's Energy Future.* Boston: Houghton Mifflin Company, 2006.

Gore, Leada. "Toyota: We're Going to Quit Making Gas-Powered Vehicles." *Al.com,* October 15, 2015. Accessed January 4, 2018. http://www.al.com/news/index.ssf/2015/10/toyota_were_going_to_quit_maki.html.

Governors' Accord for a New Energy Future. "The Accord." Accessed February 4, 2018. http://www.governorsnewenergyfuture.org/the-accord/.

Governor's Press Office. "Governor Cuomo Unveils 9th Proposal of 2018 State of the State; Calling on the NYS Common Fund to Cease All New Investments in Entities with Significant Fossil Fuel-Related Activities and Develop a De-Carbonization Plan for Divesting from Fossil Fuel." December 19, 2017. Accessed January 4, 2018. http://www.governor.ny.gov/news/govenor-cuomo-unveils-9th-proposal-2018-state-state-calling-nys-common-fund-cease-all-new.

Govtrack. "H.R. 776 (102nd): Energy Policy Act of 1992." Accessed January 2, 2018. https://www.govtrack.us/congress/bills/102/hr 776.

GPO. "Public Law 111-11-Mar. 30, 2009." Accessed August 10, 2018. https://www.gpo.gov/fdsys/pkg/PLAW-111publ11/pdf/PLAW-111publ11.pdf.

Greenpeace International. "Cracks in Nuclear Power Plant." Accessed January 11, 2018. http://www.greenpeace.org/international/en/campaigns/nuclear/safety/.

Grist. "Ice Apolcalypse," Accessed December 15, 2017. https://grist.org/article/antarctica-doomsday-glaciers-could-flood-coastal-cities/.

Gruver, Mead. "Trump Administration Rescinding Rules for Oil, Gas Drilling." *USA Today,* December 29, 2017. Accessed January 2, 2018. https://www.usatoday.com/story/news/politics/2017/12/28/trump-administration-oil-gas-drilling/989066001/.

Gustin, Georgina. "Climate Denial Pervades the Trump White House, Bit It's Hitting Some Limits." *Inside Climate News*, January 8, 2018. Accessed February 4, 2018. https://insideclimatenews.org/news/08012018/climate-change-denial-trump-hoax-2017-year-review-pruitt-tillerson-endangerment-finding.

Hamilton, Lawrence S. "Review of: Transboundary Protected Areas: The Viability of Regional Conservation Strategies." *Mountain Research and Development* 24, no. 2 (2004): 187.

Hardball, Elizabeth. "Arctic National Wildlife Refuge Battle Ends, But Drilling Not A Given." *National Public Radio*, December 21, 2017. Accessed December 29, 2017. https://www.npr.org/2017/12/21/572439797/arctic-national-wildlife-refuge-battle-ends-but-drilling-not-a-given.

Hardin, Garrett. "The Tragedy of the Commons." *Science* 162, no. 3859 (1968): 1243–1248.

Harvey, Fiona. "Calls for Greater Fossil Fuel Divestment at Anniversary of Paris Climate Deal." *The Guardian*, December 12, 2017. Accessed January 5, 2018. https://www.theguardian.com/environment/2017/dec/12/calls-for-greater-fossil-fuel-divestment-at-anniversary-of-paris-climate-deal.

Harvey, Fiona. "China Aims to Drastically Cut Greenhouse Gas Emissions Through Trading Scheme." *The Guardian,* December 19, 2017. Accessed February 4, 2018. https://www.theguardian.com/environment/2017/dec/19/china-aims-to-drastically-cut-greenhouse-gas-emissions-through-trading-scheme.

Hauserman, Jill T. "Water, Water Everywhere, But Just How Much is Clean?: Examining Water Quality Restoration Efforts Under the United States Clean Water Act and the United States—Canada Great Lakes Water Quality Agreement." *Georgia Journal of International and Comparative Law* 43, no. 701 (2015): 701–725.

Haycox, Stephen. "Battleground Alaska: Antistatism and Environmental Protection in America's Las Wilderness." *The Western Historical Quarterly* 48 (Summer 2017): 115–136.

Hays, Samuel P. *A History of Environmental Politics Since 1945*. Pittsburgh: University of Pittsburgh Press, 2000.

Hays, Samuel P. *Beauty, Health, and Permanence: Environmental Politics in the United States, 1955–1985*. Cambridge: Cambridge University Press, 1987.

Hays, Scott P., Michael Esler, and Carol E. Hays. "Environmental Commitment among the States: Integrating Alternative Approaches to State Environmental Policy." *Publius* 26, no.2 (1996): 41–58.

Helfenstein-Louw, Kate, Jennifer Bansard, Tallash Kantai, and Jennifer Lenhart. "A Brief History of the Ozone Regime." *Earth Negotiations Bulletin* 19, no. 138 (2017): 1–2. Accessed January 22, 2018. http://enb.iisd.org/ozone/cop11-mop29/.

Hinrichs, Roger A., and Merlin Kleinbach. *Energy: Its Use and the Environment*. Fort Worth: Harcourt College Publishers, 2002.

Hirji, Zahra. "Trump Delivers Two More Wins for Oil and Gas Companies in 2017." *Buzzfeed News*, December 29, 2017. Accessed January 2, 2018. https://www.buzzfeed.com/zahrahirji/trump-delivers-two-more-wins-for-oil-gas-in-2017?utm_term=.pwQ YLyD3m#.yeYAmPnJq.

Holley, Jason R. "Gifford Pinchot and the Fight for Conservation: The Emergence of Public Relations and the Conservation Movement, 1901–1910." *Journalism History* 42, no.2 (2016): 91–100.

Hoover, Katie. "Federal Lands and Natural Resources: Overview and Selected Issues for the 113th Congress." *Congressional Research Service Report 7-5700, R43429* (2014): 1–32.

Horn, Denise M. "U.S. Foreign Policy, Population Control and International Family Planning Programs." *International Feminist Journal of Politics* 15, no.2 (2013): 195–212.

Houghton Mifflin Company. "Rachel Carson, Silent Spring." Accessed August 9, 2017. www.rachelcarson.org/SilentSpring.aspx.

Hyman, Leonard, and William Tilles. "Nuclear Power's Resurgence in the Middle East." *Oilprice.com*, December 18, 2017. Accessed January 14, 2018. https://oilprice.com/Alternative-Energy/Nuclear-Power/Nuclear-Powers-Resurgence-In-The-Middle-East.html.

IAEA. "50 Years of Nuclear Energy." Accessed January 12, 2018. https://www.iaea.org/About/Policy/GC/GC48/Documents/gc48inf-4_ftn3.pdf.

IEA. "Coal." Accessed January 3, 2018. https://www.iea.org/about/faqs/coal/.

IEA. "Feed-in Tariffs." Accessed January 19, 2018. https://www.iea.org/policiesandmeasures/pams/spain/name-23929-en.php.

IEA. "Natural Gas." Accessed January 4, 2018. https://www.eia.gov/outlooks/ieo/pdf/nat_gas.pdf.

IEA. *World Energy Outlook 2016: Executive Summary.* Paris, France: International Energy Agency, 2016.

IHO. "About IHO." Accessed December 13, 2017. https://www.iho.int/srv1/index.php?option=com_content&view=article&id=298&Itemid=297&lang=en.

IMO. "Brief History of IMO." Accessed December 13, 2017. http://www.imo.org/en/About/HistoryOfIMO/Pages/Default.aspx.

IMO. "International Convention for the Prevention of Pollution from Ships (MARPOL)." Accessed December 4, 2017. http://www.imo.org/en/about/conventions/listofconventions/pages/international-convention-for-the-prevention-of-pollution-from-ships-(marpol).aspx.

Institute for Energy Research. "Biomass." Accessed January 22, 2018. https://www.instituteforenergyresearch.org/?encyclopedia=biomass-2.

Intelligence Community Assessment. "Global Water Security." *Intelligence Community Assessment Report ICA 2012-08* (2012): i–16.

International Hydropower Association. "A Brief History of Hydropower." Accessed January 17, 2018. https://www.hydropower.org/a-brief-history-of-hydropower.

International Tribunal for the Law of the Sea. "General Information." Accessed December 14, 2017. https://www.itlos.org/en/general-information/.

IPCC. "Summary for Policymakers." In *Climate Change 2013: The Physical Science Basis. Contribution of Working Group I to the Fifth Assessment Report of the Intergovernmental Panel on Climate Change*, edited by. Stocker, T.F., D. Qin, G.-K. Plattner, M. Tignor, S.K. Allen, J. Boschung, A. Nauels, Y. Xia, V. Bex and P.M. Midgley,

1–29. Cambridge University Press, Cambridge, United Kingdom and New York, NY, USA, 2013.

Iraola, Roberto. "The Bald and Golden Eagle Protection Act." *Albany Law Review* 68 (2005): 973–996.

Israel Ministry of Foreign Affairs. "Binational Red Sea Marine Peace Park." *Israel Environment Bulletin* 20, no.4 (1997), accessed November 5, 2017, http://www.mfa.gov.il/mfa/pressroom/1997/pages/binational%20red%20sea%20marine%20peace%20park%20-%20oct-97.aspx.

Ivanova, Maria. "The Contested Legacy of Rio+20." *Global Environmental Politics* 13, no.4 (2013): 1–11.

Ivanova, Maria. "UNEP in Global Environmental Governance: Design, Leadership, Location." *Global Environmental Politics* 10, no.1 (2010): 30–59.

IWC. "The International Whaling Commission." Accessed December 13, 2017. https://iwc.int/history-and-purpose.

Jaeckel, Aline. "Deep Seabed Mining and Adaptive Management: The Procedural Challenges for the International Seabed Authority." *Marine Policy* 70 (2016): 205–211.

Jaeckel, Aline, Kristina M. Gjerde, and Jeff A. Ardron. "Conserving the Common Heritage of Humankind—Options for the Deep-Seabed Regime." *Marine Policy* 78 (2017): 150–157.

Jan, Tracy. "Trumps Proposal for a 'Solar' Border Wall Now Appears Dead." *Washington Post,* October 26, 20. Accessed January 21, 2018. https://www.washingtonpost.com/news/wonk/wp/2017/10/26/trumps-proposal-for-a-solar-border-wall-now-appears-dead/?utm_term=.81807879ed00.

Johnson, Ann Marie, and Alexandru Roman. "Reflections on E-Rulemaking: Challenges, Limitations and Unrealistic Expectations." *The Electronic Journal of e-Government* 13, no. 1 (2015): 43–55.

Jones, Jason P.H., Zidong M. Wang, Bruce A. McCarl, and Minglu Wang. "Policy Uncertainty and the U.S. Ethanol Industry." *Sustainability* 9 (2017): 2056–2070.

Kaiser, Jocelyn. "The Dirt on Ocean Garbage Patches." *Science* 328, no. 5985 (2010): 1506.

Kalem, Sam, Ryan M. Seidemann, James G. Wilkins, and Megan K. Terrell. "Lingering Relevance of the Coastal Zone Management Act to Energy Development in our Nation's Coastal Waters?" *Tulane Environmental Law Journal* 24 (2010): 73–112.

Kambour, Andrew, Jerry Boese and Ryann Child. "Cleaning Up America's Nuclear Weapons Complex: 2015 Update for Governors." *National Governors Association* (2015): 1–43. Accessed August 10, 2018. https://www.nga.org/center/publications/cleaning-up-americas-nuclear-weapons-complex-2015-update-for-governors/.

Kassotis, Christopher D., Donald E. Tillitt, Chong-Ho Lin, Jane A. McElroy, and Susan C. Nagel. "Endocrine-Disrupting Chemicals and Oil and Natural Gas Operations: Potential Environmental Contamination and Recommendations to Assess Complex Environmental Mixtures." *Environmental Health Perspectives* 124, no. 3 (March 2016): 256–264.

Katona, Viktor. "The Slow Death of Nuclear Power in Europe." *Oilprice.com*, August 30, 2017. Accessed January 12, 2018. https://oilprice.com/Alternative-Energy/Nuclear-Power/The-Slow-Death-Of-Nuclear-Power-In-Europe.html.

Kauffmann, Larry. "Prospects for Nuclear Power in the U.S." *Geopolitics of Energy* (August 2017): 2–7.

Kavousi, Javid, John Everett Parkinson, and Takashi Nakamura. "Combined Ocean Acidification and Low Temperature Stressors Cause Coral Mortality." *Coral Reefs* 35 (2016): 903–907.

Kingdon, John W. *Agendas, Alternatives, and Public Policies*. New York: HarperCollins College Publishers, 1995.

Kerwin, Cornelius M. *Rulemaking: How Government Agencies Write Law and Make Policy*. Washington, D.C.: CQ Press, 2003.

Klein, Catherine. "New Leadership Needed: The Convention on Biological Diversity." *Emory International Law Review* 31(2016): 135–165.

Kopp, Robert E., Robert M. DeConto, Daniel A. Bader, Carling C. Hay, Radley M. Horton, Scott Kulp, Michael Oppenheimer, David Pollard, and Benjamin H. Strauss. "Evolving Understand of Antarctic Ice-Sheet Physics and Ambiguity in Probabilistic Seal-Level Projections." *Earth's Future* 5 (2017): 1–17. Accessed December 15, 2017. doi: 10.1002/2017EF000663.

Kraft, Michael E. *Environmental Policy and Politics*. Boston: Pearson, 2015.

Kraft, Michael E. *Environmental Policy and Politics*. New York: Routledge, 2018.

Krause, Rachel M. "Climate Policy Innovation in American Cities." In *Changing Climate Politics: U.S. Policies and Civic Action*, edited by Yael Wolinsky-Nahmias, 82–107. Thousand Oaks, CA: CQ Press, 2015.

Kullenberg, Gunnar E. B. "Ocean Dumping Sites." *Ocean Management* 2 (1974–75): 189–209.

Latschan, Thomas. "Nuclear Energy Booming in Asia." *dw.com,* November 3, 2016. Accessed January 14, 2018. http://www.dw.com/en/nuclear-energy-booming-in-asia/a-19110848.

Lander, Mark, and Jane Perlez. "Rare Harmony as China and U.S. Commit to Climate Deal." *New York Times*, September 3, 2016. Accessed February 3, 2018. https://www.nytimes.com/2016/09/04/world/asia/obama-xi-jinping-china-climate-accord.html.

Lee, Yijin J. "The Lacey Act Amendments of 2008: The World's First Ban on Illegal Logging Combats Deforestation but Gets Stumped by Foreign Laws." *San Diego Journal of Climate & Energy Law* 5 (2013–14): 187–208.

Leopold, Aldo. *Game Management*. New York: Charles Scribner Sons, 1933.

Lipton, Eric, and Barry Meier. "Under Trump, Coal Mining Gets New Life on Public Lands." *New York Times*, August 6, 2017. Accessed January 2, 2018. https://www.nytimes.com/2017/08/06/us/politics/under-trump-coal-mining-gets-new-life-on-us-lands.html.

Lueck, Dean, and Jeffrey A. Michael. "Preemptive Habitat Destruction Under the Endangered Species Act." *Journal of Law and Economics* XLVI (2003): 27–60.

Mackelworth, Peter, Drasko Holcer, and Bojan Lazar. "Using Conservation as a Toll to Resolve Conflict: Establishing the Prian-Savudrija International Marine Peace Park." *Marine Policy* 39 (2013): 112–119.

Malek, Caline. "Nuclear Power Vital to Meet Middle East's Water Demand." *The National*, June 20, 2017. Accessed January 14, 2018. https://www.thenational.ae/uae/environment/nuclear-power-vital-to-meet-middle-east-s-water-demand-1.92384.

Malthus, Thomas. *An Essay on the Principle of Population, as it Affects the Future Improvement of Society with Remarks on the Speculations of Mr. Godwin, M. Condorcet, and Other Writers*. London: printed for J. Johnson, in St. Paul's Church-yard, 1798. Accessed February 3, 2017. http://www.esp.org/books/malthus/population/malthus.pdf.

Massey, Rachel, and Molly Jacobs. "Trends and Indicators." In *Global Chemicals Output: Towards Sound Management of Chemicals,* 1–91. Geneva: UNEP, 2013.

Meadows, Donella H. Dennis I. Meadows, Jorgen Randers, and William W. Behrens III. *The Limits to Growth: A Report to The Club of Rome (1972)*. New York: Universe Books. Accessed February 6, 2017. http://www.clubofrome.org/report/the-limits-to-growth/.

Mengerink, Kathryn J. "The Pew Oceans Commission Report: Navigating a Route to Sustainable Seas." *Ecology Law Quarterly* 31 (2004): 689–718.

Mihic, Marko M., Dejan C. Petrovic, and Aleksandar M. Vuckovic. "Comparative Analysis of Global Trends in Energy Sustainability." *Environmental Engineering and Management Journal* 13, no. 4 (2014): 947–960.

Minikowski, Andrew W. "A Vision or a Waking Dream: Revising the Migratory Bird Treaty Act to Empower Citizens and Address Modern Threats to Avian Populations." *Vermont Journal of Environmental Law* 16 (2014): 153–172.

Mikesell, John L. *Fiscal Administration: Analysis and Applications for the Public Sector.* Boston: Wadsworth Cengage Learning, 2014.

Miret, Santiago. "Nearly Forgotten—Nuclear Power in Latin America." *Berkeley Energy & Resources Collaborative*, November 14, 2015. Accessed January 14, 2018, accessed January 14, 2018. http://berc.berkeley.edu/nearly-forgotten-nuclear-power-in-latin-america/.

Miskinis, Vaclovas, Juozas Baublys, Inga Konstantinaviciute, and Vidas Lekavicius. "Aspirations for Sustainability and Global Energy Development Trends." *Journal of Security and Sustainability Issues* 3, no. 4 (2014): 17–26.

Mission 2016. "Environmental Risks of Mining." Accessed January 4, 2018. http://web.mit.edu/12.000/www/m2016/finalwebsite/problems/mining.html.

Molina, Mario J., and F.S. Rowland. "Stratospheric Sink for Chlorofluoromethanes: Chlorine Atomcatalysed Destruction of Ozone." *Nature* 249 (1974): 810–812.

Montague, Ted. "World Energy Resources: Geothermal 2016." *World Energy Council* (2016): 1–52.

Moore, Steven J. "Troubles in the High Seas: A New Era in the Regulation of U.S. Ocean Dumping." *Environmental Law* 22 (1992): 913–951.

Morrisette, Peter M. "The Montreal Protocol: Lessons for Formulating Policies for Global Warming." *Policy Studies Journal* 19, no. 2 (Spring 1991): 152–161.

Mother Nature Network. "The 13 Largest Oil Spills in History." Accessed January 4, 2018. https://www.mnn.com/earth-matters/wilderness-resources/stories/the-13-largest-oil-spills-in-history.

Multilateral Fund for the Implementation of the Montreal Protocol. "Multilateral Fund." Accessed January 28, 2018. http://www.multilateralfund.org/aboutMLF/default.aspx.

Murphy, Tim. "The Radically International History of America's Best Idea." *Foreign Policy* (May/June 2017): 66–71.

NASA. "About NASA." Accessed November 16, 2016. www.nasa.gov/about/index.html.

NASA. "NASA Airborne Antarctic Ozone Experiment." Accessed January 27, 2018. https://geo.arc.nasa.gov/sge/jskiles/fliers/all_flier_prose/antarcticO3_condon/antarcticO3_condon.html.

NASA. "Global Climate Change." Accessed February 2, 2018. https://climate.nasa.gov/evidence/.

National Geographic. "Biofuels." Accessed January 22, 2018. https://www.nationalgeographic.com/environment/global-warming/biofuel/.

National Geographic. "Oceans." Accessed November 13, 2017. https://www.nationalgeographic.com/environment/habitats/ocean/.

Nelson, Robert H. "Our Languishing Public Lands." *Policy Review* February & March (2012): 45–62.

NOAA. "A Comprehensive Restoration Plan for the Gulf of Mexico." Accessed November 29, 2017. http://www.gulfspillrestoration. noaa.gov/restoration-planning/gulf-plan/.

NOAA. "About our Agency." Accessed November 16, 2016. www. noaa.gov/about-our-agency.

NOAA. "Arctic Saw 2nd Warmest Year, Smallest Sea Ice Coverage on Record in 2017." Accessed December 14, 2017. http://www. noaa.gov/media-release/arctic-saw-2nd-warmest-year-smallest-winter-sea-ice-coverage-on-record-in-2017.

NOAA. "Chlorofluorocarbons (CFCs)." Accessed January 26, 2018. https://www.esrl.noaa.gov/gmd/hats/publictn/elkins/cfcs. html.

NOAA. "Deepwater Horizon Oil Spill." Accessed November 29, 2017. https://response.restoration.noaa.gov/oil-and-chemical-spills/significant-incidents/deepwater-horizon-oil-spill.

NOAA. "Gulf Spill Restoration." Accessed November 29, 2017. http://www.gulfspillrestoration.noaa.gov/co-trustees.

NOAA. "How We Restore." Accessed November 29, 2017. http:// www.gulfspillrestoration.noaa.gov/how-we-restore.

NOAA. "Largest Oil Spills Affecting U.S. Waters Since 1969." Accessed December 29, 2017. https://response.restoration.noaa. gov/oil-and-chemical-spills/oil-spills/largest-oil-spills-affecting-us-waters-1969.html.

NOAA. "Maritime Zones and Boundaries." Accessed December 12, 2017. http://www.gc.noaa.gov/gcil_maritime.html#territorial.

NOAA. "Oceans and Coasts." Accessed November 13, 2017. http:// www.noaa.gov/oceans-coasts.

NOAA. "Seabed Management." Accessed December 4, 2017. http:// www.gc.noaa.gov/gcil_seabed_management.html.

NOAA. "What is Coral Bleaching?" Accessed December 20, 2017. https://oceanservice.noaa.gov/facts/coralreef-climate.html.

North Dakota State University Energy Publications. "Energy." Accessed January 22, 2018. https://www.ag.ndsu.edu/energy/ biofuels/energy-briefs/history-of-ethanol-production-and-policy.

NPS. "Conservation vs Preservation and the National Park Service." Accessed October 20, 2017. https://www.nps.gov/klgo/learn/ education/classrooms/conservation-vs-preservation.htm.

NPS. "Frequently Asked Questions." Accessed November 7, 2016. https://www.nps.gov/aboutus/faqs.htm.

NPS. "Hydroelectric Power in the 20th Century and Beyond." Accessed January 17, 2018. https://www.nps.gov/articles/7-hydroelectric-power-in-the-20th-century-and-beyond.htm.

NPS. "Land and Water Conservation Fund." Accessed August 10, 2018. https://www.nps.gov/subjects/lwcf/index.htm.

NRC. "Background on Chernobyl Nuclear Power Plant Accident." Accessed January 10, 2018. https://www.nrc.gov/reading-rm/ doc-collections/fact-sheets/chernobyl-bg.html.

NRCS. "Wetlands Conservation Provisions (Swampbuster)." Accessed July 20, 2017. www.nrcs.usda.gov/wps/portal/nrcs/detailfull/ national/programs/alphabetical/camr/?&cid=stelprdb1043554.

North West Council. "Columbia River Treaty." Accessed August 10, 2018. https://www.nwcouncil.org/reports/columbia-river-history/columbiarivertreaty.

Nuclear Energy Institute. "FAQ About Nuclear Energy." Accessed January 10, 2018. https://www.nei.org/Knowledge-Center/ FAQ-About-Nuclear-Energy.

Nuclear Energy Institute. "World Statistics." Accessed January 12, 2018. https://www.nei.org/Knowledge-Center/Nuclear-Statistics/ World-Statistics.

Ocean Conservancy. "Healthy Fish for a Healthy Ocean." Accessed December 18, 2017. https://oceanconservancy.org/sustainable-fisheries/.

Odum, Eugene P. *Fundamentals of Ecology*. Philadelphia: Saunders, 1953.

Office of Environmental Management. "Closing the Circle on the Splitting of the Atom: The Environmental Legacy of Nuclear Weapons production in the United States and What the Department of Energy is Doing About It." *Department of Energy DOE/EM-0266* (1996): 1–106.

Office of Environmental Management. "Linking Legacies: Connecting the Cold War Nuclear Weapons Production Processes to the Environmental Consequences." *Department of Energy DOE/EM-* 0319 (1997): 1–230.

Oleszek, Walter J. *Congressional Procedures and the Policy Process.* Washington, D.C.: CQ Press, 2007.

Olive, Andrea. "It is Just Not Fair: The Endangered Species Act in the United States and Ontario." *Ecology and Society* 21, no.3 (2016): 13. Accessed October 18, 2017. doi:10.5751/ES-08627-210313.

Olson, Trudle. "The Sagebrush Rebellion." *Rangelands* 2, no.5 (1980): 195–199.

O'Neill, Kate. "Architects, Agitators, and Entrepreneurs: International and Nongovernmental Organizations in Global Environmental Politics." In *The Global Environment: Institutions, Law, and Policy*, edited by Regina S. Axelrod and Stacy D. VanDeveer, 26–52. Los Angeles: Sage, 2015.

O'Neill, Kate. *The Environment and International Relations.* Cambridge: Cambridge University Press, 2017.

OSMRE. "Budget and Planning." Accessed November 7, 2016. http://www.osmre.gov/budget/docs/FY17_Proposed_Budget.pdf.

OSMRE. "Office of Surface Mining Reclamation and Enforcement." Accessed October 31, 2016. http://www.osmre.gov.

OSMRE. "Surface Mining Control and Reclamation Act." Accessed October 18, 2017. https://www.osmre.gov/lrg.shtm.

Ostrom, Elinor. *Governing the Commons: The Evolution of Institutions for Collective Action*. Cambridge: Cambridge University Press, 1990.

Owen, David. *Where the Water Goes: Life and Death Along the Colorado River*. New York: Riverhead Books, 2017.

Oxford University. "Oxford Geoengineering Programme." Accessed February 4, 2018. http://www.geoengineering.ox.ac.uk/.

Oxford University. "What is Geoengineering?" Accessed February 4, 2018. http://www.geoengineering.ox.ac.uk/what-is-geoengineering/what-is-geoengineering/.

Ozone Secretariat. "The Montreal Protocol on Substances that Deplete the Ozone Layer." Accessed August 10, 2018. http://web.unep.org/ozonaction/who-we-are/about-montreal-protocol.

Ozone Secretariat. "The Vienna Convention for the Protection of the Ozone Layer." Accessed August 10, 2018. https://unep.ch/ozone/pdfs/viennaconvention2002.pdf.

Ozone Secretariat. "Status of Ratification." Accessed August 10, 2018. http://ozone.unep.org/vienna-convention-protection-ozone-layer/94589.

Pachauri, R.K., and L.A. Meyer, editors. "Climate Change 2014: Climate Change Synthesis Report." *Fifth Assessment Report of the Intergovernmental Panel on Climate Change* (2015): 1–151.

Pallardy, Richard. "Deepwater Horizon Oil Spill of 2010." *Encyclopedia Britannica*. Last modified, December 15, 2017. https://www.britannica.com/event/Deepwater-Horizon-oil-spill-of-2010.

Panarella, Samuel J. "A Bird in the Hand: Shotguns, Deadly Oil Pits, Cute Kittens, and the Migratory Bird Treaty Act." *Virginia Environmental Law Journal* 35 (2017): 153–212.

Park, Sunjoo. "State Renewable Energy Governance: Policy Instruments, Markets, or Citizens." *Review of Policy Research* 32, no. 3 (2015): 273–296.

Peel, Jacqueline. "International Law and the Protection of the Global Environment." In *The Global Environment: Institutions, Law, and Policy*, edited by Regina S. Axelrod and Stacy D. VanDeveer, 53–82. Los Angeles: Sage, 2015.

Penn, Ivan. "Rooftop Solar Installations Rising but Pace of Growth Falls." *LA Times*, March 15, 2017. Accessed January 21, 2018. http://www.latimes.com/business/la-fi-rooftop-solar-20170314-story.html.

Petroff, Alanna. "These Countries Want to Ban Gas and Diesel Cars." *CNN Money*, September 11, 2017. Accessed January 5, 2018. http://money.cnn.com/2017/09/11/autos/countries-banning-diesel-gas-cars/index.html.

Perera, Frederica P. "Multiple Threats to Child Health from Fossil Fuel Combustion: Impacts of Air Pollution and Climate Change." *Environmental Health Perspectives* 125, no.2 (2017): 141–148.

Perry, Mark J. "Does the Oil-and-Gas Industry Still Need Tax Breaks?" *Wall Street Journal*, November 13, 2016. Accessed January 3, 2018. https://www.wsj.com/articles/does-the-oil-and-gas-industry-still-need-tax-breaks-1479092522.

Perry, Thomas C., and Christopher R. Abraham. "Money for Nothing: After $5 Billion, Still No Solution to Hanford's Nuclear Waste Woes." *IEEE Spectrum* (July 2002): 12–14.

Pimentel, David and Marcia Pimentel. "Global Environmental Resources Versus World Population Growth." *Ecological Economics* 59, no. 2 (2006): 195–198.

Platter, Zygmunt J. B. "A Jeffersonian Challenge from Tennessee: The Notorious Case of the Endangered "Snail Darter" Versus TVA's Tellico Dam—And Where Was the Fourth Estate, the Press?" *Tennessee Law Review* 80 (2013): 501–541.

Pollans, Margot J. "The Safe Drinking Water/Food Law Nexus." *Pace Environmental Law Review* 32, no. 2 (2015): 501–510.

Population Action International, "Why Population Matters to Water Resources." Accessed August 10, 2018. https://pai.org/wp-content/uploads/2012/04/PAI-1293-WATER-4PG.pdf.

Postel, Sandra L. "Water and World Population Growth." *Journal off the American Water Works Association* 92, no. 4 (2000): 131–138.

Potenza, Alessandra. "Trump Signs Executive Order to Expand Offshore Oil and Gas Drilling in Arctic and Beyond." *The Verge,* April 28, 2017. Accessed January 2, 2018. https://www.theverge.com/2017/4/28/15451652/donald-trump-executive-order-offshore-oil-gas-drilling-climate-change.

Powers, Martha, Poune Saberi, Richard Pepino, Emily Strupp, Eva Bugos, and Carolyn C. Cannuscio. "Popular Epidemiology and "Fracking": Citizens' Concerns Regarding the Economic, Environmental, Health and Social Impacts of Unconventional Natural Gas Drilling Operations." *Journal of Community Health* 40 (2015): 534–541.

Pump, Barry. "Beyond Metaphors: New Research on Agendas in the Policy Process." *Policy Studies Journal* 39, no. S1 (2011): 1–12.

Rabe, Barry G. "A New Era in States' Climate Policies?" In *Changing Climate Politics: U.S. Policies and Civic Action*, edited by Yael Wolinsky-Nahmias, 55–81. Thousand Oaks, CA: CQ Press, 2015.

Racioppi, Dustin. "Murphy Directs New Jersey to Re-Enter Regional Greenhouse Gas Initiative." *northjersey.com*, January 29, 2018. Accessed February 4, 2018. https://www.northjersey.com/story/news/new-jersey/governor/2018/01/29/murphy-directs-new-jersey-re-enter-regional-greenhouse-gas-initiative/1074921001/.

Rahm, Dianne. *Climate Change Policy in the United States: The Science, the Politics and the Prospects for Change.* Jefferson, NC: McFarland & Company, Inc. Publishers, 2010.

Rahm, Dianne. "Regulating Hydraulic Fracturing in Shale Gas Plays: The Case of Texas." *Energy Policy* 39 (2011): 2974–2981.

Rahm, Dianne. "Renewable Energy in Texas." In *Sustainable Energy and the States: Essays on Politics, Markets, and Leadership,* edited by Dianne Rahm, 48–63. Jefferson, NC: McFarland & Company, Inc. Publishers, 2006.

Rahm, Dianne. *United States Public Policy: A Budgetary Approach.* Belmont, CA: Thomson Wadsworth, 2004.

Reddick, Christopher G. *Public Administration and Information Technology.* Burlington, MA: Jones & Bartlett Learning, 2012.

Reisner, Marc. *Cadillac Desert: The American West and Its Disappearing Water.* New York: Penguin Books, 1993.

Rinfret, Sara, Jeffrey Cook, and Michelle C. Pautz. "Understanding State Rulemaking Processes: Developing Fracking Rules in Colorado, New York, and Ohio." *Review of Policy Research* 31, no.2 (2014), 88–104.

Rizzo, Christopher. "RCRA's 'Imminent and Substantial Endangerment; Citizen Suit Turns 25." *Natural Resources & Environment* 23, no.2 (2008): 50–51.

Roberts, Mark W. "Finishing the Job: The Montreal Protocol Moves to Phase Down Hydrofluorocarbons." *Review of European, Comparative & International Environmental Law* 26 (2017): 220–230.

Robertson, J. Alan and Michell M. Frey, "An SDWA Retrospective: 20 Years After the 1996 Amendments," *Journal of the American Water Works Association* 108, no.3 (2016): 22–30.

Rodriguez-Penalonga, Laura and B. Yolanda Moratilla Soria. "A Review of the Spent Nuclear Fuel Cycle Strategies and the Spent Nuclear Fuel Management Technologies." *Energies*10 (2017): 1235–1250.

Roman, Joe, Irit Altman, Meagan M. Dunphy-Daly, Caitlin Campbell, Michael Jasny, and Andrew J. Read. "The Marine Mammal Protection Act at 40: Status, Recovery, and Future of U.S. Marine

Mammals." *Annals of the New York Academy of Sciences* 1286 (2013): 29–49.

Romm, Joseph. *Climate Change: What Everyone Needs to Know.* Oxford: Oxford University Press, 2016.

Rosenbaum, Walter A. *Environmental Politics and Policy.* Thousand Oaks, CA: Sage/CQ Press, 2017.

Rosenbaum, Walter A. *American Energy: The Politics of 21st Century Policy.* Los Angeles: Sage/CQ Press, 2015.

Rosenberger, Randall S., Mark Sperow, and Donald B.K. English. "Economies in Transition and Public Land-Use Policy: Discrete Duration Models of Easter Wilderness Designation." *Land Economics* 84, no.2 (2008): 267–281.

Rosner, Robert, and Rebecca Lordan. "Why America Should Move Toward Dry Cask Consolidated Interim Storage of Used Nuclear Fuel." *Bulletin of the Atomic Scientists* 70, no.6 (2014): 48–62.

Rotman, Michael. "Cuyahoga River Fire." *Cleveland Historical.* Accessed July 13, 2017, https://clevelandhistorical.org/items/show/63.

Rutledge, Paul E., and Heather A. Larsen Price. "The President as Agenda Setter-in-Chief: The Dynamics of Congressional and Presidential Agenda Setting." *Policy Studies Journal* 42, no.3 (2014): 443–464.

Salcido, Rachael E. "Law Applicable on the Outer Continental Shelf and in the Exclusive Economic Zone." *The American Journal of Comparative Law* 58 (2010): 407–435.

Salzman, James, and Barton H. Thompson, Jr. *Environmental Law and Policy.* St. Paul, MN: Foundation Press, 2014.

Samal, Janmejaya, and Ranjit Kumar Dehury. "Family Planning Practices, Programmes and Policies in India Including Implants and Injectables with a Special Focus on Jharkhand, India: A Brief Review." *Journal of Clinical & Diagnostic Research* 9, no.11 (2015): 1–4.

Schoof, Renee. "EPA List Shows Dangerous Coal Ash Sites Found in 10 States." *McClatchy Newspapers,* June 29, 2009. Accessed December 29, 2017. http://www.mcclatchydc.com/news/nation-world/national/article24543913.html.

Schneider, Keith. "The Transition: Energy Policy; Clinton to Revamp Energy Dept. Role." *New York Times,* November 23, 1992. Accessed January 20, 2018. http://www.nytimes.com/1992/11/23/us/the-transition-energy-policy-clinton-to-revamp-energy-dept-role.html?pagewanted=all.

Schroder, Peter C. "UNEP's Regional Seas Programme and the UNCED Future: Apres Rio." *Ocean & Coastal Management* 18 (1992): 101–111.

Sciencing. "What Are the Environmental Impacts from Mining & Drilling." Accessed August 10, 2018. https://sciencing.com/environmental-impacts-mining-drilling-19199.html.

Scott, J. Michael, Dale D. Goble, John A. Wiens, David S. Wilcove, Michael Bean, and Timothy Male. "Recovery of Imperiled Species Under the Endangered Species Act: The Need for a New Approach." *Frontiers in Ecology and Environment* 3, no. 7 (2005): 383–389.

Seidl, Irmi, and Clem Am Tisdell. "Carrying Capacity Reconsidered: From Malthus' Population Theory to Cultural Carrying Capacity." *Ecological Economics* 31 (1999): 395–408.

Shanklin, Jonathan. "Reflections on the Ozone Hole." *Nature* 465 (May 6, 2010): 34–35.

Shaw, R. Paul. "The Impact of Population Growth on Environment: The Debate Heats Up." *Environmental Impact Assessment Review* 12 (1992): 11–36.

Shear, Michael D. "Trump Will Withdraw U.S. From Paris Climate Agreement." *New York Times,* June 1, 2017. Accessed January 2, 2018. https://www.nytimes.com/2017/06/01/climate/trump-paris-climate-agreement.html.

Sheffield, John. "World Population Growth and the Role of Annual Energy Use per Capita." *Technological Forecasting and Social Change* 59 (1998): 55–87.

Shulman, Valerie L. "Trends in Waste Management." In *Waste: A Handbook for Management.* Edited by Trevor M. Letcher and Daniel A. Vallero, 3–11, Amsterdam: Elsevier, 2011.

Shum, Robert Y. "Where Constructivism Meets Resource Constraints: The Politics of Oil, Renewables, and a U.S. Energy Transition." *Environmental Politics* 24, no.3 (2015): 382–400.

Siciliano, John. "Yucca Mountain Funding a Bright Spot for Republicans Trump's Budget." *Washington Examiner,* June 20, 2017. Accessed January 11, 2018. http://www.washington examiner.com/yucca-mountain-funding-a-bright-spot-for-republicans-trumps-budget/article/2626544.

Smith, Christopher E. *Courts and Public Policy.* Chicago: Nelson-Hall Publishers, 1995.

Sorokin, Iosif. "The UN Convention on the Law of the Sea: Why the U.S. Hasn't Ratified it and Where it Stands Today." *Berkeley Journal of International Law Blog* (March 30, 2015): 1. Accessed November 27, 2017. http://berkeleytravaux.com/un-convention-law-sea-u-s-hasnt-ratified-stands-today/.

Stoett, Peter J. *Global Ecopolitics: Crisis, Governance, and Justice.* Toronto: University of Toronto Press, 2012.

Stokes, Leah C. and Hanna L. Breetz. "Politics in the U.S. Energy Transition: Case Studies of Solar, Wind, Biofuels and Electric Vehicles Policy." *Energy Policy* 113 (2018): 76–86.

Sump, David H. "The Oil Pollution Act of 1990: A Glance in the Rearview Mirror." *Tulane Law Review* 85 (2011): 1101–1119.

Swearingen, Marshall. "Arms on the Range." *High Country News,* February 8, 2016, 22–23.

Tansel, Berrin. "From Electronic Consumer Products to E-Wastes: Global Outlook, Waste Quantities, Recycling Challenges." *Environment International* 98 (2017): 35–45.

Tear, Timothy H., J. Michael Scott, Patricia H. Hayward, and Brad Griffith. "Status and Prospects for Success of the Endangered Species Act: A Look at Recovery Plans." *Science,* November 12, 1993.

The Recycling Partnership. "The 2016 State of Curbside Report." Accessed August 10, 2018. https://recyclingpartnership.org/wp-content/uploads/2018/05/state-of-recycling-report-Jan2017.pdf.

"The Halliburton Loophole." *New York Times,* November 2, 2009. Accessed January 2, 2018. http://www.nytimes.com/2009/11/03/opinion/03tue3.html.

Thomas, David. "Going Nuclear: Africa's Energy Future?" *African Business*, January 31, 2017. Accessed January 14, 2018. http://africanbusinessmagazine.com/sectors/energy/going-nuclear-africas-energy-future/.

Thompson, Gordon R. "The U.S. Effort to Dispose of High-Level Radioactive Waste." *Energy & Environment* 19 no. 3+4 (2008): 391–412.

Thomson, Jennifer. "Toxic Residents: Health and Citizenship at Love Canal." *Journal of Social History* 50, no.1 (2016): 204–223.

Tierney, John. "The Reign of Recycling." *The New York Times,* October 3, 2015.

Treves, Tullio. "1958 Geneva Conventions on the Law of the Sea." *Audiovisual Library of International Law.* Accessed December 12, 2017. http://legal.un.org/avl/ha/gclos/gclos.html.

Turner, John H. "Off to a Good Start: The RCRA Subtitle D Program for Municipal Solid Waste Landfills." *Temple Environmental Law & Technology Journal* 15, no. 1 (1996): 1–63.

Turnquist, Kristi. "FBI Agents Posed as Filmmakers to Infiltrate the Bundy Family, 'Frontline' Documentary." *The Oregonian*, May 15, 2017. Newspaper Source Plus, 2W61362759646.

Turnipseed, Mary, Stephen E. Roady, Raphael Sagarin, and Larry B. Crowder. "The Silver Anniversary of the United States' Exclusive Economic Zone: Twenty-Five Years of Ocean Use and Abuse, and the Possibility of a Blue Water Public Trust Doctrine." *Ecology Law Quarterly* 36 (2009): 1–70.

TVA. "Hydroelectric." Accessed January 17, 2018. https://www.tva.gov/Energy/Our-Power-System/Hydroelectric.

Tyner, Wallace E. "The U.S. Ethanol and Biofuel Boom: Its Origins, Current Status, and Future Prospects." *Bioscience* 58, no.7 (July 2008): 646–653.

UN. "Conferences and Reports on the Environment." Accessed Sep 8, 2016. http://research.un.org/en/docs/environment.

UN. "Convention on the Law of the Non-navigational Uses of International Watercourses." Accessed July 19, 2017. http://legal.un.org/ilc/texts/instruments/english/conventions/8_3_1997.pdf.

UN. "Rio Declaration on Environment and Development." Accessed August 30, 2017. www.un.org/documents/ga/conf151/aconf15126-1annex1.htm.

UN. "United Nations International Year of Water Cooperation." Accessed July 19, 2017. http://www.un.org/en/events/world wateryear/.

UNDSEA. "Water Cooperation." Accessed July 19. 2017. www.unwater.org/water-cooperation-2013/water-cooperation/en/.

UNEP. "Assessment Panels." Accessed August 10, 2018. http://ozone.unep.org/science.

UNEP. "Declaration of the United Nations Conference on the Human Environment." Accessed August 10, 2018. http://www.un-documents.net/unchedec.htm.

UNEP. "Integrated Solid Waste Management." Accessed August 10, 2018. https://sustainabledevelopment.un.org/content/dsd/csd/csd_pdfs/csd-19/learningcentre/presentations/May%202%20am/1%20-%20Memon%20-%20ISWM.pdf.

UNEP. "Licensing and Quota Systems." Accessed January 28, 2018. http://web.unep.org/ozonaction/what-we-do/licensing-and-quota-systems.

UNEP. "Ozone Secretariat." Accessed August 10, 2018. http://ozone.unep.org/.

UNEP. "Regional Seas." Accessed December 13, 2017. http://web.unep.org/regionalseas/about/what-we-do/conservation-biodiversity-areas-beyond-national-jurisdiction-bbnj.

UNEP. "Rotterdam Convention." Accessed September 4, 2017. www.pic.int.

UNEP. "The Bamako Convention." Accessed August 10, 2018. https://wedocs.unep.org/bitstream/handle/20.500.11822/22491/NOTE%20ON%20THE%20BAMAKO%20CONVENTION.pdf?sequence=1&isAllowed=y.

UNEP. "The Basel Convention." Accessed August 30, 2017. www.basel.int/TheConvention/Overview/tabid/1271/Default.aspx.

UNEP. "Who We Are." Accessed December 13, 2017. http://web.unep.org/regionalseas/about/who-we-are/overview.

UNFCCC. "Adoption of the Paris Agreement." Accessed February 3, 2018. http://unfccc.int/resource/docs/2015/cop21/eng/l09.pdf.

UNFCCC. "First Steps to a Safer Future: Introducing the United Nations Framework Convention on Climate Change." Accessed

August 10, 2018. https://unfccc.int/resource/docs/publications/handbook.pdf.

UNFCCC. "Lima to Paris." Accessed February 3, 2018, http://newsroom.unfccc.int/lima/lima-call-for-climate-action-puts-world-on-track-to-paris-2015/.

UNFCCC. "Paris Agreement—Status of Ratification." Accessed January 23, 2017. http://unfccc.int/2860.php.

UNFCCC. "REDD+ Platform." Accessed February 3, 2018. http://redd.unfccc.int/.

Union of Concerned Scientists. "Coal and Air Pollution." Accessed January 5, 2018. https://www.ucsusa.org/clean-energy/coal-and-other-fossil-fuels/coal-air-pollution#.Wk_PjkxFzL8.

Union of Concerned Scientists. "Environmental Impacts of Geothermal Energy." Accessed January 22, 2018. https://www.ucsusa.org/clean_energy/our-energy-choices/renewable-energy/environmental-impacts-geothermal-energy.html#.WmYzJExFzL8.

Union of Concerned Scientists. "Environmental Impacts of Solar Power." Accessed January 21, 2018. https://www.ucsusa.org/clean_energy/our-energy-choices/renewable-energy/environmental-impacts-solar-power.html#.WmTnbkxFzL8.

Union of Concerned Scientists. "Nuclear Reprocessing: Dangerous, Dirty, and Expensive." Accessed January 11, 2018. https://www.ucsusa.org/nuclear-power/nuclear-plant-security/nuclear-reprocessing#.Wle1KExFzL8.

Union of Concerned Scientists. "The Hidden Costs of Fossil Fuels." Accessed January 4, 2018. https://www.ucsusa.org/clean-energy/coal-and-other-fossil-fuels/hidden-cost-of-fossils#.Wk5050xFzL8.

United Nations Population Division. "World Population Prospects, the 2015 Revision." Accessed February 8, 2017. https://esa.un.org/unpd/wpp/Download/Standard/Population.

USACE. "President's Fiscal 2017 Budget for U.S. Army Corps of Engineers Civil Works Released." Accessed November 7, 2016, http://www.usace.army.mil/Media/News-Releases/News-Release-Article-View/Article/652668/presidents-fiscal-2017-budget-for-us-army-corps-of-engineers-civil-works-releas/.

USAID. "USAID's Strategy for Stabilizing World Population Growth and Protecting Human Health." *Population and Development Review* 20, no. 2 (1994): 483–487.

USBR. "About Us." Accessed August 10, 2018. https://www.usbr.gov/main/about/.

USBR. "Budget Justification." Accessed November 7, 2016. https://www.usbr.gov/budget/2017/fy2017_budget_justifications.pdf.

USBR. "Hydropower Program." Accessed January 17, 2018. https://www.usbr.gov/power/edu/history.html.

USDA. "Fertilizer Use & Price." Accessed August 10, 2018. https://www.ers.usda.gov/data-products/fertilizer-use-and-price.aspx.

U.S. Department of State. "Marine Pollution." Accessed December 20, 2017. https://www.state.gov/e/oes/ocns/opa/ourocean/248163.htm.

U.S. Department of State. "'Our Oceans' Conference Outcomes: Charting a Path Toward a Global Ocean Policy." *Congressional Digest* September (2014): 11–13.

USGS. "Arctic National Wildlife Refuge, 1002 Area, Petroleum Assessment, 1998, Including Economic Analysis." Accessed October 23, 2017. https://pubs.usgs.gov/fs/fs-0028-01/fs-0028-01.htm.

USGS. "Budget Justification." Accessed August 10, 2018. https://www.doi.gov/sites/doi.gov/files/migrated/budget/appropriations/2016/upload/FY2016_USGS_Greenbook.pdf.

USGS. "Hydroelectric Power Water Use." Accessed January 18, 2018. https://water.usgs.gov/edu/wuhy.html.

USGS. "The USGA Water Science School." Accessed July 18, 2017. https://water.usgs.gov/edu/gwdepletion.html.

USGS. "Who We Are." Accessed October 31, 2016. http://usgs.gov/about/about-us/who-we-are.

USZWBC. "Zero Waste Business Council Launches Certification Program." Accessed August 10, 2018. https://www.waste360.com/zero-waste/zero-waste-business-council-launches-certification-program.

Vallero, Daniel A. "Green Engineering and Sustainable Design Aspects of Waste Management." In *Waste: A Handbook for Management*, edited by Trevor M. Letcher and Daniel A. Vallero, 11–21. Amsterdam: Elsevier, 2011.

van Beek, Christy L., Bastiaan G. Meerburg, Rene L. M. Schils, Jan Verhagen, and Peter J. Kuikman. "Feeding the World's Increasing Population While Limiting Climate Change Impacts: Linking N_2O and CH_4 Emissions from Agriculture to Population Growth." *Environmental Science & Policy* 13 (2010): 89–96.

Vangel, Inc. "Understanding Single vs. Dual Stream Recycling." Accessed August 10, 2018. https://www.vangelinc.com/single-vs-dual-stream-recycling/.

Vaughan. Adam. "Solar Power Growth Leaps by 50% Worldwide Thanks to US and China." *The Guardian*, March 7, 2017. Accessed January 21, 2018. https://www.theguardian.com/environment/2017/mar/07/solar-power-growth-worldwide-us-china-uk-europe.

Vella, Karmenu. "Maintaining Healthy Ocean Fisheries to Support Livelihoods: Achieving SDG 14 in Europe." *UN Chronicle* 54, no.1/2 (2017): 1.

Venkata, Bharadwaj. "World Energy Resources: Bioenergy 2016." *World Energy Council* (2016): 1–60.

Vig, Norman J. "Presidential Leadership and the Environment." In *Environmental Policy: New Direction for the Twenty-First Century*, edited by Norman J. Vig and Michael E. Kraft, 100–123. Washington, D.C.: CQ Press, 2006.

Vincent, Carol Hardy. "Deferred Maintenance of Federal Land Management Agencies: FY2007-FY2016 Estimates and Issues." *Congressional Research Service Report 7-5700, R43997* (2017): 1–12.

Verge, X.P.C., C. De Kimpe, and R.L. Desjardins. "Agricultural Production, Greenhouse Gas Emissions and Mitigation Potential." *Agriculture and Forest Meteorology* 142 (2007): 255–269.

Wakamatsu, Mihoko, Kong Joo Shin, Clevo Wilson, and Shunsuke Managi. "Can Bargaining Resolve the International Conflict Over Whaling?" *Marine Policy* 81 (2017): 312–321.

Waldron, Maya. "*Center for Biological Diversity v. Department of Interior*: Proper Deference." *Ecology Law Quarterly* 37 (2010): 721–726.

Walsh, James P. "The Origins and Early Implementation of the Magnuson-Stevens Fishery Conservation and Management Act of 1976." *Coastal Management* 42 (2014): 409–425.

Walters, Joanna. "Energy Agency Rejects Trump Plan to Prop Up Coal and Nuclear Power Plants." *The Guardian*, January 8, 2018. Accessed January 11, 2018. https://www.theguardian.com/environment/2018/jan/08/donald-trump-coal-industry-plan-rejected-rick-perry.

Wastler, T. A. "Ocean Dumping Permit Program Under the London Dumping Convention in the United States." *Chemosphere* 10, no. 6 (1981): 659–668.

Wiersema, Annecoos. "Uncertainty and Markets for Endangered Species Under CITES." *Review of European Comparative & International Environmental Law* 22, no. 3 (2013): 239–250.

Wild & Scenic Rivers Council. "About the WSR Act." Accessed October 4, 2017. https://www.rivers.gov/wsr-act.php.

Windworks.org. "Germany Feed Law." Accessed January 19, 2018. www.wind-works.org/cms/index.php?id=190.

"What's Next for the NRC? A Conversation with Allison Macfarlane." *Bulletin of the Atomic Scientists* 68, no. 6 (2012): 1–5.

Wolinsky-Nahmias, Yael. "Introduction: Global Climate Politics." In *Changing Climate Politics: U.S. Policies and Civic Action*, edited by Yael Wolinsky-Nahmias, 1–31. Thousand Oaks, CA: CQ Press, 2015.

World Atlas. "The Largest Countries in the World." Accessed September 25, 2017. http://www.worldatlas.com/articles/the-largest-countries-in-the-world-the-biggest-nations-as-determined-by-total-land-area.html.

World Bank. "What a Waste: A Global Review of Waste Management." Accessed August 1, 2017. http://web.worldbank.org/WBSITE/EXTERNAL/TOPICS/EXTURBANDEVELOPMENT/0,,contentMDK:23172887~pagePK:210058~piPK:210062~theSitePK:337178,00.html.

World Coal Association. "Uses of Coal." Accessed January 4, 2018. https://www.worldcoal.org/coal/uses-coal.

World Health Organization. "7 Million Deaths Annually Linked to Air Pollution." Accessed April 17, 2017. http://www.who.int/mediacentre/news/releases/2014/air-pollution/en/.

World Health Organization. "Household Air Pollution and Health." Accessed January 22, 2018. http://www.who.int/mediacentre/factsheets/fs292/en/.

World Health Organization. *World Health Statistics 2016: Monitoring Health for the SDGs*. Geneva: WHO Press, 2016.

World Nuclear Association. "Fukushima Accident." Accessed January 10, 2018. http://www.world-nuclear.org/information-library/safety-and-security/safety-of-plants/fukushima-accident.aspx.

World Nuclear Association. "Nuclear Power in Russia." Accessed January 14, 2018. http://www.world-nuclear.org/information-library/country-profiles/countries-o-s/russia-nuclear-power.aspx.

World Nuclear Association. "Nuclear Power in the USA." Accessed January 10, 2018. http://www.world-nuclear.org/information-library/country-profiles/countries-t-z/usa-nuclear-power.aspx.

World Nuclear Association. "Nuclear Power in the World Today." Accessed January 12, 2018. http://www.world-nuclear.org/information-library/current-and-future-generation/nuclear-power-in-the-world-today.aspx.

World Nuclear Association. "Online History of Nuclear Energy." Accessed January 12, 2018. http://www.world-nuclear.org/information-library/current-and-future-generation/outline-history-of-nuclear-energy.aspx.

World Nuclear Association. "Processing of Used Nuclear Fuel." Accessed January 15, 2018. http://www.world-nuclear.org/information-library/nuclear-fuel-cycle/fuel-recycling/processing-of-used-nuclear-fuel.aspx.

World Nuclear Association. "World Nuclear Power Reactors & Uranium Requirements." Accessed January 12, 2018. http://www.world-nuclear.org/information-library/facts-and-figures/world-nuclear-power-reactors-and-uranium-requireme.aspx.

World Resources Institute. "World's 36 Most Water-Stressed Countries." Accessed July 18, 2017. www.wri.org/blog/2013/12/world's-36-most-water-stressed-countries.

Wouters, Patricia. "'Dynamic Cooperation'—The Evolution of Transboundary Water Cooperation." In *Water and the Law: Towards Sustainability*, edited by Michael Kidd, Loretta Feris, Tumai

Murombo, and Alejandro Iza, 13–65. Cheltenham, UK: Edward Elgar, 2014.

Wuebbles, D.J., D.W. Fahey, K.A. Hibbard, B. DeAngelo, S. Doherty, K. Hayhoe, R. Horton, J.P. Kossin, P.C. Taylor, A.M. Waple, and C.P. Weaver. "Climate Science Special Report: Fourth National Climate Assessment, Volume I." *U.S. Global Change Research Program* (2017): 12–34, doi:10.7930/J0DJ5CTG.

WWF Global. "Working for Sustainable Fishing." Accessed December 18, 2017. www.panda.org/sustainablefishing.

Yergin, Daniel. *The Quest: Energy, Security, and the Remaking of the Modern World.* New York: Penguin, 2012.

Young, Michaela. "Then and Now: Reappraising Freedom of the Seas in Modern Law of the Sea." *Ocean Development & International Law* 47, no.2 (2016): 165–185.

Zarkin, Michael. "Unconventional Pollution Control Politics: The Reform of the US Safe Drinking Water Act." *Electronic Green Journal* 1, no.38 (2015): 1–22. Accessed July 17, 2017. http://escholarship.org/uc/item/69s0f9s0.

Zeng, Ka. "Domestic Politics and U.S.-China Trade Disputes Over Renewable Energy." *Journal of East Asian Studies* 15 (2015): 423–454.

Zhang, Junsen. "The Evolution of China's One-Child Policy and Its Effects on Family Outcomes." *Journal of Economic Perspectives* 31, no. 1 (2017): 141–160.

Zhang, Hai-Bain, Han-Cheng Dai, Hua-Xia Lai, and Wen-Tao Wang. "U.S. Withdrawal from the Paris Agreement: Reasons, Impacts, and China's Response." *Advances in Climate Change Research* 8 (2017): 220–225.

ZWIA. "ZW Definition." Accessed August 3, 2017. http://www.zwia.org/standards/zw-definition.

ZWIA. "Zero Waste Hierarchy of Highest and Best Use." Accessed August 10, 2018. http://zwia.org/standards/zero-waste-hierarchy/.

Index